MW00581352

Climbing Washington's Mountains

Selected summit hikes, scrambles, and climbs in Washington's Cascades and the Olympic Mountains

by Jeff Smoot

FALCON®

GUILFORD, CONNECTICUT
AN IMPRINT OF THE GLOBE PEQUOT PRESS

A FALCONGUIDE®

Copyright © 2002 by The Globe Pequot Press

All rights reserved. No part of this book may be reproduced or transmitted in any form by any means, electronic or mechanical, including photocopying and recording, or by any information storage and retrieval system, except as may be expressly permitted by the 1976 Copyright Act or by the publisher. Requests for permission should be made in writing to The Globe Pequot Press, P.O. Box 480, Guilford, Connecticut 06437.

Falcon and FalconGuide are registered trademarks of The Globe Pequot Press.

Cover photo of Monte Cristo Peak © Jeff Smoot
Interior photos are by the author unless otherwise noted.
Maps created by Trapper Badovinac © The Globe Pequot Press

Library of Congress Cataloging-in-Publication Data
Smoot, Jeff
    Climbing Washington's Mountains : selected summit hikes, scrambles, and climbs in Washington's Cascades and the Olympic Mountains / Jeff Smoot. — 1st ed.
        p. cm. — (A Falcon guide)
    ISBN 0-7627-1086-1
    1. Mountaineering—Washington (State)—Guidebooks. 2. Mountaineering—Cascade Range—Guidebooks. 3. Washington (State)—Guidebooks. 4. Cascade Range—Guidebooks. I. Title. II. Series.

GV199.42.W2 S642 2001
796.52'2'09797–dc21
                                                                    2001040473

Manufactured in Canada
First Edition/First Printing

The Globe Pequot Press and the author assume no liability for accidents happening to, or injuries sustained by, readers who engage in the activities described in this book.

WARNING:
CLIMBING IS A SPORT WHERE YOU MAY BE SERIOUSLY INJURED OR DIE. READ THIS BEFORE YOU USE THIS BOOK.

This guidebook is a compilation of unverified information gathered from many different sources. The author cannot assure the accuracy of any of the information in this book, including the topos and route descriptions, the difficulty ratings, and the protection ratings. These may be incorrect or misleading and it is impossible for any one author to climb all the routes to confirm the information about each route. Also, ratings of climbing difficulty and danger are always subjective and depend on the physical characteristics (for example, height), experience, technical ability, confidence, and physical fitness of the climber who supplied the rating. Additionally, climbers who achieve first ascents sometimes underrate the difficulty or danger of the climbing route out of fear of being ridiculed if a climb is later down-rated by subsequent ascents. Therefore, be warned that you must exercise your own judgment on where a climbing route goes, its difficulty, and your ability to safely protect yourself from the risks of rock climbing. Examples of some of these risks are: falling due to technical difficulty or due to natural hazards such as holds breaking, falling rock, climbing equipment dropped by other climbers, hazards of weather and lightning, your own equipment failure, and failure or absence of fixed protection.

You should not depend on any information gleaned from this book for your personal safety; your safety depends on your own good judgment, based on experience and a realistic assessment of your climbing ability. If you have any doubt as to your ability to safely climb a route described in this book, do not attempt it.

The following are some ways to make your use of this book safer:

1. Consultation: You should consult with other climbers about the difficulty and danger of a particular climb prior to attempting it. Most local climbers are glad to give advice on routes in their area and we suggest that you contact locals to confirm ratings and safety of particular routes and to obtain first-hand information about a route chosen from this book.

2. Instruction: Most climbing areas have local climbing instructors and guides available. We recommend that you engage an instructor or guide to learn safety techniques and to become familiar with the routes and hazards of the areas described in this book. Even after you are proficient in climbing safely, occasional use of a guide is a safe way to raise your climbing standard and learn advanced techniques.

3. Fixed Protection: Because of variances in the manner of placement, and weathering of fixed protection, all fixed protection should be considered suspect and should always be backed up by equipment that you place yourself. Never depend for your safety on a single piece of fixed protection because you never can tell whether it will hold weight, and in some cases, fixed protection may have been removed or is now absent.

Be aware of the following specific potential hazards that could arise in using this book:

1. Misdescriptions of Routes: If you climb a route and you have a doubt as to where the route may go, you should not go on unless you are sure that you can go that way safely. Route descriptions and topos in this book may be inaccurate or misleading.

2. Incorrect Difficulty Rating: A route may, in fact, be more difficult than the rating indicates. Do not be lulled into a false sense of security by the difficulty rating.

THERE ARE NO WARRANTIES, WHETHER EXPRESS OR IMPLIED, THAT THIS GUIDEBOOK IS ACCURATE OR THAT THE INFORMATION CONTAINED IN IT IS RELIABLE. THERE ARE NO WARRANTIES OF FITNESS FOR A PARTICULAR PURPOSE OR THAT THIS GUIDE IS MERCHANTABLE. YOUR USE OF THIS BOOK INDICATES YOUR ASSUMPTION OF THE RISK THAT IT MAY CONTAIN ERRORS AND IS AN ACKNOWLEDGMENT OF YOUR OWN SOLE RESPONSIBILITY FOR YOUR CLIMBING SAFETY.

Washington State Overview Map

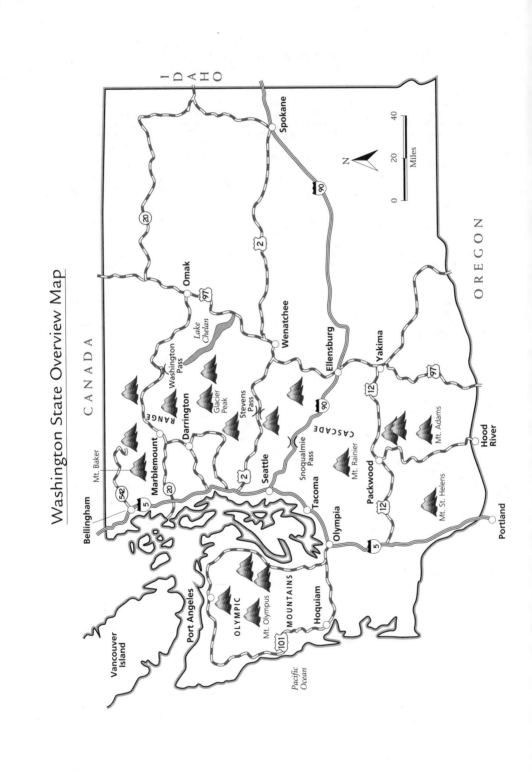

Contents

Map Legend

Interstate	(5)	State Border	WASHINGTON
U.S. Highway	(134)	City	○
State Highway	(190) (47)	Gate	•—•
Forest Road	4165 49	Cave/Mine	>—
Interstate Highway	═══⟩	Ski Area	⛷
Paved/Unpaved Road	═══⟩	Ranger Station/ Visitor Center	⚑
Trails	•-•~•-•-•	Other Buildings	▲
Cross Country Route	• • • • • •	Campground	Λ
River/Creek	⌒	Peaks	⛰
Falls	⌒//	Numbered Climbs	11
Lakes/Rivers	▬	Glacier	
Spring	○⌐	Lava Bed	
Marsh/Meadow	⋎		
National Park Boundary		Map Orientation	N
Bridge	⌣⌣	Scale	0 10 20 Miles
Pass/Saddle	)(		

Preface

Fred Beckey wrote that his *Cascade Alpine Guide* intended "an equitable rather than selective coverage of peaks and routes." This guide intends precisely the opposite—a selective rather than equitable coverage of climbing routes to the summits of many of the highest and most prominent peaks in Washington's Cascade Range and Olympic Mountains. Although this guide will certainly not replace the many past, present, and future regional guides, equitable or selective, it will hopefully provide a valuable resource for summit-bound climbers of all abilities and ambitions. At the least, this guide will provide sufficient information to get you where you want to go—provided where you want to go is to one of Washington's outstanding summits.

This book is not intended to replace Fred Beckey's venerated, three-volume series *Cascade Alpine Guide*, an excellent and well-respected series of guidebooks. Given the untold number of peaks in the Cascades and Olympics, it would be absurd to include every summit in a single volume. Beckey took three volumes to cover just the Cascade Range, and although his guides include a variety of routes up each peak, many of the easier peaks are discussed in only a brief paragraph, barely describing the route, and then often without a map, drawing, or photograph, giving little clue other than "follow ridge to summit" or some such instruction. These easier peaks and scrambles are among the most popular climbing objectives of a very large portion of the climbing community, those who enjoy climbing mountains without feeling the need to conquer them, who feel an unexplainable sense of elation, peace, or wonder atop a high summit, gazing across an endless sea of peaks and valleys that stretch out to the horizon. It is in this spirit that this guide is offered—a guide to a selection of the highest, most popular, most scenic, and most distinguished summits of the Cascade Range and Olympic Mountains.

This guide is not intended to compete with Jim Nelson and Peter Potterfield's two-volume *Selected Climbs in the Cascades*. Those well-respected and oft consulted books are guides to "climbs," not summits. While they include a smattering of scrambles and basic climbs, the two volumes primarily focus on more difficult technical rock, ice, and remote alpine climbs that are all but unapproachable by the average peak bagger. Granted, the abilities and ambitions of mountaineers have risen sharply over the past two decades, but several of the selected climbs are far too difficult for the majority of climbers.

This guide attempts to strike a balance between *Cascade Alpine Guide* and *Selected Climbs in the Cascades*, providing more detailed route information than the former, but focusing on easier summit routes than the latter—not that this is a guide only to easy climbs. Rather, the focus here is on summits. A majority of the summits included have scrambling routes. Some require glacier climbing; others require technical rock climbing. Usually, the route described is the easiest or most direct way to the summit of a given peak. Occasionally, an easier route exists; but for the sake of speed, safety, or aesthetics, a more technically difficult route is preferred by nearly everyone who climbs the peak. Likewise, sometimes a more aesthetically pleasing route exists; but for the sake of expediency or at least to avoid undue complication, the most direct route is described, warts and all. Where space permits and nature obliges, more than one route is described, allowing climbers to choose between an easier scramble or more interesting technical climb. Occasionally, a new or previously unreported summit route or variation is included, if for no other reason than to get a jump on the competition.

Rather than give vague route descriptions under the notion that this allows climbers to figure things out for themselves, I've provided a fair amount of detail about each route. Some routes may still have vaguely described sections, but for the most part, the actual climbing route is fully revealed. For those who want to discover things for themselves, this guide does offer several options, including nearby peaks and other routes that are described in less detail. I have also provided information on unreported routes, traverses, or "enchainments" that appear feasible or enjoyable.

Of course, like any guide, this guide is not perfect. The routes described are based on firsthand knowledge and from trip reports provided by many climbers, but even firsthand experience is subjective and not always fully revealing. In many cases, there may be an easier variation or more enjoyable route than described. A good spring variation is easily overlooked on a late summer ascent. Sometimes the route described is not the traditional route simply because the author or his minions missed a crucial turn and went a different way than the other guidebooks said to go. A description written after a fall climb may not accurately depict spring conditions. A snowfield encountered in July may have melted away by September. So, as with all guidebooks, trust this guide only as far as you can throw it. If the route description does not match what you encounter during your climb, follow your instincts and use your judgment. If the route described seems too difficult or dangerous, try a different way or retreat. Readers of this guide should not blindly follow words and pictures, but must exercise caution and good judgment based on what they encounter as they climb.

It is hoped that climbers still approach the mountains with a sense of exploration and discovery, without relying on any guidebook completely. Exploration and discovery, both of ourselves and our wild places, are at the very heart of why we climb. Please do not limit yourself only to the peaks and routes included in this or any other guidebook. There is usually more than one route to a summit.

Acknowledgments

If anything is true in guidebook writing, "It's not what you know; it's who you know." Without the help of others, this guidebook would have been impossible. I acknowledge and thank the following people for their assistance with this project, whether for providing route information, photographs, and chapter reviews, or for referring me along to someone who had information, including but certainly not limited to, Jim Abbie, Morgan Balogh, Paul Baugher, Darin Berdinka, Mike Bingle, Robert Bolton, Bill Boyes, Norm Buckley, Mark Dale, Pat Gentry, Colin Haley, Alex Krawarik, Matt Robertson, Gordon Schryer, Dan Smith, Michael Stanton, Martin Volken, Doug Weaver, and Ernie Zeller, as well as the many climbers who provided route information in passing during trailside, route, and summit conversations. The list goes on and on, and I have certainly forgotten someone, whom I hope is very understanding.

Special thanks to Steve Teufert, Jack Ganster, and Jim Cameron of Olympic Mountaineering for providing route information and photos for the Olympic summits. Without their help, I would not have been able to include the Olympics in this guide. Thanks also to the many staffers with the USDA Forest Service and National Park Service for their assistance in obtaining current route and trail information, rules and regulations, and permit information. My appreciation also to the Mountaineers for maintaining an exceptional outdoor library and making their resources available for my use. Also thanks to the many climbers who maintain on-line trip reports and photos of their scrambles and climbs in the Cascades and Olympics.

My sincere appreciation to Michael and Kris Stanton for inspiring and assisting me in starting the Climbing Washington Web site, which I hope will become a valuable resource for Washington climbers.

Very special thanks to my wife, Karen, and daughter, Lauren, for their tolerance throughout this and my many other projects, and as always, to my parents for letting me run wild in the mountains in my youth.

Introduction

There are hundreds if not thousands of magnificent peaks among the Cascade Range and Olympic Mountains of Washington state. All across Washington state, mountains provide a remarkable backdrop to the everyday lives of the state's residents. A panorama of high peaks surround Puget Sound, the state's most densely populated area, including the giants of the Cascade Range—Mount Rainier to the south, Mount Baker and Mount Shuksan to the north, and Glacier Peak hidden in between. A procession of lesser peaks includes Si, Baring, Gunn, Index, Pilchuck, Three Fingers, Whitehorse, Columbia, Del Campo, Sloan. And across the sound lie the peaks of the Olympic Mountains—Washington, The Brothers, Constance, and Warrior, to name only a few.

A majority of Washington's residents consider the mountains pretty scenery, lovely to look at and photograph, and they are right. But for a fortunate minority—those of us who enjoy hiking and climbing these mountains—the mountains of the Cascades and Olympics offer something far greater than mere scenery. They are places to explore, to commune with and challenge ourselves against nature, and to enjoy the company of friends or solitude. Without waxing too eloquently about the reasons we climb, suffice it to say that scrambling and climbing are very popular pursuits in the Cascades and Olympics among those of us who are not content to merely look at mountains but feel compelled to know them more intimately.

Using This Guide

This guide is intended to assist hikers, scramblers, and climbers in locating and identifying summit routes up a variety of peaks in Washington's Cascade Range and Olympic Mountains. To that end, each summit listed in this guide includes a written description of the peak and climbing route with driving directions and trail and off-trail approach routes. Maps and drawings in this guide are approximate only and should not be relied upon except to the extent that they will help get you to your chosen destination from the lowlands and help you locate the approximate line of ascent. Although maps and drawings may suffice for competent scramblers and climbers during good weather and favorable route conditions, they are not exact and cannot be a substitute for topographic maps, skilled compass use, and routefinding ability learned through experience.

In addition to maps and topographic drawings, photographs with overlays are sometimes used to show mountain features and climbing routes. Photographs will give a helpful impression, but like maps, they should not be relied upon completely, especially for judging slope, angle, or distance, or determining exact routes of ascent. Use your best judgment on each route based on what you see when you arrive, regardless of the written descriptions, illustrations, and photographs contained in this guide. Basically, this guide will show you what's there and approximately where to go; from there it's up to you.

Mark S. Dale

Climber below seracs on Mount Baker.

With the exception of roads and maintained trails, the routes listed in this guide are approximate and based upon historical and popular usage, not correctness or exactness of line. Numerous variations to these routes have been, can be, and will be done, whether for the sake of something different or to avoid occasional hazards or obstacles. All of the variations cannot possibly be listed here. On some routes, each successive party takes a slightly different variation, plus detours along the way. For most of the routes in this guide, there is no "correct" or absolute route. There are no dotted lines to follow on the mountains; you'll have to pick the best and safest route by yourself. Actually, in a few places, you may find directional arrows and dots painted on rocks; fortunately, this wilderness graffiti is not widespread. More prolific is orange and yellow flagging that marks brushy climber's trails and rock cairns in high basins and other featureless slopes. Follow these at your peril; they will sometimes lead you astray.

All route descriptions and directions assume you are facing your objective or your direction of travel, unless otherwise stated. Whenever there is possible confusion in the directions given, an approximate compass direction will be provided for clarity. All distances, including road and trail mileages, are approximate only. Your actual mileage may vary.

This guide does not presume to know every feature of every climbing route, trail, or road discussed. Mountain environs change from day to day, week to week, season to season, and year to year. Rockfall, avalanches, floods, storms, and other occasional and seasonal changes will continue to alter the nature, course, and safety of climbing routes. Trails erode, streams and rivers flood, bridges are washed out, trees fall, crevasses open and close, snow bridges collapse, seracs tumble, ice cliffs avalanche, glaciers recede and advance, rocks freeze and thaw and tumble down, volcanoes erupt, and so on. Because mountain features can change from day to day and season to season, mountain roads, hiking trails, and climbing routes will vary accordingly. A feature identified in a route description may have changed or even disappeared between now and the time you are looking for it. A road you are instructed to follow may be closed or washed out. A trail may have been re-routed. A cairn may have been knocked down. Flagging may have been removed. Changes can and do occur overnight. Again, choose your route based on what you encounter during your climb, and on instinct and judgment, rather than solely based on what is described in this guide.

PEAK SELECTION

This being a "select" guide, only a certain number of mountains could be included. After drafting an initial list of worthy inclusions, the selection process began. In order for the guide to be of practical size, an arbitrary limit of 100 peaks was imposed. Deciding which 100 peaks to include was a daunting task. Many prominent, historically important, and otherwise locally and regionally worthy peaks did not make the cut, while some seemingly unimportant, obscure peaks did. A great effort was made to cover a liberal sampling of peaks from each region of Washington's Cascades and Olympics, including the North Cascades, Glacier Peak and Monte Cristo areas, Stevens Pass and Lake Chelan, Leavenworth, Snoqualmie Pass, Mount Rainier, the South Cascades, and the Olympics. Providing a variety of climbing situations, including summit hikes, rock and snow scrambles, glacier climbs, and a few technical routes was also important. Of course, the Cascade volcanoes are included, along with many of the state's 9,000-foot summits and many of the most significant peaks of each range. However, a majority of the peaks included in this guide were selected not only for their elevation and prominence, but for the quality of climbing experience and purity of line offered.

A modest peak with a direct, interesting summit route was deemed more worthy than a higher mountain reached via a complex route, multi-day bushwhack, or glacier slog. Visibility was another factor considered in making the final selection. An important peak rising prominently above a major highway or visible from a populated city was more likely to be included than a significant peak hidden deep within the range. Accessibility was another important factor. A mountain that could be approached via a maintained trail and climbed and descended in a day or two usually won out over a peak that required a full day of hiking or extensive bushwhacking just to get to base camp. The presence of objective hazards was also considered. Summit routes with unusually high avalanche or rockfall hazard were usually avoided regardless of prominence. Another factor, and certainly not the last, was route difficulty. In order to provide a good variety of climbing opportunities in each region, not only easy scrambles or technical climbs, several peaks were cut from the list because they were too easy or too hard relative to the other peaks from that region.

CHAPTER OVERVIEW

Each "chapter" begins with the name of the mountain or peak, accompanied by a summary of information about the peak, including the peak's actual or approximate elevation in feet and meters above sea level, a rating of the route described, approximate round-trip distance, estimated climbing time from trailhead or base camp to summit, and approximate elevation gain, usually rounded up to the nearest 100 feet.

Time estimates are based on actual reports by climbing parties, but may have been adjusted to more accurately reflect a realistic time for an average party climbing at a typical pace from the trailhead to the summit. Descent times will not be included except in a few instances. These estimated ascent times assume the party is in good physical condition, prepared for the difficulties of the route, and encountering favorable climbing conditions. Poor weather, snow, ice, and rock conditions, crevasses, slow climbers ahead of you, and many other factors will render these time estimates invalid. A strong climbing team may take much less time than the estimate provided for a given route, while another team may take more time. Never try to "beat the clock," but if you are way behind schedule, don't press on into a forced bivouac or worse. Time estimates in this guide are fairly generous, assuming you will take as long as or longer than an "average" party.

ABOUT THE CLIMB

This section provides a brief description of the peak, its notable features, human or geologic history, and regional importance. You will also find general information about the climbing route, such as whether it is easy or difficult, whether it is popular or not often climbed, whether the ascent is best done during a particular season, what kind of views to expect from the summit, and so on.

Darin Berdinka

Rebecca Larsen on the South Ridge, Ingalls Peak.

HOW TO GET THERE

Usually this section is a paragraph giving brief but detailed driving directions to the trailhead. For more remote or challenging peaks with long approaches or complex climbing routes, the approach hike may be described in this section as well, although usually the approach hike is described under the heading "Route Description." In most cases, a separate description and map of the roads and approach hike is included for each peak. In some cases, a single approach description or map serves for several peaks in close proximity to each other.

ROUTE DESCRIPTION

This section includes a description of the climbing route, usually the easiest or most direct route to the summit. For easier peaks with trail approaches, the approach hike will be included here. Route descriptions will be brief on short climbs and those with few routefinding problems, and more detailed on longer routes that are complex or difficult. Usually, the higher the rating, elevation, or distance, the longer and more detailed the route description. In most cases, a map, topo, or photo of the route is included in each chapter, especially for peaks that are more difficult and complex.

OPTIONS

This section makes mention of variations and other notable or worthwhile routes up the peak, as well as other nearby peaks that can be climbed on the same trip. This information may include high traverses and enchainments, and ideas for routes or traverses that have not been reported in other guides. In some cases, a topo or photo showing another route is included. In several cases, an option is marked with an icon [♦], which denotes that additional information can be found on the Climbing Washington Web site (www.climbingwashington.com). In other cases, a reference to another guidebook is listed.

PRECAUTIONS

This last section includes a brief discussion of access, and permit considerations, and hazards commonly encountered on the peak. If a route is notorious for rockfall, avalanches, or other hazards, those hazards will be mentioned. Safety recommendations such as wearing a helmet, roping up on glaciers, or bringing an ice ax or crampons for snow and glacier climbs will not be repeated in each chapter. Wearing a helmet is a valuable safety measure on every climb. An ice ax should be carried along on all trips unless you are absolutely sure there is no snow to climb or descend. Crampons are often helpful even in late season for that one last snow patch you thought had melted away. As always, only known and obvious hazards will be mentioned in the guide. Climbing is inherently dangerous, and a variety of potential hazards exist on every peak, known and unknown, so caution must be exercised by all climbers on every climb no matter what this or any guide says.

Climbing Route Classification

The climbing and scrambling routes included in this guide will be rated using a combination of the Yosemite Decimal System (YDS) and National Climbing Classification System (NCCS) rating scheme as described here. Those unfamiliar with these rating systems are likely unfamiliar with alpine scrambling and mountaineering and should seek help from a professional before climbing in the Cascades and Olympics. Hire a guide or climb under the guidance of an experienced leader until you have gained the proper experience to climb independently.

Class 1

Off-trail hiking and easy scrambling with little or no exposure where use of hands is infrequent and there is little risk of serious injury due to falling. May include easy talus scrambling, ridge hiking, snow climbing, or any off-trail climbing.

Class 2

Easy scrambling with some exposure where you could be killed or seriously injured in a fall, but where you aren't likely to fall off unless you make a serious blunder. Use of hands and feet required. Might seem scary in places to inexperienced climbers but not technically difficult.

Class 3

More difficult rock scrambling with more severe exposure where an unroped fall would certainly lead to injury and might be fatal. Some climbers will want the safety of a belay on the hardest or most exposed sections.

Class 4

Easy technical climbing or very difficult scrambling that is so exposed that use of a rope is considered mandatory by most climbers. The leader will climb mostly unprotected, but everyone else will have the security of a belay from above. May include occasional easy technical rock climbing moves. May require placing occasional intermediate protection.

Class 5

Technical rock climbing requiring the use of a rope and intermediate protection to shorten the length of possible and sometimes imminent leader falls. Moderate to difficult rock climbing moves. Requires belaying, protecting, and rappelling or belayed downclimbing.

Class 5 is subdivided in an ascending decimal scale commonly known as the Yosemite Decimal System, where 5.0 represents the easiest Class 5 climbing and the scale progresses (e.g., 5.1, 5.2, and so on) as difficulty increases. While there are alpine rock climbs in the Cascades and Olympics of extreme difficulty, only a few Class 5 routes are included in this guide, and of those, only a few are rated as high as 5.6 or 5.7, which is relatively moderate as rock climbing goes. Don't be fooled though. A 5.4 alpine rock climb may sound easy—until you get there and find out there is no reliable protection, the rock is icy, you are wearing lug-soled boots and a heavy pack, and rope drag is becoming a major frustration.

A problem with this rating system is that one person's Class 3 is another person's Class 4, and one person's Class 4 is another's Class 5. Also, even easy scrambles become harder after a routefinding error, a very easy thing to do. A Class 3 romp can become a Class 5 nightmare just by taking the wrong gully. A one-move variation can make a scrambling route dangerously difficult to climb unroped.

A typical Cascades river crossing.

The NCCS, the Roman numeral grading system commonly used in other climbing guides, will be used sparingly here, only for technical routes (generally Class 4 and 5 only). Grades I, II, and III denote technical climbs that may take a few hours to much of a day. A Grade IV climb can easily take all day; a Grade V route will probably require a bivouac. On any Grade III, IV, and V route, be prepared for a bivouac and technical climbing. Because very few of the routes included in this guide are of sufficient length and technical difficulty to warrant its use, and because a time estimate is included for each climbing route, this system is not stressed here, thus this minimal explanation. The technical grades listed in this guide will be only for the technical portions of routes and not for any part of the route that is only glacier hiking, unroped scrambling, or a descent route.

Glacier climbs are rated generally Grade I, II, III, IV, and so on. In this guide, a Grade I glacier will involve relatively easy, non-technical glacier traversing and climbing with minimal if any crevasse exposure. A "Grade I" glacier may be stagnant or may have seasonal crevasses. Some climbers may elect not to rope up when crossing a Grade I glacier, although roping is advised on all glaciers because climbers sometimes fall into crevasses even on these low-grade glaciers. A "Grade II" glacier will be a steeper, more active glacier that shows several crevasses and has hidden crevasses as well. Climbers should definitely rope up on a Grade II glacier and have crevasse rescue experience and capabilities. A "Grade III" glacier is steeper and more technical to climb and may have difficult crevasse crossings or icefall sections. A "Grade IV" glacier would be fairly extreme with ice cliffs and such. Glacier conditions fluctuate from season to season. In late season, glaciers are icy and more difficult and hazardous than in early season. On glacier climbs, an ice ax and crampons are essential, as is roping up. Learn and practice crevasse rescue skills before you venture onto a glacier.

Ratings are not intended as an indication of actual difficulty and safety, or as a guarantee of success. The ratings included in this guide are intended to assist climbers in choosing routes that are appropriate for their abilities and experience and to let climbers know about what to expect on a given route, not to give an exact technical rating. Just because a route is rated Class 2 by this guide's definition does not mean it will never be difficult or dangerous. These ratings assume that you are on the "correct" route under perfect conditions. Straying only a few feet in the wrong direction at the wrong point can increase a route's rating and commitment factor remarkably. Again, you should rely on your judgment and base decisions on your skill, experience, and what you encounter when you are there on the mountain—not what it says in this guidebook.

Equipment

In general, climbing equipment is suggested where it may be needed; however, gear lists are not provided. You will have to rely on your own experience and judgment when selecting the clothing and equipment to bring with you. Most importantly, you need to know when, where, and how to use the stuff before you venture to the mountains. Any equipment's usefulness is wholly dependent upon its user's skill and knowledge. Practice rock climbing and placement of protection on the crags before you venture into the mountains.

There are really four essential pieces of equipment that Cascade and Olympic climbers should always bring along: helmet, ice ax, crampons, and rope. Scramblers and climbers attempting any route that might conceivably be subject to rockfall or icefall are advised to wear helmets. Many of the routes included in this guide feature sections of loose rock where the risk of injury or death from spontaneous and party-inflicted rockfall is high. Helmets are recommended on all climbs and scrambles that pass over or below alpine rock or ice. Also, helmets have saved the lives of climbers who slipped and fell on snow and ice and slid into rocks below. Use of a helmet is a personal choice, and many climbers eschew the use of a helmet on easy snow climbs and scrambles, but they wouldn't if they were smart. Helmets are recommended on every rock or snow scramble, regardless of whether a particular route description says so.

An ice ax is a critical piece of safety equipment for any snow travel. Countless climbers have avoided severe injury during slips on snow and ice by self-arresting. You should never climb or traverse a steep, exposed snow slope without an ice ax in hand and the know-how to self-arrest. Many climbers lament having packed along an ice ax only to find all the snow has melted, but those who left their ice axes behind and encountered unexpected snow have lamented louder. So, too, have those who left crampons behind and had to cut steps up a snowfield or turn around because a late-season snowfield proved too icy to climb. Many scramblers don't bring a rope, and in a majority of cases, a rope is unnecessary for Class 2 and 3 scrambles; but if a party member is injured, you get off route, an easy gully is icy, or the weather changes, a rope may be vital to assure your party's safety.

Climbers using this guide should already know what equipment and clothing to bring and how to use it. Those who don't should consult the references listed in this guide and take a mountaineering instruction course from a qualified guide service. *Mountaineering: The Freedom of the Hills* is probably the best overall comprehensive mountaineering instruction book available. This book contains instructions for nearly every aspect of mountain travel. However, be warned that you can't learn how to climb by reading a book, even a good one. Take a climbing instruction course, complete one or more guided climbs, do some easy scrambles and climbs in the company of more experienced leaders, then perfect belaying, crevasse rescue, and ice-ax arrest techniques before trying to climb these mountains on your own.

Mountain Hazards

Alpine scrambling and climbing, like other modes of wilderness travel, have numerous objective dangers, and routes described in this guide are no exception. Despite all of the obvious potential dangers, thousands of climbing and scrambling trips are made each year without incident or injury. However, we shouldn't be too smug about this. There are no guarantees of safety in the mountains, so proceed with caution and at your own risk. This guide will make an effort to point out obvious objective hazards. Warnings in this guide are intended to let users know of dangers that are frequently encountered on given routes. However, no guide can accurately or completely foresee every conceivable accident waiting to happen.

The safest mode of wilderness travel is hiking on trails, where usually only weather and your own or others' actions are reasons for concern. Of course, hiking on trails is not without objective risks. Some trails become treacherous after dark or during poor weather; losing the trail after dark is a leading cause of hiking accidents, justifying packing a flashlight, especially given the frequency that many alpine scramblers find themselves hiking out in the dark. Hikers often slip and fall off of wet rocks or footlogs while crossing streams. In certain glacier-fed stream valleys, particularly those lying at the foot of the big volcanoes, outburst floods are an infrequent but serious hazard. High rainfall causes flooding, which can erode or undermine trails. Falling trees and rocks have killed unsuspecting hikers. Snow and ice on trails can be treacherous, and you can easily break an ankle plunging through the crust. Snow bridges over streams can collapse under your weight. Streams and rivers can undermine trails. Bears and cougars lurk in the mountains, rattlesnakes in some areas, and although animal attacks are rare, they do occur. Stinging insects can cause a life-threatening allergic reaction in some people. Ticks carry Lyme disease. Simply tripping on or colliding with an exposed rock or tree root on the descent hike can cause serious injury.

When venturing off the trail, you submit yourself to greater risks, including but not limited to avalanches, rockfall, icefall, windfall, landslides, talus slides, floods, slips and falls, falls into moats and crevasses, frostbite, altitude sickness, lightning strikes, and hypothermia and other effects of weather, along with the ordinary hazards of being a frail human being. Unfortunately, no one can predict most of these occurrences, as even the weatherman cannot always predict the coming of a major storm. You should be wary of these dangers at all times and avoid them whenever possible. Indeed, climbers most often are the cause of their own and others' accidents. To climb mountains, however, you must be willing to face certain risks, even the risk that your climbing partner might make a mistake that will cost you your life. Once again, this guidebook is no substitute for good judgment gained through experience. It will try to warn you away from obvious and foreseeable hazards, but there are always unknown and unforeseeable potential hazards lurking out there that nobody knows about until it is too late.

WILDERNESS SAFETY
Any wilderness adventure includes exposure to risks and dangers, especially scrambling and climbing. All users of this guide should read it thoroughly before venturing off to climb these peaks in order to become aware of some things that might help minimize their exposure to needless risk. Scrambling and climbing are dangerous. People are injured and killed on easy climbs every year. If you have any doubt about your experience or ability to safely complete a given climb, seek professional help—hire a guide or join a mountaineering club's climbing program.

The safety suggestions contained in this book are only that, suggestions. Even if you follow these suggestions, your safety cannot be absolutely guaranteed. This is not an instruction book for hiking, climbing, or alpine scrambling. The author and publisher cannot be responsible for the consequences of your acts while traveling to or climbing on these peaks. It is assumed that those following the routes and trails listed in this guide will be experienced in wilderness travel,

Gordon Schryer

Climbers ascending Sahale Peak from the Boston-Sahale Col.

properly trained and equipped to safely complete their chosen route, and able to recognize and avoid the many avoidable dangers present in the mountain environment. Only through the exercise of good judgment, gained through experience, will you be assured of a safe trip. Even then, there simply can be no assurance of safety in the wilderness. On any given climb, anything can happen. Proceed with caution and at your own risk.

Beginning climbers and scramblers should bear in mind that the mountains of the Cascades and Olympics are no place for the unprepared and uninitiated. It is very easy to get lost if you don't know where you are going or don't have a trail to follow. If you aren't properly dressed or equipped, you are inviting trouble. Don't venture onto glaciers unless you are roped up, have an ice ax and crampons, and know how to effect a crevasse rescue. Don't try for a summit unless you have previous climbing experience and equipment or are in the company of an experienced leader or guide. Don't climb rock cliffs or mountains if you don't have rock climbing experience and equipment. Don't even go hiking if you aren't in good physical condition and well prepared for bad weather, nightfall, or minor emergencies or injuries that may and often do occur.

Experience and preparation, or lack thereof, are common factors in mountaineering accidents. Inexperienced and unprepared climbers often make fatal mistakes; experienced climbers usually know better. Inexperienced climbers should not climb on glaciers or at high elevations no matter how easy the terrain. If you have no previous mountaineering experience, you should take a climbing instruction course or go on a guided climb prior to attempting any of these routes on your own. Climb non-technical routes at first, gradually working up to more demanding routes as you gain technique, experience, and knowledge of your abilities and limitations. Practice rock, ice, self-arrest, and crevasse rescue techniques as often as possible so you know what to do when the time comes.

You should check weather and avalanche conditions before each trip. Make sure you and your entire party have adequate experience for and knowledge of your chosen routes, both for ascent and descent. Most importantly, know your limitations. Think before you act, lest you suffer the consequences of a rash or foolish choice. If conditions become dangerous for any reason, or you realize your chosen route is beyond your ability to climb safely, don't be afraid to turn back. It is wiser to descend than to continue in such instances.

MOUNTAIN WEATHER

Of all considerations of mountain travel in Washington's mountains, weather should be among the foremost to climbers and scramblers. Many a day has begun calm and clear only to end in a monsoon-like storm. Effects of weather lead to more deaths (from hypothermia) than climbing accidents. Some of the big volcanoes literally create their own weather. The mountains experience severe storms each year, and these storms cannot always be predicted. Storms often come without any warning, sometimes with fatal consequences to unprepared climbers. Prepare yourself for the worst, including wind, rain, and snow, no matter what the weatherman says.

In a nutshell, this is how Washington mountain weather works. Warm, moist air blows in off the Pacific Ocean, squeezing moisture-laden clouds against the Olympic Mountains. These clouds, like large sponges, dump excessive rain on the western slopes of the mountains until, relieved of their burden, the clouds rise over the mountains and drift eastward across Puget Sound. Here, the process is repeated with similar effect against the Cascade Range, although the volume of rainfall is generally less than that which falls on the rain forests of the Olympic Peninsula. Once the clouds have dumped their load on the western slopes of the Cascades, they again drift eastward over the eastern slopes of the range, which are markedly drier and less heavily vegetated. This warm, moist marine air condenses and freezes very rapidly when it hits the cold, snowy Cascades and Olympics, which accounts for high winds and the tremendous snowfalls each year. This is a bit simplistic, but it is close enough for this guide's purposes.

Winter climbers should go prepared for the worst weather imaginable. Fierce storms, with high winds and volumes of snowfall, can rage for days and sometimes come without warning. Winter climbing is not recommended for any but the most experienced. Plan winter climbs carefully; your life will depend on it. Weather changes can occur suddenly and dramatically, which is well illustrated by a mining-era report of over 100-degree temperatures on the summit of Mount Adams in an afternoon followed within 12 hours by a storm with minus 48-degree temperatures. Just because it is sunny and calm doesn't mean it won't soon be freezing and blustery. A light dusting of snow or overnight icing can turn an easy scramble into a serious ordeal.

The majority of weather-related problems occur when climbers are unable to find their way down out of a storm or are trapped in a storm with no shelter.

Morgan Balogh

The summit of Mount Daniel.

Whiteout conditions are frequent on the volcanoes and high peaks and are particularly problematic on featureless terrain. It is very easy to get lost in a whiteout on glaciers and easier routes, even on approach hikes above treeline. Carry a compass and take bearings here and there along the way. Also flag your route so you can more easily find your way down if the weather deteriorates.

Many peaks east of the Cascade crest are subject to daily thunderstorms during summer months. Climbers who find themselves on high ridges or summits should descend quickly when storm clouds threaten or when they see lightning or hear thunder nearby.

Check the weather forecast and avalanche conditions before any climbing or scrambling trip. Although the weatherman is not always right about good weather, when it comes to poor weather, considering your life may be in the bargain, you should give him the benefit of the doubt. Avalanche hazard, snow information, and other weather resources, including on-line weather reports and web-cam sites, are listed in Appendix C.

When to Climb

When you make your climb should be determined by several factors, such as weather, snow and glacier conditions, trail conditions, permit requirements, and of course, your personal preferences. Some people prefer summer and autumn climbing, favoring snow-free approach hikes and more reliable weather; others prefer spring and early summer snow climbs with ski descents. Many people don't mind the season as long as they can go climbing. Some climbs are easy in the spring and early summer when snow slopes and gullies offer easy passage, but are a chore in summer and fall when brush and scree make for tedious going.

Some climbs are popular in winter when snow and ice offer more challenge. Other climbs are dangerous in winter and spring due to avalanches or during the fall when snow in gullies is undermined or loose rock is exposed.

Wilderness Regulations

Regulations vary from wilderness to wilderness and park to park, but all have approximately the same limitations. If you follow these regulations, you will probably not run afoul of the regulations in effect in most areas of the Cascades and Olympics.

- Maximum group size is eight to twelve, which includes all people and stock. In sensitive or overused areas, maximum group size is five to eight.
- No motorized or mechanized equipment is allowed. That means no motorbikes, bicycles, chainsaws, carts, aircraft, or pneumatic drills.
- Many areas have camping restrictions such as distance from lakes or designated sites, usually no closer than 200 feet.
- Campfires not allowed above 4,000 or 5,000 feet, if at all.
- Cutting switchbacks is not allowed. Stay on established trails.
- Caching of supplies for longer than 48 hours is prohibited.
- Do not cut trees, snags, or boughs. Do not walk or camp in areas closed for restoration.
- Pack out all litter.
- Bury human waste and pet waste well away from camps and water sources. Dispose of wash water well away from water sources.
- Do not install fixed anchors. Temporary installations are allowed if not left in place for more than a full climbing season.

Check current park and wilderness rules, regulations, and permit requirements before your climb. You can call the appropriate park or forest service office, or log on to one of the Web sites listed in Appendix C.

WILDERNESS PERMIT REQUIREMENTS

Many of the wilderness areas and national parks covered in this guide have established quotas on the number of persons who may occupy certain campsites and who may climb certain routes. Permit systems have been implemented at some areas. Permit fees and advance reservations are required at a few. These measures, though occasionally restrictive, are meant to help reduce the harm humans have done and continue to do to these fragile mountain environments. The management plans governing wilderness areas have established "limits of acceptable change" for certain high-use areas. When an area exceeds the limits of acceptable change, access is often restricted. Examples of areas where human use has had significant adverse impact are Camps Muir, Schurman and Hazard on Mount Rainier, the South Climb on Mount Adams, the Enchantment Lakes of the Alpine Lakes Wilderness, and various places in Olympic National Park. The more popular the corridor of travel, the more likely it will be overused and abused, not only by climbers but by other wilderness visitors as well.

Michael Stanton/Mountainwerks

Climber on the West Ridge, Prusik Peak.

Permit systems and overnight quotas were implemented to relieve the burden wilderness users have imposed upon the mountains. A good way to ensure permit availability and some solitude is to plan your trip during the work week when the mountains are relatively void of human visitors. On weekends, they are packed full of us. Campsites crowded on Saturday night are usually vacant on Tuesday and Wednesday nights. Specific wilderness and national park regulations (including permits and quotas) will be discussed where appropriate in the following chapters. Please do your best to follow these regulations, and please do what you can to minimize your impact.

To check current permit requirements, contact the appropriate park or forest service office, or log on to one of the Web sites listed in Appendix C.

Zero-Impact

Because of the popularity of climbing in the Cascades and Olympics, many popular trails, campsites, and climbing routes are showing signs of overuse. Zero-impact use of the wilderness areas of the Cascade Range is urged by the NPS and Forest Service. Here are some simple suggestions to help minimize your impact on the mountain environment:

- Travel in small groups to do less damage to meadows and campsites.
- Use a stove for cooking and bring a tent rather than relying on scarce natural resources. No campfires.
- Use pit toilets or practice accepted human waste disposal practices (packing it out in plastic bags). Do not eliminate waste near water sources.
- Plan your actions so as to make the least impact on the environment.
- Stay on trails, even when muddy, to avoid causing erosion; and do not take shortcuts on switchbacks.
- Tread gently on vegetation, which is often fragile on high mountain slopes.
- Hike on snow or talus whenever possible rather than causing unnecessary erosion on pumice slopes and vegetation.
- Choose stable sites for camps and rest stops rather than fragile vegetation.
- Use existing campsites rather than creating new ones.
- Camp on snow instead of bare ground whenever possible.
- Don't construct rock windbreaks or clear ground of rocks or vegetation for any reason.
- Don't leave routes flagged after you depart; remove plastic tape and other markers during your descent.
- Use slings that blend in with the color of the mountain environment instead of bright colors that attract attention and draw complaints. Pack out old slings instead of throwing them off the cliff.
- Avoid having leftover food so you won't attract wildlife to your camp. Do not feed wildlife.
- Don't bring your pets with you.
- Pack out your own trash and any litter you find along the way.

Although we won't likely wear the mountains down with our boot soles, we may greatly detract from the beauty and serenity of the mountain environment unless we think and act in ways appropriate to preserving our wilderness areas.

HUMAN WASTE DISPOSAL

Human waste disposal is a major problem on many peaks included in this guide. With so many climbers using the same camps, sanitation is a real concern. On Mount Rainier and Mount Olympus, the NPS requires the use of plastic bags ("blue bags") for human waste disposal. Putting any refuse into crevasses or burying it in snow, in soil, or under rocks is not acceptable. Use pit toilets and trash containers where available; otherwise, pack it out, particularly in high-use areas. In lowland forests, bury it in a cat hole well away from any water source. If you are on a remote, infrequently traveled route, you might be okay, even environmentally correct, to leave your offering out in the open where wind and sun will decompose it. But on crowded routes, unless you want to drag your rope through it, it is best to use a well-sealed plastic bag and take it out where it can be disposed of properly. Instructions for use of blue bags are provided by the NPS. It's not only easy, it's the law.

Trailhead Theft

Nearly every trailhead along a major highway suffers from car prowling and vandalism. You can protect yourself by leaving nothing of value in your car, visible or not. Thieves are reported to be after purses and wallets, especially credit cards and personal identification, so don't lock your wallet or purse in the trunk and think it's safe there. Plan your trip so that you are able to carry everything you bring with you in your pack. Be suspicious of anyone loitering at the trailhead and report them to the authorities if you suspect they are up to no good. Likewise, if you notice someone driving back and forth past a trailhead for no apparent purpose, make note of their license number and report it. Some trailheads are monitored by the county sheriff's office, but that has only barely deterred car prowlers. There was a rash of incidents involving vandals shooting guns at cars parked at trailheads along the Stevens Pass Highway, but that seems to have subsided for the time being.

In Case of Emergency

To report a climbing or scrambling accident, or any other life-threatening emergency, call 911. If the situation is less critical, or you don't feel it is an emergency worthy of dialing 911, contact the nearest park or forest service office, campground ranger or host, or local sheriff or police department. See Appendix C for a list of park and forest service phone numbers.

It is now common for climbers and backcountry travelers to pack a cellular phone. Increasingly, injured and distressed climbers have summoned backcountry rescues via telephone. This practice allows rescuers to begin efforts hours or days sooner than they would otherwise, but as often as not, the use of a phone in an initial distress call has led to what is referred to as a "bastard search" (a response by rescuers for a situation that does not require a rescue). The NPS recommends that you follow these guidelines when calling in a distress situation:

- Always state your location and cell phone number early in the call in case the connection fails and a call back is necessary.
- Communicate your situation clearly and indicate whether you are requesting assistance or just advising the authorities of your situation. If you are making an advisory call and plan to call back later, be sure to say so. If you are not clear, a rescue may result even if you didn't ask for and don't need one.
- Remember that just because you got through the first time, you may not be able to get through again, even from the exact same location. Give as much information as you can during your first contact.

Climbers should be aware that, while cellular reception is often good, at times it can be bad or nonexistent. Don't trust your cell phone to get you out of a jam. Rely instead on experience and good judgment and avoid situations where you might get yourself into trouble.

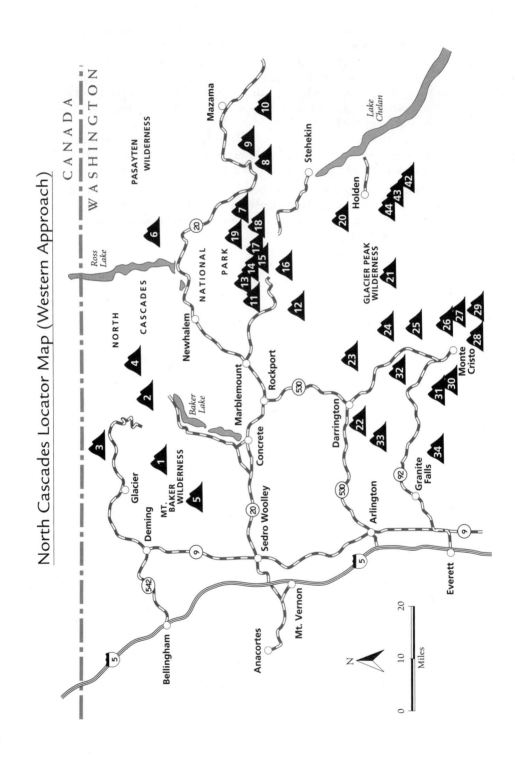

North Cascades Locator Map (Western Approach)

The North Cascades

The peaks of the North Cascades are among the most complex, varied, and challenging mountains in North America. In contrast to the gentle woodland peaks and high volcanoes of the southern Cascade Range, the North Cascades are rugged beyond compare. Actually, the range has been likened to the Swiss Alps, not as high in elevation, but equaled if not exceeded in sheer relief and volume of ice. Uplifted by colliding continental plates and scoured and carved by glaciers, the mountains of the North Cascades rise abruptly from deep glacial valleys in steep cliffs terminating in sharp rocky points and crests. Rugged glaciers drape the highest peaks and hang menacingly from north facing cirques and basins.

As climbing objectives, the peaks of the North Cascades offer great variety from easy scrambles to extreme alpine rock climbing, snow, ice, and glacier climbing, and high traverses. While a majority of climbers climb the big peaks, there are many other worthy peaks scattered throughout the range. A majority of the summits can be climbed via scrambling routes, especially those farther south; but the northern peaks, with few exceptions, involve glaciers and steep, technical snow, rock, and ice climbing. The rock formations of the North Cascades are primarily granite and gneiss, most of which is reasonably sound and reliable for climbing, although loose rock is a constant threat. There are several peaks of volcanic origin here. The obvious stratovolcanoes, which have less reliable rock, are usually ascended via glacier routes.

This guide includes a very small sampling of what the North Cascades have to offer. To find out more about climbing routes and summits in the North Cascades, read Fred Beckey's compelling *Challenge of the North Cascades* and refer to the *Cascade Alpine Guide* and other references listed in Appendix D.

The North Cascades are usually deemed to extend only as far south as Glacier Peak, but for purposes of this guide, the term North Cascades refers to all of the peaks from Snoqualmie Pass north to the Fraser River in British Columbia and includes the following Wilderness areas: Alpine Lakes, Glacier Peak, Chelan-Sawtooth, and Pasayten. For the most part, the peaks of the Alpine Lakes Wilderness and Monte Cristo region are not considered part of the North Cascades, but they exhibit many of the same characteristics. From Snoqualmie Pass north, the peaks become increasingly glaciated, craggy, and alpine, in contrast to the peaks lying between Snoqualmie Pass and Mount Rainier, which are for the most part indistinct, gentle, heavily logged mountains of absolutely no interest to climbers. Some may criticize the southern extension of the North Cascades, but the peaks along the Snoqualmie Crest, including Chimney Rock and Mount Daniel, and the peaks of the Stuart Range, certainly share many if not all of the characteristic traits of mountains farther north.

North Cascades Locator Map (Eastern Approach)

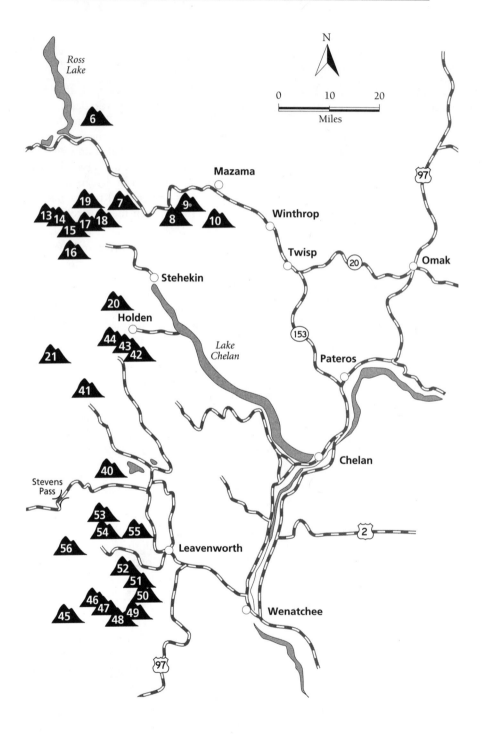

Backcountry Use Permit
A backcountry use permit is required for all overnight climbing trips in the national park. The permit is free and must be obtained in person on the day of your trip (or the day before) from the Wilderness Information Center in Marblemount or from another NPS office depending on where your trip originates (see chart below). A backcountry use permit must be carried by an individual or group leader on the trip. If you don't have a permit, you may be fined or removed from the park, or both. For more information, contact North Cascades National Park at (360) 837-4500, extension 39, or log on to the NPS Web site at www.nps.gov/noca/permits.htm.

Trip Originates In	Obtain Permit At
Baker Lake Area	NPS headquarters in Sedro Woolley
Mount Baker Highway (Washington Highway 542)	Glacier Public Service Center
Washington Highway 20 east of Marblemount (if not passing through)	Visitor center in Newhalem or Winthrop
Twisp River Drainage	Methow Valley Ranger District, Twisp Office
Stehekin Valley	Golden West Visitor Center in Stehekin
All Others	Marblemount Wilderness Information Center

Party Size Limit
In most cases, the maximum number of persons allowed per party is twelve when hiking on trails. If you bring stock animals, your total number of persons and stock is twelve (i.e., six people and six stock animals). In designated cross-country zones near Mount Shuksan, Eldorado Peak, and Forbidden Peak, party size is also limited to twelve. In all other cross-country zones, the limit is six per party.

Marblemount Ranger Station is the clearinghouse for all climbing and backcountry information for the Skagit District. The Golden West Visitor Center provides climbing and backcountry information for the Stehekin District.

North Cascades National Park recommends that you use their form *Wilderness Trip Planner* to plan your trip to the North Cascades. You can obtain one from the Marblemount Ranger Station or Golden West Visitor Center, and on-line via the park's climbing home page at www.nps.gov/noca/home.htm. Climbers should log on to this Web site before visiting the area. It is a valuable source of route and permit information, safety tips, accident reports, and other useful details about climbing in the North Cascades.

In Case of Emergency
To advise of a distress situation or to summon a rescue in North Cascades National Park, the NPS suggests that you call the park dispatcher at (360) 873-4500, extension 37, rather than 911. This will save time. You can still call 911 or the local sheriff's office, but the 911 operator will have to forward your call to the park dispatcher.

Matt Arksey descending Coleman Glacier, Mount Baker.

1. MOUNT BAKER

Elevation: 10,785 feet/3,288 meters
Route: Coleman Glacier/Easton Glacier
Rating: Grade II glacier
Distance: 10 miles round trip
Elevation Gain: 7,100 feet
Time: 8 to 10 hours trailhead to summit; best done as two- or three-day climb
Maps: USGS Mount Baker; Green Trails No. 13 (Mount Baker)

ABOUT THE CLIMB

Mount Baker, the "northern sentinel" of the Cascade Range, is the fourth highest summit in Washington State. It is also one of the iciest of the Cascade volcanoes, with 44 square miles of ice spread out among its twelve glaciers. By comparison, Mount Rainier has only 35 square miles of ice. Rising a short distance south of the Canadian border on the 49th parallel, only 50 miles from Bellingham Bay, Mount Baker is a dominating presence from any vantage around northern Puget Sound and from any high ridge or peak in the northern Cascades and Olympics. Its stark white glaciers are clearly visible from Seattle, and on a clear day, you can see it quite well from Mount Rainier, more than 100 miles away.

Mount Baker was "discovered" in 1792 by Captain Vancouver's first mate, Joseph Baker, for whom the peak was named. Long before that, local Nooksack tribespeople knew the mountain as "Koma-Kulshan," translated as "Wounded Mountain," among other things. A native legend had it that an angry god struck

THE NORTH CASCADES 25

the mountain with a lightning bolt, wounding or breaking the great peak and causing it to "bleed" molten rock, undoubtedly the best explanation of a volcanic eruption that could be mustered by the superstitious inhabitants of the mountain's foothills. The mountain was supposedly more precipitous prior to the mid-1800s, but a summit "slump" or partial collapse is thought by some geologists to have occurred, giving the summit, Grant Peak, its somewhat rounded appearance.

Mount Baker volcano was active during the mid-1970s, when Sherman Crater broke open and began spewing steam and ash—a minor event compared with the 1980 eruption of Mount St. Helens, but of great concern at the time. The peak has settled down, but seismic activity continues beneath the peak. There is little doubt among geologists that Mount Baker may erupt again in the not-too-distant future.

The first ascent of Mount Baker was claimed in 1868 by Edmund T. Coleman, David Ogilvy, Thomas Stratton, and John Tennant. Coleman, an English librarian living in Victoria, B.C., had made two previous attempts to climb the mountain and was dedicated to the task. His detailed journals and artwork provide a remarkable glimpse of early climbing attempts on the mountain.

The generally accepted elevation of Mount Baker is 10,778 feet, but according to the USGS database, it is 10,785 feet, which is the elevation listed here.

HOW TO GET THERE

If climbing Coleman Glacier, drive the Mount Baker Highway (Washington Highway 542) for about 37 miles east from Bellingham to Glacier. Register at the Glacier Ranger Station. About 1 mile past the Glacier Ranger Station, turn south on Forest Road 39 and follow it for about 8 miles to the Mount Baker Trail trailhead on the left.

If climbing Easton Glacier, register at the NPS headquarters at Sedro Woolley. Drive the North Cascades Highway (Washington Highway 20) to Baker Lake–Grandy Creek Road, which leaves Washington Highway 20 about 22.5 miles east of Interstate 5 (exit 230). After about 13 miles, the road forks; take unpaved Forest Road 12 on the left and follow it for just over 3 miles, then turn right onto Forest Road 13 and follow it for 4 miles to the road's end at the trailhead "Schreibers Meadow." The road is well signed, so finding the trailhead should be easy. If approaching from the east on Washington Highway 20, register at Marblemount Ranger Station, then drive to Concrete and turn right on a signed road pointing to Baker Lake, just past the concrete silos; this road leads north just over 4 miles to connect with Baker Lake Road (Forest Road 11). Proceed north just over 5 miles to the turnoff for Forest Road 12.

A Northwest Forest Pass is required at each trailhead. Refer to Appendix B for information about obtaining this pass.

ROUTE DESCRIPTION

The Coleman Glacier is the line of the original ascent in 1868 and remains the most popular route to Mount Baker's summit. From Forest Road 39, hike about 2 miles up Mount Baker Trail (Trail 677) to the former site of Kulshan Cabin at

Mount Baker Area

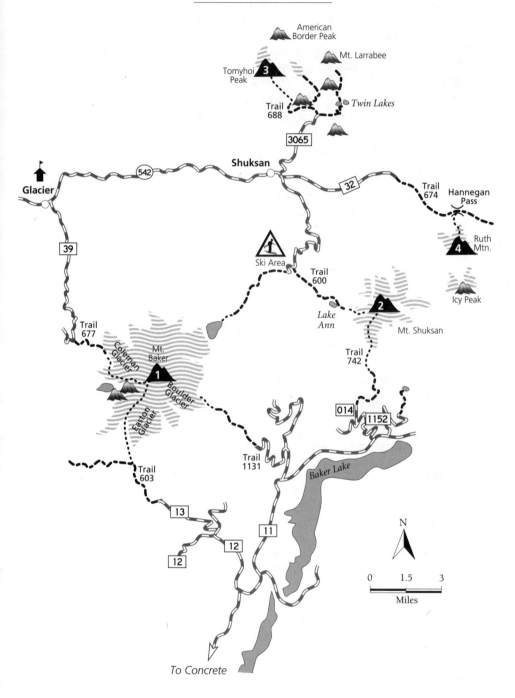

American Border Peak

Mt. Larrabee

Tomyhoi Peak

3

Twin Lakes

Trail 688

3065

Shuksan

542

32

Glacier

Trail 674

Hannegan Pass

39

Ruth Mtn.

4

Ski Area

Trail 600

Icy Peak

Lake Ann

2

Mt. Shuksan

Trail 677

Coleman Glacier

Mt. Baker

Trail 742

1

Boulder Glacier

014

1152

Easton Glacier

Baker Lake

Trail 1131

Trail 603

13

11

12

12

To Concrete

N

0   1.5   3

Miles

USGS

North Ridge

Easton Glacier

Black Buttes

Coleman Glacier

Hogback

timberline. From the trail's official end, continue another 0.5 mile up a climber's trail to a narrow lateral moraine dubbed the "Hog's Back" or "Hogback." There is a popular campsite at the top of the Hogback, which is often crowded.

From the Hogback, continue up the climber's trail to the glacier. In early season, it may be difficult to determine where the snow ends and glacier begins. Rope up early to be on the safe side. Ascend the right flank of the glacier, which is usually less crevassed, toward and beneath the Black Buttes to the saddle between Colfax Peak and Grant Peak. Some climbers camp at about 7,000 or 9,000 feet on the Coleman Glacier below the Black Buttes to gain a head start on climbers coming from the Hogback, or when that site is crowded. From the saddle, ascend to the left up a pumice ridge, staying right of the Roman Wall, and continue pretty much straight up the glacier headwall, bearing right toward the

top to the summit dome. The actual summit is a small mound at the southeast edge of the summit dome, reached via an easy snow hike across the dome.

The Easton Glacier, another popular route, is not as long and is less demanding than the Coleman Glacier. This is a popular winter route, especially among ski mountaineers, and unfortunately among snowmobilers, at least on the glacier and occasionally on the summit. From the trailhead, hike about 3 miles up Baker Pass Trail (Trail 603) to Morovitz Meadow, where a climber's trail ascends to the Railroad Grade moraine. Most climbers bivouac on the Railroad Grade or at Morovitz Meadow. From the top of the Railroad Grade, rope up and ascend the Easton Glacier, following the line of least resistance. The glacier is usually less crevassed on the west side, near the Easton-Deming Glacier divide. Ascend the right flank of the Deming Glacier headwall or traverse over to the left flank to the Coleman-Deming saddle and finish via the Coleman Glacier route.

To descend, downclimb the route. Resist the urge to glissade on the glaciers or on the slopes below the glaciers. Several fatal accidents have occurred involving climbers glissading into hidden crevasses and moats.

OPTIONS
There are several other summit routes, the best of which include the Boulder Glacier, the classic North Ridge◆, and the challenging Coleman Headwall. Refer to *Climbing the Cascade Volcanoes* or one of the other guides listed in Appendix D for route information.

PRECAUTIONS
Mount Baker's glaciers are heavily crevassed; one of them swallowed a snowmobile recently. A large number of climbers have been injured or killed falling into

crevasses on Mount Baker. Lately, there have been numerous incidents of climbers glissading down the Coleman Glacier and alongside the Hogback and sliding into hidden crevasses and moats, which has resulted in injury and death. A July 1939 avalanche high on the Deming Glacier killed six climbers, an event repeated more than once since. Rockfall off the Black Buttes is not uncommon. Fierce storms may set in without much warning. Descend immediately if a storm develops.

2. MOUNT SHUKSAN

Elevation: 9,127 feet/2,782 meters
Route: Sulphide Glacier
Rating: Class 4 to 5; Grade I or II glacier
Distance: 14 miles round trip
Elevation Gain: 6,600 feet
Time: 8 to 10 hours trailhead to summit; best done as a two- or three-day climb
Maps: USGS Mount Shuksan; Green Trails No. 14 (Mount Shuksan)

ABOUT THE CLIMB

Mount Shuksan, Washington's tenth highest mountain, is one of the most recognized peaks in Washington due to the fact that its likeness graces a variety of postcards, brochures, magazine covers, maps, and books. It's often seen in television commercials. Shuksan is best known by its west face, as viewed from Picture Lakes, a 4,000-foot wall of rock and ice punctuated by the distinct summit pyramid. It is a classic alpine peak, a sharp rock horn set atop a craggy, steep-walled, glaciated massif, that rises dramatically above a subalpine meadow valley. Due to local topography, it is one of the few interior peaks of the North Cascades that is visible from Puget Sound.

As one of the most visible, accessible, and visually stunning 9,000-foot peaks in Washington, it is a very popular climb especially by the fairly easy route via the south ridge and Sulphide Glacier. Another popular route to the summit, the Fisher Chimneys, is a challenging mixed route up the west face. Although it is well regarded for its alpine nature and climbing challenge, Mount Shuksan is notorious for bad weather and difficult climbing conditions. Like Mount Baker, Shuksan is subject to fierce storms, sometimes even during the summer months. Climbing conditions can deteriorate rapidly, and the summit pyramid and Fisher Chimneys become difficult and dangerous during poor weather and after snowfall, as many climbers have discovered the hard way. But during good weather, Mount Shuksan is one of the best climbs in the North Cascades—and most crowded. Summit views include nearby Mount Baker, as well as a panorama of high peaks to the north, east and south, including the American Border Peaks, the Picket Range and the Chilliwack Range.

HOW TO GET THERE

The Sulphide Glacier route begins from Shannon Creek Road at the north end of Baker Lake. If approaching from the west, take exit 230 off Interstate 5 and register at the NPS headquarters at Sedro Woolley. Drive the North Cascades Highway (Washington Highway 20) east to the turnoff for Baker Lake, about

Summit pyramid, Mount Shuksan.

22.5 miles east from Interstate 5. Turn north onto Baker Lake-Grandy Creek Road and follow it for about 24 miles to Shannon Creek Campground near the north end of Baker Lake. Turn left on the Shannon Creek spur (Forest Road 1152) and follow it up several switchbacks to another spur road on the right (Forest Road 1152-014) at about 3.5 miles. Follow this spur about 1 mile to a gate. Park here. If approaching from the east on Washington Highway 20, register at Marblemount Ranger Station, then drive to Concrete and turn right on a signed road pointing to Baker Lake, just past the concrete silos; this road leads north just over 4 miles to connect with Baker Lake Road (Forest Road 11). Proceed north to Shannon Creek. A Northwest Forest Pass is required even though this is an "abandoned" trail.

ROUTE DESCRIPTION

Sulphide Glacier is the fastest, easiest, and consequently, the most popular route up Mount Shuksan. The route involves a relatively gentle glacier climb to the summit pyramid, then a Class 4–5 scramble to the summit. This is a very popular winter and spring ski mountaineering route.

From the gate, hike up the abandoned but heavily used Shannon Ridge Trail (Trail 742) for about 3 miles to the 4,800-foot ridge crest. The trail begins on an old road grade, then climbs through a small clearcut. This initial section is brushy and can be hot by midday. Once past the brush, the trail ascends through shady old-growth forest for some distance to the ridge crest. Follow the crest another 0.5 mile to where a short climb up a gully gains a pass. The entire route to the pass is on an established but unmaintained climber's trail with snow patches until summer. From the pass, contour on the northeast side of the ridge

Sulphide Glacier

Summit Pyramid

Crystal Glacier

Sulphide Glacier

Trail 742

Shuksan Lake

Shannon Creek

FR 1152-014

Trail 608

FR 1160

FR 1152

FR 11

Baker Lake

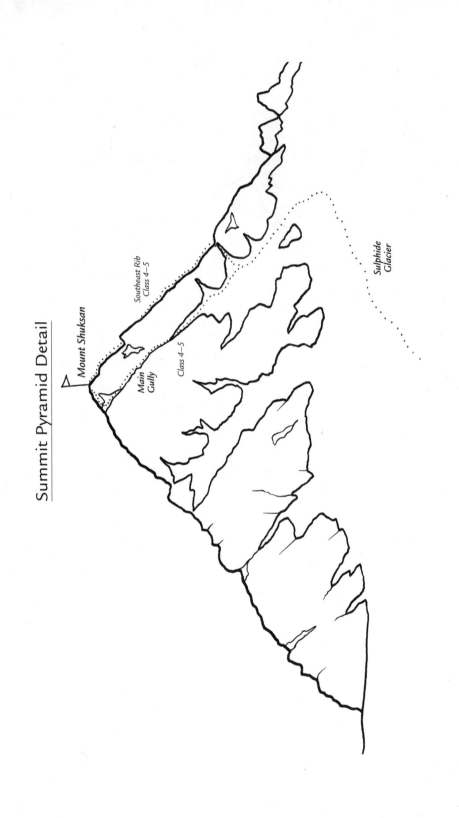

Summit Pyramid Detail

Mount Shuksan

Southeast Rib
Class 4–5

Main
Gully

Class 4–5

Sulphide
Glacier

to the Sulphide Glacier. Most parties camp just below the glacier at about 6,200 feet and begin their climb early in the morning. The park service has installed a composting toilet here and recommends that climbers camp near enough that they can use the toilet to alleviate sanitation problems in and around the camp.

From high camp, rope up and ascend the glacier, skirting crevasses as necessary and aiming for the base of the summit pyramid. The glacier is generally less crevassed on the west side nearer the ridge. By summer, there is usually an established trail on the glacier. The summit pyramid is most often ascended via the obvious steep gully on the right side of the southern face. In winter and early season, this is a moderately steep snow or ice climb to just below the summit, with only a brief section of rock climbing or scrambling near the top. Later in the season, it is a mixed snow and rock scramble up a steep snowpatch and a moderately angled open book with a brief lieback crack. Variations of the gully route may be required due to snow conditions. By late season, it is usually all rock scrambling from the glacier to the summit. The summit route is generally reported as Class 3, easy enough that most parties ascend and descend it unroped; however, many climbers feel it is more difficult and exposed than they would have preferred to climb unroped. General consensus is that the summit pyramid is Class 4-5.

To descend, downclimb the route. A single-rope rappel (or two) down the steepest rock sections may be desired. Some parties fix a rope on a snow traverse at the top of the snowpatch, but a rope should be carried to the summit so a rappel or belay can be made if desired, especially when the rock is wet, snowy, or icy, or the party includes less-experienced climbers.

OPTIONS
The Fisher Chimneys♦, a series of snow and rock gullies splitting the northern headwall of lower Curtis Glacier, is the most popular route from Mount Baker Highway. This is a more challenging route, involving moderately steep rock, snow, and ice climbing (in season) and requiring good routefinding and all-around mountaineering skills. It is not recommended for climbers lacking good routefinding skills and steep snow, ice, and rock experience, or for climbers who are not able to move rapidly and make quick transitions between differing terrain. Those climbers are better off climbing the Sulphide Glacier route. There are several other popular routes up Mount Shuksan, including the challenging North Face and classic Price Glacier. A direct route up the White Salmon Glacier is frequently climbed as well. Refer to *Cascade Alpine Guide* and other guides listed in Appendix D for route details.

PRECAUTIONS
Mount Shuksan is one of the most rugged peaks in the North Cascades and is a serious mountaineering objective that should not be taken lightly even on its easier routes. Mount Shuksan's glaciers are heavily crevassed, so rope up and be prepared for crevasse rescue. Steep, hard snow or ice may be encountered on any route. There is rockfall and icefall exposure on and below the summit pyramid. Mount Shuksan is subject to sudden storms, so be prepared for bad weather and descend immediately if a storm develops. Ice ax and crampons required; helmet recommended.

There are several routes up the summit pyramid, but the summit scramble described above is the route of choice for a majority of climbers, which creates a bottleneck on busy weekends. Climbers are often forced to turn back because of delays in the final gully. Overcrowding can create potentially dangerous climbing conditions here. A recommended alternative is to climb the southeast rib of the summit pyramid, the right skyline as viewed from the Sulphide Glacier. This route is said to be an airy, enjoyable Class 4 rock climb. Other parties climb Class 3–4 rock to the left of the main gully on "funky" but interesting rock.

The summit pyramid's rock is green gneiss, which is sharp and slick. Climb carefully when the rock is wet, or when patchy snow and ice, fresh snowfall, or verglas covers the rock. There is some loose rock, and rockfall is not uncommon. Because the summit pyramid involves fairly exposed Class 4–5 rock, belaying and rappelling the steepest sections is recommended. Peer pressure (i.e., faster climbers behind or party members climbing unroped) should not force a hasty unroped ascent; belay and rappel as desired, for safety's sake.

3. TOMYHOI PEAK

Elevation: 7,451 feet/2,271 meters
Route: East Ridge
Rating: Class 3; Grade I glacier
Distance: 12 miles round trip
Elevation Gain: 4,500 feet
Time: 5 to 7 hours trailhead to summit
Maps: USGS Mount Larrabee; Green Trails No. 14 (Mount Shuksan)

ABOUT THE CLIMB

Tomyhoi Peak is one of a group of peaks located north of Mount Baker, near the U.S.-Canada boundary. Although these peaks are relatively insignificant compared to other nearby peaks, especially Mount Baker and Mount Shuksan, they are interesting, accessible summits offering some of the most spectacular views in the North Cascades. Tomyhoi is not the highest of the group, but it is the most enjoyable to climb and hence the most popular. Alpine scramblers and climbers heap superlative praise upon Tomyhoi Peak even though it is relatively unknown and often overlooked in favor of its more prominent neighbors. Some call it the best alpine scramble in the North Cascades.

The climb is not especially difficult. The route follows a boot path along a high ridge to very near the summit, then a snow and rock scramble leads to the top. The approach hike is great in the fall, through vast meadows of heather and huckleberry. The hues of red, orange, and yellow will leave a lasting impression. Summit views are phenomenal. A panorama of the peaks of North Cascades includes Mount Baker, Mount Shuksan, the Picket Range, the American and Canadian Border peaks, the Chilliwacks, and the mysterious Coast Range.

HOW TO GET THERE

This climb begins from Gold Run Pass trailhead, just north of Shuksan on the Mount Baker Highway. Drive the Mount Baker Highway (Washington Highway 542) east from Bellingham and continue 13.5 miles past the Glacier Visitor Center to Shuksan. Just past the snow equipment maintenance shed, turn left on

Tomyhoi Peak

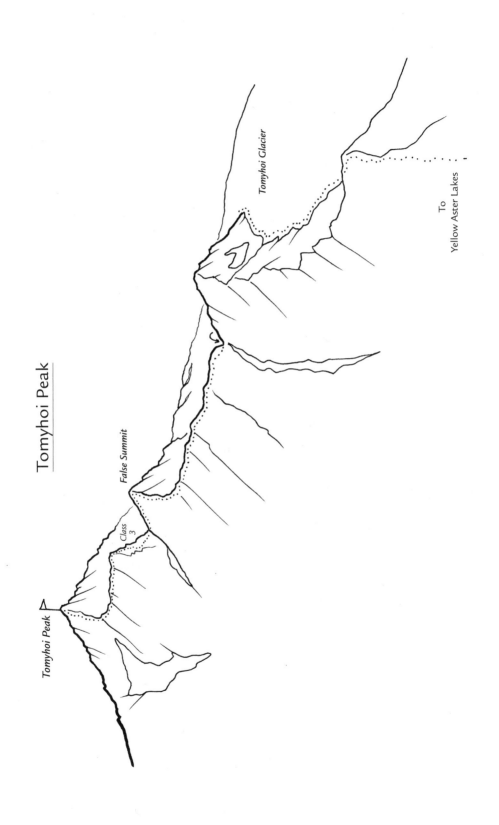

Tomyhoi Peak

Class 3

False Summit

Tomyhoi Glacier

To
Yellow Aster Lakes

Twin Lakes Road (Forest Road 3065) and follow it for about 4.2 miles to the trailhead. A Northwest Forest Pass is required.

ROUTE DESCRIPTION

The old Keep Kool Trail has been decomissioned and replaced by a shorter, more scenic, and gentler trail. Hike up Gold Run Pass Trail (Trail 688) almost to the pass, then follow the new trail, which traverses westward across the southern slopes of Yellow Aster Butte, then descends to Yellow Aster Lakes. From the lakes, follow a climber's trail or snow slopes up to and along the ridge toward Tomyhoi Peak. At one point midway along the ridge, descend about 200 feet of easy but exposed rock, then rejoin the boot path following the ridge. Where the going gets tough, traverse a snow patch curving to the right around to the north flank of Tomyhoi Peak. This leads to the upper slopes of the Tomyhoi Glacier. Traverse the glacier's upper slopes, which are usually unbroken except for a bergschrund, around to the northwest side. Climb to an obvious gap in the ridge, then cross over to the south side of the ridge and continue along rubble-strewn benches, easy but exposed, to the false summit. Stay high on these benches, just below the ridge crest; careful routefinding is required here to avoid loose, exposed scrambling. From the false summit, descend to the gap and climb about 150 feet of Class 3 rock to gain the summit ridge. This wall is steep and exposed with some loose rock and looks "impossible" from the false summit, but it turns out to be quite reasonable. Once atop this obstacle, traverse the ridge a few hundred feet to the rocky summit. To descend, downclimb the route.

OPTIONS

There are several other climbable peaks in the vicinity. Yellow Aster Butte (6,145 feet), the most popular, is reached via a straightforward scramble from either Gold Run Pass or Yellow Aster Lakes.

PRECAUTIONS

There is rockfall hazard and some loose, exposed scrambling on the summit ridge. Careful routefinding on the climb is critical. A wrong turn could lead to exposed Class 4–5 climbing. Stay high on the glacier to avoid crevasses. Roping up on glaciers is always recommended, but most parties don't rope up on the glacier because they are traversing above the bergschrund. Stay close to rock to avoid crevasses.

4. RUTH MOUNTAIN

Elevation: 7,106 feet/2,166 meters
Route: Ruth Glacier
Rating: Class 2; Grade I glacier
Distance: 10 miles round trip
Elevation Gain: 4,300 feet
Time: 5 to 6 hours trailhead to summit
Maps: USGS Mount Shuksan; Green Trails No. 14 (Mount Shuksan)

ABOUT THE CLIMB

Ruth Mountain is a relatively modest glaciated peak located about 5 miles northeast of Mount Shuksan. It is not a difficult climb, but it is fairly popular because

Ruth Mountain from near Hannegan Pass.

it is a straightforward glacier to a high summit at the edge of the most rugged portion of the North Cascades and provides breathtaking views of the Picket Range, Mount Shuksan, Mount Baker, and many other craggy, glaciated peaks. Its glacial mantle belies the mountain's origins. Ruth Mountain is a remnant of an ancient volcano. The mountain is composed of breccia, a volcanic rock common in the Cascades but seemingly out of place in the North Cascades. A black rock outcrop near the summit, known as "Rest Rock" by climbers, is composed of black phyllite rubble that has been cemented together. However, Ruth Mountain offers a fantastic, accessible introduction to glacier climbing, and the glacier portion of the route is so gentle that many climbers don't bother roping up. Because it is so easy and accessible, many climbers continue on to Icy Peak to add some challenge and length to the ascent. The Ruth-Icy Traverse makes a great weekend climb, although a one-day ascent of Ruth Mountain alone is well worth the long drive.

HOW TO GET THERE

This climb begins via Hannegan Pass Trail just east of Shuksan on the Mount Baker Highway. Drive the Mount Baker Highway (Washington Highway 542) east from Bellingham and continue 13.5 miles past the Glacier Visitor Center to Shuksan. Turn left onto Ruth Creek Road (Forest Road 32) just before the Nooksack River bridge and follow it for about 5.5 miles to Hannegan Campground and the trailhead at the road's end. A Northwest Forest Pass is required.

ROUTE DESCRIPTION

Hike up Hannegan Pass Trail (Trail 674) about 3.5 miles to Hannegan Pass, elevation 5,068 feet. From the pass, a climber's trail leads southward up the ridge toward Ruth Mountain, which looms invitingly nearby. The initial climb up

Ruth Mountain

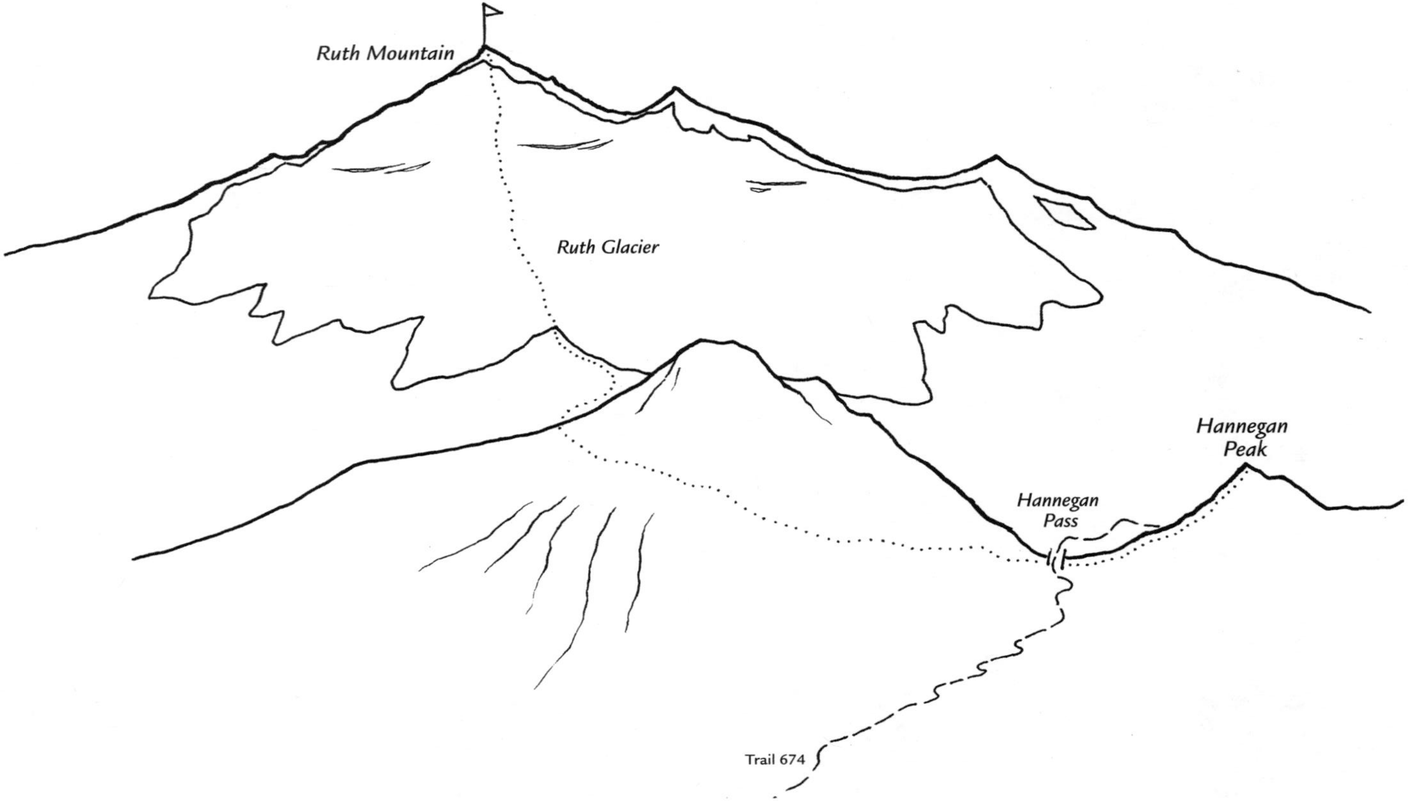

Ruth Mountain

Ruth Glacier

Hannegan Pass

Hannegan Peak

Trail 674

from the pass is steep but not too difficult, following a climber's path that skirts the only intervening ridge point on the left (east) side. This traverse is snowy until late season, and although it is straightforward, the slope is moderately steep and has a short runout to an abrupt drop-off, so cross with care. Once on the upper ridge, traverse gentle slopes to the edge of Ruth Glacier. Rope up and ascend the glacier, avoiding or crossing crevasses as necessary, to the summit. You may need to skirt crevasses lower on the glacier; the final climb is directly up firn slopes to the summit. To descend, downclimb the route.

OPTIONS

You can ascend the glacier to the saddle just west of the summit, then scramble up a few hundred meters of broken rock to the summit. This option is recommended if a late-season bergschrund is difficult to pass, which is rare. An ascent of 7,070-foot Icy Peak can be combined with Ruth Mountain via a southwest traverse from the saddle just west of the summit. The Mountaineers make this a regular early summer weekend traverse. Refer to *Cascade Alpine Guide* for route details.

PRECAUTIONS

The steep snow slopes on the approach from Hannegan Pass are avalanche prone and have a dangerous runout above cliffs. Many climbers complete the glacier ascent unroped, but roping up is recommended because there are crevasses.

5. NORTH TWIN

Elevation: 6,570 feet/2,003 meters
Route: West Ridge
Rating: Grade III, Class 4
Distance: 15 miles round trip
Elevation Gain: 3,200 feet from Dailey Prairie to summit
Time: 4 hours from Dailey Prairie to summit; 7 to 10 hours round trip depending on descent route and conditions
Maps: USGS Twin Sisters Mountain; Green Trails No. 45 (Hamilton)

ABOUT THE CLIMB

The Twin Sisters are the highest peaks of the Twin Sisters Range, a subrange of craggy peaks lying about 9 miles southwest of Mount Baker. Although the 6,932-foot South Twin is the highest of the group, the North Twin is the most popular because it is easiest to approach and descend, and because the West Ridge is a classic alpine scramble. The North Twin is an attractive rock peak. The West Ridge is a sweeping ridge of mostly solid, orange-hued rock, rising nearly 2,000 feet from base to peak and providing a long, interesting rock scramble. Approaching the peak is complicated by a gated logging road that requires a 5-mile hike or bike ride to get to Dailey Prairie, which is where the climbing route begins. Given favorable weather and route conditions, you can make a one-day ascent from the road, but most parties make it a two-day climb. Those who plan to climb the North Twin and South Twin usually add an extra day. Summit views are grand and include many peaks of the North Cascades, a close look at Mount Baker, and views west across Puget Sound to the Olympic Mountains.

West Ridge (left) of North Twin.

HOW TO GET THERE

The Twin Sisters are located about 20 miles due east of Bellingham. The route begins via Gailbraith Creek Road from Middle Fork Nooksack River Road. If you are coming from Bellingham, drive Washington Highway 542 to Deming, then continue 2.5 miles from the Washington Highway 9 junction to Mosquito Lake Road and follow it about 5 miles to Middle Fork Road. If you are coming from Seattle, drive Interstate 5 north to the Bow Hill Road exit and head east on Prairie Road to the Washington Highway 9 junction at the town of Prairie. Then head north through Wickersham to Acme and turn right on Mosquito Lake Road, continuing to a fork just past Porter Creek. Follow Middle Fork Road (Forest Road 38) 4.4 miles to Clearwater Creek bridge, then another 0.3 mile to Gailbraith Creek Road, a spur road on the right. Follow Gailbraith Creek Road a short distance to a gated bridge over the Middle Fork Nooksack River. Park here but do not block the gate or road.

The access road is gated, necessitating the use of mountain bikes to avoid a 5.2-mile approach hike up Gailbraith Creek Road. Not that climbers can't handle a 5-mile approach hike up a logging road, but it goes much faster if you can bike in. At least, it's faster on the way out, which is mostly downhill.

ROUTE DESCRIPTION

Pass the gate and cross the river, then hike or bike up the road, which begins as a long uphill traverse heading southeast. After about 2 miles the road crosses Gailbraith Creek. Continue about 0.5 mile from the creek until an overgrown spur road cuts back right at about 2,600 feet elevation. Follow this spur road south. It opens up into a large clearing after several hundred yards and is then blocked by several rock-filled water bars. This spur leads 1.5 miles to a fork at the

North Twin Approach

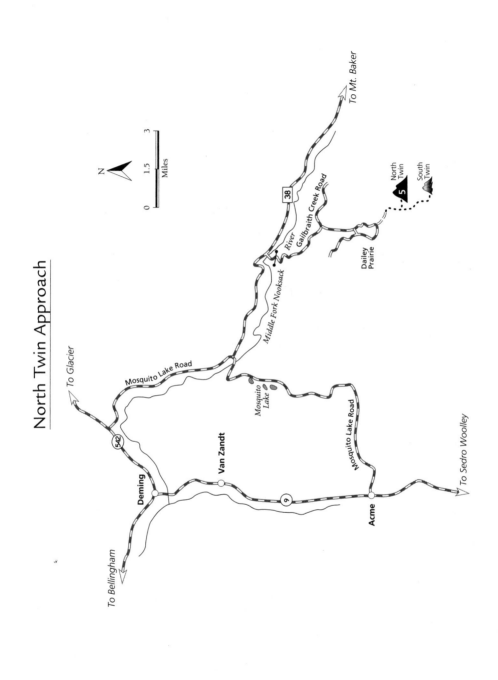

North Twin

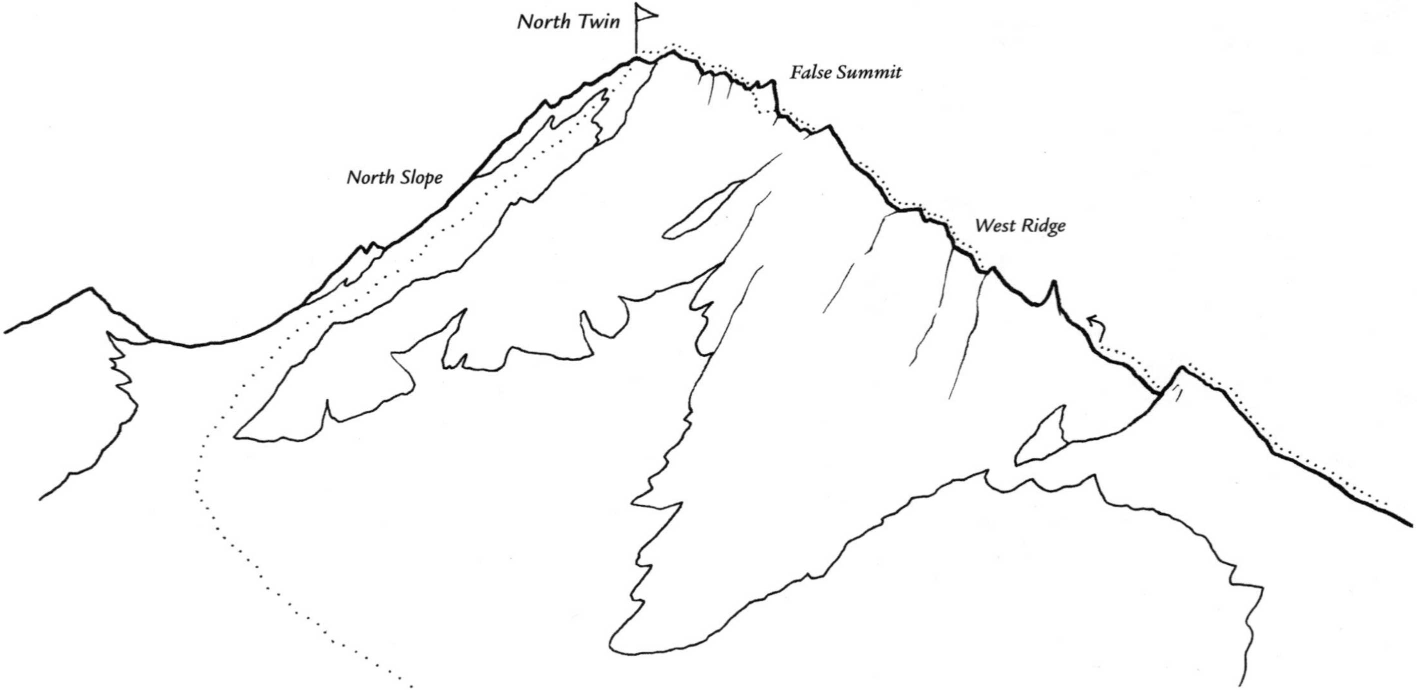

North Twin

North Slope

False Summit

West Ridge

north end of the Dailey Prairie loop. Stay left and continue 0.9 mile to the "trail-head" at the southeast corner of Dailey Prairie where you'll find a logging spur with a large dead tree beside the road and a second downed log shortly up the road. This is the middle of the three spur roads depicted on the USGS topo map. Ascend this old logging spur about 1.5 miles to the base of the West Ridge. From the road's end, a climber's trail continues directly up the ridge. If there is not a good trail at the road's end, backtrack and find the right road.

From the base of the ridge, scramble up Class 2 rock to the top of a small, prominent peak visible on the approach about a third of the way up the ridge. Scramble down to the notch on the upper side of this ridge peak and continue scrambling up the south side of the ridge, skirting a very prominent orange rock pinnacle (the "obelisk"). Gain the ridge crest again shortly above the pinnacle by Class 3–4 climbing. Follow the sometimes narrow ridge crest several hundred feet until you reach a short headwall just below the false summit. When free of snow, this obstacle is most easily passed by scrambling on the north side. How-ever, you can climb it directly (Class 4) or pass via a right traverse over a sharp southwest spur ridge and an exposed traverse on loose yellow rock (Class 3–4). Via any option, a simple scramble continues from the false summit to the sum-mit. Although Class 4 climbing is encountered, many climbers complete the ascent unroped. Many variations are possible, and Class 4 or even Class 5 rock climbing awaits those who get "off route."

The standard descent route is down the snowfield on the North Slope, then across brushy slopes back to the base of the ridge. However, several accidents and a death have occurred on this descent due to steep snow and an inability to self-arrest. Some parties elect to downclimb the West Ridge instead. Do not descend the North Slope without an ice ax and confidence in your self-arrest skills. Moats atop the snowfield may complicate the descent. Descending into the forest is not recommended due to brush and routefinding difficulties; a traverse contouring back to the base of the ridge is recommended. This descent has very loose rock when not covered in snow.

OPTIONS

The North Slope (the descent route described previously) is a simple early season snow climb with little routefinding difficulty once you get to the snowfield below the north face. It is the easiest summit route, but definitely not the route of choice for a majority of climbers. Come prepared for steep snow climbing; ice ax recommended, crampons may be useful. Not particularly recommended in late season due to loose rock. Be very careful when descending this route.

The West Ridge of South Twin is a popular Class 3 scramble. North Twin and South Twin can be climbed in a weekend outing, especially if you hike in on Fri-day evening. Refer to *Cascade Alpine Guide* for route details.

PRECAUTIONS

The access road is usually gated, and even if it isn't, do not drive past the gate because it will soon be locked. Although most of the route is Class 3 scrambling and many climbers complete the route unroped, you will likely encounter Class 4 climbing and a wrong turn can lead to very exposed Class 4–5 climbing. Descending the North Slope route can be treacherous.

6. JACK MOUNTAIN

Elevation: 9,066 feet/2,764 meters
Route: Southeast Slope via Jerry Lakes
Rating: Class 3–4
Distance: 22 miles round trip
Elevation Gain: 7,400 feet
Time: 6 to 8 hours from Jerry Lakes to summit; best done as a two- or three-day climb
Maps: USGS Jack Mountain; Green Trails No. 17 (Jack Mountain)

ABOUT THE CLIMB

Jack Mountain is the highest summit in the Pasayten Wilderness. It is a big, somewhat remote, glaciated peak with a few interesting summit routes that all require at least a strenuous full-day approach. Fast climbers might manage the ascent in a day from a trailhead bivouac, but for most, Jack is a two- or three-day climb, which probably accounts for the fact that very few climbers attempt the peak. If Jack Mountain was not one of the state's 9,000-foot summits, it probably would not be climbed very often. However, because it is one of the few 9,000-foot peaks north of Cascade Pass with a scrambling route that does not require glacier travel, and is one of the supreme viewpoints of the Pasayten Wilderness, it deserves greater popularity. Summit views are supreme and include close views across Ross Lake to the Pickets and north to Mount Redoubt, Mount Spickard, Mox Peak, and Hozomeen Mountain as well as eastward across the Pasayten Wilderness and south to Black Peak, Ragged Ridge, Snowfield Peak, Eldorado Peak, Forbidden Peak, and Boston Peak. You will also see 9,000-footers Buckner Mountain, Mount Logan, and Goode Mountain poking up in between, and Glacier Peak in the distance.

HOW TO GET THERE

The climb begins via Crater Mountain Trail from the North Cascades Highway just east of Ross Lake. Drive the North Cascades Highway (Washington Highway 20) to Canyon Creek, about 20.2 miles east from Newhalem and 17.6 miles west from Rainy Pass. Park at the trailhead turnout. A Northwest Forest Pass is required.

ROUTE DESCRIPTION

The easiest and most direct route to the summit is the South Face. There are two standard approaches: Crater Mountain Trail and the Southeast Ridge or Little Jack Mountain and the Southwest Ridge. The Crater Mountain approach is preferred because it is easier and faster, assuming the link to Canyon Creek Trail is passable. Call the Newhalem Visitor Center in advance for current trail conditions.

From the highway, hike 0.2 mile down across Granite Creek and Canyon Creek to the junction with Ruby Creek Trail (Trail 736). A segment of this trail is subject to washouts and may be impassable or dangerous if bridges are out. Once across the creeks, take a right at the trail junction and hike up Crater Mountain Trail (Trail 738) for about 4 miles to a junction with the Crater Lake Trail Spur

Jack Mountain

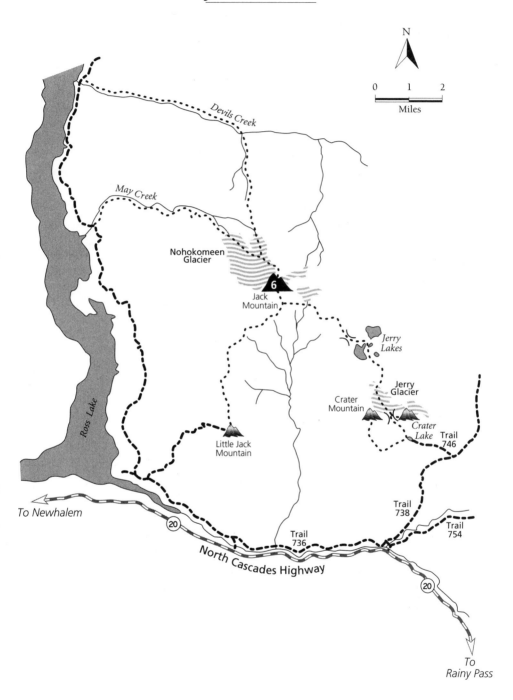

N

0   1   2
Miles

Devils Creek

May Creek

Nohokomeen
Glacier

6

Jack
Mountain

Ross Lake

Jerry
Lakes

Jerry
Glacier

Crater
Mountain

Crater
Lake

Trail
746

Little Jack
Mountain

To Newhalem

20

Trail
736

Trail
738

Trail
754

North Cascades Highway

20

To
Rainy Pass

Jack Mountain

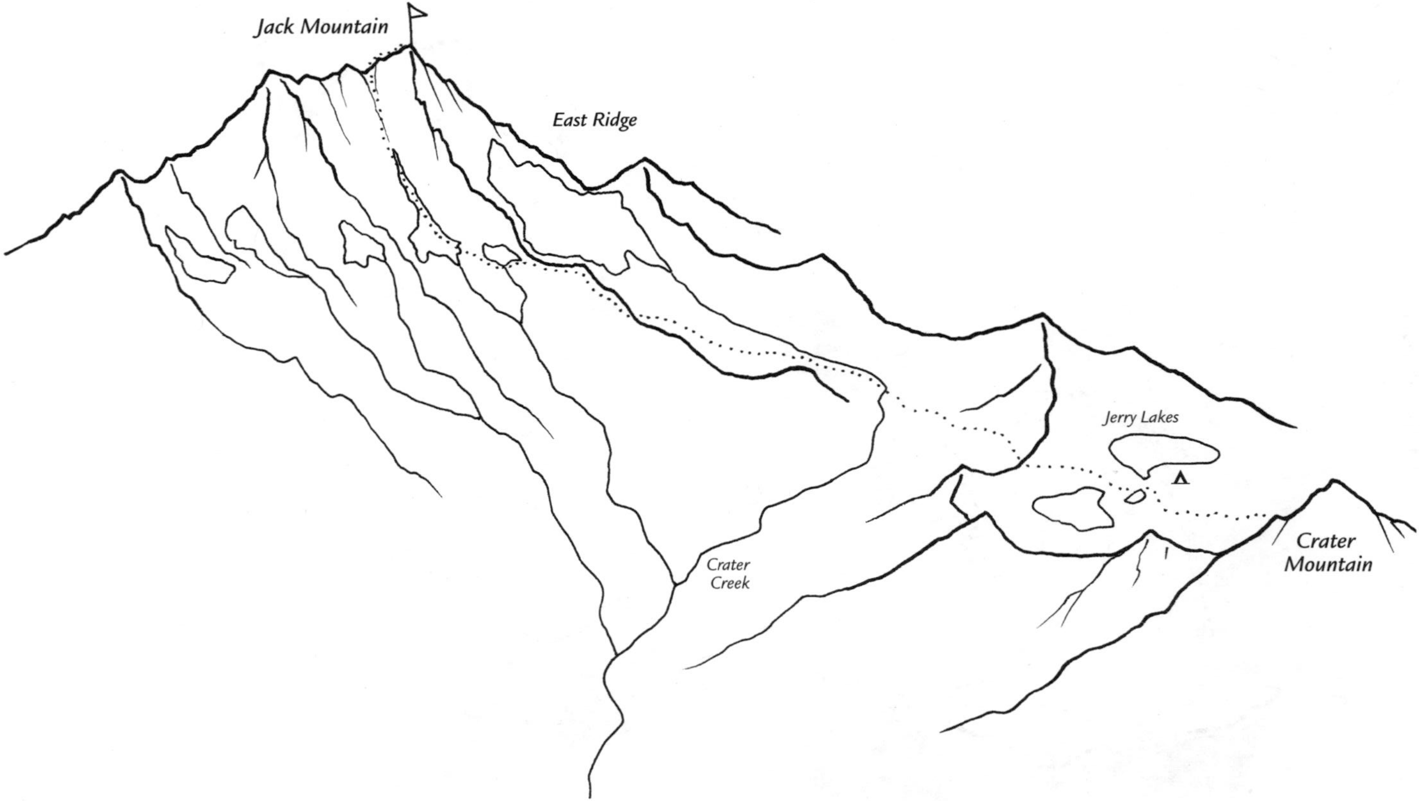

Jack Mountain

East Ridge

Jerry Lakes

Crater Creek

Crater Mountain

(Trail 746). Hike the old trail about 1.8 miles to Crater Lake, then scramble up to the obvious 7,180-foot saddle between the east and west summits of Crater Mountain. From the saddle, rope up and descend Jerry Glacier, contouring northwest to a ridge and descending to Jerry Lakes, elevation about 5,900 feet. Beckey's guide describes a scrambling shortcut that avoids elevation loss getting to the lakes, but most parties opt for the easier route and a convenient camp at Jerry Lakes. However, if pushing for a two-day round trip, bivouac higher up. From Jerry Lakes, continue northwest up and over the broad saddle in the ridge dividing Crater Creek and Jerry Lakes and contour northwest below a spur ridge onto the south face of Jack Mountain. Ascend an obvious snow or scree gully leading to the slight notch in the ridge crest shortly west of the summit, then scramble eastward to the summit. There are several gullies and more than one feasible route up the south face. Whichever gully has the most snow is probably the best option. Otherwise, loose rock scrambling gains the ridge. To descend, downclimb the route.

OPTIONS
There are several other routes up Jack Mountain, including the North Ridge and East Ridge, both Class 4 rock routes with glacier traverses. Refer to *Cascade Alpine Guide* for approach and route details. You can readily make an ascent of the 8,128-foot Crater Mountain via the old lookout trail leading up the southeast slope from Crater Lake and a short Class 2 rock scramble up the south ridge.

PRECAUTIONS
The approach is long and strenuous. The south face slopes and gullies are avalanche prone in winter and early season. There is rockfall hazard in the south face gullies and loose rock on the summit scramble. Roping up on the Jerry Glacier is recommended even if no crevasses show.

7. BLACK PEAK

Elevation: 8,970 feet/2,734 meters
Route: South Slope
Rating: Class 3
Distance: 14 miles round trip
Elevation Gain: 4,200 feet
Time: 7 to 8 hours trailhead to summit
Maps: USGS Mount Arriva; Green Trails No. 49 (Mount Logan)

ABOUT THE CLIMB
Black Peak is the highest summit in the vicinity of Rainy Pass. It is a big, accessible peak with a relatively easy approach and little routefinding or climbing difficulty, making it very popular, despite some poor quality rock. Rising to nearly 9,000 feet near the center of the range, its summit provides outstanding views of the North Cascades, with especially good views of the north face of Goode Mountain to the south. It is feasible as a one-day climb, including driving to and from Seattle, although a majority of climbers make it an overnight climb with a camp at Wing Lake or at least a bivouac at the Pacific Crest Trail (PCT) trailhead.

View from the summit of Black Peak down to Wing and Lewis Lakes and Heather Pass.

Morgan Balogh

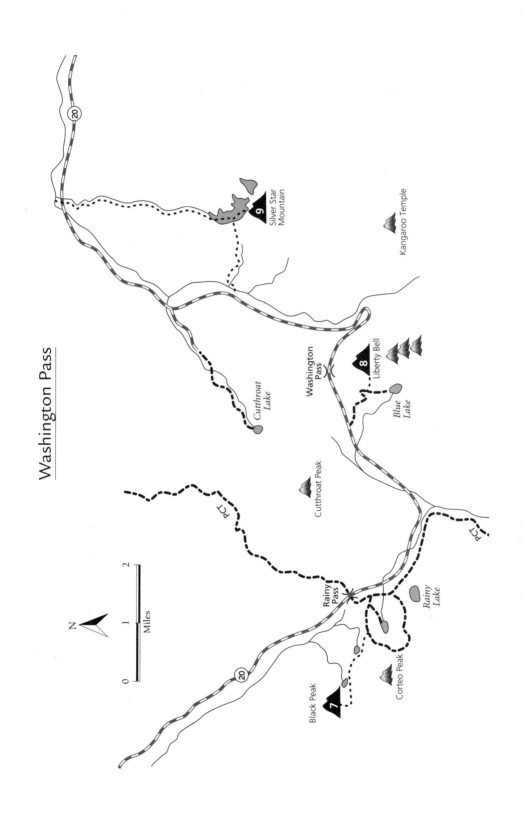

Washington Pass

N

0   1   2
Miles

20

Black Peak
7
Corteo Peak

Rainy Pass
Rainy Lake

PCT
Cutthroat Peak

PCT

Blue Lake
Liberty Bell
8
Washington Pass

Cutthroat Lake

Silver Star Mountain
9

Kangaroo Temple

20

Black Peak

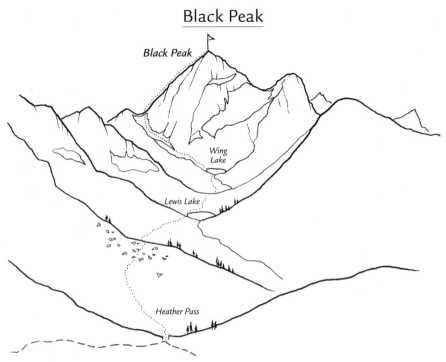

HOW TO GET THERE

The climb begins via Lake Ann Trail from Rainy Pass on the North Cascades Highway. Drive to Rainy Pass and park at the PCT trailhead. The trail begins from the picnic area. A Northwest Forest Pass is required. This is a high "car-prowl" trailhead, so leave nothing of value inside your car.

ROUTE DESCRIPTION

Hike the Lake Ann Trail for 3 miles, staying right at the Lake Ann junction and climbing to Heather Pass (elevation about 6,200 feet) from where Black Peak is plainly visible to the west, assuming good weather. Leave the trail here and follow an old unmaintained trail westward, first descending about 600 feet on talus then traversing another mile of talus to Lewis Lake. Continue from Lewis Lake up to and along the base of an old terminal moraine (or over and up the basin on the other side if there's snow) and up a dusty trail to Wing Lake (elevation about 6,900 feet), which is the popular campsite for summit-bound climbers. Expect to take about three hours from Heather Pass to Wing Lake, longer if packing in for an overnight stay.

From Wing Lake, hike southward up a talus and snow-filled basin below Black Peak's southeast face. Either ascend a long, steep snowfield to the head of the basin, or scramble up loose rocks on the right to reach the col. The snowfield is steep at the top; it may be easier if you leave the snow on the right where it gets steep and scramble up rock to the col. From the col, ascend easy rock, talus, or snow up the gradual south slope to the summit. The route from the col to the summit was described by one climber as "about 1,000 feet of crappy scrambling on loose rock, then about 20 feet of exposed scrambling to the top." The route is easiest following the line of least resistance, traversing right and resisting the urge to summit too soon. A Class 3 ramp leads to the top. If you are stopped by a drop-off, you have gone too far; 20 feet of exposed Class 4 climbing leads to the top. To descend, downclimb the route.

OPTIONS
A route ascends the East Buttress directly from Wing Lake, following a vertical band of dark rock. It is reportedly Class 4 with a bit of Class 5 climbing and some loose scrambling, especially if you get "off route," which is apparently easy to do. Refer to *Cascade Alpine Guide* for route details.

PRECAUTIONS
There is loose rock on much of the route and exposure to rockfall, especially climber-induced. Expect steep snow even in late season; crampons recommended. Avalanche danger on approach early in season from Heather Pass to Lewis Lake.

8. LIBERTY BELL MOUNTAIN

Elevation: 7,740 feet/2,359 meters
Route: Beckey Route
Rating: Grade II, 5.6
Distance: 5 miles round trip
Elevation Gain: 2,300 feet
Time: 4 to 5 hours trailhead to summit
Maps: USGS Washington Pass; Green Trails No. 50 (Washington Pass)

ABOUT THE CLIMB
Liberty Bell Mountain is the northernmost summit of the Liberty Bell massif, an impressive group of granite peaks towering over the North Cascades Highway. Liberty Bell is the most obvious of the group, a golden bell-shaped shaft with a striking 1,200-foot east face. There is no easy way to the top and the peak was not climbed until 1946, when Fred Beckey, Jerry O'Neil, and Charles Welsh made the ascent.

This is probably because of access problems prior to 1972 (when the North Cascades Highway was completed) and the fact that Liberty Bell is not the highest peak of the group. The original route is the fastest and easiest summit route, and thus remains the most popular. Although technically the southwest face, the route is called the Beckey Route in honor of one of the most prodigious new route pioneers of the Cascade Range. Of course, there are several other excellent routes up Liberty Bell. Its impressive east face has three direct, distinct Grade V climbs, including the classic Liberty Crack. Most climbers are content to summit via the easier route.

HOW TO GET THERE
Drive the North Cascades Highway to Blue Lake trailhead, about 1 mile west of Washington Pass. A Northwest Forest Pass is required.

ROUTE DESCRIPTION

The route described is the southwest face, or Beckey Route as it is more popularly known. Hike up Blue Lake Trail until the trail breaks into a small meadow and bends eastward toward the lake, then leave the trail and follow a steep, well-worn climber's path through boulder-strewn sub-alpine slopes into a basin below the west face of the Early Winter Spires. Ascend toward the gully leading to the Liberty Bell-Concord notch, scrambling up talus (often snow through early summer) to the notch. Just downhill from the notch, on the west side, is a brushy ledge. Traverse left along the ledge and belay at the base of the obvious blocky chimney. Ascend the chimney

Colin Haley leading up the Beckey Route, Liberty Bell Mountain.

and blocky slabs to a small roof, from where a clean crack leads to easier slabs up the summit shoulder. A short scramble, including Class 3–4 ledges and a 5.6 bouldering move up a 10-foot slab, leads to the summit. Most parties belay three roped pitches and scramble the remainder of the route. The route is well worn and should not be difficult to follow. Bring a medium rack up to 3 inches and several slings, including a couple of long slings for the fixed pins on the third pitch to minimize rope drag. Some recommend skipping the fixed pin clips to avoid rope drag, but they're hard to resist, so bring long slings. Rock shoes recommended.

To descend, scramble back toward the top of the third pitch, carefully downclimbing the 5.6 slab. Follow the obvious tree-filled gully east about 100 feet until you can follow ledges to a two-bolt rappel station. Eventually you will find the rappel anchors; one double-rope rappel or two single-rope rappels will get you to the notch. Some parties start rappelling sooner, or belay down to the rappel anchors. A single rope will suffice, but double ropes are recommended.

Liberty Bell Mountain, Beckey Route

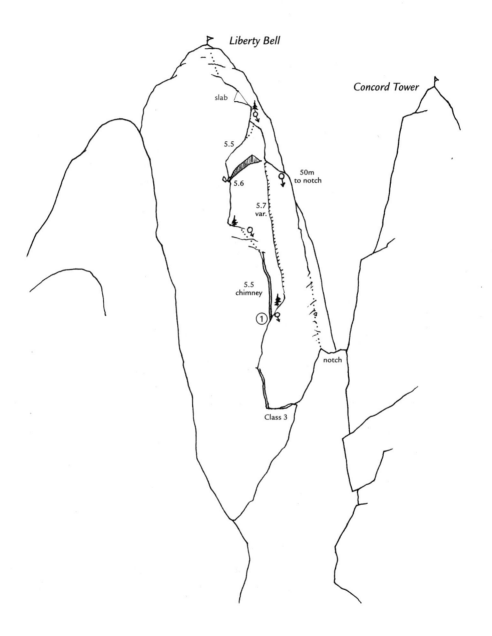

Liberty Bell

Concord Tower

slab

5.5

5.6

50m
to notch

5.7
var.

5.5
chimney

①

notch

Class 3

OPTIONS

A direct route (II, 5.7) leads from the Liberty-Concord notch to the summit of 7,560-foot Concord Tower, making both summits feasible in a single day, unless one or other of the routes is clogged up with climbers, which is a common occurrence. From the Liberty Bell-Concord notch, climb a short, direct crack to a ledge. Traverse right, then up left-trending cracks to the base of the summit block. Finish via a ramp and crack on the left (5.6) or a crack and arete on the right (5.7). Bring gear up to 4 inches and a few long slings. Two double-rope rappels down the route reach the notch.

PRECAUTIONS

Steep snow lingers in the approach gully until summer. Icy conditions and patchy snow in the approach gully and on the route can be hazardous, especially for climbers who didn't come prepared. Double ropes are recommended for the descent. If bivouacking below the cliffs, bring insect repellent, especially during the summer months when the mosquitos and biting flies are at their peak voracity.

9. SILVER STAR MOUNTAIN

Elevation: 8,876 feet/2,706 meters

Route: Silver Star Glacier

Rating: Class 3–4; Grade I glacier

Distance: 8 miles round trip

Elevation Gain: 4,700 feet

Time: 5 to 6 hours trailhead to summit

Maps: USGS Silver Star Mountain; Green Trails No. 50 (Washington Pass)

ABOUT THE CLIMB

Silver Star Mountain is one of the major peaks in the vicinity of Washington Pass. It is a big, craggy peak with some of the best alpine rock climbing in the state on its many sharp granite ridges and faces. It has a few scrambling routes to its summit, the most popular of which is the Silver Star Glacier route, a varied, distinctly alpine scramble. Silver Star has a reputation for tedious scree and steep snow climbing in gullies, which has not endeared the mountain to many climbers. However, Silver Star is regionally important and a worthwhile climb, especially via the glacier route. Silver Star is a popular spring and early summer climb because snow makes for easier going on the approach and it is much more aesthetic than climbing late-season scree in the gullies leading to Burgundy Col and the West Peak notch. The mountain is near enough to the North Cascades Highway that it can be climbed in a day from as far away as Seattle or Wenatchee if you start driving early in the morning. Most parties make it an overnight climb with an approach hike in the evening and a bivouac below the glacier. Summit views are excellent and include Liberty Bell Mountain, the Early Winter Spires, Mount Logan, Goode Mountain, Bonanza Peak, Glacier Peak, and the many high summits of the Pasayten Wilderness.

HOW TO GET THERE

This climb begins from North Cascades Highway just east of Washington Pass. If approaching from the east side of the mountains, drive the North Cascades

Silver Star Mountain. Burgundy Col is the deep notch on the left.

Highway (Washington Highway 20) to the turnoff for Cutthroat Creek and continue about 0.5 mile beyond to a large pullout on the east side of the highway, just below the confluence of Early Winters Creek and Willow Creek. (Willow Creek is easily identified by its prominent waterfall.) If coming from the west side, drive about 4 miles east from Washington Pass to the same pullout. A Northwest Forest Pass is not required because this is not an official trailhead. This is a high "car-prowl" trailhead, so leave nothing of value in your car.

ROUTE DESCRIPTION

The climb described is the Silver Star Glacier via Burgundy Col, the most popular summit route, although it is not necessarily the best route. Before leaving the highway, it is useful to make a visual note of the lay of the land. From the highway, hike briefly down to Early Winters Creek and cross the creek via a footlog below its confluence with Willow Creek. Some parties, unable to find a good footlog, have forded the creek, which is not recommended in early season when high water makes such a crossing hazardous.

Once across Early Winters Creek, locate a rough trail on the north side of Burgundy Creek. (Burgundy Creek drains the basin below the Wine Spires and will most likely be up the valley from your crossing of Early Winters Creek.) This steep climber's trail ascends the forested slope on the left side of Burgundy Creek to a plateau-like basin at about 6,400 feet, just below Burgundy Col where many parties bivouac. Some have trouble finding the trail and encounter a rugged climb to the basin. Ascend steeply from the basin to Burgundy Col. A short but steep, gravelly climb (or snow in early season) leads to the col (elevation about 7,800 feet). A variation approach to the col, preferred by some, follows a boot path up and left of the gully, then traverses right into the gully higher up. Some parties bivouac at the col, though space and water are limited.

Silver Star Mountain

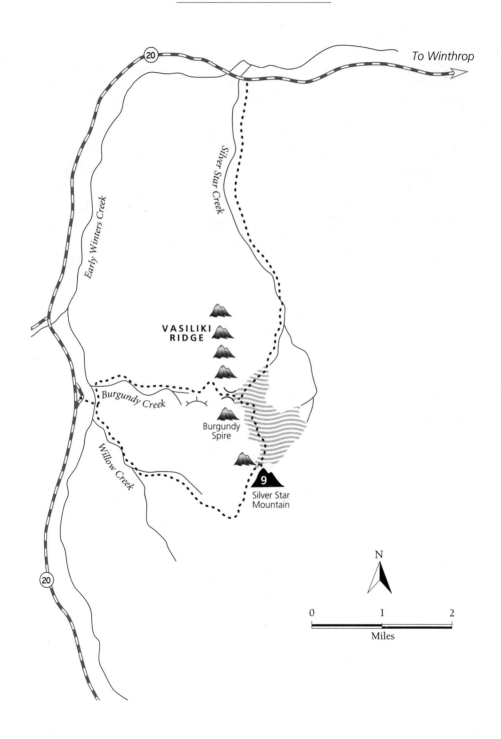

Silver Star Mountain

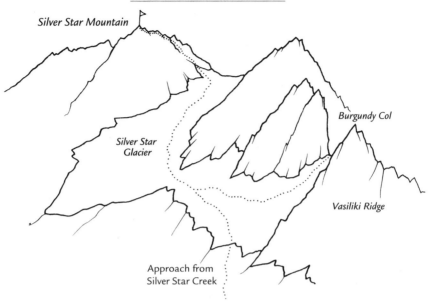

From the col, descend briefly then contour southward to the northern lobe of the Silver Star Glacier. Rope up and ascend the glacier, skirting below the wine spires and continuing up the glacier toward the saddle between the summit and West Peak. You can climb to the upper saddle and continue from there directly to the summit (Class 3–4), but the easier route leaves the glacier about 100 feet or so below the saddle and leads up slabby rock directly to the summit. Keep to the left to avoid exposed ledges, but not too far left. The summit is a small, sharp block. There are several possible variations here, some involving roped climbing over short steep slabs and walls. Although most consider the easiest route to be Class 3 scrambling, many encounter what they consider Class 4 or 5 climbing. Snow on the summit rocks may make the climbing either easier or harder, depending on conditions and the exact route taken. To descend, downclimb the route.

OPTIONS

A longer but highly recommended approach is via Silver Star Creek, about 3.7 miles farther east from the turnoff for Cutthroat Creek. This option involves about 3 miles of sometimes steep cross-country hiking from the head of Silver Star Creek to Burgundy Col, which makes it less popular than the Burgundy Col approach described earlier but with somewhat easier routefinding. This is considered by many to be a safer early season alternative because the slopes leading up to Burgundy Col are avalanche prone. Note: this route is not entirely protected from avalanches. In early season, a long ski descent may be made from just below the summit all the way to the highway. Silver Star Creek is just 0.1 mile east of the bridge crossing Early Winters Creek. Park here and follow a rough trail on the east side of the creek for about 2 miles to a steep headwall. The trail climbs steeply up the west side of this headwall before traversing back toward the

Silver Star Glacier just below Burgundy Col. Here the route continues up the glacier to the summit. In early season, just follow the creek up the valley until you break out of the trees, then follow the valley bottom to the base of the glacier. This route can be done in a single day even without skis, but it is even faster and more enjoyable with a ski descent.

PRECAUTIONS
The gullies on either side of Burgundy Col are avalanche prone. The approach gullies involve either steep snow or gravelly scree and can be hot and unpleasant by midday. The Silver Star Glacier shows crevasses by late season, so roping up is recommended although many parties don't bother. Most climbers regard the summit scramble as Class 3, although some references list it as Class 4. Bring a rope in case any party member desires a belay, or to rope up on the glacier.

10. NORTH GARDNER MOUNTAIN

Elevation: 8,956 feet/2,730 meters
Route: South Slope
Rating: Class 2
Distance: 27 miles round trip via Wolf Creek Trail
Elevation Gain: 8,100 feet
Time: 10 to 12 hours; best done as a two- or three-day climb
Maps: USGS Mazama; Green Trails No. 50 (Washington Pass), 51 (Mazama), and 83 (Buttermilk Butte)

ABOUT THE CLIMB
North Gardner Mountain is the highest of the Methow Mountains, an old subrange of gentle peaks rising west of the Methow Valley. It is also the highest summit in Okanogan County. Although it rises to within a stone's throw of 9,000 feet, most climbers have never heard of North Gardner. This is probably because it is a non-technical climb and fairly remote. North Gardner gets barely more than a paragraph's worth of ink in Beckey's guide and no map or photo. Because North Gardner doesn't rise above 9,000 feet elevation, about the only people who aspire to climb North Gardner are either looking for some solitude or on a personal quest to climb Washington's 25, 50, or 100 highest mountains. Fortunately, this lack of press and popularity means the peak isn't often overcrowded and provides more of a wilderness experience than its less lofty neighbors to the west. Summit views are splendid and include the many high peaks of the Pasayten Wilderness and eastern North Cascades, Silver Star Mountain, Bonanza Peak, and Glacier Peak.

HOW TO GET THERE
This climb begins via Wolf Creek Trail just east of Winthrop. Drive the North Cascades Highway (Washington Highway 20) to Winthrop. At the south end of town, follow Twin Lakes Road west about 1.5 miles to a fork. Take the right fork and follow Wolf Creek Road, staying left at the final fork, to Wolf Creek trailhead at the road's end. A Northwest Forest Pass is required.

North Gardner Mountain

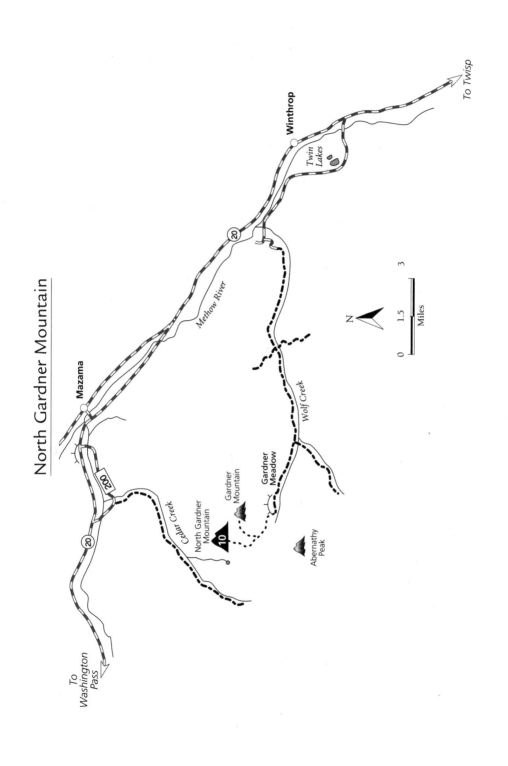

To Twisp

Winthrop

Twin Lakes

20

Methow River

Mazama

200

20

Cedar Creek

North Gardner Mountain

10

Gardner Mountain

Gardner Meadow

Wolf Creek

Abernathy Peak

To Washington Pass

N

0   1.5   3
Miles

North Gardner Mountain

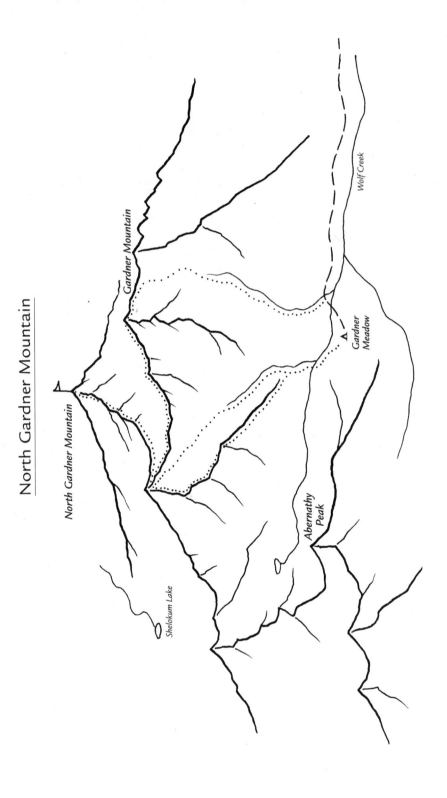

North Gardner Mountain

Gardner Mountain

Wolf Creek

Gardner Meadow

Abernathy Peak

Shelokum Lake

ROUTE DESCRIPTION

The easiest route, if not the fastest, ascends scree slopes and ridges northward from Wolf Creek Basin, a remote subalpine basin west of Winthrop. Hike Wolf Creek Trail (Trail 627) about 12 miles to the trail's end in Gardner Meadow (elevation about 5,700 feet). Most parties camp in the meadows. From the end of the trail, hike cross-country alongside Wolf Creek to a meadow basin at about 6,200 feet elevation. Proceed northward from here into the basin lying south of the ridge connecting Gardner Mountain and Point 8,487, then head up the scree slopes to the ridge crest. Alternatively, scramble up the ridge to the left of the scree field on the west side of the basin to the ridge crest and up to Point 8,487. From there, traverse just over 0.5 mile north along the connecting ridge to the summit of North Gardner Mountain. The climb is not technically difficult, just scree scrambling and ridge traversing. Expect to take about four to five hours from Wolf Creek Basin to the summit. To descend, downclimb the route.

OPTIONS

An ascent of 8,897-foot Gardner Mountain is often combined with North Gardner via their connecting ridges.

PRECAUTIONS

The slopes above Gardner Meadow are avalanche prone in winter and spring. There is loose rock on the route, and the upper mountain is dry by late season. Bring plenty of water. Be wary of bears and cougars in late season.

11. HIDDEN LAKE PEAK

Elevation: 7,088 feet/2,160 meters
Route: North Ridge
Rating: Class 2
Distance: 8 miles round trip
Elevation Gain: 3,200 feet
Time: 2 to 3 hours
Maps: USGS Eldorado Peak and Sonny Boy Lakes; Green Trails No. 80 (Cascade Pass)

ABOUT THE CLIMB

Hidden Lake Peak is a small, attractive rocky peak rising above the Cascade River Valley about 7 miles due west of Cascade Pass. Its isolated position at the foot of the Eldorado-Triad ridge gives it an unobstructed view of the peaks around Cascade Pass: Johannesburg Mountain, Sahale Peak, Boston Peak, Forbidden Peak, Eldorado Peak, and Snowking Mountain. You will also see the Ptarmigan Traverse peaks, as well as many high summits throughout the range including excellent views of Mount Baker, Mount Shuksan, Glacier Peak, Mount Rainier, the Twin Sisters, and the Picket Range.

Hidden Lake Peak is a popular climb because it is one of few Cascade Pass area summits that can be attained by hikers, although the hiking trail leads to a lookout cabin on the lower south summit. An ascent of Hidden Lake Peak is a wonderful introduction to the joys of climbing in the North Cascades, especially for

Morgan Balogh on the North Ridge, Hidden Lake Peak.

non-climbers, and experienced climbers will also find some appeal. The routes are mostly easy talus and snow scrambling with infinite variation and without the rigors of most North Cascades climbs. Hidden Lake Peak is a good early season climb when much of the route is up snow. Whatever the season, just be sure to climb on a clear day in order to fully appreciate the magnificent views.

HOW TO GET THERE

The climb begins via Hidden Lake Trail from just off of Cascade River Road. Drive the North Cascades Highway (Washington Highway 20) to Marblemount. Turn off onto Cascade River Road (Forest Road 15) and follow it for 9.7 miles to the turnoff for Hidden Lake Peak Trail. Follow Forest Road 1540 for 4.6 miles to the Hidden Lake trailhead at the road's end. This is a popular trailhead with limited parking. The road is steep and narrow in a few places but not as bad as it used to be. A Northwest Forest Pass is required.

ROUTE DESCRIPTION

Hidden Lake Peak can be climbed via several routes. The popular scrambling route is via the north ridge from Sibley Creek Pass. Hike Hidden Lake Peak Trail (Trail 745) for about 2 miles to the top of the switchbacks at the head of Sibley Creek Basin. Depart the trail at the high point in the basin and follow a boot path up rocky heather slopes and scree gullies to 6,050-foot Sibley Creek Pass. Follow a climber's trail southward up the ridge, first over a dusty ridge point to a saddle, then up granite blocks and boulders, for about 0.8 mile to the blocky summit. The ridge is described in a popular hiking guide as a "moderate rock scramble," but it's pretty easy going over big granite blocks, ledges, and slabs. You might manage the ascent without the use of hands, but it is great fun to vary

Hidden Lake Peak

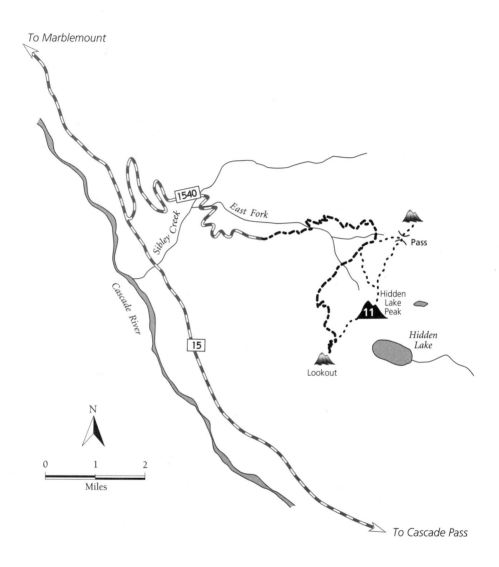

Hidden Lake Peak

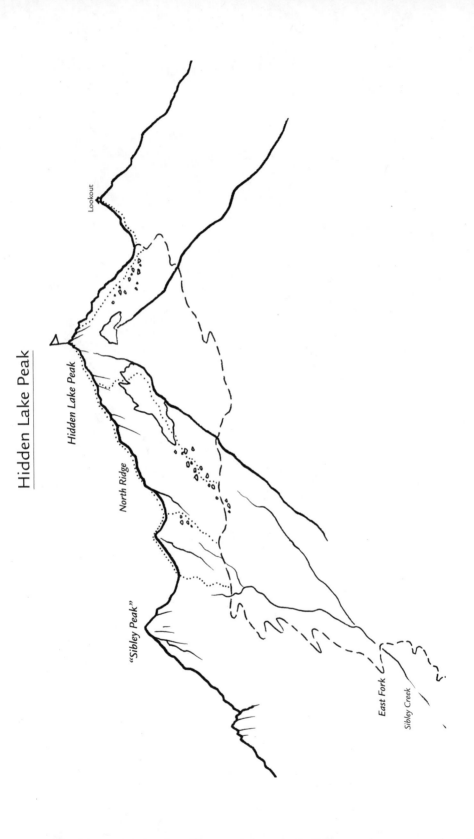

Lookout

Hidden Lake Peak

North Ridge

"Sibley Peak"

East Fork

Sibley Creek

the route by climbing the many short chimneys, cracks, slabs, and corners along the ridge.

To descend, downclimb the route, or go down the south ridge and loop out via Hidden Lake Peak Trail.

OPTIONS

The easier route is a talus and snow hike via the south ridge from the saddle at the trail's end. Another good route leaves the trail at the talus field shortly past the upper crossing of Sibley Creek, climbs big talus blocks into the snow basin just northwest of the summit, and then ascends snow or slabby rock up the headwall to join the north ridge route shortly north of the summit. You can also hike up to the abandoned lookout cabin atop the 6,890-foot south peak. Also, many hikers scramble up the craggy 6,480-foot peak north of Sibley Creek Pass. This peak is visible from the trailhead.

PRECAUTIONS

The slopes below Sibley Creek Pass are avalanche prone. Snow lingers until late summer most years making the trail and upper slopes treacherous for those without an ice ax. The north-south ridgeline of Hidden Lake Peak forms the national park boundary; a permit is required if bivouacking on the summit ridge or at Hidden Lake.

12. SNOWKING MOUNTAIN

Elevation: 7,433 feet/2,266 meters
Route: Kindy Ridge
Rating: Class 3 (minimal glacier climbing)
Distance: 20 miles round trip
Elevation Gain: 5,400 feet
Time: 10 to 12 hours; best done as a two- or three-day climb
Maps: USGS Snowking Mountain and Sonny Boy Lakes; Green Trails No. 79 (Snowking Mountain) and 80 (Cascade Pass)

ABOUT THE CLIMB

Snowking Mountain is a relatively modest but very attractive glaciated peak rising south of the Cascade River about 10 miles west of Cascade Pass. Snowking is very heavily glaciated, surprisingly so for a peak of such modest elevation. It is one of the most remote peaks included in this guide. Because there is not a true approach trail, relatively few climbers visit Snowking Mountain. The road leading to the "trailhead" is often blocked by fallen trees or washouts. If you are able to manage the road, you will have to follow a steep, brushy old boot path that leads up to the high point of Kindy Ridge. From there, the route is pure cross-country, either along a high ridge crest or down in the valley among turquoise-hued lakes. But if you manage the approach, you will probably have the mountain all to yourself. The summit views are spectacular and include the Ptarmigan Traverse and peaks around Cascade Pass; south to Glacier Peak, Sloan Peak, Whitehorse Mountain, White Chuck Mountain, and Three Fingers Mountains; north to Mount Baker and Mount Shuksan, and a glimpse of the Picket Range. Early season ascents are favored, although the weather is less reliable.

Snowking Mountain from Hidden Lake Peak.

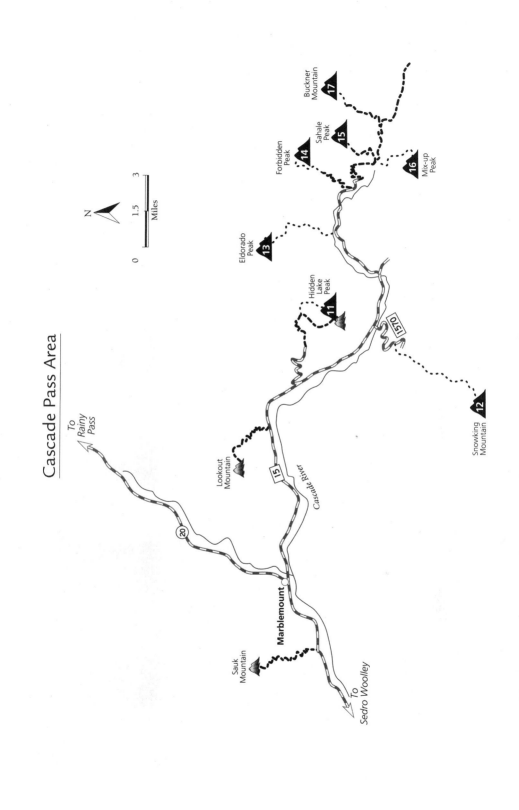

Cascade Pass Area

N

0   1.5   3
Miles

To
Rainy
Pass

Buckner
Mountain
▲ 17

Forbidden
Peak
▲ 14

Sahale
Peak
▲ 15

Mix-up
Peak
▲ 16

Eldorado
Peak
▲ 13

Hidden
Lake
Peak
▲ 11

Lookout
Mountain

15

Cascade River

20

Snowking
Mountain
▲ 12

1570

Marblemount

Sauk
Mountain

To
Sedro Woolley

HOW TO GET THERE

The climb begins via Kindy Ridge "trail" from Cascade River Road just west of Cascade Pass. Drive the North Cascades Highway (Washington Highway 20) to Marblemount. Unless you are trying this climb in a single day, get an overnight permit at the Marblemount Ranger Station. Turn off onto Cascade River Road (Forest Road 15) and follow it 14.1 miles to Kindy Creek Road (Forest Road 1570) on the right. Follow this road down to the river (stay left at first fork at about 0.1 mile) and up the other side. Take a right at the fork 0.4 mile beyond the river crossing, then a left at the next fork 0.7 mile along. Continue about 0.6 mile beyond this fork to where the road is blocked. Supposedly, you can continue driving, but most wisely park and start hiking from here. At last report, there were trees across the road well below the "trailhead." If the road is blocked, park off to the side and start walking.

ROUTE DESCRIPTION

Hike up the road along a ridge to where it curves eastward and descends across a stream gully at about 2,200 feet elevation. Leave the road here and follow a boot path southwest up the timbered slope (an old clearcut). The trail climbs up, and up, steeply to the ridge. The trail here is not often hiked, so it is easy to lose the path in the brush; flagging may help keep you on course but don't rely on it. If you lose the trail, you'll be bushwhacking up the steep slope to the ridge crest. Hike along the crest to a 5,116-foot ridge point, then descend to a saddle at about 4,800 feet elevation. A way trail continues along the ridge to the 5,791-foot high point of Kindy Ridge. From here, hike cross-country along the ridge crest directly toward Snowking Mountain. You can follow a faint boot path part of the way, and you can drop off the ridge and bivouac at one of the lakes on the west side or at the base of the snowfields.

The final climb is straightforward. Ascend directly up rocky heather slopes, then up snow and firn slopes toward the summit, and finally via a short rock scramble. Stay left to avoid crevasses on the Snowking Glacier. To descend, downclimb the route.

OPTIONS

You may vary the approach by dropping down from Kindy Ridge saddle to Found Lake, then hiking up the valley to Cyclone Lake and rejoining the route. You can also climb a variation up the Snowking Glacier to the ridge connecting the summit and Southwest Peak. Either or both summit peaks can be readily ascended. Beckey's guide lists a few other routes, all of which involve somewhat long wilderness approaches and relatively easy climbing. Refer to *Cascade Alpine Guide* for route details.

PRECAUTIONS

The approach "trail" is not frequently hiked and is steep, faint, and hard to follow. A map, compass, and altimeter may help. Cornices form on Kindy Ridge; be especially careful if traversing the ridge in spring during poor visibility. Although crevasses are usually not a problem, roping up on the glacier is recommended.

Snowking Mountain

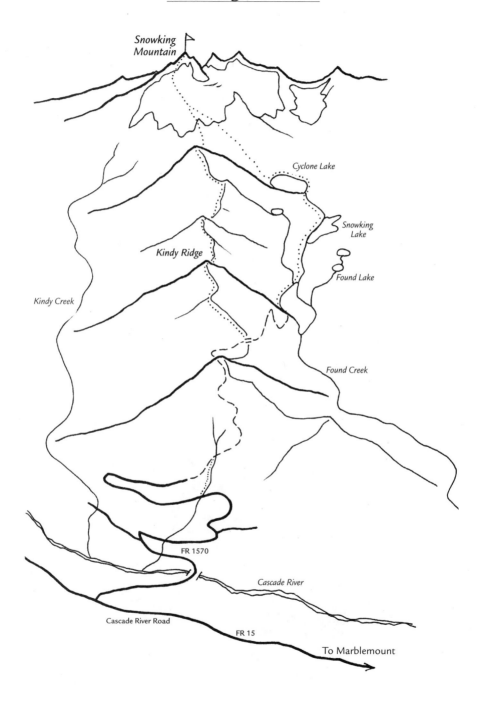

Snowking Mountain

Cyclone Lake

Snowking Lake

Kindy Ridge

Found Lake

Kindy Creek

Found Creek

FR 1570

Cascade River

Cascade River Road

FR 15

To Marblemount

Darin Berdinka

Eldorado Peak.

13. ELDORADO PEAK

Elevation: 8,868 feet/2,703 meters
Route: East Ridge
Rating: Class 3; Grade I glacier
Distance: 10 miles round trip
Elevation Gain: 6,700 feet
Time: 6 to 8 hours trailhead to summit
Maps: USGS Eldorado Peak and Sonny Boy Lakes; Green Trails No. 80 (Cascade Pass) and 48 (Diablo Dam)

ABOUT THE CLIMB

Eldorado Peak is one of the premier peaks of the Cascade Pass area and is among the most popular climbs in the North Cascades. Although not as high as its 9,000-foot neighbors to the east (Buckner Mountain, Goode Mountain, and Mount Logan), Eldorado is more impressive owing to its size, relief, and glacier mantle, as well as its situation. Where other peaks in the region, impressive as they are, rise up from a common ridge or divide, Eldorado stands alone in majestic proportion and deserves the superlatives heaped upon it by climbers.

Although there are other routes up the peak, climbers swarm up the East Ridge, which features a long, airy traverse up a "knife-edge" snow ridge to the summit. It is a popular spring ascent, especially with ski mountaineers and telemarkers who can enjoy a long, exhilarating descent into Eldorado Basin whether or not they bag the summit. Some climbers won't climb Eldorado except when the snow ridge is "in shape," but it is still an enjoyable ascent later in the season. Most parties make an overnight climb of Eldorado Peak, although it is feasible as a one-day climb if you start early and climb fast. The presence of other climbers on the summit ridge, which tends to clog up the route, may dictate the speed of your ascent. Be prepared to wait if you're behind other climbers. Etiquette dictates that climbers on the way up the ridge step aside for those heading down.

HOW TO GET THERE

This climb begins from Cascade River Road just west of Cascade Pass. Drive the North Cascades Highway (Washington Highway 20) to Marblemount. If you are making Eldorado an overnight climb, get a permit from the Marblemount Ranger Station. Drive east on Cascade River Road (Forest Road 15) for 19.9 miles to a large turnout on the right just before mile 20 and park here. In early season, the road may be gated here, in which case the parking lot may be crowded. Because this is not an official trail, a Northwest Forest Pass is not required.

ROUTE DESCRIPTION

The approach hike to Eldorado Peak is via a climber's trail most of the way or snow in early season. It is regarded by climbers as either horrendous or not so bad. (It's not so bad.) The East Ridge is very popular, the trail is well established, and the approach has even been re-routed to avoid erosion even though it is not officially a trail. From the parking turnout, backtrack down the road about 50 yards to find the trail leading into the brush toward the river. The trail is well

Eldorado Peak

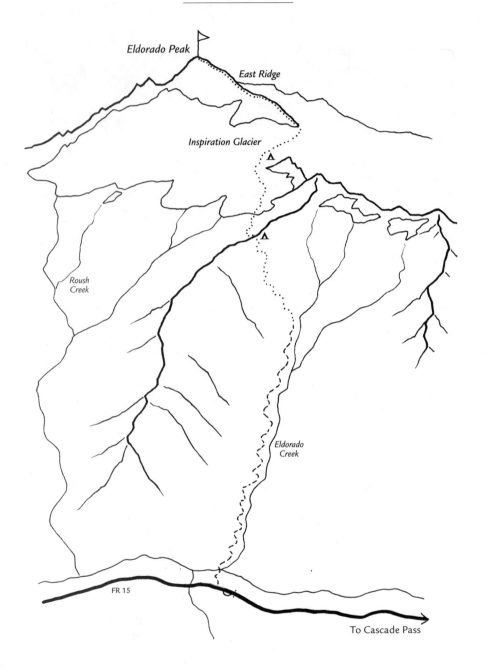

Climber on the summit ridge, Eldorado Peak.

used and easy to follow. Cross the river via a convenient footlog and hike up the climber's trail along Eldorado Creek. To get up on the log, you might have to climb up its roots if the river is running high. The trail leads gently upriver at first, then begins a steep climb within earshot of Eldorado Creek. At about 4,000 feet elevation, the trail enters a talus field. Follow cairns up through the middle of the large talus blocks, then over a short, steep brushy section to a higher, larger talus field. A faint path marked with cairns leads along the right edge of this talus field before climbing steeply uphill again. Follow the most obvious path, crossing beneath a waterfall before reaching an open basin and campsites at about 5,400 feet. Continue up the left side of the basin to about 6,100 feet elevation, then cross the ridgeline bordering the west side of the basin just below a steep step. Many parties camp here at a big flat area on the ridge, which is known as "Hammered Ridge" due to the impacts of too many campers. From the ridgeline, drop down about 100 feet into Roush Basin. There are several variations here; most climb down an obvious gully, which may have a difficult moat crossing. Continue up the right side of Roush Basin, first on talus, slabs, and snow, then on a lobe of the Eldorado Glacier.

Rope up and ascend the glacier, which flattens out at about 7,400 feet. Traverse the glacier to the base of the East Ridge. Many parties bivouac on the glacier; there are some good bivy sites on the lower third of the ridge as well. Follow the crest of the East Ridge directly to the summit. The ridge is easy and straightforward; no routefinding difficulty here. If the ridge becomes too narrow to climb directly, drop down slightly and traverse steep snow slopes on one side or the other. The upper ridge is quite exposed in places. The difficulty and danger of the route will vary depending on snow and weather conditions. Usually it is quite easy going, but can be difficult and dangerous if loose wet snow or icy conditions are encountered. To descend, downclimb the route.

OPTIONS
There are only a few other routes up Eldorado Peak, none of which is even close to being as popular as the ridge route. Refer to *Cascade Alpine Guide*.

PRECAUTIONS
The upper slopes of Eldorado Basin and Roush Basin, and the summit foundation, are avalanche prone. Periods of warm weather can destabilize snow on the summit ridge and basin headwalls. Be careful on the approach when traversing from talus to snow so you don't break through the snow and injure yourself on the rocks as many climbers have done. The descent from "Hammered Ridge" into Roush Basin is steep. The glacier is crevassed, so roping up is recommended even if no crevasses show. Bring a picket or two to belay any portion of the ridge and to avoid one climber having to jump off one side of the ridge to prevent a partner from falling down the other side.

14. FORBIDDEN PEAK

Elevation: 8,815 feet/2,687 meters
Route: West Ridge
Rating: Grade III, 5.6; Grade II glacier
Distance: 10 miles round trip
Elevation Gain: 5,600 feet
Time: 6 to 8 hours trailhead to summit
Maps: USGS Forbidden Peak and Cascade Pass; Green Trails No. 80 (Cascade Pass) and 48 (Diablo Dam)

ABOUT THE CLIMB
Forbidden Peak, located on the Cascade Pass crest north of Boston Peak, is one of the most impressive peaks in the North Cascades. It is a classic alpine horn, carved out by glaciers on three sides with sharp rock ridges and steep rock headwalls. The first ascent of Forbidden Peak was made by Lloyd Anderson, Fred Beckey, Helmey Beckey, Jim Crooks, and Dave Lind in July 1940. Forbidden's West Ridge is considered one of the most classic alpine rock climbs in the Cascade Range and was featured in *Fifty Classic Climbs in North America*. The West Ridge is regarded as one of the true classic routes of the Cascade Range. This route is so overwhelmingly popular that everyone has it on their list. Just hope they don't all arrive on the same day you choose to climb it.

Fortunately, the West Ridge is not Forbidden's only classic route, as many climbers will attest. The peak's East Ridge has gained favor as an equal for alpine purity. Both routes are easily approached via Boston Basin and can be climbed in a long day, although most parties bivouac in the basin. Due to the classic status of the West Ridge, it is often overcrowded, resulting in delays both going up and coming down and causing problems when bad weather sets in. If you should happen to have Forbidden Peak to yourself on a clear summer or fall day, consider yourself blessed.

Forbidden Peak from Hidden Lake Peak.

Forbidden Peak

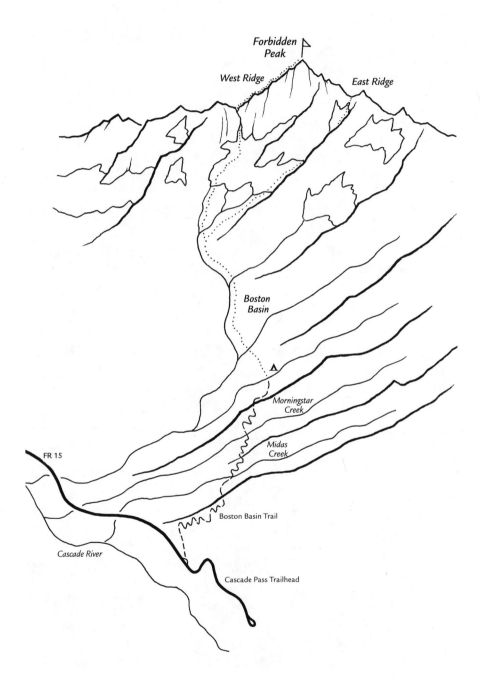

HOW TO GET THERE

This climb begins via Boston Basin Trail from Cascade River Road just west of Cascade Pass. Drive the North Cascades Highway (Washington Highway 20) to Marblemount. Unless you are making a one-day ascent, get a permit at the Marblemount Ranger Station. Follow Cascade River Road (Forest Road 15) east for 22.4 miles to the Boston Basin trailhead on the left. There are usually several cars parked here. A Northwest Forest Pass is required.

ROUTE DESCRIPTION

Hike up Boston Basin Trail, a steep, strenuous boot path. The path leads about 1 mile up a couple of switchbacks to the Diamond Mine and continues very steeply up through brush to a fork. Take the left fork and follow the old trail across Midas Creek. Then travel up a sweltering avalanche slope to Morning Star Creek and switchback up moderate timber slopes to Boston Basin. The trail is steep, strenuous, and heavily used. In early season, a faster route climbs the timbered ridge before Midas Creek to the upper slopes of Boston Basin. Ford or boulder hop across an arm of Boston Creek, then continue on the trail to a high camp either at about 5,200 feet or about 6,400 feet. The creek is sometimes running high even in late summer, so cross carefully. Both camps have toilets (with awesome views) and are infested with rodents. Expect to take three or four hours to high camp.

Traverse northwest across Boston Basin toward Forbidden Peak, then ascend glacier-polished slabs and snowfields up to the small unnamed glacier and the base of the south face. Be sure to scout the route from a distance to avoid ascending the wrong glacier basin. This may seem unlikely, but parties have done so, especially when clouds set in. From the glacier, climb the obvious couloir on the left to gain a notch in the ridge at about 8,300 feet elevation. In early season, the couloir may be moderately steep snow (45 degrees) and can be quickly climbed; while in late season, moats, crevasses, and a bergschrund may make progress difficult and hazardous. Some parties avoid this by climbing slabby rock on the right side of the gully. A few pitches of dubious Class 3-4 rock up a gully lead to the notch. There are a couple of bivy spots at the col, but don't count on finding them unoccupied. Keep your crampons and ice ax with you until you are on the ridge; you may need them to get up an unexpected moat wall, and you can retrieve them on the descent assuming you choose to descend the West Ridge.

An alternative route to the ridge crest climbs gullies left of the couloir. Approach the glacier, then skirt it on the west side, eventually traversing back east on clean slabs or snow slopes to an obvious rock promontory that sits above the glacier just west of the snow couloir. Several obvious gullies lead up from here, paralleling the couloir on the west side. The leftmost, largest gully offers a reasonable approach to the ridge crest. From the promontory, rappel slings should be visible about 100 feet up this gully. Climb Class 4 rock to the slings, then scramble sandy Class 3 to the ridge crest at the top of the couloir. This is said to be a good approach variation that avoids the problematic glacier and couloir. This option may allow snow-free climbing by late season some years.

The ridge itself is straightforward and joyous. Just climb up the narrow, exposed (but relatively easy) rock ridge. Enjoy airy traverses around rock towers all the way to the summit. The climbing is mostly Class 4 with a few Class 5 sections (reports vary between 5.3 and 5.6) on mostly solid rock. You can avoid most of the harder or more exposed sections by traversing left (north) of the ridge crest and then climbing back up to it. A short rock step above an old bolt higher on the ridge is the technical crux (rated 5.6). Expect to take three or four hours from the glacier to the summit, longer if slower climbers clog up the route or if you belay each pitch. Many parties simul-climb the majority of the ridge to save time. Bring a moderate rack with gear up to 3 inches, including several cams and extra runners.

To descend, downclimb and rappel the ridge and rappel down the gully to the glacier. Unfortunately, descending the route clogs up the ridge for other climbers. A recommended alternative descent is to make several rappels down the Northeast Face, then traverse Class 4 ledges to the East Ridge notch. Be careful not to rappel too far down the face or you will have to climb back up to the traverse ledges. Also be careful on the traverse; many parties climb it unroped, but it is very exposed and can be treacherous when wet, snowy, or icy. Finally, be careful when descending from the ridge back to Boston Basin because there are some cliffs to negotiate. It helps to have climbed the East Face previously to be familiar with the terrain before attempting this descent.

OPTIONS
There are several other routes up Forbidden Peak. The East Face ♦ (III, Class 4) is the easiest and most direct route up Forbidden Peak. The East Ridge ♦ (III, 5.8) ascends the east ridge directly.

PRECAUTIONS
The slopes of Boston Basin and Forbidden Peak are very avalanche prone in winter and spring. In late season, the couloir may be difficult due to moats and a bergschrund. Accidents and fatalities have occurred on both the West Ridge and East Face. The ascent is more hazardous with snow or ice on the upper ridges, after a snowfall, or during poor weather. All routes are committing, and retreat can be complicated by bad weather and slow climbers. Be sure to start down early if the weather deteriorates. Descending during a storm can be difficult and time consuming, especially when there are several parties on the ridge. The need to beat a hasty retreat off the ridge may arise, so come prepared.

15. SAHALE PEAK

Elevation: 8,700 feet/2,652 meters
Route: Sahale Glacier
Rating: Class 4; Grade I glacier
Distance: 14 miles round trip
Elevation Gain: 5,100 feet
Time: 5 to 7 hours trailhead to summit
Maps: USGS Cascade Pass; Green Trails No. 80 (Cascade Pass)

ABOUT THE CLIMB
Sahale Peak (officially Sahale Mountain but climbers know it as Sahale Peak) is the sharply pointed peak rising immediately north of Cascade Pass. It is an

Alex Krawarik

A climber high on Sahale Peak.

attractive peak, accessible and relatively simple to climb with remarkable panoramic views. The summit is a sharp rock peak. Sahale is a popular climb, largely because of its relatively easy access compared to other summits around Cascade Pass, and also because of its central location and views. From the summit, you get a grand view of the Cascade Pass peaks—Johannesburg Mountain, Cascade Peak, the Triplets, Mix-up Peak, Magic Mountain, Pelton Peak, Buckner Mountain, Boston Peak, Forbidden Peak, Eldorado Peak, and Hidden Lake Peak. The many summits in the near and far distance include Snowking Mountain, Mount Logan, Goode Mountain, MacGregor Mountain, Mount Baker, Mount Shuksan, Mount Rainier, Glacier Peak, the Monte Cristo peaks, and an incredible view down the Stehekin River Valley all the way to the northern tip of Lake Chelan.

Although Sahale Peak is regarded by many climbers as an easy climb, the final rock scramble to the summit is fairly rugged and exposed with a few moves that may cause even experienced climbers a moment's pause. On a clear, dry day, the summit climb is enjoyable and airy, but if the rock is wet, icy, or snow covered, or visibility is poor, it is a more serious climb. Many climbers have stopped short of the summit, unwilling to climb the final pitch unroped. The USGS survey marker on the summit mistakenly identifies the mountain as Boston Peak.

HOW TO GET THERE

This climb begins from Cascade Pass trailhead at the end of Cascade River Road. Drive the North Cascades Highway (Washington Highway 20) to Marblemount. If you are camping overnight, register at the Marblemount Ranger Station. Follow Cascade River Road (Forest Road 15) east about 23 miles to the Cascade Pass trailhead at the road's end. The last bit of the road is paved, a big improvement over the rough road that used to force many hikers and climbers to park much lower. In early season, though, the last 2 miles of the road may be gated. This is a very popular trailhead, so expect crowds. A Northwest Forest Pass is required.

ROUTE DESCRIPTION

The popular route up Sahale Peak is via the Sahale Arm and Sahale Glacier. This route is reasonably done in a day or with a camp at Sahale Glacier.

Hike Cascade Pass Trail for about 3.7 miles to Cascade Pass, elevation 5,392 feet. Cross over the pass, dropping down briefly to the junction with Sahale Arm Trail. Then hike north up Sahale Arm for about 1.9 miles to the terminus of Sahale Glacier, elevation about 7,700 feet. The trail degenerates near the end and may be difficult to follow. If you lose the trail, just climb up through the moraine rubble and snow to the top of the moraine. Sahale Glacier Camp is officially the highest developed campsite in North Cascades National Park. There are several bivy sites here with rock windbreaks and a pit toilet west of the campsite on the moraine ridge. Camping is allowed only above the second moraine ridge at the foot of the glacier. Camping is not allowed anywhere on Sahale Arm. The Sahale Glacier Camp is one of the longest and most arduous advance base camps in the Cascades. Because the climb can be done in a day, most opt to climb light instead of carrying a heavy pack up to the glacier camp.

From the moraine, ascend the glacier directly, staying on the west side higher up to avoid a mid-level crevasse, and continue directly up the steep firn slopes to

Sahale Peak

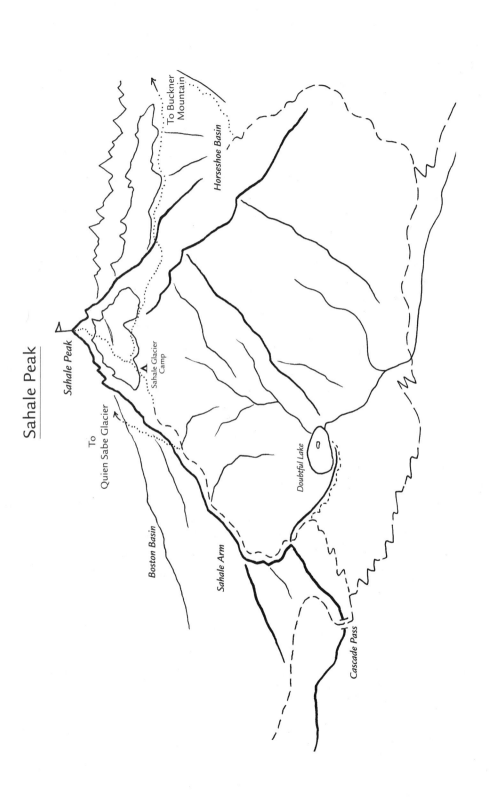

To Buckner Mountain

Horseshoe Basin

Sahale Peak

To
Quien Sabe Glacier

Sahale Glacier Camp

Boston Basin

Doubtful Lake

Sahale Arm

Cascade Pass

Sahale Peak Summit Pyramid

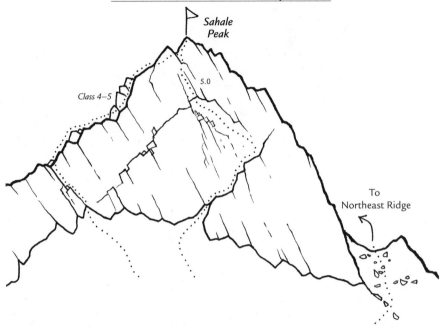

the base of the summit rocks. A short "scramble" up the summit rocks completes the ascent. There are three commonly used routes. The standard route is on the right side of the south face. Scramble right up slabby rock nearly to the southern ridgeline, then left to an alcove, and finally up a short Class 4–5 step to the summit. The blocky west ridge is straightforward ridge scrambling with a short, exposed Class 4 section if you pick your route carefully among the big blocks, which seem precariously perched. There is also a Class 4 route skirting the summit rocks right around the north side of the summit rocks and up the northeast ridge.

To descend from the summit, either downclimb or rappel from the summit block. Rappel down to the alcove, then again down to the base of the summit rocks. Two single-rope rappels suffice. Bring a couple of long slings to back up or replace the old slings tied around the summit block.

OPTIONS

Another popular route up Sahale Peak climbs the west side via Quien Sabe Glacier. It is more challenging and a bit longer, and thus not as popular as the Sahale Glacier route. However, this straightforward route is climbed fairly often. It may be approached either from Boston Basin or by traversing across talus slopes from Sahale Arm. Refer to *Cascade Alpine Guide*.

PRECAUTIONS

Although mild as glaciers go, the Sahale Glacier is crevassed, and roping up is recommended, although many climbers foolishly don't bother. In early season, cornices form on the upper ridge. The summit peak is sharp and exposed with room for only a few climbers at a time. The summit scramble is mostly easy, but involves loose blocks, some downsloping rock, and exposed Class 3 climbing with a couple of Class 4 moves. Many climbers feel there are low Class 5 moves on the summit climb. Most climbers complete the climb unroped, but many balk at the prospect of soloing the last 100 feet to the summit. Definitely belay if the summit rocks are wet or icy. Bring a rope, a small rack up to 2 inches, and some slings just in case.

Remember to get a permit at Sedro Woolley or Marblemount Ranger Station if making an overnight climb. Camping is not permitted on Sahale Arm, only at the Sahale Glacier Camp.

16. MIX-UP PEAK

Elevation: 7,420 feet/2,262 meters
Route: East Face
Rating: Grade II, 5.0; Grade I glacier
Distance: 10 miles round trip
Elevation Gain: 3,800 feet
Time: 8 to 10 hours trailhead to summit
Maps: USGS Cascade Pass; Green Trails No. 80 (Cascade Pass)

ABOUT THE CLIMB
The East Face of Mix-up Peak is one of the overlooked classics of the North Cascades. It's a popular route with some very enjoyable scrambling and easy climbing, but it is routinely left out of "select" guides, probably because it isn't one of the lords of the Cascade Pass area. Although it is a big peak with steep, impressive rock walls and buttresses, it pales in comparison with its neighbors like the imposing Johannesburg Mountain and the more isolated peaks across the way (Forbidden Peak, Eldorado Peak, and Sahale Peak). Part of Mix-up's identity crisis is that its summit is far to the south, hidden from view until you get up and over Cascade Pass. Until then, all you see is a bulky, steep-walled, fairly unattractive peak without a defined summit. However, once you get above Cascade Pass onto Sahale Arm, you can see Mix-up's east ridge in profile, a long, narrow, sweeping crest rising some 900 feet from a narrow notch to its craggy summit.

From afar, and even from closer up, Mix-up Peak's easiest route seems improbably steep and rocky. However, aside from some Class 4 climbing at the start and finish, with a move or two of low Class 5, the route is a reasonable, enjoyable scramble. Mix-up can be climbed in a long day but is best climbed with a trailhead bivouac because camping is not allowed near Cascade Pass and there are no good bivy sites. Summit views are excellent, including impressive views of Sahale Peak and Buckner Mountain, the Ptarmigan Traverse, Glacier Peak, Snowking Mountain, and along the ridge to the Triplets, Cascade Peak, and Johannesburg Mountain.

HOW TO GET THERE
This climb begins from Cascade Pass trailhead at the end of Cascade River Road. Drive the North Cascades Highway (Washington Highway 20) to Marblemount,

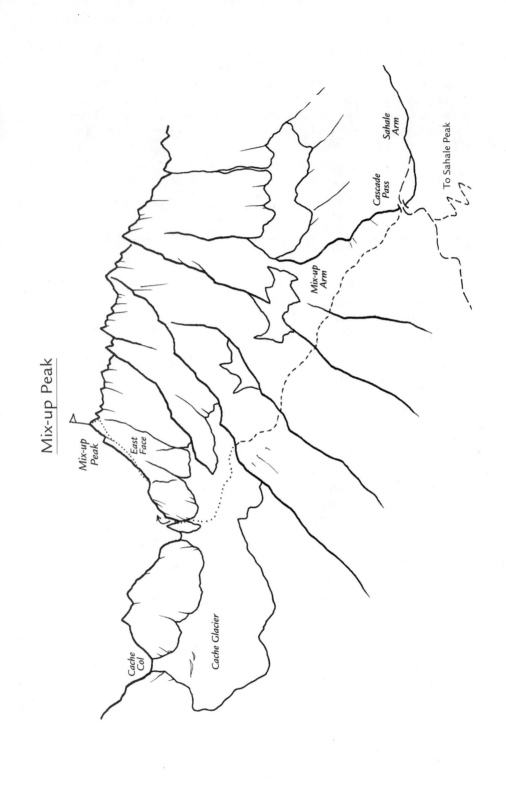

Mix-up Peak

Mix-up
Peak

East
Face

Cache
Col

Cache Glacier

Mix-up
Arm

Cascade
Pass

Sahale
Arm

To Sahale Peak

then follow Cascade River Road (Forest Road 15) east for about 21 miles to the road's end and the trailhead. This is a very popular trailhead, so expect crowds. A Northwest Forest Pass is required.

ROUTE DESCRIPTION

The route described is popularly known as the East Face, an improbably steep-looking face that turns out to be quite reasonable. Hike Cascade Pass Trail for about 3.7 miles to Cascade Pass, elevation 5,392 feet. Leave the trail at the pass and traverse southeast on a climber's trail on Mix-up Arm. This path traverses scree and snow slopes along the east side of Mix-up Peak to the glacier basin below the east face. Cross the glacier and ascend to the notch at the base of Mix-up Peak's East Ridge. In late season, a moat forms between the snow and rock in the gully leading up to the gap, adding a difficult bit of climbing to get established on rock and up the chute to the notch. In early season, climb steep snow to the notch.

From the notch, cross over and descend about 10 feet to the right (left if you are facing the rock, westerly direction) and start climbing up the rock face. The first 30 feet are Class 4, which eases to Class 3 but becomes very exposed. Alternatively, descend about 100 feet and start climbing back up to the ridge crest (also Class 4). Cross over the ridge and ascend a small chute, then traverse right to some trees and continue upward to the top of the ridge. Cross over to the north (right) side of the ridge and traverse to a large white granite "staircase," a series of short walls and ledges leading up toward the summit. Climb this staircase for several hundred feet to within about 70 feet of the summit. A final Class 5.0 pitch climbs right to a small notch, then traverses to the summit.

To descend, downclimb back to the notch, rappel back to the top of the granite staircase, and scramble/climb back down the route. Rappel or downclimb the final step to the notch.

OPTIONS

The East Ridge is reported as a Class 4–5 rock climb with some devious routefinding and loose rock. It is not popular. Refer to *Cascade Alpine Guide* for route details.

PRECAUTIONS

In late season, expect difficult climbing out of the moat to reach the notch. Although commonly reported as Class 4, some feel the route has a little bit of low Class 5 climbing. Many parties belay only the first and last pitches, but the route is exposed Class 3, so belay if any member of your party feels the need. There is some loose rock, and spontaneous rockfall has resulted in a fatality here. Be careful not to knock rocks down on other climbers. The approach crosses a lobe of the Cache Glacier, but few parties rope up. This climb can be done in a day, but it is a long haul when driving time is factored in. Start early from the trailhead and be prepared for the possibility of an unplanned bivouac.

A permit is required for overnight camping. Camping is not permitted on Mix-up Arm. Most parties who make an overnight climb bivouac at the trailhead. Register at Marblemount Ranger Station.

Buckner Mountain and Goode Mountain (right) from Sahale Peak.

17. BUCKNER MOUNTAIN

Elevation: 9,112 feet/2,778 meters
Route: Southwest Slope
Rating: Class 3
Distance: 19 miles round trip
Elevation Gain: 7,300 feet
Time: 9 to 12 hours; best done as a two- or three-day climb
Maps: USGS Cascade Pass and Goode Mountain; Green Trails No. 80 (Cascade Pass) and 81 (McGregor Mountain)

ABOUT THE CLIMB

Although not the highest peak of the Cascade Pass area of the North Cascades, Buckner Mountain is considered the "king" of the region by virtue of its great size and location. Because it is nearer to Cascade Pass than its higher neighbor, Goode Mountain, Buckner gets all the glory. A relatively simple route up the Southwest Slope makes Buckner one of the more accessible 9,000-foot summits of the Cascade Range, but its size and position make it a very big climb even without technical difficulty. The approach over Cascade Pass gains and loses some 1,800 feet of elevation before climbing about 5,500 feet more to the summit. While very strong climbers may manage the climb in a long day, most will wisely bivouac in Horseshoe Basin or higher up.

According to Beckey, the southwest peak is an estimated 2 feet higher than the northwest peak. While the exact height of the true summit is unknown, the southwest peak appears to be barely higher. Both peaks may be climbed via a loose ridge scramble, although the traverse adds unnecessary risk. A steep glacier

Buckner Mountain

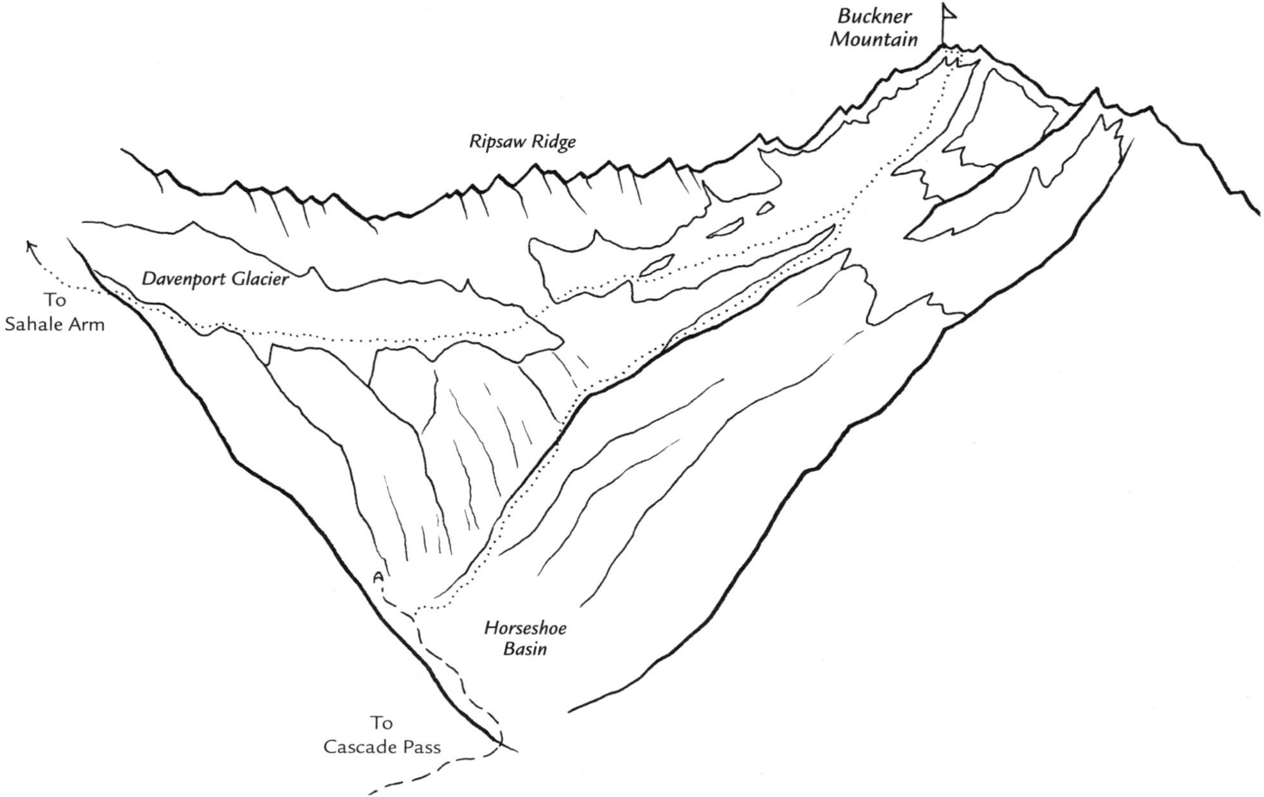

Buckner
Mountain

Ripsaw Ridge

Davenport Glacier

Horseshoe
Basin

To
Sahale Arm

To
Cascade Pass

route up the North Face of Buckner Mountain has become very popular in recent years, although the scrambling route is still the route of choice for a majority of climbers. Due to its height and position, Buckner provides supreme views of the heart of the North Cascades, including the peaks of Cascade Pass and the Ptarmigan Traverse, and Mount Logan, Goode Mountain, Bonanza Peak, and Glacier Peak, to name only a few.

HOW TO GET THERE

This climb begins from Cascade Pass trailhead at the end of Cascade River Road. Drive the North Cascades Highway (Washington Highway 20) to Marblemount, then follow Cascade River Road (Forest Road 15) east for about 24 miles to the road's end and trailhead. This is a very popular trailhead, so expect crowds. A Northwest Forest Pass is required.

ROUTE DESCRIPTION

The standard route up Buckner Mountain is via Horseshoe Basin, just east of Cascade Pass. Hike Cascade Pass Trail about 3.7 miles to Cascade Pass, elevation 5,392 feet. Continue down the other side another 2.7 miles to a junction with Horseshoe Basin Trail and hike 1.5 miles up into Horseshoe Basin. In early season, the lower basin is covered in avalanche snow and debris. The trail (an old mine road) leads to a mine at the head of the basin. Steep, brushy cliffs seem to bar further progress, but an old miner's trail leading up the less steep slopes on the east side of the basin gives access to the upper basin. Leave the trail just below the mine and follow a boot path across the creek and up the opposite slope. Scramble up brushy, slabby rock several hundred feet to gain the gentler upper basin slopes. If you lose the path, just scramble up wherever seems easiest, skirting cliffs until you regain it. Once past the steepness, ascend scree and snow slopes upward seemingly forever toward the summit ridge. The route steepens near the top. Once the summit ridge is gained, a short rock scramble leads to the top. Except for the initial climb out of Horseshoe Basin, the route is very straightforward in clear weather. The southwest peak is reputedly the highest point, which is just as well, because the traverse to the northwest peak is a bit loose and scary. To descend, downclimb the route.

OPTIONS

There are several other routes up Buckner Mountain, most of which are technical rock or ice ascents. Since being featured in *Selected Climbs in the Cascade Range*, the North Face has become one of the most popular routes up the mountain.

A descent variation commonly used by climbers coming down from the North Face is to traverse upper Horseshoe Basin toward Sahale Peak, contouring to the base of a broad gully leading about 1,000 feet up to the Sahale Glacier, then hiking out via Sahale Arm to Cascade Pass. This variation has far less elevation loss and gain than hiking all the way out via Horseshoe Basin. This is a feasible approach variation as well, especially from a bivouac at Sahale Glacier. The gully is steep, requiring care when climbing down, but it isn't much steeper than the rest of the climb up Buckner Mountain.

PRECAUTIONS

The slopes below Cascade Pass and in and above Horseshoe Basin are very avalanche prone. The route ascending from lower Horseshoe Basin is not especially
difficult but can be hard to follow. A wrong turn can lead to exposed, loose
scrambling.

18. GOODE MOUNTAIN

Elevation: 9,220 feet/2,810 meters
Route: Northeast Buttress
Rating: Grade IV, 5.6; Grade III glacier
Distance: 32 miles round trip
Elevation Gain: 6,600 feet on the ascent; at least 1,900 feet on the descent
Time: Allow at least three days, including a full day for the summit climb and
descent
Maps: USGS Goode Mountain; Green Trails No. 81 (McGregor Mountain)

ABOUT THE CLIMB

Goode Mountain (or Mount Goode, depending on your reference) is the highest
and most outstanding of the Cascade Pass area peaks. Goode is also one of the
most remote of Washington's 9,000-foot summits. The mountain is situated
almost directly between Rainy Pass and Cascade Pass, a full-day's hike at best
from the nearest trailhead. Just getting to the peak is a strenuous ordeal of expe-
ditionary proportion. You have your choice of hiking in at least 14 miles, or taking the ferry to Stehekin and shuttling closer to the mountain. Then you have to
climb it, a task complicated by the mountain's extreme relief (nearly 6,000 feet
rise from base to peak on the east face) and lack of a truly easy summit route.

Goode Mountain was one of the Cascade's most sought after unclimbed summits. It resisted many attempts over the years until 1936, when Wolf Bauer, Phil
Dickert, Jack Hossack, Joe Halwax, and George McGowan made the first ascent
via the Southwest Chimney route. These Mountaineers club climbers felt a special urgency to summit because a pair of Mazama club climbers on the boat with
them were also bound for Goode. The group was nearly stopped just short of the
summit but prevailed in overcoming the final rock pitch by means of a lasso and
prusik, then a piton-protected finger traverse by Bauer gained the summit ridge.
Bauer hastily built a cairn on the summit, then told the others that the Mazamas
had beat them to the summit. They were not amused.

A variation of their route, the Southwest Couloir, is easier than the chimney
and is one of the standard summit routes, although it and other gully climbs on
the west face involve steep, brushy approaches, and infamously loose scree.
Goode's classic route, the Northeast Buttress, is a 2,600-foot rock buttress (IV,
5.6) that includes a long, difficult approach involving strenuous bushwhacking,
Class 3-4 scrambling, and a difficult glacier climb. Although the Northeast Buttress is popular and highly recommended, it is also a serious, committing technical route. Given the difficulties encountered just on the approach to the peak,
Goode Mountain is not a popular climb. But popular or not, it is climbed fairly

Goode Mountain

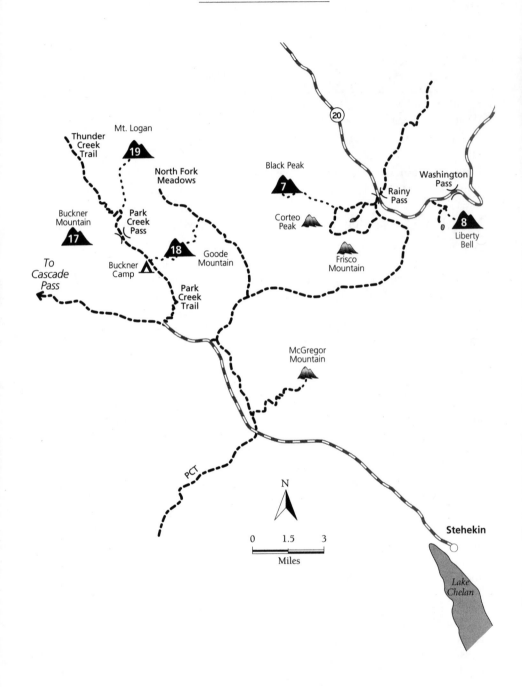

Thunder Creek Trail

Mt. Logan

19

North Fork Meadows

Black Peak

7

Washington Pass

Buckner Mountain

17

Park Creek Pass

Corteo Peak

Rainy Pass

Liberty Bell

8

To Cascade Pass

Buckner Camp

18

Goode Mountain

Frisco Mountain

Park Creek Trail

McGregor Mountain

PCT

N

Stehekin

0   1.5   3

Miles

Lake Chelan

often, or at least attempted, usually by climbers intent upon summiting all of this state's 9,000-foot peaks, often by climbers out to prove themselves against one of the state's most difficult high mountains, and sometimes by climbers lured by the mountain's isolation and savage beauty. Summit views are commanding, but views are not why people climb Goode Mountain. Better views can be had with far less suffering or commitment.

HOW TO GET THERE

The shortest hiking approach is via the Lady of the Lake ferry to Stehekin, then a shuttle bus and NPS van to Park Creek. Refer to the information under "Stehekin and Holden Village Transportation" in Appendix A. However, this is a longer approach overall considering the time necessary to drive to Chelan, take the ferry to Stehekin, and wait for the van to drive you up to the trailhead. If you use this approach, consider bringing a mountain bike with you to the trailhead so you can ride down the road to Stehekin on the way out instead of waiting for the van. The recommended approach option is via the PCT from near Rainy Pass. For this approach, drive the North Cascades Highway (Washington Highway 20) to the PCT trailhead about 2 miles southeast of Rainy Pass. A Northwest Forest Pass is required. This is a high "car-prowl" trailhead, so leave nothing of value in your car.

ROUTE DESCRIPTION

Hike about 10 miles south on the PCT to the junction with North Fork Bridge Creek Trail. Hike up this trail for about 3.5 miles to where it crosses Grizzly Creek. Continue about 0.6 mile beyond Grizzly Creek and find a climber's trail descending to North Fork Bridge Creek. The trail begins just past the last stand of trees before crossing an avalanche path, opposite an obvious waterfall. If you reach a big grassy meadow, you have gone too far. Descend the trail to the creek and cross via a knee-to-waist-deep ford, or try to find a footlog just downstream. Once across, ascend the opposite slope, angling left through stands of subalpine fir and hemlock, then bushwhacking through slide alder to a talus slope leading right and up to the base of the slabby cliffs. Scramble up to the base of a waterfall, then scramble up Class 4 slabs right of the falls. From the top of the slabs, climb upward through brush, then up a rocky heather ridge to the base of the cliffs below the glacier seracs. There are two small bivy sites at the base of the cliffs. This is a long, brushy, complex approach. You can follow a climber's trail for much of the way, but you may lose the path in brush, and there are several slabby cliffs that you must pass via Class 3 and 4 scrambling. Climb carefully.

From camp, scramble left up to the glacier. In early season, snow slopes lead almost directly up; later, you must take a longer traverse to pass loose cliffs and seracs. Once on the glacier, rope up and ascend the glacier, which is steep and can be icy and difficult by late season. Double tools and ice screws are recommended for the 50- or 60-degree glacier ice. Climb as high as feasible on the glacier to gain the rock buttress, then climb a couple of rock pitches (reported 5.4–5.6) to gain the buttress proper. A moat crossing to get on the rock may be the crux of the climb. The climbing is reportedly easier as you go higher on the buttress. Climb heather benches to and up the northeast buttress proper. The lower portion of the buttress is enjoyable Class 4 climbing, fairly easy but increasingly exposed.

Goode Mountain Northeast Buttress

Goode
Mountain

Descent

Northeast
Buttress

Goode Glacier

⛺ bivy

brushy

falls

slabs

falls

Class 4
slabs

falls

waterfall

brushy

ford

North Fork

Bridge Creek

Grizzly Creek

The buttress steepens, and the climbing becomes more difficult, especially in the middle pitches where the buttress flattens out. Higher up, about 500 feet below the top, the buttress becomes more distinct, and the climbing is more difficult, continuously Class 4 up to mid-Class 5. Eventually the climbing eases up and soon ends at a shelf just south of the summit, immediately right (north) of a deep notch in the summit ridge. Some parties bivouac here; most leave their packs and continue to the summit. Some 200 feet of easier climbing gains the airy summit. Bring ice ax, crampons, double ropes, a moderate rack including gear and cams up to 3 inches, and several slings. Although light travel is definitely preferred, be prepared for the possibility of an unplanned bivouac or a forced retreat down the buttress.

The standard descent is down the Southwest Couloir via several rappels at the top, some scrambling, and scree or snow glissading down to the climber's trail leading to Park Creek. A descent over the Goode-Storm King col is suggested in *Selected Climbs in the Cascade Range*, but by late season the glacier is usually icy and broken, making this descent more difficult than necessary. Unless there is a compelling reason to go back to Goode Glacier, the most expedient retreat is to hike out via Park Creek Trail.

OPTIONS
There are two "easy" routes to the summit of Goode Mountain, the Bedayn Couloir and the Southwest Couloir, and both are approached via Park Creek Trail and Buckner Camp. These routes involve mostly scree or snow climbing up gullies with a few rock pitches of Class 4–5 difficulty. Refer to *Cascade Alpine Guide* for approach and route details.

PRECAUTIONS
All routes on Goode Mountain are committing and exposed, and should not be attempted by inexperienced climbers. There is avalanche and rockfall hazard on all routes. Be aware of climber-induced rockfall in the gullies and couloirs. Overnight snow or ice can make the routes much more difficult and serious. The Goode Glacier is steep and broken, and more technical than many Cascades glacier climbs. Those climbing the Northeast Buttress should be proficient on Class 5 rock and steep ice climbing. The descent is complicated and time consuming.

19. MOUNT LOGAN

Elevation: 9,087 feet/2,770 meters
Route: Fremont Glacier
Rating: Class 3; Grade I glacier
Distance: 25 miles round trip
Elevation Gain: 7,500 feet
Time: Allow at least 3 days; a full day for the summit climb and descent
Maps: USGS Mount Logan; Green Trails No. 49 (Mount Logan)

ABOUT THE CLIMB
Mount Logan is a broad, glaciated mountain located in the heart of the North Cascades. Situated some 10 miles due west of Rainy Pass and hidden from view by intervening ranges, Logan is one of the least known and least accessible of

Mount Logan

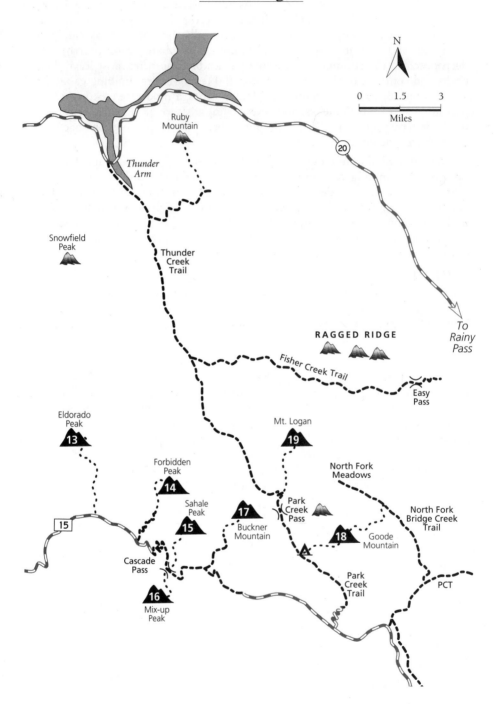

N

0   1.5   3
Miles

Thunder Arm

Ruby Mountain

20

Snowfield Peak

Thunder Creek Trail

RAGGED RIDGE

Fisher Creek Trail

To Rainy Pass

Easy Pass

Eldorado Peak

13

Mt. Logan

19

North Fork Meadows

Forbidden Peak

14

Sahale Peak

15

Park Creek Pass

North Fork Bridge Creek Trail

15

17

Buckner Mountain

18

Goode Mountain

Cascade Pass

16

Mix-up Peak

Park Creek Trail

PCT

Mount Logan (left) and Buckner Mountain from Sahale Peak.

Washington's 9,000-foot summits. Like Goode Mountain, Logan has a long, strenuous approach. Fortunately, Logan is not nearly as difficult to climb. The popular route is the Fremont Glacier on the southwest flank. The climbing is mostly glacier traversing with some exposed Class 3 scrambling to the summit. Although relatively simple, Logan is a serious climb that should be approached with caution. Due to the peak's isolation, a rescue would be long in coming. Excellent views from the summit include Buckner Mountain, Sahale Peak, Boston Peak, Eldorado Peak, Snowfield Peak, Ragged Ridge, Black Peak, Goode Mountain, Jack Mountain, Glacier Peak, Mount Baker, and Bonanza Peak, to name only a few.

HOW TO GET THERE

There is no fast or short route to Mount Logan. The shortest hiking approach is via the Lady of the Lake ferry to Stehekin, then a shuttle bus and NPS van to Park Creek. Refer to the information under "Stehekin and Holden Village Transportation" in Appendix A. The shortest alternative approach to Park Creek is to hike in 19-plus miles from the North Cascades Highway via Thunder Creek Trail. Another alternative is to hike in 22.5 miles via Cascade Pass, an option that is sometimes used by climbers approaching from the west side. A final option is to approach as for Goode Mountain via the PCT from near Rainy Pass, which is also a 20 mile plus affair but mostly downhill from the trailhead to Park Creek.

ROUTE DESCRIPTION

From Park Creek, hike up Park Creek Pass Trail for about 5.2 miles to Buckner Camp, the traditional climber's base camp for Mount Logan and Goode Mountain. If you take the morning ferry from Stehekin and no ferry or shuttle connections are missed, you should arrive at Park Creek in the late afternoon with

Mount Logan Fremont Glacier

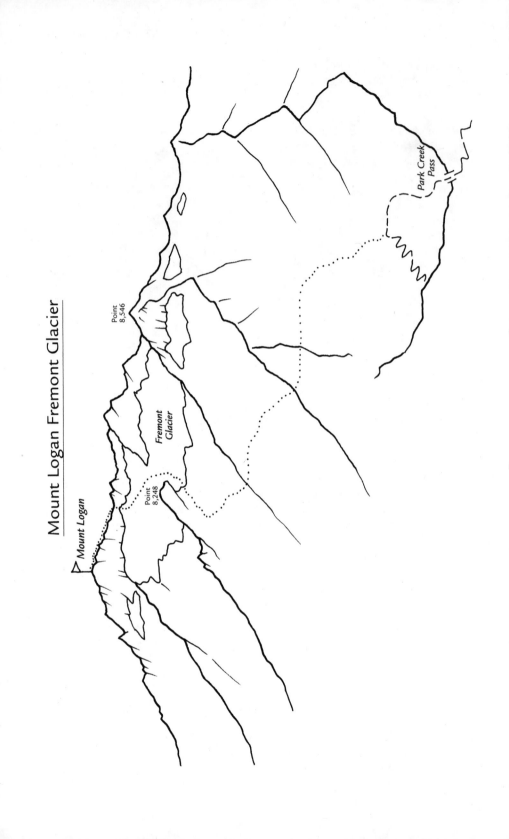

Mount Logan

Point
8,546

Point
8,248

Fremont
Glacier

Park Creek
Pass

enough time to hike in to Buckner Camp or beyond. If there's extra time, push over Park Creek Pass and camp at the edge of the meadow or along the climber's trail to the Fremont Glacier, which enables a shorter summit climb the next morning.

From Buckner Camp, hike another 2.7 miles up and over 6,060-foot Park Creek Pass. Follow the trail briefly down the north side of the pass for about 0.7 mile to a meadow and find the obvious climber's path leading off to the right (northeast). Do not start down the switchbacks toward Thunder Creek; the route leaves the trail above the switchbacks. Follow the climber's trail that traverses open slopes around a ridge and up to the base of the Fremont Glacier. When the climber's trail disappears, contour the slopes below the Fremont Glacier (6,400 feet), then ascend directly to the glacier just south of Point 8,248 to avoid cliffs farther south. Rope up and cross the gentle glacier, ascending from just south of Point 8,248 more or less directly to an obvious gap in the summit ridge. From here, a rock scramble up exposed ledges on the east side of the ridge leads to the summit. To descend, downclimb the route.

OPTIONS
Beckey's guide reports routes up Banded Glacier and Douglas Glacier, both of which look interesting, but neither of which is as popular as Fremont Glacier due to long approaches. Of course, long approaches are what climbing Mount Logan is all about. Refer to *Cascade Alpine Guide* for route details.

PRECAUTIONS
The Fremont Glacier is deceptively gentle, but crevasses do open up and catch an occasional climber. Roping up is recommended. The ridge traverse is relatively easy scrambling but very exposed with some loose rock. The ridge traverse is risky when snow-covered or icy, justifying roping up and belaying if not turning back.

20. BONANZA PEAK

Elevation: 9,511 feet/2,899 meters
Route: East face via Mary Green Glacier
Rating: Grade III, Class 4–5; Grade II glacier
Distance: 14 miles
Elevation Gain: 6,200 feet
Time: Best done as a three-day climb, which includes a full-day for the summit climb and descent
Maps: USGS Holden; Green Trails No. 113 (Holden)

ABOUT THE CLIMB
Bonanza Peak is the highest non-volcanic peak in the Cascade Range and one of the most challenging summits included in this guide, all things considered. Bonanza Peak is a precipitous, heavily glaciated granitic peak rising about 15 miles west of Lake Chelan. It is a relatively remote peak with a complicated approach and without an easy route to its summit. You cannot drive there but must take a ferry halfway up Lake Chelan, then hire a "taxi" 12 miles just to get to the trailhead. This deters many from making the ascent, but the mountain's sheer height and regional prominence make it a compelling climb.

Bonanza Peak

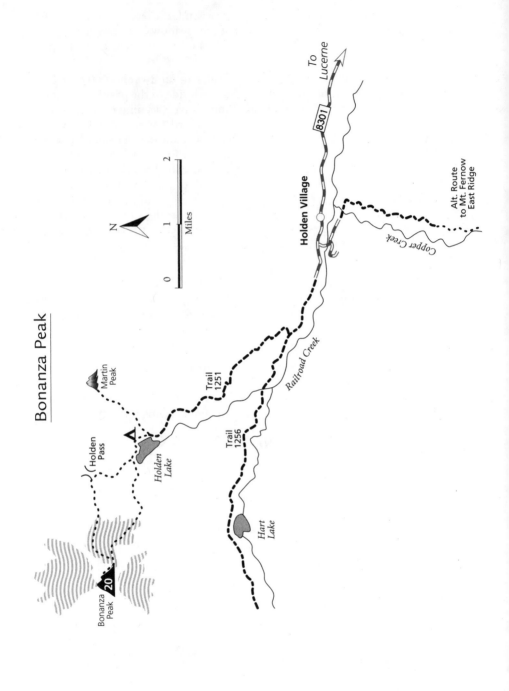

The easiest route is via the Mary Green Glacier and the east face, a fairly straightforward but very committing route that combines steep glacier and rock climbing. Although the climbing is mostly Class 3–4, the rock is notoriously loose. Nary an ascent is made without report of a near miss by a boulder dislodged by a party member or random rockfall started by rain or a puff of wind. Fortunately, most parties survive the climb intact, although luck may play as large a role as skill in that regard. As the highest peak in eastern section of the North Cascades, Bonanza Peak has supreme views, a sublime panorama of the Chelan, Entiat, and Sawtooth Mountains, and the peaks in Pasayten Wilderness and Glacier Peak Wilderness; northwest to Mount Logan and Goode Mountain, west to the Ptarmigan Traverse, and far south to Mount Stuart and Mount Rainier, to name only a few.

HOW TO GET THERE

Bonanza Peak is most easily approached from Holden Village on the west shore of Lake Chelan. From Wenatchee, follow U.S. Highway 97 Alternate north along the west side of the Columbia River through Entiat, then follow Washington Highway 971 north to Lake Chelan where signs lead to Field's Point Landing. Take the *Lady of the Lake* ferry to Lucerne. (You can also catch the ferry at Chelan.) From Lucerne, bike or hitch a ride 12 miles up Forest Road 8301 to the old mining town of Holden, which is now used as a retreat center affiliated with the Lutheran Church. The ride to Holden Village costs $10 per person round trip at last report, so bring some cash. Travel to the road's end and the Hart Lake trailhead. Refer to the information under "Stehekin and Holden Village Transportation" in Appendix A.

ROUTE DESCRIPTION

Hike Hart Lake Trail a long 0.5 mile to its junction with Holden Lake Trail (Trail 1251). Take a right and follow Holden Lake Trail for about 3.6 uphill miles to Holden Lake, elevation 5,250 feet. Holden Lake is a popular campsite for summit-bound climbers. Holden Pass is supposedly more popular because it is closer to the summit than the lake, and because Beckey's guide says so, although most climbers make a direct approach from Holden Lake.

If approaching via Holden Pass, skirt around the east side of the lake, crossing a stream, and ascend easy slopes to the pass (elevation 6,405 feet). From the pass, head west toward Mary Green Glacier, traversing a climber's trail across talus slopes and below cliffs to steep snow or rocky slopes to the northeast edge of the glacier, then traverse the glacier toward the snow thumb described below.

The alternate route—favored by most—climbs directly west from the northeast corner of Holden Lake. Ford an icy stream, then ascend the brush-lined talus cone on the left to its apex, continuing up a difficult vine maple slope a short distance to where the gully narrows to a waterfall. Exit right onto slabby rocks and follow a wall around to the next waterfall, then climb easy slabs to the glacier's southeast terminus. Expect a bit of scrambling here, up to Class 3. Flag the position at the top of the gullies so you can find the route on the descent, which could be difficult with the onset of poor weather.

In early season, snowfields may make it difficult to tell where the snow ends and glacier begins. If in doubt, rope up early. Once on the glacier, ascend to the

Bonanza Peak

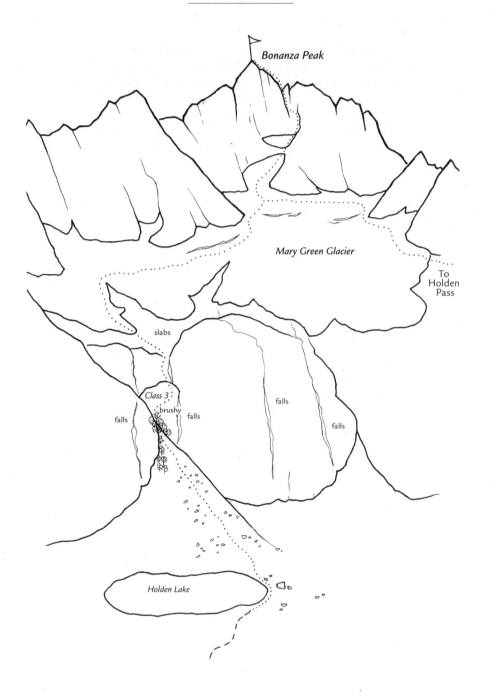

Bonanza Peak

Mary Green Glacier

To
Holden
Pass

slabs

Class 3

falls

brushy   falls

falls   falls

Holden Lake

obvious wide snow gully ("thumb" according to Beckey) in the middle of the east face, skirting crevasses as necessary. The glacier is usually less crevassed on the north side, an advantage to approaching from Holden Pass. If you take the direct approach, the glacier is more rugged. A bergschrund may bar access to the snow thumb by late season. Ascend the snow thumb's right side to an obvious gully. The snow gets quite steep near the top; pickets are recommended for belay anchors. Climb the gully (rock or snow in early season) or easier rock just right (scantily protected Class 3-4, maybe a little Class 5 depending on the route taken), taking care not to rain rocks down the gully. About two thirds of the way up the face, traverse left past a small rock outcropping to a gully that leads to the prominent notch just below the summit. Do not take the gully on the right; it leads nowhere. From the notch, pass a short, moderately difficult step, then scramble up exposed, broken rock to the summit.

The majority of the rock climbing on the route is Class 3-4, with one or two short Class 5 sections. Protection is difficult, and there is abundant loose rock on the route. The descent involves several rappels and substantial downclimbing. Double ropes are recommended for the descent.

OPTIONS

An ascent of 8,511-foot Martin Peak can be combined with Bonanza Peak in the same trip, or substituted if you are not up to the difficulties of the latter. Hike in to Holden Lake, then ascend northeast either from the lake or from the meadow slopes below Holden Pass, toward Martin Peak. Traverse moderate scree slopes on the south side of the west ridge to a central gully system, which you ascend to the summit ridge. Expect a long snow climb in early season, some patchy snow and scree later. A straightforward Class 2-3 rock scramble gains the summit.

PRECAUTIONS

An ascent of Bonanza Peak is a serious undertaking, not at all suitable for inexperienced climbers. Like all routes up Bonanza Peak, the Mary Green Glacier route is complex and involves steep snow, brush, and rock scrambling on the approach, a heavily crevassed glacier, a difficult bergschrund crossing, exposed firn slopes, rock scrambling, and technical rock climbing up a 2,200-foot face. These challenges are all complicated by snow, fragile rock, and often unreliable weather. Start early, rope up on the glacier, and be prepared to cross snow bridges or to find other ways across or around crevasses and the bergschrund later in the season. The rock gullies and the slab traverse are hazardous under even the best conditions. The gullies have loose rock poised and waiting to be knocked loose, and sometimes they don't wait. The gullies and snow thumb are prone to avalanches in early season and are treacherous when mixed snow and rock, or when wet. Rock is very friable in places, and there is a lot of loose rubble on the summit scramble. Spontaneous rockfall is frequently reported. Be careful not to knock rocks down on other climbers or to pull off a loose block while climbing. Early season ascents are recommended (June to mid-July); the glacier opens up later in the year. Wand the glacier in case bad weather or darkness sets in during the climb.

Mountain Loop and Index Area

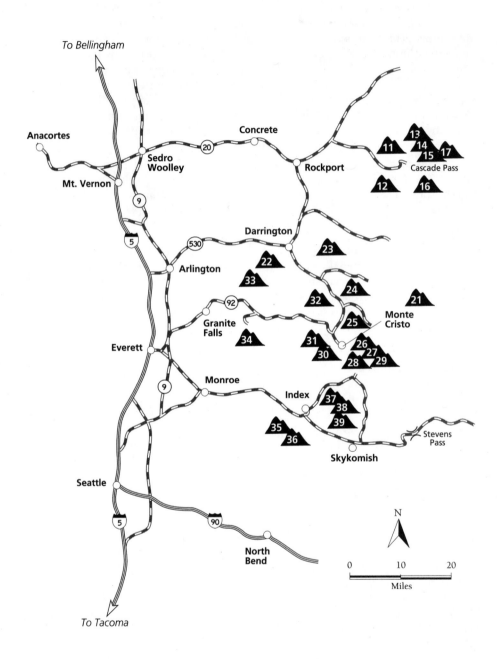

Mountain Loop and Index Area

The Mountain Loop Peaks are a group of mountains flanking the western boundary of the Glacier Peak Wilderness. Most of these peaks are within the Boulder River Wilderness and Henry M. Jackson Wilderness. The name derives from the Mountain Loop Road, the main thoroughfare between Darrington and Granite Falls, which is used to approach the many hiking trails in this region.

Although the Mountain Loop Peaks are among the most rugged of the Cascade Range, nearly every peak has a relatively easy route to the top. Some of the routes are devious, starting on one side of the mountain and winding around via ledges and gullies to the summit. The rock is sometimes good, but mostly not so good, especially among the Monte Cristo Peaks, which are notorious for their loose rock. Due to the area's proximity to Puget Sound, most of the peaks in this area can be approached and climbed in a single day, although a few, including Glacier Peak and Sloan Peak, are best climbed over two or three days. Most of these peaks are also best climbed in early season, when snow allows easier passage. Helmets are highly recommended for all of the climbs in the Mountain Loop region.

Included with the Mountain Loop Peaks are several high summits in the vicinity of the town of Index in the Skykomish River Valley. Although not normally associated with the higher summits of the Monte Cristo region, the Index-area peaks are geographically contiguous and similar in geology, with some very rugged topography and dubious rock quality in places. Like the Mountain Loop Peaks, each peak has a relatively easy scrambling route to the summit.

As with other areas included in this guide, a Northwest Forest Pass is required to park at all Forest Service trailheads. For more information, contact the Forest Service's Darrington Ranger District Office listed in Appendix C.

21. GLACIER PEAK

Elevation: 10,541 feet/3,213 meters
Route: Sitkum Glacier
Rating: Class 2; Grade I–II glacier
Distance: 20 miles round trip
Elevation Gain: 8,200 feet
Time: 8 to 12 hours trailhead to summit; best as a two-day climb
Maps: USGS Glacier Peak West and East; Green Trails No. 112 (Glacier Peak)

ABOUT THE CLIMB

Tucked away within the interior of the Cascade Range of central Washington, Glacier Peak is the most remote and the least prominent of Washington's high volcanoes. No road penetrates within 8 miles of the mountain, and most approach hikes are over 10 miles long. When viewed from the lowlands of Puget Sound, the mountain barely stands out above lesser surrounding peaks. If you didn't know better, you might not guess it was one of the state's highest summits.

Glacier Peak is a heavily glaciated, significantly eroded dacite volcano. The mountain has a long history of building and explosive eruptions, the last major

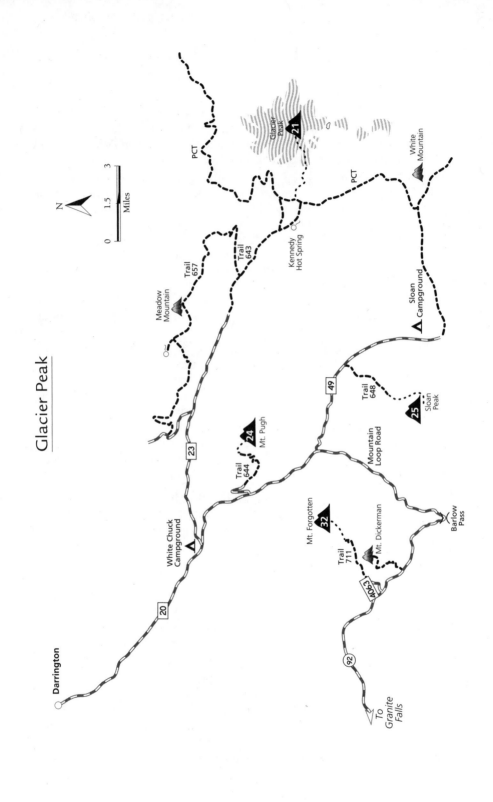

Glacier Peak

N

0   1.5   3
Miles

PCT

Glacier Peak [21]

White Mountain

PCT

Trail 657

Meadow Mountain

Trail 643

Kennedy Hot Spring

Sloan Campground

[23]

White Chuck Campground

Mt. Pugh [24]

Trail 644

[49]

Trail 648

Sloan Peak [25]

Mt. Forgotten [32]

Mountain Loop Road

[20]

Trail 711

Mt. Dickerman

Barlow Pass

[A063]

Darrington

[92]

To Granite Falls

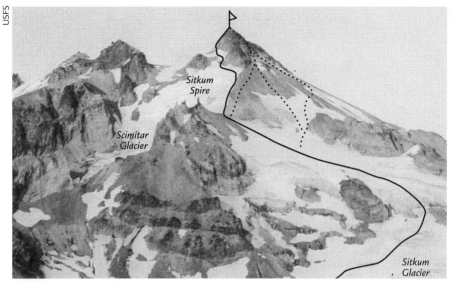

Sitkum Glacier Route, Glacier Peak.

eruption occurring at least 12,000 years ago. There is no evidence of significant eruptions since that time, except for the extrusion of Disappointment Peak, a dacite plug, but hot springs near the base of the peak are a sign that volcanic forces are still at work beneath the mountain. There is evidence to suggest that the mountain was once a bit higher than its present altitude; however, it is likely that the eruption 12,000 years ago, or earlier eruptions, and not glaciation alone, lowered the elevation of Glacier Peak.

Because of its remoteness and its unassuming skyline presence, Glacier Peak is not as popular an ascent as most of the other Cascade volcanoes. However, it is enjoyable and mostly private except during the weekend on popular routes. Because of its central location and relative height, Glacier Peak offers perhaps the best views of the North Cascades available without chartering an airplane. An unobstructed panorama overlooks every high summit from Mount Baker to Mount Rainier.

HOW TO GET THERE

This climb begins via Kennedy Hot Springs Trail from White Chuck River Road. From Darrington, follow the Mountain Loop Road (Forest Road 20) south about 9 miles to White Chuck Campground; from Granite Falls, follow Mountain Loop Road about 45 miles east to White Chuck Campground. From the campground, follow White Chuck River Road (Forest Road 23) another 10.5 miles to the Kennedy Hot Springs trailhead at the road's end. A Northwest Forest Pass is required.

ROUTE DESCRIPTION

The most popular route up Glacier Peak is the Sitkum Glacier, probably due to its reasonably short and direct approach. Register at the trailhead, then hike Kennedy Hot Springs Trail (Trail 643) almost 5 miles to a junction near Kennedy Hot Springs. From the hot springs, take White Chuck Trail Spur (Trail 643A)

USFS

Climbers on upper Scimitar Glacier, Glacier Peak.

about 2 miles to its junction with the PCT, then take a left, following the PCT northward another 0.5 mile to where a climber's trail departs. This steep trail climbs pretty much straight up a wooded spur ridge and rocky slopes above (some gravelly scrambling) to reach Boulder Basin, a small basin below the toe of the northern lobe of Sitkum Glacier, the customary bivouac spot for summit-bound climbers. Protect your food from hungry marmots, who have taken a liking to climbers' chow. Some parties prefer to camp higher up, on moraine slopes at the toe of the glacier. Some manage the ascent with a base camp at Kennedy Hot Springs, but most bivy higher up.

There are several possible routes from Boulder Basin. Most climbers ascend steep, rocky slopes and moraines directly to the toe of the glacier, then climb the left flank of the lower lobe of the glacier (less crevassed than the right flank), avoiding mid-level crevasses. Then traverse the upper lobe to a saddle above Sitkum Spire and continue up snow or pumice on the ridge, or just left on the upper Scimitar Glacier, to the summit. Many parties continue directly from the glacier to the summit without going to the saddle via a fairly direct snow gully or another, which is an easier, more direct option in early season when snow covers pumice slopes.

OPTIONS
Other variations from Boulder Basin are not as popular because they take longer and have more difficulties (crevasses, ice gullies, tedious pumice slopes), but they do have fewer climbers, a plus for those seeking escape from the masses. There are several other good routes up Glacier Peak, including Kennedy Glacier and Frostbite Ridge. Refer to *Climbing the Cascade Volcanoes* for route details.

PRECAUTIONS
Glacier Peak is regarded as an easy climb by most, but it has had its share of accidents and fatalities due to falls, crevasses, avalanches, and poor weather. Climbers must be self-sufficient on Glacier Peak, perhaps more so than on some of the other Cascade volcanoes, where rescues are easier.

Boulder Basin is a heavily used base camp and suffers from adverse impacts, primarily erosion and improper human waste disposal. There is a pit toilet here, but prior to July it is buried in snow. Please be mindful of these problems and take appropriate measures to minimize impacts.

22. WHITEHORSE MOUNTAIN

Elevation: 6,852 feet/2,088 meters
Route: West Ridge via Lone Tree Pass
Rating: Class 3–4; Grade I glacier
Distance: 12 miles round trip
Elevation Gain: 6,000 feet
Time: 8 to 10 hours trailhead to summit; easiest with a bivouac
Maps: USGS Whitehorse Mountain; Green Trails No. 110 (Silverton)

ABOUT THE CLIMB
Whitehorse Mountain is one of the most outstanding peaks of the western front of the Cascade Range. It rises dramatically above a deep, verdant glacial valley

Whitehorse Mountain

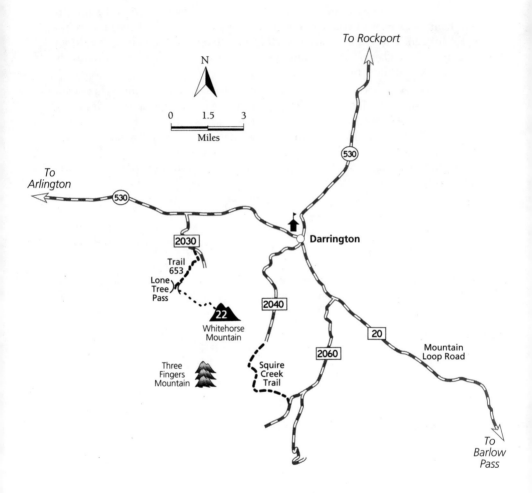

Whitehorse Mountain from near Lone Tree Pass.

just southwest of the town of Darrington to a craggy, glaciated summit. White-horse is reminiscent of peaks of the Swiss alps, except for the brush, which detracts from the romantic appeal of the peak, at least from a climber's perspective. Whitehorse is visible from Puget Sound as the first major peak north of Three Fingers Mountain. Legend has it that the peak was named in jest after a local farmer's horse went missing. In summer, from certain vantages, the glacier does somewhat resemble a white horse. The peak enjoyed fleeting stardom in the early 1980s as the setting for a forgettable made-for-television movie, *High Ice*, that featured such ingenious plot development as shooting missiles at a perfectly stable snowfield to reduce supposed avalanche danger. This caused a massive avalanche to fall on a climbing party stranded on a ledge with a homicidal maniac, or some such nonsense.

For us real climbers, Whitehorse is a popular early season climb, when snow allows easier passage over brush and scree. Its popularity wanes later in the season, not only because of tedious off-trail travel, but because the glacier becomes very broken and is all but impassable by late summer. With just over 6,000 feet of elevation gain from trailhead to summit, the climb is strenuous and more time consuming than most climbers anticipate. The usual route is over Lone Tree Pass and up through High Pass to the Whitehorse Glacier, a fairly direct and uncomplicated route that is often done in a single long day but is more enjoyable with a high camp in the vicinity of Lone Tree Pass. If you are making a one-day ascent, get an early start. Summit views are excellent and include Mount Baker, Mount Shuksan, and other North Cascades summits; Glacier Peak and the Monte Cristo peaks, Three Fingers Mountain, and unobstructed views west across the lowlands of Puget Sound to the Olympic Mountains.

Whitehorse Mountain

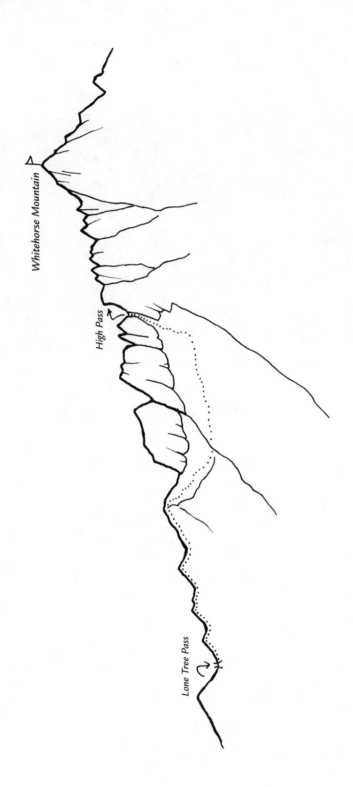

Whitehorse Mountain

High Pass

Lone Tree Pass

HOW TO GET THERE

This climb begins via Whitehorse Trail just off of Washington Highway 530 east of Darrington. Drive Interstate 5 to Arlington (exit 208), then follow Washington Highway 530 east about 26 miles to Whitehorse. From Granite Falls, follow the Mountain Loop Road or Washington Highway 530 south from Rockport to Darrington, then continue 5.3 miles west on Washington Highway 530 to Whitehorse. Turn south and follow Mine Road about 1.8 miles to the Whitehorse trailhead on the right. A highway sign points to the Whitehorse trailhead. A Northwest Forest Pass is required.

ROUTE DESCRIPTION

Hike Whitehorse Trail (Trail 653) about 3 miles to Lone Tree Pass. The trail officially ends about 0.5 mile short of the pass, but a climber's trail or moderate snow slope continues from the upper meadows to the pass (elevation about 4,800 feet). From Lone Tree Pass, scramble eastward along the ridge crest about 0.7 mile to a high point with magnificent views up the ridge to the Whitehorse Glacier. Further progress on the ridge is soon blocked by a cliffy buttress. Descend from the viewpoint southeast into a basin with a small lake, then contour along the base of the cliffs eastward into the upper basin below High Pass, the obvious notch in the ridge just left of the 6,357-foot west summit of Whitehorse Mountain.

The west summit is a rounded rock tower that is difficult to mistake for anything else when viewed from the traverse toward High Pass. The route stays about 500 feet below the ridge, traversing a bench into High Pass basin, where a moderately steep snow or scree gully leads to the pass. Many parties traverse too high on an open shelf close to the base of the ridge cliffs where the going is much steeper and more difficult. Some parties are fooled into climbing the wrong gully, only to find themselves at an impassable spot on the ridge. The correct route stays low until directly below High Pass, then climbs directly up the gully.

From High Pass, rope up and cross the Whitehorse Glacier (or "So-Bahli-Ahli" Glacier, after the native name for the peak), then ascend the obvious steep gully to the summit ridge. A late-season bergschrund may bar easy progress to the gully and force an end run and some rock scrambling (possibly Class 4–5) to get to the top. Some blocky scrambling is usually required on the last bit to the summit, even in winter and spring.

OPTIONS

Beckey's guide shows a few other routes up Whitehorse Mountain, including a direct route from the valley to the Whitehorse Glacier. This steep, brushy affair offers the shortest route to the summit but at a price higher than many are willing to pay. The route is featured in *Selected Climbs in the Cascade Range* (Volume 2). The Southeast Ridge is said to be an enjoyable, moderate Class 5 climb, although it has a fairly rugged approach. Refer to *Cascade Alpine Guide* for route details.

PRECAUTIONS

Most winter and spring ascents report recent or imminent avalanche activity on the slopes leading up to Lone Tree Pass. During poor visibility, climbers may unwittingly cross a big cornice that forms on the ridge above the pass.

White Chuck Mountain

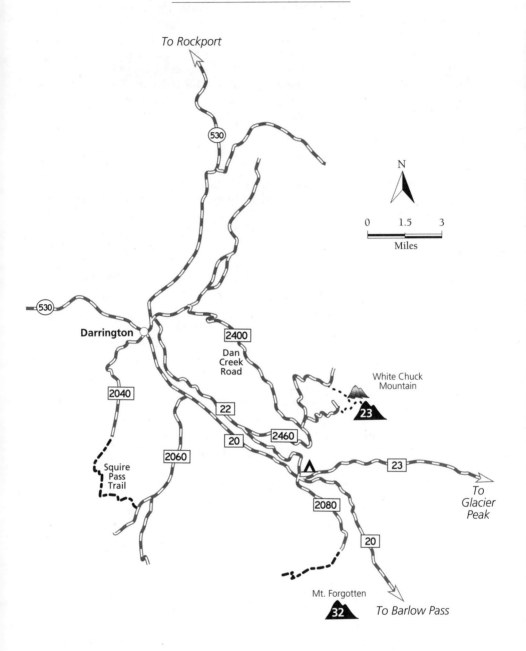

To Rockport

530

N

0   1.5   3
Miles

530

Darrington

2400

Dan
Creek
Road

White Chuck
Mountain

2040

22

2460

23

20

2060

Squire
Pass
Trail

23

To
Glacier
Peak

2080

20

Mt. Forgotten

32

To Barlow Pass

White Chuck Mountain.

23. WHITE CHUCK MOUNTAIN

Elevation: 6,989 feet/2,130 meters
Route: Northwest Gully/Ridge
Rating: Class 3
Distance: 4 miles round trip
Elevation Gain: 3,800 feet from the spur road to summit
Time: 4–5 hours from the spur road to summit
Maps: USGS White Chuck Mountain; Green Trails No. 111 (Sloan Peak)

ABOUT THE CLIMB

White Chuck Mountain is another of the major peaks of the Darrington region, but it is not one of the most popular. White Chuck has an unfortunate reputation, largely undeserved, of having a difficult approach drive and a bushwhack approach hike. True, the approach drive is up a maze of logging roads, and there is some brush on the approach, but neither is as bad as usually reported. The scrambling route is a straightforward scree climb and ridge traverse, mostly following a boot path, sometimes exposed but not especially difficult. The summit is craggy and exposed, providing airy views of Mount Pugh, Sloan Peak, Glacier Peak, the Monte Cristo peaks, Mount Rainier, Mount Baker, and Mount Shuksan, the Picket Range, the peaks around Cascade Pass, and many, many more summits.

HOW TO GET THERE

This climb begins via a climber's trail from Forest Road 2436 east of Darrington. Most climbers approach from Darrington, which is reached by driving Washington Highway 530 east from Arlington via Interstate 5, south from Rockport via

White Chuck Mountain Route

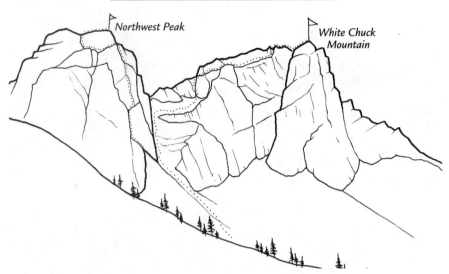

Washington Highway 20, or northeast from Granite Falls via Mountain Loop Road. There are two commonly used approaches from Darrington.

One follows Dan Creek Road (Forest Road 24), but most climbers use the Sauk River Road approach. Drive south from Darrington on the Mountain Loop Road (Forest Road 20) about 9 miles to Forest Road 22, the turnoff for White Chuck Campground. Turn left and cross the Sauk River. Drive past the campground and continue about 3.7 miles north on Forest Road 22 to its junction with Forest Road 24.

From the junction, follow Forest Road 24 about 4 miles to the Forest Road 2430 fork. Stay right on Forest Road 2430 for about 0.5 mile to the Forest Road 2435 fork. Stay right again and follow Fores. Road 2435 another 0.5 mile to the Forest Road 2436 fork. All roads are clearly marked at last check. Turn right on Forest Road 2436 and follow just over 3 uphill miles to a spur road at about 4,200 feet elevation. The spur road is decommissioned. Park here and start hiking. Following the directions from White Chuck Campground, your total driving distance on gravel roads is about 14.5 miles to the spur road.

ROUTE DESCRIPTION

From Forest Road 2436, hike up the decommissioned spur road, passing several drainage ditches, until you leave a clearcut and come to a stand of older open timber. Leave the spur road and hike east toward the mountain, ascending through open forest for about 15 minutes and veer slightly left as you ascend until you reach Conn Creek. Veer right and follow the creek upward until you reach a small open meadow, where you will find a boot path on the left side of the stream that leads to Black Oak Creek. Climb steeply up the left side of Black Oak Creek, veering north, still on the climber's trail. The path may be muddy until late summer because it serves as an intermittent streambed. Toil upward another twenty minutes or so until the path reaches open slopes directly below White Chuck Mountain. Continue up and across several small creeks that flow down from the snowfields below Northwest Peak, then ascend the scree slope (snow in early season) directly between White Chuck and Northwest Peak.

From the top of the scree slope, scramble up loose rock a short distance toward the gap between White Chuck Mountain and Northwest Peak and pick up a climber's trail that traverses right and up along a broad, sloping heather and scree shelf. Follow the trail toward the right and up several switchbacks until below low-angle slabs. Continue traversing right along the shelf, then climb an open gully to gain the ridge crest. Pick up the trail on the ridge and follow it to a vertical abutment, then traverse ledges on the right side of the ridge crest, angling upward toward the summit. Some parties climb back up to the ridge crest and traverse the crest, sometimes dropping down onto the east side. Each route eventually regains the ridge just short of the summit formation. Scramble down an exposed rock step, then traverse heather and scree slopes to the summit. To descend, downclimb the route.

OPTIONS

For a longer drive but simpler approach hike, continue on Forest Road 2435 just over 5 miles from the Forest Road 2436 fork to a spur road at about 4,500 feet elevation, then take a right and follow the spur road briefly to its end. From the road's end, hike up to a ridge and follow the ridge up toward the Northwest Peak, then traverse a talus and scree slope right and down to the base of the scree slope below White Chuck's west face. This approach hike is said to be much faster and easier than the usual approach hike and may gain favor as the preferred approach to the mountain, although it does involve more uphill hiking on the way out.

PRECAUTIONS

This approach hike is notoriously brushy but not as bad as some reports indicate. Spring ascents would be favored except for avalanche-prone slopes in the upper basin and gully and on the upper shelf and ledge traverses, which are dangerously exposed when snow-covered. The angle is moderate, but the traverse is above a 700-foot cliff with no runout. If snow lingers, rope up and belay across the most exposed sections; a couple of pickets might be helpful. The gully leading to the notch has loose rock. Be careful not to send rocks hurtling down on other climbers. The route is very exposed in places along the ridge and shelf traverse.

24. MOUNT PUGH

Elevation: 7,201 feet/2,195 meters
Route: Northwest Ridge
Rating: Class 2
Distance: 10 miles round trip
Elevation Gain: 5,300 feet
Time: 4 to 6 hours to summit
Maps: USGS White Chuck Mountain; Green Trails No. 111 (Sloan Peak)

ABOUT THE CLIMB

Mount Pugh is one of the landmark peaks of the western Cascades. Rising to a height of 7,201 feet with a vertical rise of over 5,000 feet from the Sauk River, Pugh stands aloof among the Mountain Loop peaks and is a close rival of nearby

Mount Pugh from Mount Forgotten.

Morgan Balogh

Sloan Peak for sheer size and regional dominance. As a climbing objective, Pugh is an accessible mountain. A trail leads to a high pass on the summit ridge and an old lookout trail continues to the summit. The hiking trail officially ends at Stujack Pass, but adventuresome hikers and alpine scramblers frequently continue to the top. The summit is the site of a former fire lookout.

The summit trail was constructed in the 1910s to facilitate installation of a summit lookout. There are places where you have to climb slabby rock and traverse snow, but most of the climb is on an established trail. The trail is faint or nonexistent in places, true; but even when the trail vanishes, the route is never truly difficult unless you get way off route. Like most former lookout sites, the summit of Mount Pugh offers superb views, especially of nearby Glacier Peak, Sloan Peak, and the Monte Cristo peaks; north to Mount Baker, Mount Shuksan, and the peaks around Cascade Pass; and south to Mount Daniel, Mount Hinman, Mount Stuart, and Mount Rainier.

HOW TO GET THERE

This climb begins via Mount Pugh Trail from Forest Service Road 2095 south of Darrington. From Darrington, follow Mountain Loop Road (Forest Road 20) south about 9 miles to White Chuck Campground and continue 3.8 miles to Forest Road 2095. If you're coming from Granite Falls, follow Washington Highway 92 about 41 miles east to Forest Road 2095. A sign points the way to Mount Pugh Trail. Follow the spur road 1.1 miles to the trailhead. (See the map for Glacier Peak.) A Northwest Forest Pass is required.

ROUTE DESCRIPTION

Hike Mount Pugh Trail (Trail 644) 1.6 miles to the 3,180-foot Lake Metan, then hike another 2.4 steep miles to Stujack Pass, elevation about 5,500 feet. From the

Mount Pugh

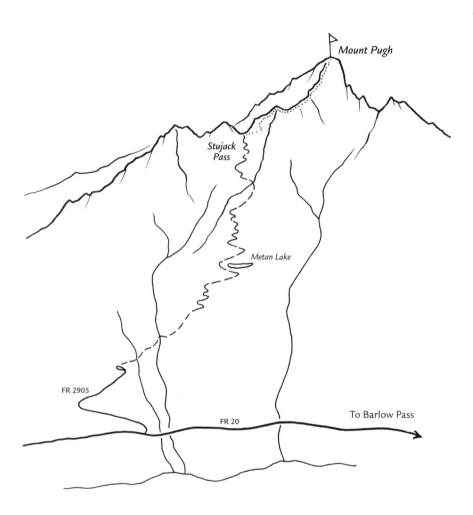

pass, follow the old summit trail up the ridge, crossing an occasional snowfield and scrambling up slabby rocks to the summit. The route is straightforward, mostly following the old trail with only a few scrambling sections.

OPTIONS
Beckey's guide reports a variation up the upper northeast face, but little is known about this route. Other routes seem possible but appear to have significant approach difficulties. Refer to *Cascade Alpine Guide* for details.

PRECAUTIONS
Although the route follows remnants of the old trail, it involves a fair amount of snow hiking and rock scrambling with some exposure, particularly near the summit. The trail can be difficult to follow when snow lingers on the upper ridge.

Sloan Peak. The Corkscrew Route crosses the upper snow shelf.

Colin Haley

25. SLOAN PEAK

Elevation: 7,835 feet/2,388 meters
Route: Corkscrew Route
Rating: Class 3; Grade II glacier
Distance: 11 miles round trip
Elevation Gain: 6,000 feet
Time: 6 to 8 hours to summit
Maps: USGS Sloan Peak; Green Trails No. 111 (Sloan Peak)

ABOUT THE CLIMB

Sloan Peak is the highest mountain in the Henry M. Jackson Wilderness and in the Cascades between Glacier Peak and Puget Sound. It is a large, glaciated citadel that has been compared with the Matterhorn, which it somewhat resembles from some vantages, albeit with a definite slouch compared with its Swiss counterpart. Although Sloan Peak looks like a difficult ascent—and is from most sides—it has a scrambling route to its summit. This devious route winds around the peak and exploits the mountain's weakness. It requires good routefinding and climbing skills, including glacier travel and exposed rock scrambling, but it provides a good, well-rounded summit adventure without too much difficulty. It's not a scrambling route in the truest sense because it traverses a very active glacier.

Sloan Peak is widely regarded as one of the best climbs in the region. Alas, this means you will rarely have this peak to yourself. Because of its regional dominance and height, Sloan Peak offers unmatched views, a star-studded panorama including Mount Baker, Mount Shuksan, Eldorado Peak, Forbidden Peak, Buckner Mountain, Goode Mountain, Logan Peak, Dome Peak, Glacier Peak, the Dakobed Range, the Stuart Range, Mount Daniel, Mount Hinman, Chimney Rock, Mount Thompson, Mount Rainier, the Monte Cristo peaks, the Three Fingers, Whitehorse Mountain, White Chuck Mountain, and Mount Pugh, to name only a few.

HOW TO GET THERE

This climb begins via Sloan Peak Trail from North Fork Sauk River Road south of Darrington. Drive Mountain Loop Road to Bedal, 17 miles south of Darrington via Forest Road 20 and 6.2 miles north of Barlow Pass via Granite Falls and Washington Highway 92. Turn up North Fork Sauk River Road (Forest Road 49) and follow it 3.5 miles to a spur road on the right with signs pointing the way to Sloan Peak Trail. Follow this spur to the trailhead at the road's end. (See map for Glacier Peak.) A Northwest Forest Pass is required.

ROUTE DESCRIPTION

This climb is referred to as the Corkscrew Route because it circles around from the north to the south and up the west face to the summit. Given the mountain's topography, this is actually the fastest route to the summit.

Hike Sloan Peak Trail (Trail 648) about 3.5 miles to the trail's end in a small meadow basin at about 4,800 feet on the north slope of Sloan Peak. There is presently no bridge or reliable footlog, so ford the river. This deters many early

Sloan Peak Lower Corkscrew Route

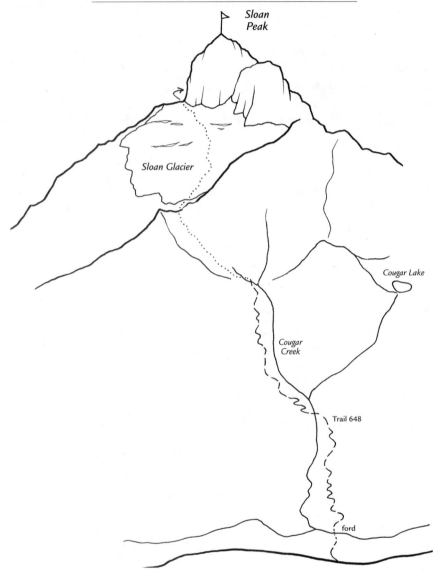

season ascents. The usual ford is just downstream from the trail and may be flagged. In early season, the trail through the forest is easily lost under snow. From the trail's end, ascend southward up an obvious wide snow gully or follow a climber's trail up the heather ridge by late season to the ridge crest at the edge of the Sloan Glacier. Some parties bivouac in the meadows, some near the glacier's edge.

Rope up and traverse the glacier southward as crevasses permit to its upper southwest edge at the base of the east face. A bergschrund or moat crossing may

Sloan Peak Upper Corkscrew Route

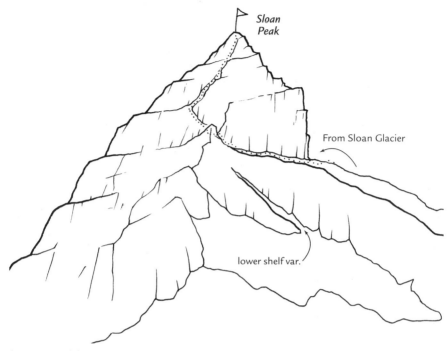

Sloan
Peak

From Sloan Glacier

lower shelf var.

be required here. Ascend snow or easy rock to the crest of the east ridge, then turn the corner and traverse westward following a boot path across the rocky heather shelf, skirting beneath the upper south face and around the corner to a sandy gully on the west face. Ascend the gully directly to the blocky summit. The path is pretty well worn; and by late season, there may be a climber's trail to follow much of the way from the glacier to the summit. To descend, downclimb the route.

OPTIONS
An alternate approach from Bedal Creek climbs a lower shelf and chimney to join Corkscrew Route. This approach used to be the popular route, but now it is rarely used because Sloan Peak Trail provides faster access to the peak. Refer to *Cascade Alpine Guide* for route details.

PRECAUTIONS
Fording the Sauk River can be very hazardous during early season and on hot afternoons when the water level may be high. Cross carefully. The glacier is crevassed, and climbers have been seriously or fatally injured in falls into crevasses and moats on the glacier. Roping up is highly recommended. The upper shelf traverse, gully, and final summit scramble are exposed with some loose, sandy scrambling, and treacherous places when snow- or ice-covered. There is rockfall hazard on the glacier, shelf traverse, and especially in the upper gully with climbers above. Be careful not to knock rocks loose on other climbers.

Monte Cristo Peaks

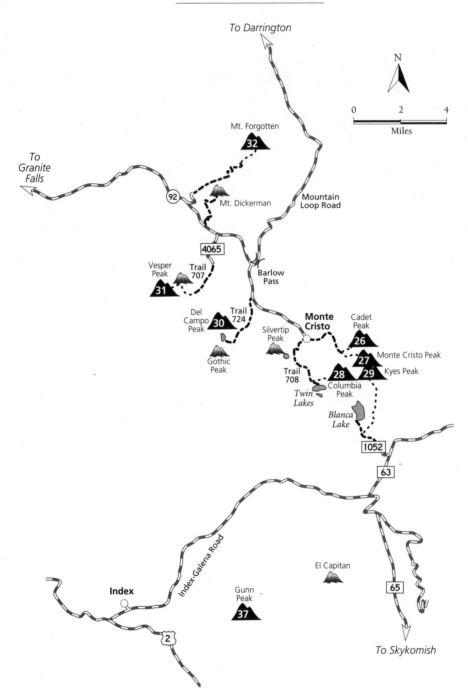

To Darrington

To Granite Falls

N

0   2   4
Miles

Mt. Forgotten
32

Mt. Dickerman

92

Mountain Loop Road

4065

Vesper Peak
Trail 707
31

Barlow Pass

Del Campo Peak
Trail 724
30

Gothic Peak

Silvertip Peak

Monte Cristo

Cadet Peak
26

Monte Cristo Peak
27
Kyes Peak

Trail 708
28
29

Columbia Peak

Twin Lakes

Blanca Lake

1052

63

El Capitan

Index

Index-Galena Road

Gunn Peak
37

65

2

To Skykomish

Cadet Peak from Twin Lakes trail.

26. CADET PEAK

Elevation: 7,186 feet/2,190 meters
Route: West Slope
Rating: Class 2–3
Distance: 8 miles round trip
Elevation Gain: 4,600 feet
Time: 4 to 6 hours to summit
Maps: USGS Monte Cristo and Blanca Lake; Green Trails No. 111 (Sloan Peak) and 143 (Monte Cristo)

ABOUT THE CLIMB

Cadet Peak is one of a cluster of 7,000-foot summits in the Monte Cristo region, including Monte Cristo Peak, Kyes Peak, and Columbia Peak, and is probably the easiest of the group from a technical standpoint, though it is fairly strenuous. Cadet is an abrupt, rocky peak, especially on its south and east sides, with a long, craggy summit ridge. Although the mountain has the aspect of a long, rocky ridge when viewed from the west, its summit appears as a sharp rock horn when viewed from the south, especially from the summits of the other Monte Cristo peaks.

On USGS maps, Cadet Peak is shown as the 7,186-foot peak on the south end of the summit ridge, although the north summit is listed at 7,197 feet elevation. The north summit does not appear higher than the south summit; in fact, it seems to be quite a bit lower. The Mountaineers have installed a summit register on the 7,186-foot summit, which is regarded as the true summit, and rightly so. Whichever summit is higher, though, Cadet Peak is definitely higher than its neighbors across Glacier Basin.

Of the Monte Cristo peaks, only 7,280-foot Kyes Peak is higher. Because of its height, accessibility, and central location within the range, Cadet is a good climb for those seeking a high summit without too much difficulty. The standard route is steep and strenuous, but not technically difficult, and is very scenic. Cadet Peak is a good late spring and early summer climb, when snow slopes and gullies can be ascended much of the way. It's a good late season climb too, if you don't mind tedious hiking up steep heather meadows and scrambling up a couple of loose gullies and rocky slopes. The summit views alone are worth the trip. A panorama of peaks presents itself, including close views of the other Monte Cristo peaks, plus Wilmans Peak and Williams Spires, Del Campo Peak, Gothic Peak, Sloan Peak, Mount Pugh, Glacier Peak, Mount Baker, Mount Shuksan, Mount Stuart, Chimney Rock, Mount Daniel, Mount Hinman, and Mount Rainier to the south, as well as nearly every other high peak of the central and north Cascades.

HOW TO GET THERE

This climb begins via Glacier Basin Trail from Monte Cristo south of Barlow Pass on the Mountain Loop Road. From Granite Falls, drive east on Mountain Loop Road 30.2 miles to the Monte Cristo turnoff at Barlow Pass. From Darrington, drive south on Mountain Loop Road to Barlow Pass. Park at the Barlow Point trailhead just west across the road from the gate or in the wide turnout just across the road from the trailhead parking lot. A Northwest Forest Pass is required. This is a high "car-prowl" trailhead, so leave nothing of value in your car. Do not block the gate or the road leading to the gate. If for some reason the gate is open, drive in at your own risk because the road may be impassable or the gate may be locked when you try to get out. Hike or ride a mountain bike about 4 miles up Monte Cristo Road to the Monte Cristo townsite. Cross the river via the footbridge on the right and hike up the gravel road to the Glacier Basin trailhead. Riding a mountain bike in to Monte Cristo will save considerable time going both ways.

ROUTE DESCRIPTION

Hike up Glacier Basin Trail (Trail 719) about 2.5 rocky miles to Glacier Basin (about 4,400 feet). Continue into the basin, aiming for the big, pointed boulder on the east side of the basin. Beckey's guide refers to this as "the house-sized boulder," as if there was only one, but there are at least three boulders of equal size in the basin, none of which is as big as your average house. Anyway, from this boulder, cross the creek and hike several hundred feet up the talus/scree slopes just right of a narrow snow gully, or right up the gully in early season. Near the top of the gully is a band of rust-colored rock, on the left side. Cross the gully and traverse left to and across this loose dirt and rock slope to the base of a narrow, rocky gully. Ascend this gully a couple hundred feet to its head, then exit left and traverse a brushy slope to a wooded ridge. Here, pick up a climber's trail that continues up the ridge. Follow the trail upward some distance, staying right of the ridge rather than on the brushy crest, until it crosses over the ridge into a broad heather gully opposite a cliff of orange-colored rock. Continue up steep heather slopes to the head of the gully, then cross back right over the ridge and continue upward to the head of a rocky gully. Scramble back to the ridge crest,

Cadet Peak

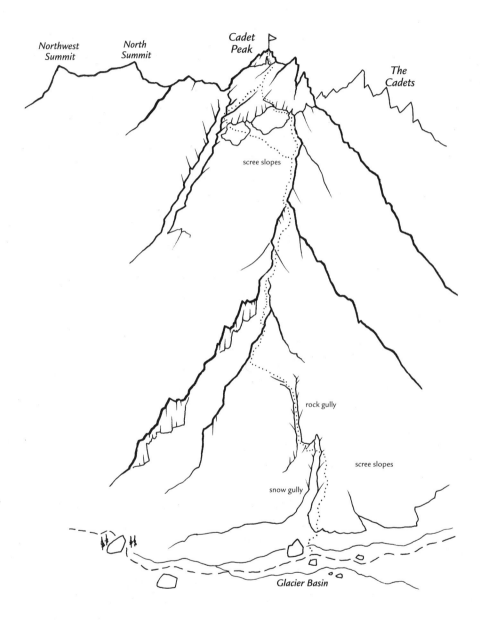

then climb more steep, rocky heather meadows, following the trail or game traces to where the ridge ends at the base of a rocky headwall (about 6,800 feet elevation) on the southwest shoulder. The most direct route is to traverse left on scree or snow slopes along the base of the headwall to its apex (at the top of the highest snow patch or scree slope). From here, you can traverse a ledge and climb a short, exposed rocky slope to reach the easier upper slopes. Alternatively, traverse farther left across scree and snow slopes to the southern edge of the steep, rocky gully, then scramble up to a rocky shelf and climb right up the shelf several hundred feet to the easier upper slopes. There are several possible routes here; all involve loose Class 2–3 rock scrambling with some exposure getting past the headwall. Once past the headwall, continue hiking up heather and scree slopes to the base of the summit rocks, then scramble up easy rock on the west side to the summit.

OPTIONS
The north summit is listed at 7,197 feet elevation on the USGS map, but it appears lower than the south summit. For those intent upon climbing the north summit, the easiest option is to traverse the summit ridge 0.4 mile from the south summit.

PRECAUTIONS
The slopes of Glacier Basin are highly avalanche prone in winter and spring. The gullies and headwall have loose rock. Spontaneous and climber-caused rockfall are definite hazards. The scramble up the headwall to the upper summit slopes is not difficult with careful routefinding, but you may encounter steep, exposed, loose rock. The big snow gully is not recommended due to avalanche and rockfall hazard. A helmet is definitely recommended if the gully option is taken and is a good idea for the lower gully and upper headwall sections. When descending, follow the climber's trail (or your tracks in the snow) faithfully to avoid straying too far left or right down the fall line and becoming stranded among steep, brushy cliffs.

27. MONTE CRISTO PEAK

Elevation: 7,136 feet/2,175 meters
Route: North Face via North Col
Rating: Class 4
Distance: 10 miles round trip
Elevation Gain: 4,600 feet
Time: 5 to 6 hours trailhead to summit
Maps: USGS Monte Cristo and Blanca Lake; Green Trails No. 111 (Sloan Peak) and 143 (Monte Cristo)

ABOUT THE CLIMB
Monte Cristo Peak is one of the major peaks of the Monte Cristo region, but it is probably the least popular climb due to a reputation for loose rock and exposed climbing. At 7,136 feet elevation, Monte Cristo is the fourth highest of the group including Cadet Peak, Columbia Peak, and Kyes Peak, and the most difficult to

Monte Cristo Peak from Glacier Basin.

climb. The popular route, via the North Col, is a simple, straightforward snow and scree climb to within a few hundred feet of the summit, but the final climb to the summit involves loose Class 4 rock climbing, deterring many from attempting the peak. A moat often prevents an ascent of the last 400 feet of rock to the summit.

Despite this, the North Col is still the favored summit route because the Class 3 scrambling route up the west face gully and west ridge is loose and exposed. A recent fatality on the easy route up the peak has underscored the objective hazards of climbing Monte Cristo Peak. Approach the peak with caution and respect, and climb carefully. The climb is not outright dangerous, nor is it unworthy. It is an interesting peak with varied climbing and good summit views, including a close look at the other Monte Cristo peaks, as well as more distant peaks like Glacier Peak, Mount Baker, and Mount Rainier.

HOW TO GET THERE
This climb begins as for Cadet Peak, via Glacier Basin Trail from Monte Cristo. Drive Mountain Loop Road to Barlow Pass and hike or bike in the 4 miles to Monte Cristo and the Glacier Basin Trail. A Northwest Forest Pass is required. This is a high "car-prowl" trailhead, so leave nothing of value in your car.

ROUTE DESCRIPTION
The standard route ascends the northwest face to the North Col. This route is popular because it is the first route listed in Beckey's guide, it is one of the Mountaineers' basic climbs, and it is one of the most direct summit routes with the least amount of loose rock.

Hike up Glacier Basin Trail (Trail 719) about 2.5 rocky miles to Glacier Basin (about 4,400 feet elevation). Follow way trails up into the upper basin, staying left of Ray's Knoll (the rocky, tree-covered hump in the middle of the basin), and ascend the obvious broad scree slope in the middle of the headwall to pass the lowest cliff band. From the top of the scree slope, a gully angles left through the cliffs to the upper slopes. Continue up a long, left-angling snow slope, staying right of the late season scree slope (unless climbing loose scree is preferred), to the base of the northwest face, then traverse steep snow left and climb a snow chute to the North Col or "V-notch," the obvious sharp notch north of the summit formation (elevation about 6,760 feet). The route is all snow from the top of the talus slide to the col through late summer most years. From the col, descend snow slopes on the east side briefly, then traverse southward along the base of the summit rocks about 300 feet to an obvious gully. Assuming the moat is passable, ascend the gully about 80 feet until it becomes too steep and blocky, then exit via easier ledges that lead up to the summit. The gully is Class 3-4; many parties belay the gully. An option is to climb the face just right of the gully, which is loose Class 4. Once above the gully, Class 2-3 scrambling leads to the broad, flat summit area. A large, flat rock provides a perfect spot to sit and enjoy the view.

To descend, downclimb the route, belaying or rappelling as necessary. Glissading down the northwest face snow slopes is a popular and quick way to descend, but be careful not to lose control and wipe out on the rocks or go flying over a cliff.

Monte Cristo Peak

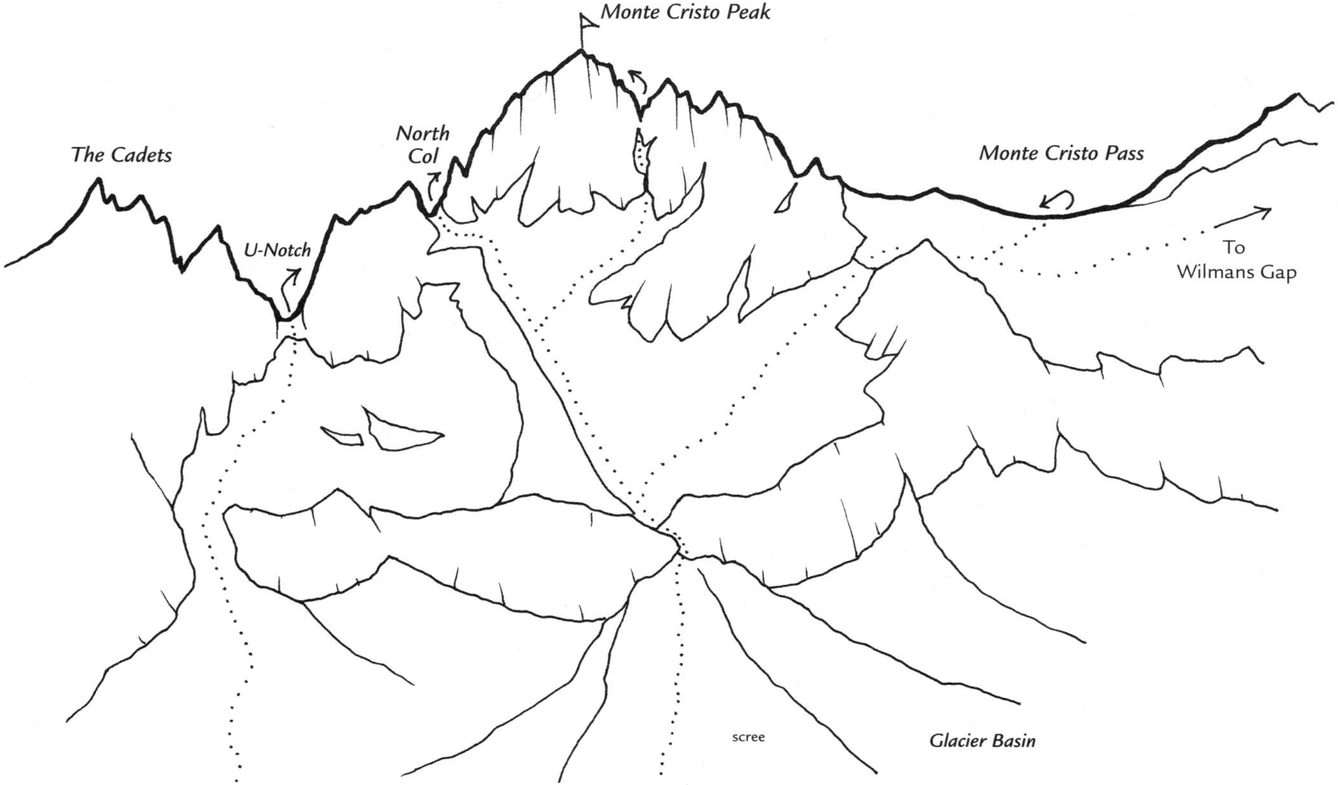

The Cadets

U-Notch

North Col

Monte Cristo Peak

Monte Cristo Pass

To Wilmans Gap

Glacier Basin

scree

Monte Cristo Peak Summit Detail

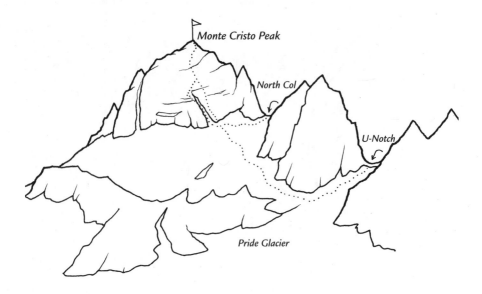

OPTIONS

The peak can be climbed via the "U-notch," the obvious 6,480-foot pass north of and below the North Col. From Glacier Basin, hike up into the gully below the notch, skirting the low cliff bands on the left, then climb scree or snow slopes and scramble a short rocky section to the notch. Cross over the notch and traverse snow and easy rock slopes, skirting under cliffs on the east side of the north ridge, to gain the upper snowfield and join the North Col route to the summit. Also, there is a semi-popular scrambling route via the West Face gully♦. It is mostly Class 3 scrambling but has higher avalanche and rockfall hazard.

PRECAUTIONS

The slopes of Glacier Basin are highly avalanche prone, especially below the northwest face and in the gullies leading up to the North Col and U-notch. This route is best done in late spring or early summer, after avalanche hazard has passed, when snow covers loose scree, and before the moat becomes a problem. By late season, the moat between the upper snowfield and summit rocks may be difficult to pass. Later in the season, the route may involve loose scree climbing. You will definitely encounter loose rock, especially on the summit formation, where gravelly scree can cause insecure footing. The lower part of the route climbs below and up to a rockfall and avalanche gully and beneath loose cliffs. The final climb to the summit involves a pitch of Class 4 climbing before easing up. Bring a rope and a light rack, including several slings, and be prepared to belay at least 1 pitch. There is a definite risk of spontaneous and climber-initiated rockfall.

Columbia Peak from Twin Lakes Trail.

28. COLUMBIA PEAK

Elevation: 7,172 feet/2,186 meters
Route: West Ridge
Rating: Class 3
Distance: 10 miles round trip
Elevation Gain: 4,600 feet
Time: 5 to 6 hours trailhead to summit
Maps: USGS Monte Cristo and Blanca Lake; Green Trails No. 111 (Sloan Peak) and 143 (Monte Cristo)

ABOUT THE CLIMB

Columbia Peak, another of the major summits of the Monte Cristo region, is one of the best climbs of the group and involves a reasonable approach with a fun, varied 800-foot summit scramble up the west spur. Columbia Peak is a good early summer climb because snow slopes can be ascended much of the way. It's a good late season climb too, with a good trail approach, a short ridge scramble, and a steep, enjoyable final scramble up snowfields and a long, rock gully to the summit. The best time to climb Columbia is after snow has melted off the summit area; when snow lingers on the upper ledge traverse, the route is too risky for mere scrambling, although a reasonable alternative route exists. In winter conditions, Columbia is a challenging intermediate climb. Summit views are impressive, including a great view of the other Monte Cristo peaks, plus Del Campo Peak, Gothic Peak, Sloan Peak, Mount Pugh, Glacier Peak, Mount Baker, Mount Shuksan, Mount Stuart, Chimney Rock, Mount Daniel, Mount Hinman, and Mount Rainier to the south, as well as nearly every other high peak of the central and north Cascades, and west to the Olympic Mountains.

HOW TO GET THERE

This climb begins as for Cadet Peak, via Mountain Loop Road to Barlow Pass and a 4-mile hike or ride to Monte Cristo. The only difference is that this climb is approached via Poodle Dog Pass Trail. A Northwest Forest Pass is required. This is a high "car-prowl" trailhead, so leave nothing of value in your car.

ROUTE DESCRIPTION

The route described is the West Spur, the easiest and most direct line up Columbia Peak, and hence the most popular. From Monte Cristo, hike 1.5 steep, rocky miles up Poodle Dog Pass Trail (Trail 708) to Poodle Dog Pass (elevation 4,350 feet). Some parties camp at Silver Lake, just 0.2 mile down from the pass. From the pass, turn south on Twin Lakes Trail and follow that trail southward along a ridge. This is a way trail, mostly good but occasionally narrow and brushy. The trail traverses the west side of the ridge but regains the ridge crest after about 1.5 miles, offering an outstanding view of Columbia Peak. Near the end of the ridge, the trail climbs a steep, rocky slope, the final climb before the trail traverses to Twin Lakes saddle (elevation about 5,300 feet).

The usual climber's route begins from the saddle, but a faster route starts earlier on the trail. Just before the start of the rocky section of the trail, a distinct trail leads off to the left and down a rocky heather gully. Descend the gully and traverse snow slopes and heather benches eastward about 0.2 mile, then go up a talus slope or snow gully to the ridge crest. Alternatively, just hike the ridge from Twin Lakes saddle, staying on the crest except where necessary to skirt granite cliffs. Either way, you will arrive at a small boulder basin on the north side of the ridge where the trail continues through the boulders and right up a steep heather slope that bypasses a rock buttress. After a short climb, the trail rounds the ridge and crosses meadow benches, then angles left to the ridge crest and crosses a gravelly rock slope. The easiest way across this slope is high, along the base of the cliffs. Once across, a scree and heather slope climbs back to the ridge crest, where the trail leads briefly to a rocky shelf just below a craggy, dark rock buttress at about 6,300 feet elevation.

From here, climb snow or scree up into the snow basin immediately left of the buttress, then go up moderately steep snow (or scree just left) to the head of the basin. Traverse right across a loose shelf just below the headwall cliffs and around the corner about 100 feet to the base of a broad rock gully. Pass a short rock step, then scramble up the slabby gully about 300 feet to the base of a 30-foot rock band. Pass this obstacle on the left via a right-angling blocky gully to gain the upper gully. Scramble another 300 feet up the gully to its head at the base of the summit block. The gully scramble varies from Class 2 to Class 3 depending upon the route taken. It is generally easier to stay left but involves more loose rock. From the head of the gully, traverse left on a gravelly ledge around to the northeast side of the summit block where a blocky gully and brief rock scramble reach the airy summit.

OPTIONS

The summit block can be climbed by traversing rightward beneath the summit block and then traversing across the west face to the base of the final gully. This

Columbia Peak

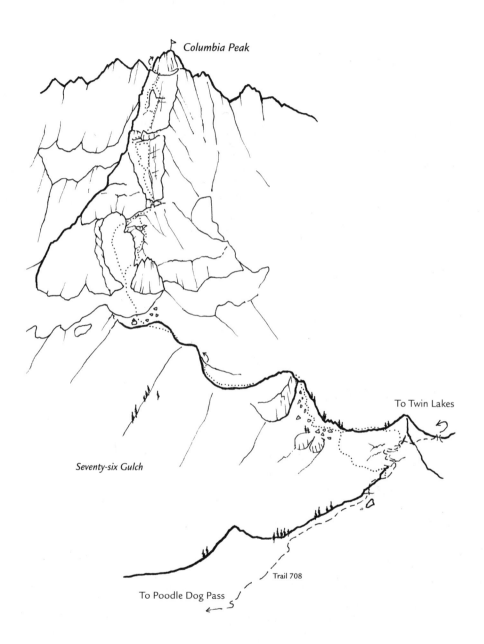

Columbia Peak

To Twin Lakes

Seventy-six Gulch

Trail 708

To Poodle Dog Pass

option has proven useful when the upper ledge is snow-covered. It is just as difficult as the standard route but has a few exposed Class 3 moves and more overall exposure. An alternate approach is from Glacier Basin via Wilmans Glacier and Seventy-six Glacier.

PRECAUTIONS

The approach trail, ridge slopes, upper snowfield, and gully are highly avalanche prone in winter and spring. The upper gully and summit block are more difficult and exposed when covered with snow or ice and may require steep ice or rock climbing with an unprotected traverse at the top. The upper snowfield is moderately steep and can be difficult when icy; definitely bring crampons. There is abundant loose rock in the gully, making it difficult to climb (and especially to descend) without starting rocks down the gully. Spontaneous rockfall has been reported, especially in early and late season when snow is melting. Gravelly rock here could cause you to lose your footing and slide down the gully. The upper ledge traverse is easy but very exposed with loose rock. Be especially careful if the ledge or summit block are covered with snow or ice.

29. KYES PEAK

Elevation: 7,285 feet/2,221 meters
Route: South Ridge
Rating: Class 3
Distance: 12 miles round trip
Elevation Gain: 5,400 feet
Time: 5 to 6 hours trailhead to summit
Maps: USGS Blanca Lake; Green Trails No. 143 (Monte Cristo)

ABOUT THE CLIMB

Kyes Peak is the highest of the Monte Cristo peaks and probably the best climb of the bunch. It is a long, craggy peak with glaciers on all sides. Kyes (rhymes with "wise") was named after Commander Jimmy Kyes, a member of the first ascent party. After his death, his old climbing buddy, Senator Henry "Scoop" Jackson, had the peak (and a naval destroyer) named in honor of Kyes. The peak seems somewhat remote from Monte Cristo, but it is fairly accessible from Index and Skykomish.

The popular scrambling route begins from the south via Lake Blanca Trail and involves a long, low elevation ridge traverse that is more difficult than the summit scramble. The western slopes of the peak are rocky and alpine with lovely talus and heather basins and snowfields rising to craggy rock cliffs and peaks. This long route is varied, interesting, and enjoyable. Views from the exposed summit include a close look at the other Monte Cristo peaks; more distant views of Glacier Peak, Mount Baker, and other peaks to the north; and unobstructed but distant views of the central Cascades: Mount Daniel, Mount Hinman, the Wenatchee Mountains, Dakobed Range, Mount Index, Mount Persis, Baring Mountain, Gunn Peak, and Merchant Peak, plus great views down to Columbia Glacier and Blanca Lake.

Kyes Peak

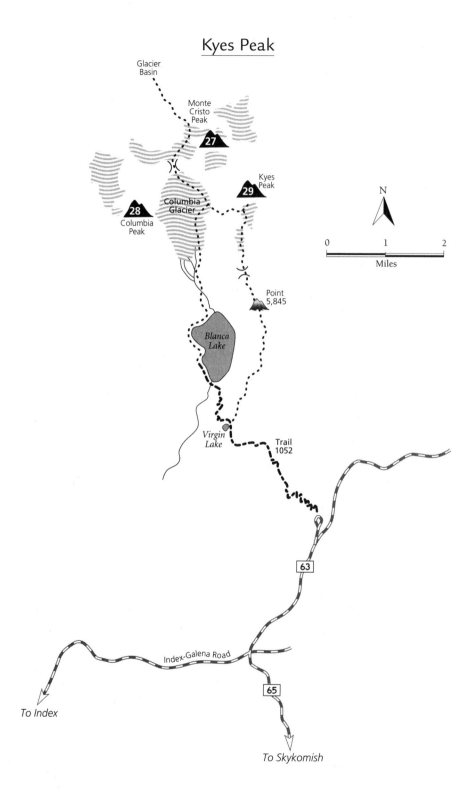

Kyes Peak from Columbia Peak.

HOW TO GET THERE

This climb begins via Blanca Lake Trail from Forest Road 63 north of Index and Skykomish. If approaching from the west, drive U.S. Highway 2 to the turnoff for Index. Follow Index-Galena Road about 15 miles (all nicely paved) from U.S. Highway 2 to an intersection with Forest Roads 63 and 65. Turn left on Forest Road 63 and follow it for about 2 miles to the turnoff for Blanca Lake Trail. Take the left fork and travel 0.1 mile to the trailhead. If approaching from the east, drive U.S. Highway 2 to Skykomish and turn north up Forest Road 65 to an intersection and proceed straight through on Forest Road 63 to the turnoff for the trailhead. A Northwest Forest Pass is required.

ROUTE DESCRIPTION

Hike up Blanca Lake Trail (Trail 1052) about 3 uphill miles to Virgin Lake. A climber's trail departs the trail on the lake's north shore at a small blazed hemlock tree on the right. Follow the faint, sparsely flagged trail up through the woods to the ridge crest; a small meadow here makes a good campsite. Pick up the trail on the left side of the meadow and follow it up subalpine slopes, passing the initial ridge rocks on the right via gullies and rocky slopes or a lower, less exposed forest traverse. Once the ridge is regained, the trail follows close to or on the ridge crest the rest of the way, passing directly over the high point of the ridge and along the rocky spine beyond. A couple of rock points must be skirted on the west side. One especially exposed rock peak can be passed either by descending a gully and traversing heather slopes about 100 feet below the ridge on the west side, or via a Class 3 traverse on the left, starting at a group of bleached snags. Generally, staying low on the west side avoids the most difficult sections of the ridge.

Kyes Peak (Upper South Ridge)

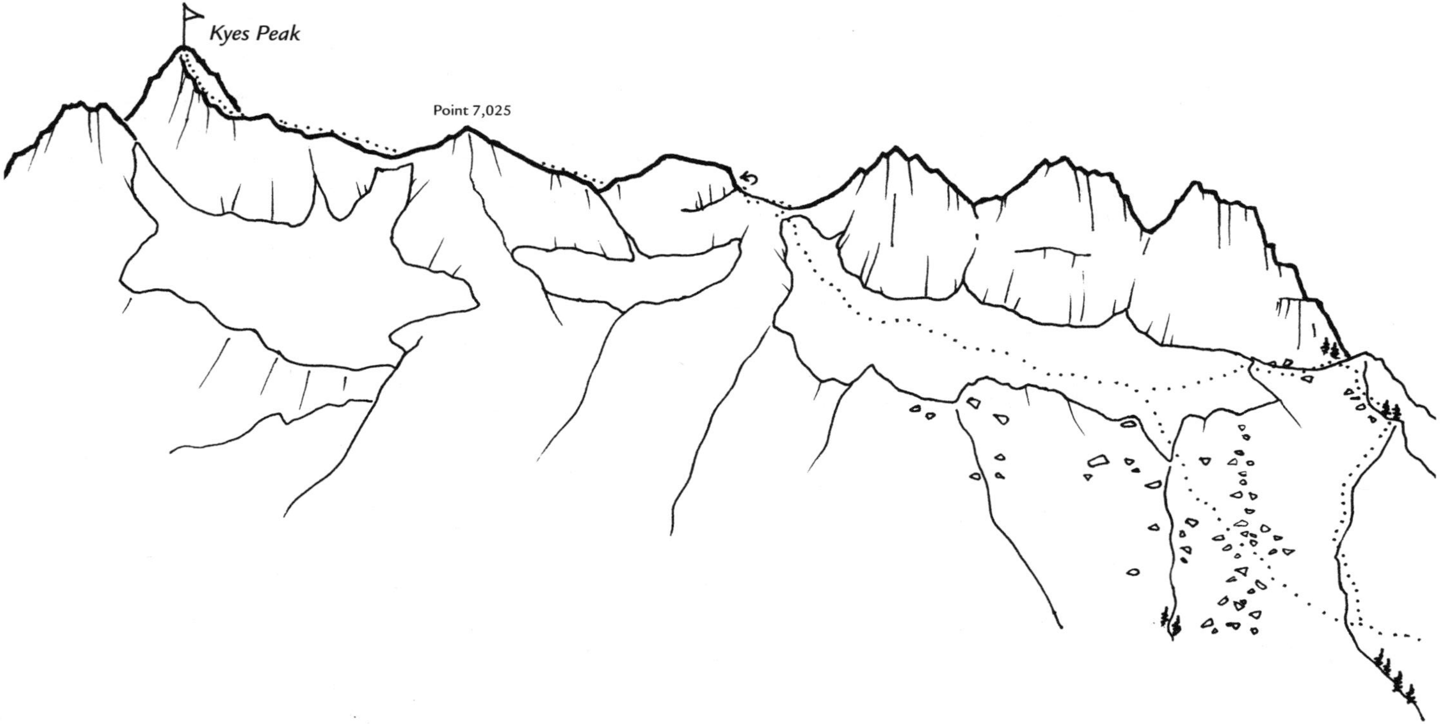

Kyes Peak

Point 7,025

Once past the difficulties, continue along the ridge trail to a saddle, then climb the opposite ridge slope northward until it meets a western spur ridge descending from the rock peaks at the south end of the summit ridge. Here, either follow the trail up the steep ridge, through trees and talus slopes just left, to a lovely heather basin below craggy cliffs, or traverse hemlock and heather slopes left into a broad talus basin below the west face snowfields. Either way, traverse talus slopes and snowfields left below the three rock peaks on the south ridge of Kyes Peak, then ascend the broad central gully between the third rock peak and the flat-topped ridge. Scramble up gravelly scree to gain the saddle, then traverse northward up the ridge via loose rock and scree slopes to the base of the ridge rocks. Traverse a loose, exposed scree shelf around to the right to gain the upper ridge and a permanent snowfield on the east side of the ridge. Hike up snow or scramble up rocks on or right of the ridge past Point 7,025 and right toward the summit formation. The final climb is up ledges and gullies on the southwest side of the summit rocks, then across a gravelly ledge to the narrow, exposed summit.

OPTIONS
There is a route from Glacier Basin that climbs over Monte Cristo Pass and down to Columbia Glacier, then up snowfields and gullies on the west face. Refer to *Cascade Alpine Guide* for route details.

PRECAUTIONS
The ridge slopes and western snow slopes are avalanche prone in winter and spring. Beware of cornices on the approach ridge and upper ridge. There is some Class 3 scrambling on the approach ridge with loose rock in places, although the most difficult sections can be bypassed. There is rockfall hazard on the final summit climb and in places on the approach ridge. You will encounter much loose scree on the summit ridge. Gravel on ledges makes footing insecure in places, so climb with care.

30. DEL CAMPO PEAK

Elevation: 6,610 feet/2,015 meters
Route: South Gully
Rating: Class 3
Distance: 10 miles round trip
Elevation Gain: 4,300 feet
Time: 5 to 6 hours to summit
Maps: USGS Monte Cristo; Green Trails No. 111 (Sloan Peak) and 143 (Monte Cristo)

ABOUT THE CLIMB
Del Campo Peak is one of the major peaks of the Monte Cristo region. Although it stands only 6,610 feet high—small compared with the several 7,000-foot summits only a few miles east—Del Campo seems relatively isolated. This craggy, angular peak is one of the most popular scrambling summits in the region, mostly because it is accessible, but also because of its interesting climbing and

dramatic summit views. The peak rises above Gothic Basin, one of the most lovely subalpine basins in the Monte Cristo region, making this a great weekend trip in which you can include ascents of both Del Campo Peak and Gothic Peak.

HOW TO GET THERE

This climb begins via Weden Creek Trail from Monte Cristo Road south of Barlow Pass on Mountain Loop Road. From Granite Falls, drive east on Mountain Loop Road 30.2 miles to the turnoff for Monte Cristo at Barlow Pass. From Darrington, drive south on Mountain Loop Road (Forest Road 20) to Barlow Pass. Park at the Barlow Point trailhead just west across the road from the gate. A Northwest Forest Pass is required. This is a high "car-prowl" trailhead, so leave nothing of value in your car. Do not block the gate or the road leading to the gate. If for some reason the gate is open, drive in at your own risk because the road may be impassable and the gate may be locked when you try to get out. Hike or ride a mountain bike about 1 mile down the Monte Cristo Road to the Weden Creek trailhead on the right just before you cross the creek.

ROUTE DESCRIPTION

Hike up Weden Creek Trail (Trail 724), popularly known as Gothic Basin Trail, about 3.2 miles to Gothic Basin, a lovely subalpine basin dotted with several small lakes and one big lake. There are many good campsites in the basin.

There are several possible approach routes from the trail to Del Campo Peak. The easiest approach to describe and follow without getting lost (best for parties camping at Gothic Basin) is to hike the trail all the way through Gothic Basin to Foggy Lake (also known as Crater Lake), then angle northeast up a draw via talus or snow and slabby rock to the saddle northwest of Point 5,415. Contour northeast to the angling talus/snow shelf where a long left traverse up snow and talus slopes leads to the base of a gully leading up to the obvious notch just east of the summit. A more direct approach from the lake climbs the steep-looking talus/snow slope from the northwest corner of the lake directly to the upper gully. Another popular approach route leaves the trail sooner, at the last creek crossing before the trail dips over the ridge into Gothic Basin, and ascends a talus or snow basin toward the saddle northwest of Point 5,415, or directly up a snow gully on the east side. However you go, expect extended snow travel in early season and mixed snow and scree by midsummer with some slabby scrambling. By late season, follow a faint boot path from the pond on the south side of Foggy Lake to the talus slope below the summit gully.

Once at the base of the gully, ascend the gully to the notch between the summit and lower east peak. Scramble up Class 3 rock to the notch, staying to the left near the top on easier rock (or a Class 4 rock step directly to the notch), then cross just over the notch and scramble up easier rock and roots on the northeast side of the mountain to the blocky summit. Routefinding is not complicated except getting to the notch and finding the easiest route leading up from the notch.

OPTIONS

The Southwest Buttress (I, 5.0) offers a slightly more technical route with interesting climbing on flakes and incuts. An ascent of 6,213-foot Gothic Peak from

Del Campo Peak and Gothic Peak

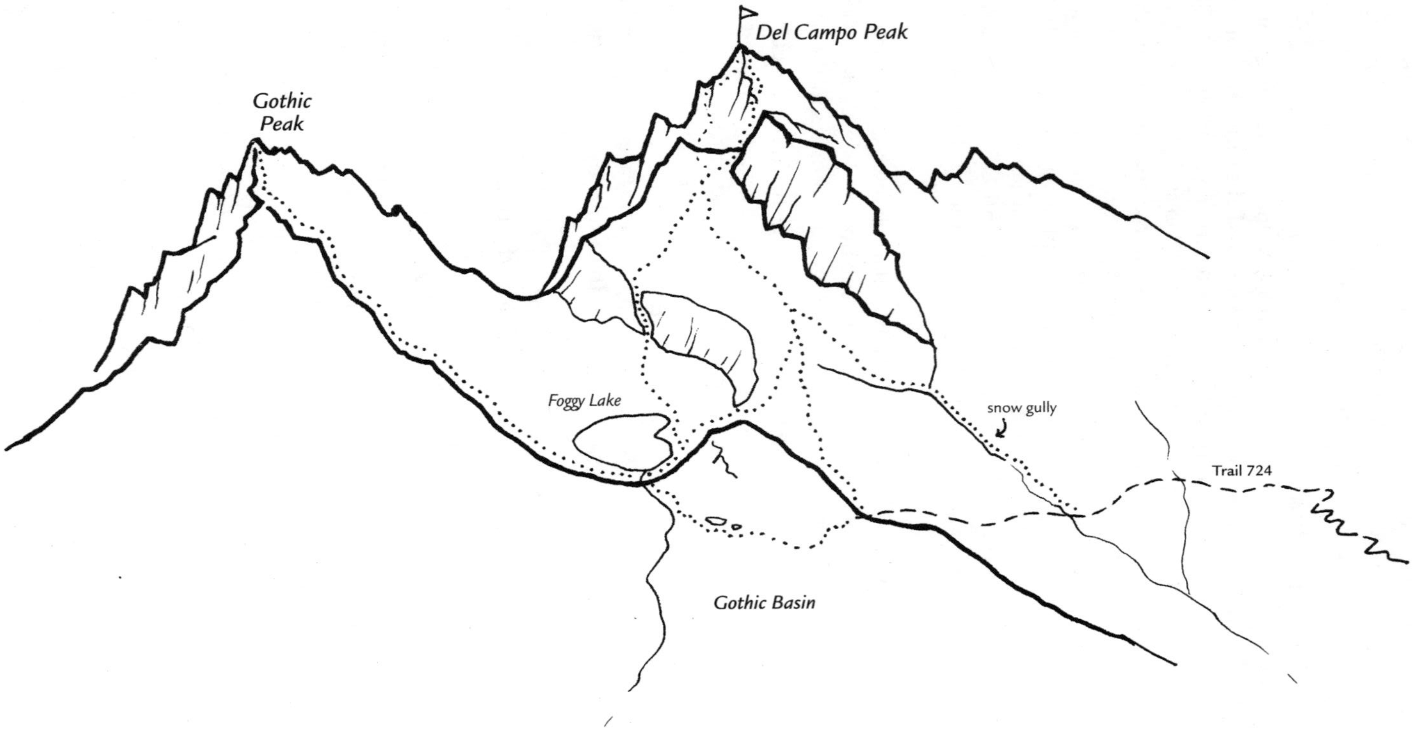

Del Campo Peak

Gothic Peak

Foggy Lake

Gothic Basin

snow gully

Trail 724

Del Campo Peak Summit Detail

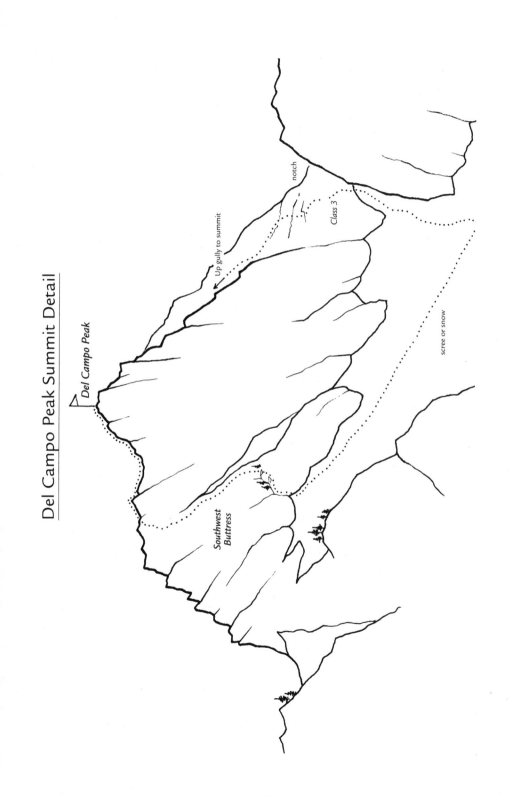

Del Campo Peak

Up gully to summit

notch

Class 3

Southwest Buttress

scree or snow

Foggy Lake is an obvious option. Climb easy slopes to the base of the southeast ridge, then up the final ridge, which is exposed Class 2 with only a little bit of Class 3 climbing to the top. This is mostly a simple snow ascent in early season.

PRECAUTIONS
Steep snow may linger on the route well into summer. The south and east slopes of Del Campo Peak and the east slope of Gothic Peak are avalanche prone in winter and spring. A lot of early season climbers seem to slip and fall on steep snow slopes while descending to the trail. Beware of shifting talus and rockfall, especially party-inflicted rockfall in the upper gully.

31. VESPER PEAK

Elevation: 6,214 feet/1,894 meters
Route: Northeast Slope via Headlee Pass
Rating: Class 2
Distance: 8 miles round trip
Elevation Gain: 4,300 feet
Time: 4 to 6 hours to summit
Maps: USGS Bedal and Silverton; Green Trails No. 111 (Sloan Peak) and 110 (Silverton)

ABOUT THE CLIMB
Vesper Peak is one of the lesser stars of the Monte Cristo area. Although modest compared with its neighbors to the east and relatively hidden from view except from surrounding summits and ridges, Vesper is a prominent summit with a very popular scrambling route. The usual route is a simple, straightforward snow climb or talus scramble. Vesper has an imposing north face, featuring several long technical rock routes that have seen increasing traffic in recent years, despite being relatively inaccessible. Many who climb Vesper Peak also summit nearby Sperry Peak, which provides somewhat better views despite its lower elevation.

HOW TO GET THERE
This climb begins via Sunrise Mine Trail east of Silverton on Mountain Loop Road. From Granite Falls, drive east on Mountain Loop Road (Washington Highway 92) 28.3 miles to Sunrise Mine Road (Forest Road 4065). From Darrington, drive south to Barlow Pass and travel another 1.9 miles west to Sunrise Mine Road. Follow this to the Sunrise Mine trailhead at the road's end. A Northwest Forest Pass is required.

ROUTE DESCRIPTION
Hike Sunrise Mine Trail (Trail 707), a strenuous, rugged path leading across the South Fork Stillaguamish River (no bridge) and up into Wirtz Basin, a bouldery meadow basin. Ascend the steep, broad gully dividing Sperry Peak and Morning Star Peak. An old miner's trail switches back many times up Wirtz Basin to Headlee Pass (4,500 feet). The ascent to Headlee Pass is considered by many to be the most difficult part of the climb. Expect steep snow (until late season) and loose rock in the upper gully. From the pass, the trail continues downward briefly, then contours westward to a basin with a small lake, dubbed Lake Elan (about 5,100 feet) in upper Vesper Creek Basin.

Vesper Peak and Mount Forgotten

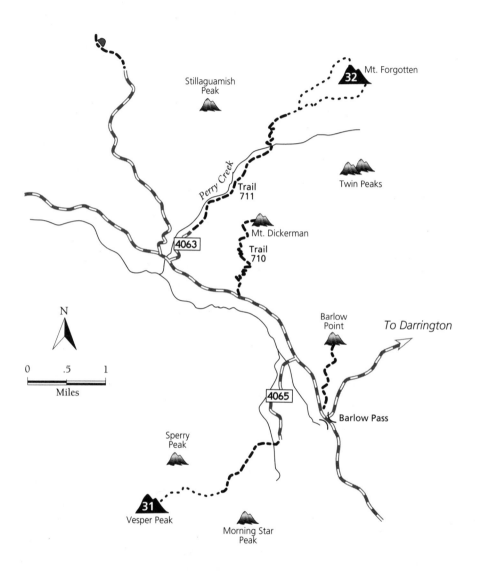

Stillaguamish Peak

Mt. Forgotten

32

Twin Peaks

Perry Creek

Trail 711

Mt. Dickerman

Trail 710

Barlow Point

To Darrington

N

0   .5   1
Miles

4063

4065

Barlow Pass

Sperry Peak

31

Vesper Peak

Morning Star Peak

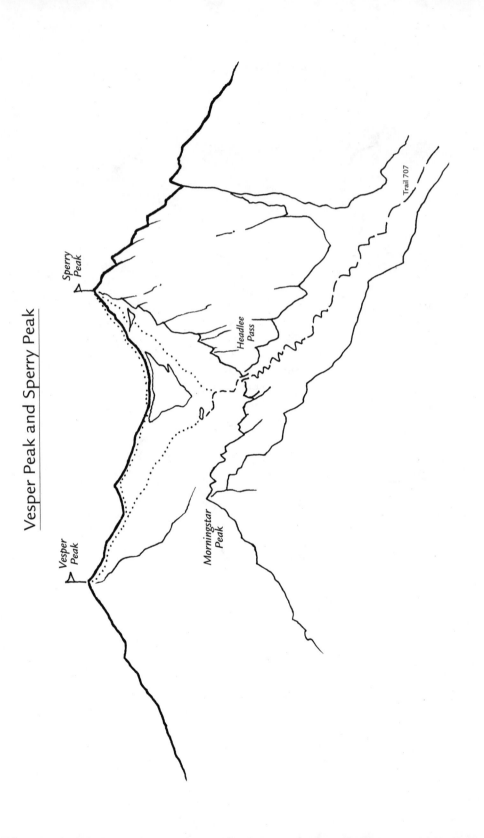

Vesper Peak and Sperry Peak

Sperry
Peak

Vesper
Peak

Morningstar
Peak

Headlee
Pass

Trail 707

From the lake, ascend the climber's trail westward up the east slope of Vesper Peak. When the trail peters out, easy rock scrambling up enormous granite blocks and slabs continues to the summit. Until late season most years, this is a straightforward snow ascent.

OPTIONS
An ascent of 6,002-foot Sperry Peak is often combined with an ascent of Vesper Peak. Two Class 3–4 scrambling routes are popular, one up the ridge and one up the face above Lake Elan. Both routes are obvious, following well-established climber's trails much of the way with some bushwhacking through subalpine forest on the upper slopes.

PRECAUTIONS
There is presently no bridge crossing the South Fork Stillaguamish River. There are two river/creek crossings on the approach that can be hazardous during high water, which is commonly in early season. Wirtz Basin presents an obvious avalanche hazard in winter and early season.

32. MOUNT FORGOTTEN

Elevation: 6,005 feet/1,830 meters
Route: East Rib/Gully
Rating: Class 2–3
Distance: 9 miles round trip
Elevation Gain: 4,000 feet
Time: 4 hours to summit
Maps: USGS Bedal; Green Trails No. 111 (Sloan Peak)

ABOUT THE CLIMB
Mount Forgotten is an inconspicuous peak located just north of Barlow Pass on the Mountain Loop Road. Rising to a height of 6,005 feet, it is not one of the high peaks of the region, considering that several 7,000-foot peaks rise up on the other side of the Sauk River Valley. However, it occupies a fairly commanding position as the highest summit between Three Fingers Mountain and Sloan Peak, with a significant 4,700-foot rise (base-to-peak) from the Sauk River on the east. It is a moderately popular scrambling objective reached via a good trail and providing excellent views of the Monte Cristo peaks, Glacier Peak, and Mount Baker. An old hiking guide suggests that hardy hikers can manage the climb without trouble, although it is a Class 3 scramble, definitely not for those lacking prior scrambling experience or good leadership.

HOW TO GET THERE
This climb begins via Perry Creek Trail east of Silverton on Mountain Loop Road. From Granite Falls, drive Mountain Loop Road (Washington Highway 92) east 27 miles to Perry Creek Campground. From Darrington, drive Mountain Loop Road (Forest Road 20) south 23.5 miles to Barlow Pass, then west another 3.5 miles to Perry Creek Campground. Turn up Forest Road 4063, staying left at a fork, to the Perry Creek trailhead at the road's end. A Northwest Forest Pass is required.

Mount Forgotten (East Gully)

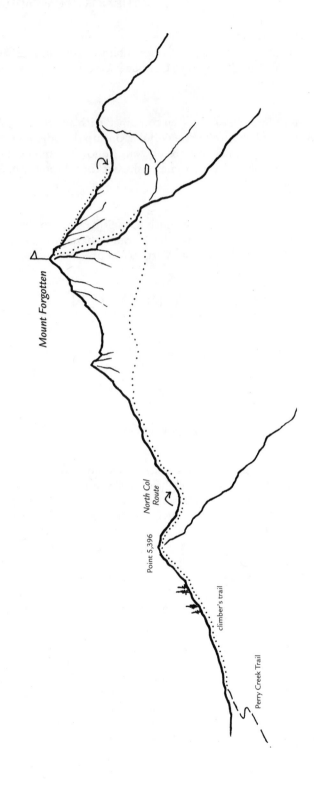

Mount Forgotten

North Col
Route

Point 5,396

climber's trail

Perry Creek Trail

ROUTE DESCRIPTION

Hike Perry Creek Trail (Trail 711) 3.3 miles to the trail's end at about 5,000 feet on the ridge dividing Perry Creek and Shake Creek. Continue up an obvious climber's trail leading northeast up the ridge past Point 5,396 (shown on USGS map) staying on the east side to avoid west side cliffs, and descend to a 5,150-foot saddle. From here, two routes are possible.

The popular route, sometimes referred to as the East Rib but better described as the East Gully, continues from the first saddle directly up the southwest ridge via a climber's trail, then contours across the mountain's south slope, around to a bench on the northeast side, and up the northeast side to the summit. This route is obvious; follow a boot path most of the way, then a gully above a tarn on the upper bench, which leads to easier scrambling of heather and rock slopes to the rocky summit.

OPTIONS

The erstwhile standard route (sometimes referred to as the North Col route) crosses over to the north side of the ridge and traverses northward across the basin below Mount Forgotten's west face. The route then circles around to the 5,530-foot saddle directly north of the summit and heads left, traversing a bit around to the northeast side finishing up Class 3 rock to the summit.

PRECAUTIONS

The upper slopes are avalanche prone in winter and spring. There is rockfall hazard on the summit scramble.

33. THREE FINGERS MOUNTAIN

Elevation: 6,854 feet/2,089 meters
Route: Three Fingers Trail
Rating: Class 2–3
Distance: 12 miles round trip
Elevation Gain: 4,100 feet
Time: 4 to 5 hours trailhead to summit
Maps: USGS Whitehorse Mountain; Green Trails No. 110 (Silverton)

ABOUT THE CLIMB

Three Fingers Mountain is one of the landmark peaks of the Puget Sound region. The source of its name is obvious; it has three rocky summit peaks of about equal height set above a modest glacier, the Queest Alb or Three Fingers Glacier (the former being the native name for the mountain). South Peak was originally the highest but lost that distinction as a result of blasting for a lookout cabin built in the 1930s; now North Peak is considered the true summit, but it is not the most popular because the old lookout trail provides an easier route that is often followed by adventuresome hikers as well as climbers. Legend has it that South Peak was unclimbed prior to the blasting. Whichever summit you choose to climb, expect commanding views of Puget Sound and surrounding peaks, including Glacier Peak, Mount Baker, Mount Shuksan, Whitehorse

Three Fingers Mountain

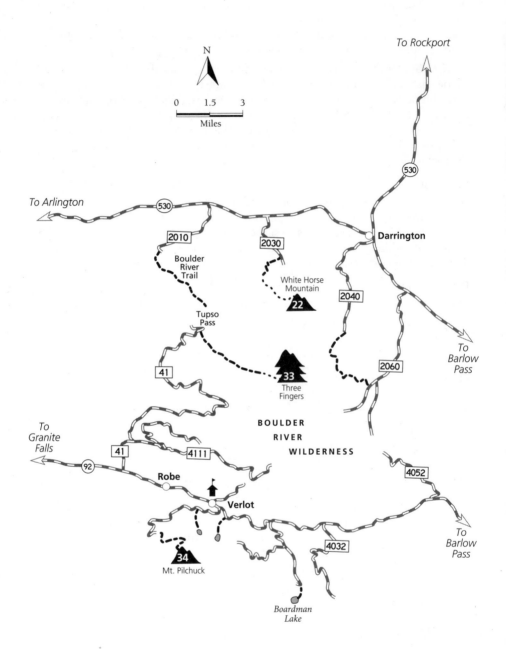

The North Peak of Three Fingers Mountain, as seen from the South Peak.

Mountain, the Monte Cristo peaks, Mount Daniel, Mount Hinman, the Snoqualmie Pass peaks, Mount Rainier, and across Puget Sound to the Olympic Mountains.

HOW TO GET THERE

This climb begins via Three Fingers Trail from Forest Road 41 east of Granite Falls on Mountain Loop Road. From Granite Falls, drive the Mountain Loop Road (Washington Highway 92) east about 7.5 miles and turn left onto Forest Road 41. Follow this gravel road just over 17 miles to Tupso Pass. The trail begins here. A Northwest Forest Pass is required.

ROUTE DESCRIPTION

Hike Three Fingers Trail (Trail 641) 2.5 miles to Saddle Lake, then 2.5 miles more across Goat Flat to Tin Can Gap (elevation about 5,700 feet).

To climb the 6,854-foot South Peak, follow the old lookout trail from Tin Can Gap up the ridge as far as it goes, then scramble up the summit rocks and the ladders to the lookout. The trail is easy to follow by late summer most years, but occasional snow patches may obscure the trail. If you lose the trail, stay to the right of the ridge crest on snow instead of rock. Some parties drop down onto the glacier and traverse the glacier until they can regain the ridge higher up; this is only recommended for experienced climbers equipped for glacier travel. After some easy rock scrambling and a lingering snowfield, climb the ladders to the exposed summit lookout. The ladders are easy to climb but very exposed. You may spend the night in the summit lookout if it is not already occupied (don't count on it), but be aware that at least one party was trapped on the summit by an overnight snowstorm.

Three Fingers Mountain

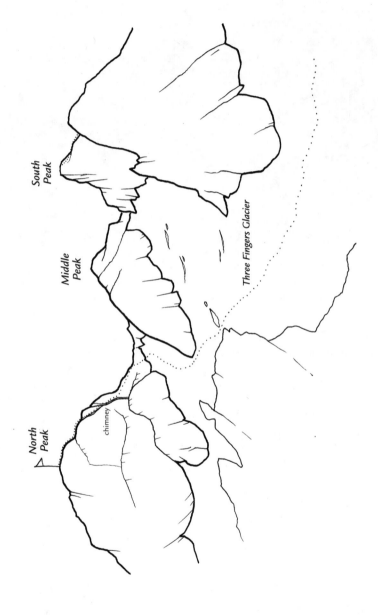

South Peak

Middle Peak

North Peak

chimney

Three Fingers Glacier

OPTIONS

To climb North Peak, the true summit, leave the trail at Tin Can Gap or at the higher Camp Saddle (elevation 5,850 feet) and descend to the glacier. Getting down to the glacier from Tin Can Gap may require a rappel. Traverse the glacier and ascend a snow finger toward the saddle dividing North Peak and Middle Peak. Just below the saddle, traverse blocky ledges left and up to the ridge crest. Continue along ledges to the base of the obvious chimney on the north buttress. Some parties start belaying before the chimney. Climb the chimney to the top of the first buttress, then scramble easier rock up the ridge and just right to the summit. Expect 2 to 4 roped pitches of Class 4 and low Class 5 climbing, which is not especially well protected. Bring a light rack and some slings. A single rope will suffice. Downclimb and rappel the route.

PRECAUTIONS

Although much of the route to South Peak is on a trail, the path is rugged and unmaintained and has some serious exposure, especially on the summit ladders and the summit where the east face falls away some 2,000 feet. All three summits involve exposed rock scrambling or climbing, so be prepared for snow travel with ice ax and crampons, especially if crossing the glacier. The upper slopes are avalanche prone in winter and spring. Beware of cornices on the ridges.

34. MOUNT PILCHUCK

Elevation: 5,324 feet/1,623 meters
Route: Mount Pilchuck Trail
Rating: Class 2
Distance: 6 miles round trip
Elevation Gain: 2,200 feet
Time: 2 hours trailhead to summit
Maps: USGS Verlot; Green Trails No. 109 (Granite Falls)

ABOUT THE CLIMB

Mount Pilchuck is one of the most visible mountains on the western front of the Cascade Range. Although not a high peak, Pilchuck stands out from other higher peaks because of its westerly position. A popular hiking trail leads to its summit, where there is a former lookout cabin that has been converted to accommodate a large number of visitors. The final climb to the summit involves a bit of scrambling through big granite blocks, then up a ladder. The hiking trail is too crowded to make it a popular ascent for climbers, although there are scrambling routes up the east ridge that deserve attention. Mount Pilchuck is a lonesome winter and spring snowshoe climb. The summit offers excellent views of the Monte Cristo peaks, Glacier Peak, Mount Baker, and Mount Rainier, and west across the Puget Sound lowlands to the Olympic Mountains.

HOW TO GET THERE

This climb begins via Mount Pilchuck Trail from Mount Pilchuck Road east of Verlot on Mountain Loop Road. From Granite Falls, follow Mountain Loop Road (Washington Highway 92) east 10.8 miles to the Verlot Ranger Station.

Mount Pilchuck

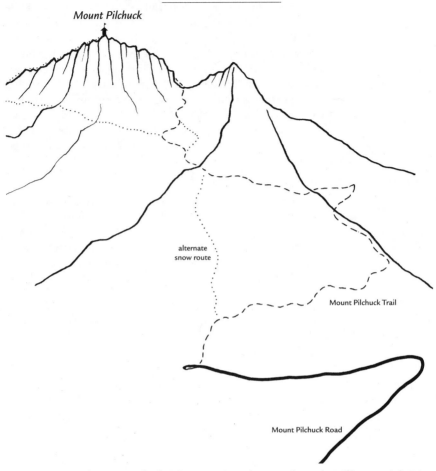

Mount Pilchuck

alternate
snow route

Mount Pilchuck Trail

Mount Pilchuck Road

Continue 1 mile east to the bridge crossing the South Fork Stillaguamish River, then take the first right turn up Mount Pilchuck Road. The road is paved at first but soon becomes a bumpy gravel road that leads about 7 miles to the trailhead. A Northwest Forest Pass is required. This is a high "car-prowl" trailhead, so leave nothing of value in your car.

ROUTE DESCRIPTION

The trail begins on an old road grade but soon angles right into the woods and climbs a ridge at the edge of a clearcut, then switches back at a talus slope and cuts back across the west shoulder of Mount Pilchuck. After about 2 miles, the trail begins climbing a lovely subalpine rock slope over polished granite slabs, around heather, fir, and hemlock, and past several relics of past mining operations. This area of the trail can be confusing because there are many "trails," some beaten out by boots, some taken by opportunistic scramblers, and then the official trail. Choose any path, aiming for the west ridge saddle, where the trail angles onto the south slope of the mountain and switching back up a few hundred feet to reach the edge of a large talus slope. Here, for some unknown reason, the Forest Service has blasted a new trail through the old, weathered granite blocks that used to offer a fun scrambling variation to the old trail. Presumably, the new trail is better because it doesn't get muddy and can't suffer erosion, but from an aesthetic standpoint, the new trail leaves a lot to be desired, although a majority of hikers seem to like it. Anyway, hike up the trail to the summit lookout, which is perched on the very edge of the north face and reached via a steep ladder. Enjoy the view.

OPTIONS

Mount Pilchuck is a very enjoyable and accessible winter and spring climb, assuming there is no avalanche danger and if the road isn't buried in feet of snow. The winter route climbs directly up the old ski slope, then up a gully or snow slopes on the left. Here, it follows the approximate line of the trail up to the west ridge saddle, then up the ridge to the summit. Several variations are possible to the ridge; the route will vary depending on snow conditions and other factors.

PRECAUTIONS

There are some steep drop-offs along the trail, especially near the summit. The summit ridge is very exposed, so be very careful and stay back from the edge. Snow lingers in the upper basin well into summer, so an ice ax is recommended, especially if an off-trail variation is chosen. In winter, beware of avalanches on the old ski slope and below the saddle, and watch out for cornices on the summit ridge. The summit area can be unsanitary because there is no toilet to accommodate the many hikers who visit this popular lookout. Please use the trailhead toilet.

35. MOUNT PERSIS

Elevation: 5,452 feet/1,662 meters
Route: West Ridge Trail
Rating: Class 1
Distance: 6 miles round trip
Elevation Gain: 2,800 feet
Time: 2 to 3 hours trailhead to summit
Maps: USGS Index, Gold Bar; Green Trails No. 142 (Index)

ABOUT THE CLIMB

Mount Persis is one of the landmark peaks of the Skykomish River Valley. Although it lacks the sheer relief of its more well-known neighbor, Mount Index, the peak occupies a commanding position at the foot of the valley. It forms a long rampart with a broad, steep north face rising some 5,000 feet from the valley floor and culminates in innumerable rock faces and buttresses including a 900-foot vertical cliff directly below the summit. Mount Persis is an enjoyable, easy climb. The summit is readily reached via a popular hiking trail—not a

Mount Persis.

maintained forest service trail, mind you, but a steep, sometimes rugged path beaten out by hikers and climbers. Road access problems (i.e., a locked gate) sometimes make the approach too long for all but a determined few, but usually the summit hike is an easy morning or afternoon jaunt. Mount Persis is a very popular winter and spring snowshoe climb. Summit views are excellent, including the Monte Cristo peaks, Mount Baker, Glacier Peak, Mount Rainier to the south, distant views of Seattle and the Puget Sound lowlands, west to the Olympic Mountains, and of course, close-up views of the dizzying peaks and walls of Mount Index and the bustle of the Skykomish River Valley.

HOW TO GET THERE

This climb begins from Forest Road 62 just off of Stevens Pass Highway west of Index. Drive U.S. Highway 2 to Proctor Creek Road (Forest Road 62), about 2.5 miles east from Zeke's Drive-In and 2.1 miles west from the Mount Index Cafe. If the gate is open, drive 3.6 miles up the road to the Proctor Creek fork and take the left fork (Forest Road 6220). Follow that spur road just over 1 mile to another fork. Turn left and continue to the trailhead where the road is blocked off.

ROUTE DESCRIPTION

From the Mount Persis trailhead, hike up the decommissioned spur road for about 0.5 mile to the start of the west ridge "trail." Hike the obvious path ascending directly up the clearcut slope into the forest, negotiate a maze of windfall, and go up to the ridge proper. Continue along the boot path as it ascends directly up the ridge slope through some brush and talus. Higher up, the slope drops off steeply on the left. Eventually the route crosses a rocky false summit that offers great views of the summit and north face of Mount Persis and across to Mount Index. From the false summit, the trail descends briefly along the

Mount Persis and Mount Index

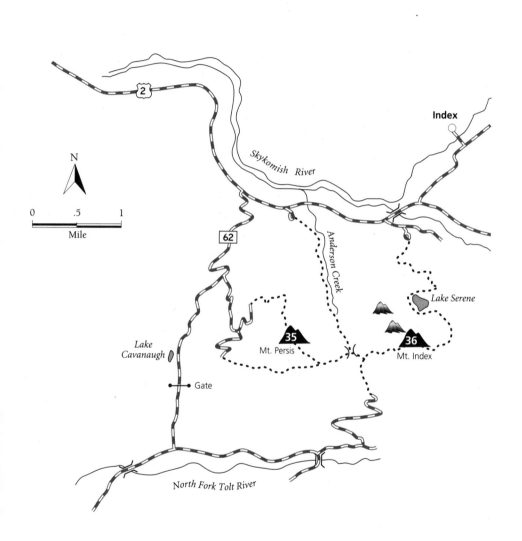

Index

Skykomish River

N

0   .5   1
Mile

2

62

Anderson Creek

Lake Serene

35
Mt. Persis

36
Mt. Index

Lake
Cavanaugh

Gate

North Fork Tolt River

ridge, crosses a divide, then climbs gradually to the flat, rocky summit. To descend, hike down via the trail.

OPTIONS

Mount Persis is a popular winter and spring snowshoe ascent with very little avalanche exposure and fairly easy routefinding. It is a long climb, though, when snow covers the road, and winter conditions can be punishing. Although Persis is considered an easy day hike in summer, the difficulty and commitment of a winter or spring climb should not be underestimated, especially during adverse conditions or when the road is gated or buried under several feet of snow. Beware of cornices, which are very common in winter and spring. Flag or wand key points of the route to avoid missing a turn on the way down, but please remove flagging on the descent.

PRECAUTIONS

Getting off route on Mount Persis could have serious consequences, especially in winter. It would be easy to get off route when the mountain is enshrouded by clouds, and remember rocks and roots are slippery when wet. During all seasons, be careful not to lose the route on the way down. It is easy to miss a crucial turn and end up hiking down the wrong ridge. With steep cliffs lurking close by, descending too far down the ridge or following the wrong ridgeline could be unpleasant or worse. In winter and spring, flagging or wanding key points of the route will help locate the route during the descent, especially if visibility is limited. Please remove flagging on the way down, though, to avoid misleading hikers later in the year. Beware of cornices on the summit ridge; stay well back from the edge. Bring an ice ax if snow lingers.

The access road crosses Weyerhaeuser land, and in 1998 the gate adjacent to U.S. Highway 2 was locked, purportedly to keep out vandals, trash dumpers, and rogue loggers. The gate is open now but could be closed again without warning.

36. MOUNT INDEX

Elevation: 5,979 feet/1,822 meters
Route: West Ridge/Slope
Rating: Class 2 to 3
Distance: 11 miles round trip from North Fork Tolt River Road
Elevation Gain: 3,000 feet
Time: 6 to 8 hours trailhead to summit
Maps: USGS Mount Index; Green Trails No. 142 (Index)

ABOUT THE CLIMB

Mount Index, the most striking mountain visible along the entire length of Stevens Pass Highway, is a jagged spine rising abruptly from the Skykomish River Valley. The impossibly vertical and overhanging walls are gouged by steep avalanche gullies and soar thousands of feet above the steep-walled valley below. With a 5,000-foot plus vertical rise from the valley to the summit, Mount Index rivals many of the giants of the Cascade Range in sheer relief. It is an awesome sight to behold, at least from the Skykomish River Valley. From the Puget Sound

Michael Stanton/Mountainwerks

Mount Index in winter from Mount Persis. The scrambling route follows the ridge on the right.

lowlands, however, it is just another ordinary looking mountain, a rounded, forested, talus-strewn hump that is barely distinguishable from its neighbors.

Despite impressive north and west faces, Mount Index is not a particularly appealing climb, at least not by its easiest routes, which are steep, brushy scrambles up forest slopes, snow gullies, and talus slides. But the mountain occupies such a commanding position above the confluence of the North Fork and South Fork of Skykomish River that it simply demands to be climbed. Fortunately, the scrambling routes are not difficult, at least not in a technical sense. Gated logging road gates and difficult lowland forest terrain pose the biggest obstacles to a successful ascent of Mount Index. Indeed, although more direct routes exist, many parties approach via a high ridge traverse from Mount Persis just to avoid hiking up brushy forest slopes. Ridge and summit views are spectacular, including nearby Baring Mountain and Gunn Peak, Mount Daniel, Mount Hinman, the Monte Cristo peaks, Mount Rainier, Mount Baker, and Glacier Peak, as well as distant views of Seattle and the Puget Sound lowlands, west to the Olympic Mountains, and of course, a vertigo-inducing look down the north face to the Skykomish River Valley.

HOW TO GET THERE

The route described begins from Forest Road 62 just off of U.S. Highway 2 west of Index. Drive U.S. Highway 2 to Proctor Creek Road (Forest Road 62), about 2.5 miles east from Zeke's Drive-Inn and 2.1 miles west from the Mount Index Cafe. If the gate is open, drive 3.6 miles up the road to the Proctor Creek fork and take the right fork, staying on Forest Road 62 until you reach Weyerhaeuser gate. Park off the road, being careful not to block the road or gate.

Mount Index

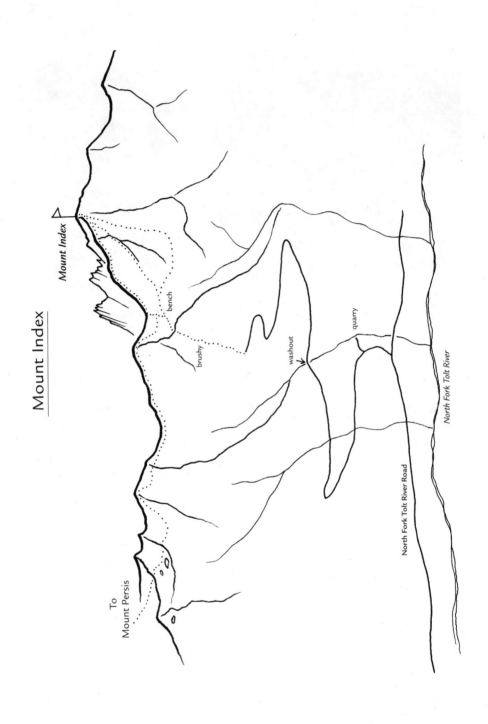

ROUTE DESCRIPTION

From the gate on Forest Road 62, hike or ride up the road to the junction with North Fork Tolt River Road. Turn left and continue east along the north bank of the North Fork Tolt River for about 2.7 miles to a fork. Take the left fork and follow the road another mile upriver to another fork. Turn left again and follow this logging spur road, staying left at all forks, to the road's end at about 3.5 miles. At last report, the road was washed out at about 3,000 feet elevation. Hike up the logging road to the road's end at about 4,000 feet elevation, then ascend timbered slopes directly upslope, bearing in a northeast direction to a shoulder. From here, traverse right across a broad bench at about 4,700 feet elevation into the basin below the Index-Persis divide. From the basin, ascend the west ridge proper or the basin's eastern headwall to the summit.

There are three feasible routes. One climbs the west ridge directly and involves some Class 3 rock scrambling. Another climbs a narrow gully at the head of the basin just south of the ridge and involves mostly talus and snow climbing. A third climbs a gully farther south on the basin headwall and is reportedly the easiest but longest option. A snowfield lingers high up until late season, so bring an ice ax. This route is not often climbed; expect bushwhacking and difficult routefinding. To descend, downclimb the route.

OPTIONS

A traverse along the Index-Persis divide is a popular approach in theory if not in practice. Although many climbers consider this the best option, very few seem to have actually done the traverse. Beckey's guide describes a route ascending from the east shore of Lake Serene up northeast slope gullies. This route is long and steep with unavoidable exposure to rockfall and avalanches. It is not recommended. The North Face of the North Peak of Mount Index◆ is a popular route (IV, 5.6). Index Peaks Traverse (V, 5.7) is also popular although not often completed. Refer to *Cascade Alpine Guide*.

PRECAUTIONS

Come prepared for serious bushwhacking. Avalanche hazard can be extreme in winter, spring, and early summer. Beware of cornices on the ridges and summit. Loose rock is prevalent on Mount Index.

37. GUNN PEAK

Elevation: 6,245 feet/1,904 meters
Route: Barclay Creek Route
Rating: Class 3
Distance: 8 miles round trip
Elevation Gain: 4,200 feet from Forest Road 6024 to summit
Time: 5 to 6 hours from road to summit
Maps: USGS Baring; Green Trails No. 143 (Monte Cristo)

ABOUT THE CLIMB

Gunn Peak is the prominent, sharp rock rising to the east above the town of Index. It is the highest of a group of craggy 6,000-foot peaks rising between the

Gunn Peak and Vicinity

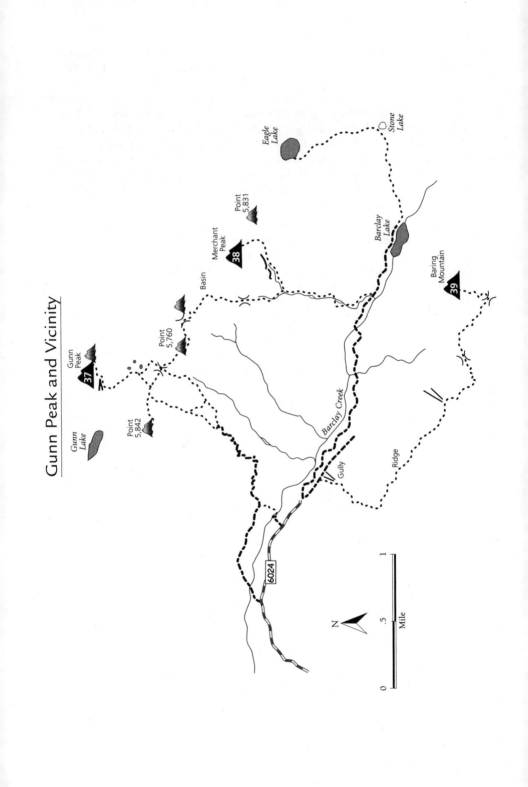

Gunn Lake

Gunn Peak **37**

Point 5,842

Point 5,760

Basin

Merchant Peak **38**

Point 5,831

Eagle Lake

Stone Lake

Barclay Lake

Barclay Creek

Gully

Ridge

Baring Mountain **39**

6024

N

0   .5   1
Mile

North Fork and South Fork Skykomish River. This group includes Merchant Peak and Baring Mountain. Despite its visibility from the Skykomish River Valley and the Puget Sound lowlands, and proximity to the Stevens Pass Highway, Gunn is a fairly remote peak from a climber's perspective because there are no trails leading close to the mountain. A number of different approaches exist but none is especially popular because they all involve off-trail hiking up steep, brushy slopes and gullies. Still, Gunn Peak is an attractive summit, and thus a fairly popular climbing objective despite its modest approach difficulties.

The approach "trail" is difficult to find and follow. Many parties can't find it at first and simply bushwhack across Barclay Creek and up toward the mountain until they stumble upon the trail. Some hikers have given up in frustration, unable to find any trace of a trail. If you don't find the trail, expect an arduous bushwhack. In addition to its reputation for brush, Gunn takes about two hours longer to climb than Baring Mountain or Merchant Peak, which makes it the least-climbed peak of the group. Of course, that means you may have the mountain all to yourself. The upper ridges, basins, and summit scramble are open and enjoyable. The summit scramble is exposed but fairly secure. The summit is exposed on all sides, providing airy views of Baring Mountain and Merchant Peak (close-up), north to the Monte Cristo peaks, Glacier Peak, and Mount Baker; south to Mount Daniel, Mount Hinman, and Mount Rainier; west to Mount Index and across the Puget Sound lowlands to the Olympic Mountains; and into the depths of the Skykomish River Valley.

HOW TO GET THERE
This climb begins from Barclay Creek Road just north of Baring on the Stevens Pass Highway. Drive U.S. Highway 2 to the small "town" of Baring, about 5.6 miles east from the Index Galena Road and 7.7 miles west from Skykomish. Turn north onto Barclay Creek Road (Forest Road 6024) just across the highway from Der Baring Store. Cross the railroad tracks and continue 4 miles to a spur road on the left, just 0.2 mile short of the Barclay Lake trailhead. Don't drive down the spur road; it dead-ends at Barclay Creek. Park at a turnout near the junction or at the Barclay Lake trailhead. A Northwest Forest Pass is apparently required because this road is within 0.25 mile of the trailhead.

ROUTE DESCRIPTION
From Barclay Creek Road, hike briefly down to the end of the spur road at the edge of Barclay Creek. Take a trail leading off to the right, then hop boulders upstream to an old footlog. Cross the creek, then bushwhack northward, trending left through timber and brush for about 0.2 mile to join the old approach trail on an overgrown logging road. Continue northward up the old road grade, then follow a blazed trail upslope through dense, young fir and alder trees, trending right to the edge of an old clearcut. Once out of the clearcut, the trail is easy to follow as it climbs steeply up open forest slopes and passes a waterfall (heard but not seen) off to the right. Many parties get lost in the brush approaching through the old clearcut. Others bushwhack to the base of the waterfall, then climb the steep slope on the left to join the trail above the clearcut.

Gunn Peak

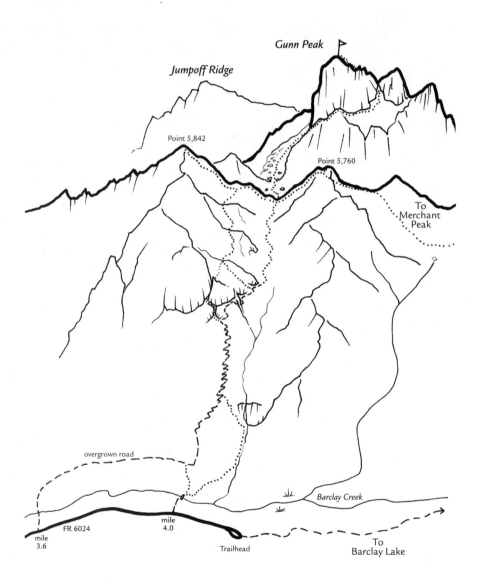

Continue climbing until the trail breaks into the open just below a big rock buttress at about 4,000 feet elevation. Two options present themselves. The standard route angles left up the gullies to the base of the buttress, then climbs the steep, loose gully right and up along the base of the buttress, and finally goes up a brushy ridge slope to rocky heather meadows leading to the Gunn-Barclay divide. The other option is to follow a boot path right around the toe of the initial slabby ridge and along the base of overhanging, blocky cliffs to the broad, brushy gully that leads to the saddle in the ridge giving access to Gunn Peak. The latter option has a tricky gully crossing midway, then is straightforward to the saddle. The upper gully is a long, direct snow climb in early season, but by summer it is a miserable bushwhack. A variation follows this traversing path to cliffs at the edge of the main gully, then bushwhacks left and up to the rocky heather meadows like the gully option.

Once on the Gunn-Barclay divide, traverse to the saddle and descend snow and talus slopes into the tarn-dotted meadow basin on the other side, then traverse to the base of the broad talus gully below Gunn Peak. Ascend the talus slope several hundred feet until just below the steep southwest buttress of Gunn Peak, then climb the obvious steep rock gully on the right. Climbing the gully directly would be difficult; it is often wet and has loose rock. Stay just right of the gully, climbing a short section of Class 3 rock and find a hidden trail leading up through hemlocks. Traverse talus and snow slopes right below the south face of Gunn Peak, then up a narrowing gully to the sharp notch in the summit ridge about 300 feet east of the summit. Cross over to the north side and traverse an exposed dirt ledge briefly, then scramble up the blocky ridge crest to the airy summit.

To descend, downclimb the route. Some parties rappel the Class 3 gully, especially when it's snowy or icy, or when the rock is wet.

OPTIONS

The other approach begins via an inconspicuous, overgrown logging road 3.6 miles up Barclay Creek Road. Although it is flagged, many who try this approach get lost in the clearcut. The other route, although more brushy, is shorter and more direct. A scrambling ascent of either Point 5,842 or Point 5,760 can be made from the Barclay-Gunn divide. Gunn Peak can be enchained with Merchant Peak via an enjoyable high route.

PRECAUTIONS

The approach is a notorious bushwhack, especially if you miss the "flagged" trail. There is a trail, but it can be hard to find and follow, especially in the clearcut area. The approach gully and slopes leading up to the peak are avalanche prone in winter and spring, and brushy in summer and fall. The crux gully is steep rock scrambling that is more difficult when snowy, icy, or wet. Some parties belay and rappel this gully. In early season, snow and ice may linger on the north side of the summit ridge, making the initial ledge traverse very tricky and exposed. Belaying across the ledge is recommended under these conditions. Protection is possible in good cracks in the rock here; a small rack up to 2.5 inches and some slings should suffice.

Norm Buckley

Tom Barnhart looks back at Baring Mountain from Merchant Peak.

38. MERCHANT PEAK

Elevation: 6,113 feet/1,863 meters
Route: South Gully/Slope
Rating: Class 3
Distance: 6 miles round trip
Elevation Gain: 3,800 feet
Time: 3 to 4 hours trailhead to summit
Maps: USGS Baring; Green Trails No. 143 (Monte Cristo)

ABOUT THE CLIMB

The second highest of the Skykomish River group that includes Gunn Peak and Baring Mountain, Merchant Peak is perhaps its most obscure. Merchant Peak is the culmination of a craggy ridge rising prominently between the more distinguished peaks of Gunn Peak and Baring Mountain. Even though it rivals its neighbors in height and scale, it is mostly overlooked. Too bad, because Merchant Peak is a significant summit with an enjoyable, varied summit scramble and impressive summit views. Although the standard route is marred by loose rock, undermined snow, and avalanche danger depending on the season, it is still a moderately popular climb. Because the route climbs a notorious avalanche and rockfall gully, it is best done in late spring or early summer when avalanche danger has passed and snow covers loose rock—but before the snow has been seriously undercut by the stream flowing down the gully. The close views of Baring Mountain's north face are inspiring. Summit views stretch out to include Mount Index, Mount Daniel, Mount Hinman, the Monte Cristo peaks, Glacier Peak, and Mount Baker, as well as distant views across Puget Sound to the Olympic Mountains.

HOW TO GET THERE

This climb begins from the Barclay Lake trailhead, just north of Baring on the Stevens Pass Highway. Drive U.S. Highway 2 to the small "town" of Baring, about 5.6 miles east from the Index-Galena Road and 7.7 miles west from Skykomish. Turn north onto Barclay Creek Road (Forest Road 6024) just across the highway from Der Baring Store. Cross the railroad tracks and continue 4.2 miles to the trailhead at the road's end. A Northwest Forest Pass is required.

ROUTE DESCRIPTION

Hike Barclay Lake Trail (Trail 1055) about 1 mile to the bridge crossing Barclay Creek. Continue briefly beyond the bridge, up a rise to where the trail levels out, then leave the trail and follow a rocky streambed left and upstream. You may leave the trail just after crossing the stream and bushwhack directly north to the streambed. The streambed doubles back to the west at first, then curves northward and up to the base of an obvious broad gully. Pass a steep rock step with a waterfall by scrambling up the left side and across the top of the cliff, which gives access to the upper gully. A bit higher up is another rock step and waterfall; pass this step more directly via moderate slabby scrambling. About halfway up the gully, at about 4,100 feet elevation, is a narrow, steep-walled basin that is usually snow-filled through summer. A stream flows in through a gully on the right side

Merchant Peak

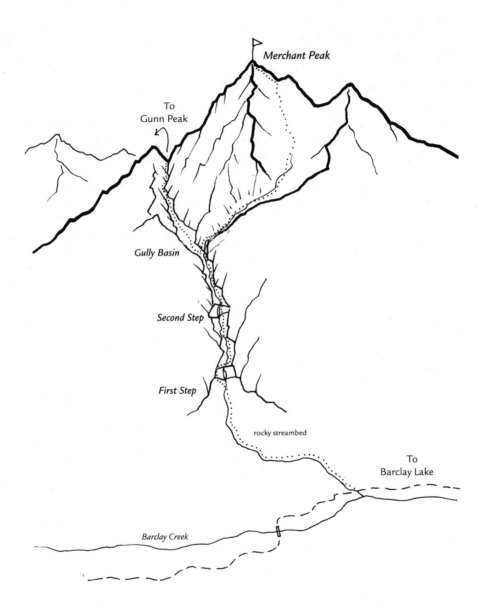

Merchant Peak

To
Gunn Peak

Gully Basin

Second Step

First Step

rocky streambed

To
Barclay Lake

Barclay Creek

of the basin. Angle right out of the basin and follow a climber's trail across an inobvious sloping dirt ledge leading diagonally right below cliffs, then up an easier slope into a widening brushy gully that opens into a broad heather basin on the south slope. From here, ascend rocky heather or snow slopes to the summit. In early season, the route is all snow except for the rock steps and ledge traverse. To descend, downclimb the route.

OPTIONS
You may approach Gunn Peak via the Merchant Peak gully and a high route over Point 5,670. Climb the gully to its head at a notch overlooking a broad heather basin. Descend and cross the basin and climb to the 5,220-foot saddle just east of Point 5,760. Hike westward up the ridge to a steep rock buttress. An inconspicuous but very exposed goat trail leads right along a ledge about 50 feet to the northeast corner of the summit block, where a short ridge scramble (blocky Class 3) gains the summit of Point 5,760. Alternatively, traverse left across rocky slopes and climb a short rock step (Class 3–4) to gain the southwest slope just below the summit rocks. Just below the summit is debris from the 1965 plane crash mentioned in Beckey's guide. From here, descend talus slopes briefly to the Barclay-Gunn divide where an ascent of Gunn Peak is straightforward.

PRECAUTIONS
The main gully is an obvious avalanche chute with severe avalanche hazard in winter and early season. The upper slopes are also avalanche prone. The gully is an obvious rockfall channel as well. There is high rockfall hazard in the gully, especially climber-caused rockfall. The upper gully has very loose rock. The rock steps low in the gully are exposed and very slippery when wet or icy. Climbers should beware of undermined snow in the gully. There are many late-season snow bridges to fall through and moats on the edges, so be careful.

39. BARING MOUNTAIN

Elevation: 6,125 feet/1,867 meters
Route: West Ridge/South Slope
Rating: Class 2
Distance: 6 miles round trip
Elevation Gain: 3,900 feet
Time: 3 to 4 hours
Maps: USGS Baring; Green Trails No. 143 (Monte Cristo)

ABOUT THE CLIMB
Mount Baring is one of the most dramatic peaks of the western Cascade Range, although you wouldn't know it unless you viewed the mountain from the proper vantage point. The mountain is craggy and precipitous on all sides but especially on the north side, which falls away in a massive, nearly unbroken 3,000-foot cliff of vertical and overhanging rock. Mount Baring's north wall is legendary among climbers and was the site of one of the most epic first ascents ever undertaken in Washington's Cascades. The tale is of sacrifice and persistence, of resignation and despair, of death, and finally, of success over seemingly impossible odds.

Although the shroud of impossibility has been lifted in recent years, the north face of Mount Baring remains a classic testpiece for local mountaineers and rock climbers.

Fortunately for the rest of us, there is a scrambling route to the summit of Mount Baring up the west ridge and south slope. Although rated Class 2, the route is mostly a strenuous hike up steep forest, heather, and talus slopes with just a few places where you are really scrambling. Baring is a good winter and spring climb when avalanche danger is low. Incredible summit views await, including Merchant Peak, Gunn Peak, Mount Index, Mount Daniel, Mount Hinman, the Monte Cristo peaks, Glacier Peak, Mount Baker, and Mount Rainier, as well as distant views across the Puget Sound lowlands to the Olympic Mountains.

HOW TO GET THERE
Follow the directions for Merchant Peak via Forest Road 6024 from Baring to the Barclay Lake trailhead. A Northwest Forest Pass is required.

ROUTE DESCRIPTION
From the trailhead, don't take Barclay Lake Trail; instead hike up the old road grade just right of and uphill from the trail. This road now serves as a path to a trailhead toilet "hidden" behind a boulder about 10 feet up the trail. Follow the road grade about 600 feet to a narrow dirt and rock gully on the right. A steep, slippery climber's trail—the worst part of the climb—leads several hundred feet up the gully. Once above this initial gully, the trail climbs steeply through hemlock and silver fir forest, occasionally clambering up roots and rocks, but is mostly a pleasant, strenuous forest hike to the ridge crest (elevation about 4,000 feet). Continue eastward, following the trail up and down along the verdant ridge crest or just right to a notch above a steep north-side gully. Drop down on the south side of the ridge and traverse to a broad forest gully, then climb directly to the ridge crest at the edge of a broad talus basin (about 4,800 feet elevation). Cross the basin, on the rocks, or on a faint trail on the left, and ascend the steep talus gully (snow in early season) on the other side to the saddle between the south and main summit, about 400 vertical feet below the summit. From the saddle, scramble northward up rocks, or take a hidden trail through the trees just left, and continue up wide open heather and talus slopes to the rocky summit. To descend, downclimb the route.

OPTIONS
There is a route ascending the south slope via an old logging road above Baring and joining the route described just below the talus basin. This option is longer and not as popular. The road has grown over with alders, fir saplings, and brush, which makes for tedious going.

PRECAUTIONS
The initial gully is steep and can be muddy when wet. The talus gully is prone to climber-caused rockfall and is avalanche prone in winter and spring. Beware of cornices on the ridge, at the saddle, and on the summit. The summit area is quite exposed; be very careful here because the north face drops away thousands of feet to the valley floor. In places, old flagging from winter and spring ascents can be confusing. Stick to the boot path to avoid routefinding problems.

Baring Mountain

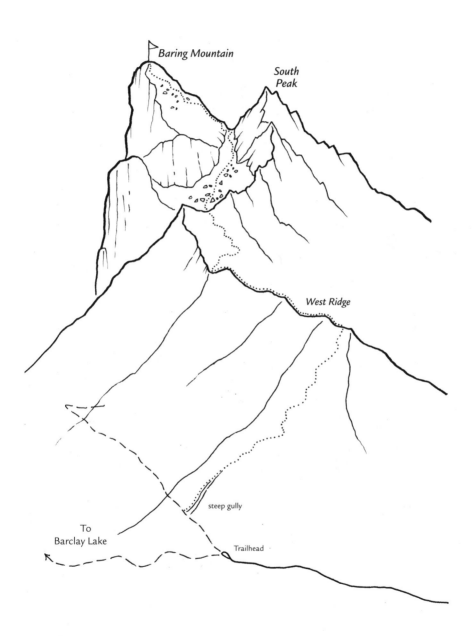

Baring Mountain

South
Peak

West Ridge

steep gully

To
Barclay Lake

Trailhead

Morgan Balogh

Mount Howard from Rock Mountain. The route ascends the righthand slope.

40. MOUNT HOWARD

Elevation: 7,063 feet/2,153 meters
Route: South Slope
Rating: Class 2
Distance: 12 miles round trip
Elevation Gain: 4,200 feet
Time: 4 to 5 hours trailhead to summit
Maps: USGS Mount Howard; Green Trails No. 145 (Wenatchee Lake)

ABOUT THE CLIMB

Mount Howard is the highest peak of Nason Ridge, the long, moderately craggy ridge on the north as you drive along U.S. Highway 2 about 10 miles east of Stevens Pass. The mountain rises as a prominent pyramid from certain vantage points, especially from U.S. Highway 2 as you drive west toward Stevens Pass, making it easily distinguishable from other nearby peaks. The peak is often climbed by hikers because it is easy to access via the popular Nason Ridge Trail. This is a pleasant early season snow climb, best attempted in late spring after the approach trails have mostly melted out and avalanche hazard has diminished, but while snow still provides for easy travel on the upper slopes and ridges. Later in the year, this is a simple talus and meadow climb.

Mount Howard is not a technical ascent but a strenuous one, gaining over 4,000 feet of elevation from the trailhead to the summit, most of that in the first 4 miles. The views alone are worth the effort. Mount Howard offers a panoramic view of the surrounding mountainscape with the Stewart Range and Wenatchee Mountains to the south; and Glacier Peak, the Dakobed Range, Entiat Mountains, Bonanza Peak, and a multitude of other high peaks to the north.

HOW TO GET THERE

This climb begins from Rock Mountain trailhead just off of U.S. Highway 2 about 8.8 miles east from Stevens Pass (just east of the highway maintenance shed) and 11.7 miles west from Coles Corner (the turnoff for Lake Wenatchee). A Northwest Forest Pass is required. This is a high "car-prowl" trailhead, so leave nothing of value behind.

ROUTE DESCRIPTION

Hike up Rock Mountain Trail (Trail 1587), a steep, switchbacking path that climbs up and up (and up!) to its junction with Nason Ridge Trail (Trail 1583) after 4 grueling miles. Turn right and descend eastward to Rock Lake, then continue along Nason Ridge Trail about 1 mile to Crescent Lake, tucked in a basin just south of Mount Howard. Cross the outlet stream and skirt the lakeshore, then ascend directly northward from the lake up rocky meadows and talus (snow in early season), angling right to the southeast summit ridge, and continue up the easy subalpine ridge slope to the summit. To descend, downclimb the route.

OPTIONS

Mount Howard can be climbed just as easily via Merritt Lake Trail (Trail 1588), which begins about 2.9 miles east of the Rock Mountain trailhead on U.S. Highway 2. Rock Mountain Trail was highlighted because it is more direct and offers

Mount Howard

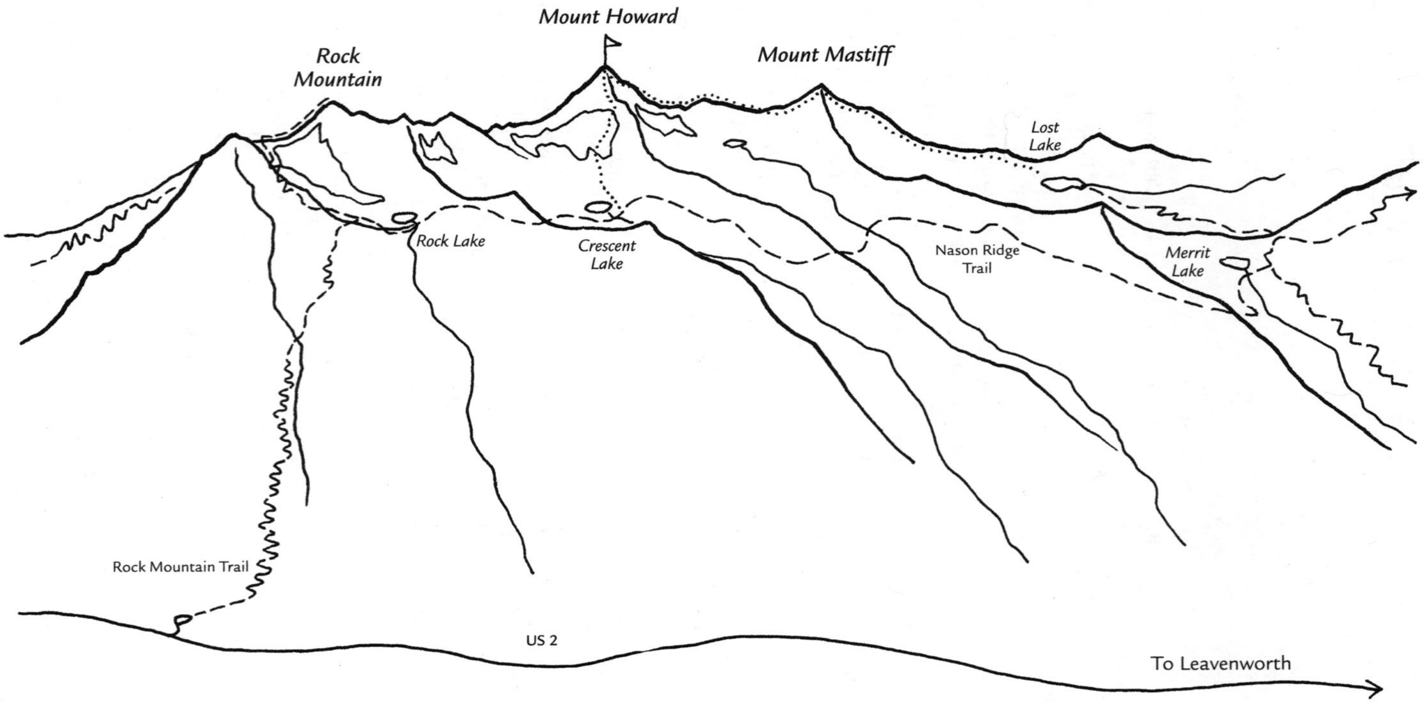

Rock
Mountain

Mount Howard

Mount Mastiff

Lost
Lake

Merrit
Lake

Nason Ridge
Trail

Rock Lake

Crescent
Lake

Rock Mountain Trail

US 2

To Leavenworth

better options for the summit-minded scrambler. The two other Nason Ridge summits, Rock Mountain and Mount Mastiff, can be climbed during a long day or two-day trip.

PRECAUTIONS
As with other summits lying east of the Cascade crest, Mount Howard is subject to afternoon thunderstorms, particularly during late summer. The upper ridge and basin slopes are avalanche prone in winter and spring. Cornices form in many places along the crest of Nason Ridge.

41. CLARK MOUNTAIN

Elevation: 8,576 feet/2,614 meters
Route: Southeast Slope
Rating: Class 3
Distance: 22 miles round trip
Elevation Gain: 6,200 feet
Time: 8 to 10 hours trailhead to summit; best done as a two- or three-day climb
Maps: USGS Clark Mountain; Green Trails No. 113 (Holden)

ABOUT THE CLIMB
Clark Mountain is the highest summit of the Dakobed Range, a modest subrange of 8,000-foot peaks rising above the White River Valley, only a few miles southeast of Glacier Peak. Clark is an attractive peak, especially when viewed from the south where it presents itself as a modest snowy pyramid with a rocky, sharp-ridged summit. The mountain is flanked by glaciers on its north side and shows evidence of glacial carving on its southeast and southwest flanks. It is a remote but moderately popular climb with a trail approach to its southeast slope and easy meadow hiking and rock scrambling to the top. The Walrus Glacier on the mountain's northeast flank is also a popular route. Clark Mountain is a popular late spring climb when snow leads much of the way to the summit. Summit views are outstanding and include a panorama of eastern side of the Cascade Range with a close-up view of Glacier Peak. You will have views west to the Monte Cristo peaks; south to Mount Stuart and Mount Rainier; and north to the Entiat Mountains, Bonanza Peak, and Mount Baker, plus innumerable peaks in every direction.

HOW TO GET THERE
This climb begins from White River trailhead, many miles north of Lake Wenatchee on White River Road. Drive U.S. Highway 2 to Coles Corner, 20.5 miles east of Stevens Pass and 14.5 miles northwest of Leavenworth. Turn right on Washington Highway 207 toward Lake Wenatchee, stay left where the road forks, and continue along the lake's north shore another 6.7 miles past the Lake Wenatchee Ranger Station to a fork. Take the right fork, following White River Road (Forest Road 64) about 9 miles to the White River trailhead at the road's end. A Northwest Forest Pass is required.

ROUTE DESCRIPTION
The easiest and most direct route is the Southeast Slope, a traversing meadow hike, rock scramble, and snow climb from Boulder Pass Trail. Hike White River

Clark Mountain

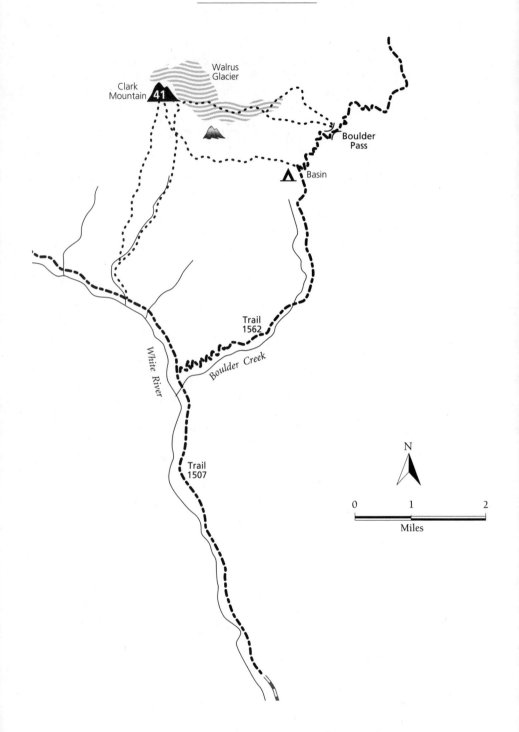

Clark Mountain

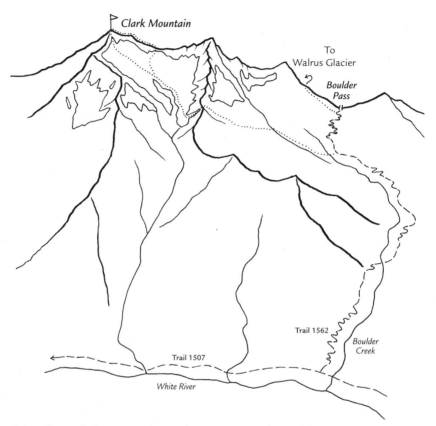

Trail (Trail 1507) about 4 miles to the junction with Boulder Pass Trail. Hike up Boulder Pass Trail (Trail 1562) another 5 steep miles to a broad meadow basin at the head of Boulder Creek. There are several campsites in the basin.

Find the faint climber's trail leading westward up the basin, through brush at first but clearing higher up, and contouring the western basin headwall to the southern ridge descending from Clark's rocky east peak. The trail may be diffi-cult to find if snow lingers in the basin or where obscured by brush. The trail or cross-country hiking leads you to a flat area on the ridge at about 7,000 feet ele-vation, where a steep gully leads down into the broad south slope basin. In early season, the gully is a steep snow descent where crampons and a rope may be desirable; by late season, this is a loose, insecure Class 2–3 rock scramble. From the base of the gully, continue upward and across the broad south slope basin, traversing and climbing heather, talus, and snow slopes directly to the summit. You may vary the route by climbing directly to the summit ridge and scrambling westward to the summit. Several variations appear to be possible. In early season and through summer most years, the route is mostly, if not all, snow with just a bit of rocky scrambling to the summit. To descend, downclimb the route.

OPTIONS
The Walrus Glacier route♦ on the mountain's northeast flank offers a much more alpine climbing experience. It is also approached via Boulder Pass. There are other summit routes on Mount Clark. A high traverse enchaining all of the Dakobed Range summits appears to be a good multi-day traverse. Refer to *Cascade Alpine Guide* for details.

PRECAUTIONS
Clark Mountain's upper slopes are avalanche prone in winter and spring. The gully on the south slope traverse involves steep Class 3 downclimbing with loose rock and definite rockfall hazard, especially party-inflicted. The gully may have steep snow or ice; a belay may be desired.

42. MOUNT MAUDE

Elevation: 9,082 feet/2,768 meters
Route: South Shoulder
Rating: Class 3
Distance: 16 miles round trip
Elevation Gain: 5,600 feet
Time: 8 to 10 hours; best done as a two- or three-day climb
Maps: USGS Holden and Trinity; Green Trails No. 113 (Holden)

ABOUT THE CLIMB
Mount Maude is the second highest and most popular summit of the Entiat Mountains, a subrange of mountains dividing the upper tributaries of the Entiat River that is about midway between Glacier Peak and Lake Chelan. While Mount Maude is an imposing peak from the north and east, its south and west slopes are fairly direct and simple, making it one of the easiest of Washington's 9,000-foot peaks to climb. Adventuresome hikers sometimes make the ascent, despite some steep snow and exposed rock scrambling. Hermann F. Ulrichs and John Burnett are credited with the first ascent of Mount Maude in July 1932, although mountain goats certainly preceded any human summit climbers.

Maude is fairly remote, at least in terms of driving, making it an unlikely one-day climb, although motivated climbers sometimes manage it in a long day. Most climbers prefer a more leisurely two- or three-day climb, including a traverse of the Carne Mountain high route, one of the scenic highlights of the area. Maude is best climbed in early summer when snow makes for easy going up gullies and slopes that are long, tedious scree and talus slogs in late season. Summit views are outstanding and include close-ups of the Entiat Mountains and Bonanza Peak to the north; plus Glacier Peak and the Chiwawa Mountains to the west, the Dakobed Range and Mount Stuart to the south, and the Chelan Mountains to the east.

HOW TO GET THERE
This climb begins from the Phelps Creek trailhead, many miles north of Lake Wenatchee on Chiwawa River Road. Drive U.S. Highway 2 to Coles Corner, 20.5 miles east of Stevens Pass and 14.5 miles northwest of Leavenworth. Turn north

Entiat Mountains

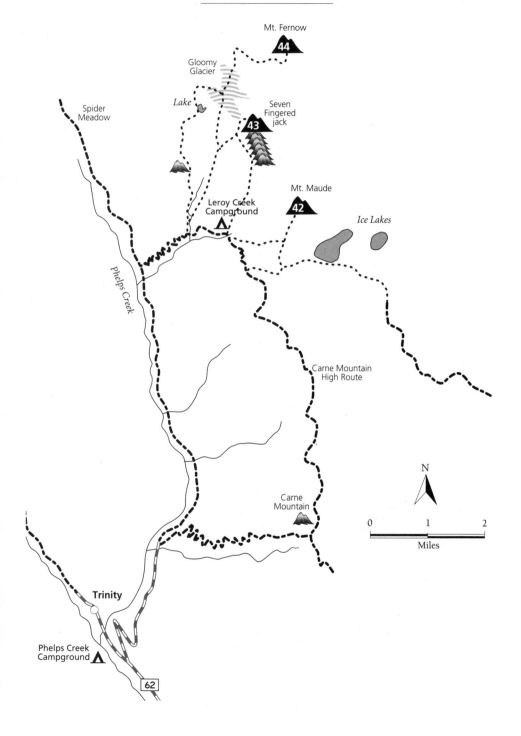

Mt. Fernow

44

Gloomy Glacier

Spider Meadow

Lake

Seven Fingered Jack

43

Mt. Maude

42

Ice Lakes

Leroy Creek Campground

Phelps Creek

Carne Mountain High Route

N

Carne Mountain

0   1   2
Miles

Trinity

Phelps Creek Campground

62

on Washington Highway 207 toward Lake Wenatchee and stay right at the Fish Lake fork. About 1.2 miles from the fork, turn left onto Chiwawa River Road (Forest Road 62). Follow Forest Road 62 about 25 miles to Alpine Meadow Campground. Continue 1.4 miles to a spur road on the right. Turn right and follow the spur road nearly 2.5 miles to the Phelps Creek trailhead at the road's end. A Northwest Forest Pass is required.

ROUTE DESCRIPTION
The route described is the South Shoulder, the most popular route up Mount Maude. The shortest approach is to hike Phelps Creek Trail (Trail 1511) about 3.5 miles to Leroy Creek. Find the abandoned but heavily traveled Leroy Creek-Carne Mountain Trail (Trail 1512) and follow it, climbing steeply via many switchbacks about 2 miles to Leroy Creek Basin, elevation about 5,400 feet. Leroy Creek Basin is the traditional base camp for climbers ascending Mount Maude, Mount Fernow, and Seven Fingered Jack. There are several campsites in the basin.

From Leroy Creek Basin, follow a trail southward out of the basin and up to a slight spur ridge saddle (about 6,800 feet elevation). Leave the trail here and contour southeast into a basin and up to a saddle about 7,600 feet just west of upper Ice Lake. Traverse northward from the saddle across a bench just east of the ridge, and climb a steep snow/scree gully that gains the south shoulder at about 8,300 feet elevation. Hike up the broad pumice ridge toward the summit. The going is mostly easy, except the final scramble to the summit up Class 3 ledges.

The recommended descent is via the route of ascent. Some parties take a shortcut, descending the west slope more directly. Begin from a flat area of the south shoulder at about 8,000 feet elevation, descend scree slopes into a steep gully, and go down through the trees just south of the gully. This descent is steep with loose rock and not highly recommended by those who have done it.

OPTIONS
A better but longer approach is via the Carne Mountain high route. From the Phelps Creek trailhead, hike up Carne Mountain Trail (Trail 1508) about 3 steep miles to a junction and take the left trail (Trail 1512) northwest over 7,085-foot Carne Mountain and along the ridge slopes toward Mount Maude. In late summer, this is an enjoyable, airy meadow hike bursting with wildflowers. The trail leads to the saddle (about 6,800 feet) above Leroy Creek Basin where the climbing route begins. Some parties descend into Leroy Creek Basin and camp, then complete the climb the next day; others bivouac higher up. Another alternate approach to the South Shoulder is via Entiat River Trail and Ice Lakes. From upper Ice Lake, the route ascends toward the 7,600-foot saddle, then continues as described. This longer option is best done over three days.

PRECAUTIONS
The slopes above Leroy Creek Basin are avalanche prone in winter and spring. The gully leading to the south shoulder is steep, with icy snow in early season and loose rock later in the year. Snow may linger in the gully through summer some years. The Entiat Mountains have a well-earned reputation for loose rock, and climber-caused rockfall is common. As one of the easiest 9,000-foot peaks in the state, Maude is often underestimated. The upper slopes are dry by late season; bring plenty of water.

Mount Fernow, Seven Fingered Jack, and Mount Maude

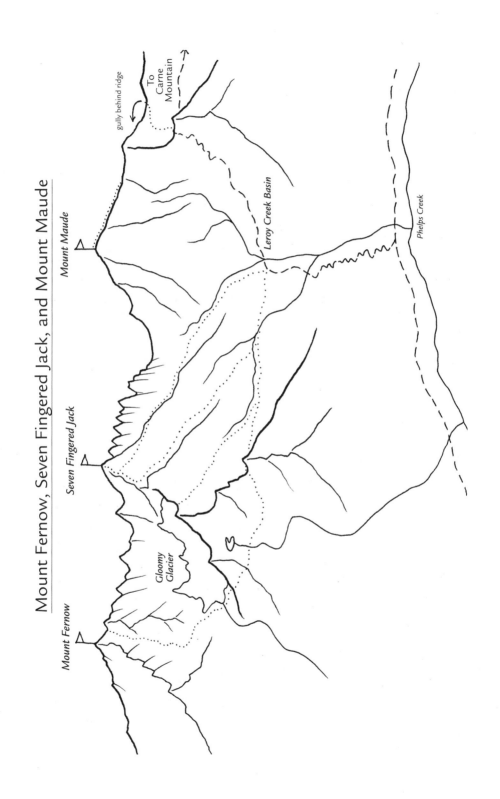

Mount Fernow

Seven Fingered Jack

Mount Maude

gully behind ridge

To Carne Mountain

Leroy Creek Basin

Phelps Creek

Gloomy Glacier

Seven Fingered Jack (left) and Mount Maude.

43. SEVEN FINGERED JACK

Elevation: 9,077 feet/2,767 meters
Route: Southwest Slope
Rating: Class 2–3
Distance: 16 miles round trip
Elevation Gain: 5,600 feet
Time: 6 to 8 hours to summit; best done as a two- or three-day climb
Maps: USGS Holden and Trinity; Green Trails No. 113 (Holden)

ABOUT THE CLIMB

Seven Fingered Jack is the third highest summit of the Entiat Mountains. It is a craggy peak with seven prominent rock points along its spine. Richard Alt and partner are credited with the first ascent of Seven Fingered Jack in July 1932, although mountain goats certainly preceded any human summit climbers. Jack is not a difficult climb from the south. Easy rock slopes and a summit scramble lead to the top. It is a fairly remote peak, at least in terms of driving, although from the trailhead it's a reasonable day climb.

The usual route isn't very interesting, just a long snow or scree slog with a little bit of rock scrambling, but Seven Fingered Jack is climbed quite often because it rises to over 9,000 feet elevation. It is best climbed during a multi-day trip including Mount Maude and Mount Fernow, although most climbers, having summited Maude and Seven Fingered Jack, give up and head home without tagging the higher summit. It is a recommended early season climb unless you prefer tedious scree and talus climbing. Jack has excellent summit views including the Entiat Mountains, Glacier Peak, Bonanza Peak, the Chelan Mountains, the Dakobed Range, the Stuart Range, and Mount Rainier.

HOW TO GET THERE
This climb begins from Phelps Creek trailhead, many miles north of Lake Wenatchee on Chiwawa River Road. Approach as for Mount Maude via Forest Road 62 to the Phelps Creek trailhead at the road's end. A Northwest Forest Pass is required.

ROUTE DESCRIPTION
Hike Phelps Creek Trail (Trail 1511) about 3.5 miles to Leroy Creek. Find the abandoned but heavily used Leroy Creek–Carne Mountain Trail (Trail 1512) and follow it, climbing steeply via many switchbacks about 2 miles to Leroy Creek Basin, elevation about 5,400 feet. There are many campsites in the basin.

From Leroy Creek Basin, there are several possible routes, all of which are straightforward and obvious. One route ascends a broad heather gully toward the saddle dividing Mount Maude and Seven Fingered Jack, skirts a rocky heather shelf below the south crags (the "seven fingers") to the broad southwest shoulder, and then involves scree and easy rock scrambling to gain the summit. Another route ascends the gentle southwest shoulder directly from Leroy Creek Basin to the summit. In early season, a central snow gully invites an ascent to the summit shoulder. None of these routes involves more than a bit of Class 2–3 scrambling. The rest is hiking up heather meadows and scree slopes or snow in early season. To descend, downclimb the route.

OPTIONS
Climbers often ascend both Seven Fingered Jack and Mount Maude on the same trip. Mount Fernow can be included if an extra day is allowed.

PRECAUTIONS
All precautions listed for Mount Maude apply equally to Seven Fingered Jack, except concerning Maude's gully.

44. MOUNT FERNOW

Elevation: 9,249 feet/2,819 meters
Route: Southwest Slope
Rating: Class 3–4
Distance: 22 miles round trip
Elevation Gain: 5,900 feet
Time: 10 to 12 hours; best done as a two- or three-day climb
Maps: USGS Holden; Green Trails No. 113 (Holden)

ABOUT THE CLIMB
Mount Fernow is the highest summit of the Entiat Mountains, a subrange of 9,000-foot peaks dividing the Entiat River and Leroy Creek about midway between Glacier Peak and Lake Chelan. Like other Entiat peaks, it is somewhat remote with abundant snow, scree and talus slopes, and gullies on all sides—a

Copper Peak, Mount Fernow, and Seven Fingered Jack from Bonanza Peak.

fairly long, tedious climb by any route. But more than the others, Mount Fernow
has a reputation for loose rock. In reality, much of the climbing is on reasonably
sound rock, or at least the loose rock scrambling isn't terrifyingly exposed. And
for that matter, the rock isn't any looser than on Mount Maude or Seven Fingered
Jack. Still, there are sections of very loose rock that require careful climbing.

Although Fernow is the highest summit of the range with a reasonably good
scrambling route to its summit, it is often overlooked in favor of Mount Maude
and Seven Fingered Jack. About the only reason anybody climbs Fernow, aside
from its excellent views, is to tick off another 9,000-footer and earn a club pin.
Either that, or to get away from the hordes on Mount Maude. Summit views are
outstanding and include a panorama of peaks: Bonanza Peak, Goode Mountain,
Buckner Mountain, Glacier Peak, the Chiwawa Mountains, and the Dakobed
Range. You can look south to Mount Stuart and Mount Rainier, and east to the
Chelan Mountains and beyond.

HOW TO GET THERE
Approach as for Mount Maude and Seven Fingered Jack. Start at the Phelps
Creek trailhead and hike to Leroy Creek Basin. A Northwest Forest Pass is
required.

ROUTE DESCRIPTION
The Southwest Slope is the most accessible and least difficult summit route. The
route described here is a better variation of the route described in Beckey's guide.

Approach via Phelps Creek Trail to Leroy Creek Basin (as described under
Mount Maude). From the basin, climb heather and scree slopes directly north to

a slight saddle in the ridge, just east of a ridge point at about 7,000 feet elevation. Cross over the saddle and descend 100 feet or so, then traverse heather slopes northward and up to or just below a small lake. There is a possible bivy site near the lake. Continue north across a slight saddle in the ridge and descend heather and talus slopes about 300 feet, then traverse right around to the foot of the diminutive Gloomy Glacier. Cross the glacier or moraine slopes just below the glacier, then climb the rocky slope on the northeast side to a higher basin. From this basin, climb the steep, rocky gully slope and gentler upper snow slopes to the ridge saddle just a few hundred yards south of Fernow's summit. Head north- ward up the ridge toward the summit, passing a large block by tunneling through or scrambling around to reach the east side of the ridge, then traverse scree slopes to the northeast ridge and scramble a short distance to the summit. To descend, downclimb the route.

OPTIONS
The East Ridge described in Beckey's guide is not a popular route because of a reputation for very loose rock and the complexity of the approach. However, climbers already at Holden Village may prefer this approach. Refer to *Cascade Alpine Guide* for route details.

PRECAUTIONS
All precautions for Mount Maude apply equally to Mount Fernow. Mount Fer- now's rock is very loose in places.

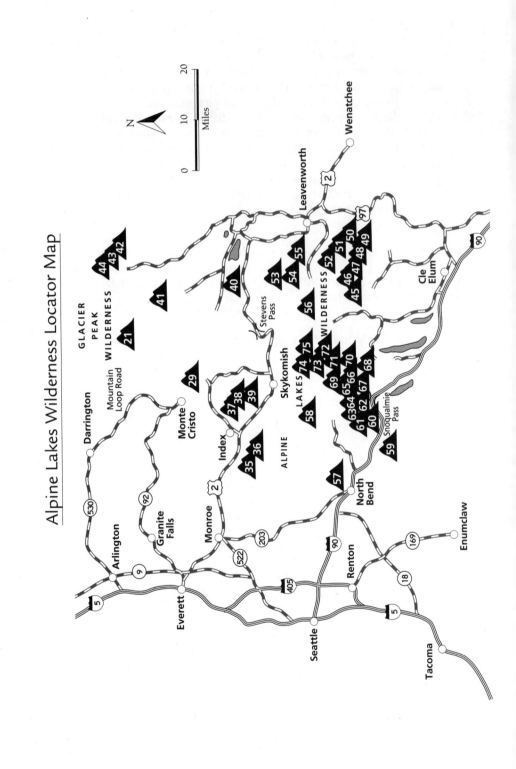

Alpine Lakes Wilderness Locator Map

Alpine Lakes Wilderness

The Alpine Lakes Wilderness is one of the most rugged areas of the Cascade Range. Although in terms of sheer relief it does not quite compare with the North Cascades, it is still a sublime region of deep, glacier-carved valleys, pristine subalpine meadows, and craggy peaks rising to over 9,000 feet. It is also an accessible wilderness. Most of the trails of the Alpine Lakes Wilderness are within a one- or two-hour drive for a majority of Washington state's population, making it one of the most crowded "wilderness" areas in the state.

The peaks of the Alpine Lakes Wilderness present varied challenges. The several summits in the Snoqualmie Pass and Index areas provide accessible scrambling and technical rock routes, some of which can be climbed in half a day including driving time from Puget Sound. The Snoqualmie Crest Peaks provide more rugged and remote scrambling and technical climbing. The older Wenatchee Mountains provide high mountain rambling and some snow and rock scrambling. The Stuart Range is the climax of the Alpine Lakes Wilderness, a rugged ridge of craggy granite spires and walls hung with precipitous glaciers rising thousands of feet above the valley floor. The Stuart Range offers some of the best technical mountaineering in Washington, as well as some of the best alpine scrambling.

The Alpine Lakes Wilderness is encircled by two major highways, U.S. 2 and U.S. 97, and an interstate highway, I-5. All of the approach trails begin either from one of these highways or a Forest Service road. Most of the trailheads are well marked and easy to find. A Northwest Forest Pass is required to park at Forest Service trailheads. For more information, contact the Forest Service's North Bend, Cle Elum, Leavenworth, or Skykomish Ranger District Offices listed in Appendix C.

45. INGALLS PEAK

Elevation: 7,662 feet/2,336 meters
Route: South Ridge
Rating: Grade II, 5.2 to 5.6
Distance: 8 miles round trip
Elevation Gain: 3,400 feet
Time: 4 to 6 hours trailhead to summit
Maps: USGS Mount Stuart; Green Trails No. 209 (Mount Stuart)

ABOUT THE CLIMB

Ingalls Peak is a craggy mountain rising directly west of Ingalls Lake. Although Ingalls pales in comparison to its neighbor, Mount Stuart, it is a popular, accessible climb on good rock. Unlike Mount Stuart, Ingalls Peak is feasible as a day climb for a majority of climbers. However, many prefer a more alpine-style ascent and bivouac before making their ascent early the next morning.

Ingalls is a short but rugged ascent, even by its easiest route. Although only Class 4 to moderate Class 5 in difficulty, and only a few pitches in length, Ingalls

Aidan Haley

Colin Haley leading on the South Ridge, Ingalls Peak.

Ingalls Peak, Mount Stuart, and Sharps Peak

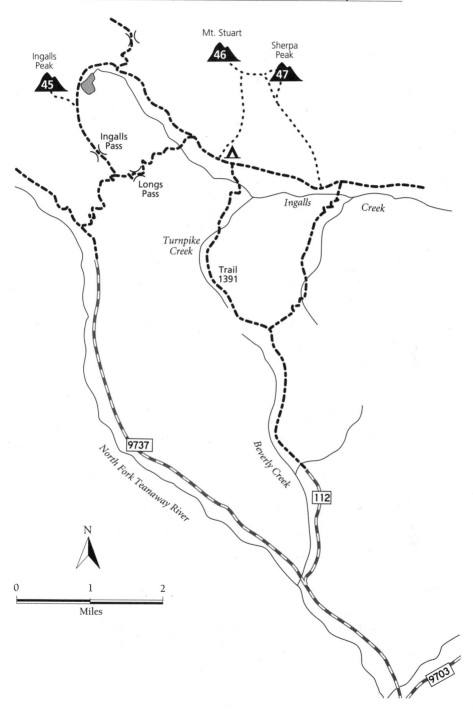

Ingalls Peak
45

Mt. Stuart
46

Sherpa Peak
47

Ingalls Pass

Longs Pass

Ingalls   *Creek*

Turnpike Creek

Trail 1391

North Fork Teanaway River

9737

Beverly Creek

112

9703

N

0   1   2
Miles

Ingalls Peak South Ridge

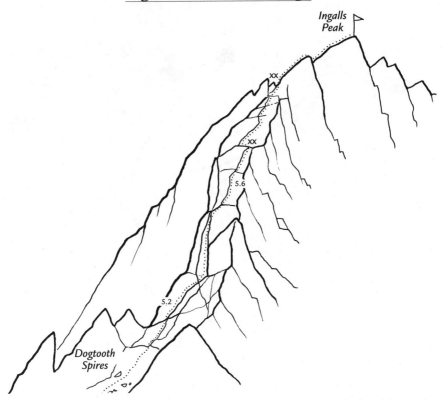

Peak's standard routes are serious climbing objectives and should not be attempted by anyone lacking alpine rock climbing experience. That said, an ascent of Ingalls Peak is more like cragging than alpine mountaineering. The popular route is short, accessible, and often crowded. Come on a weekday to avoid crowds, but even then, don't expect to have the mountain to yourself.

HOW TO GET THERE
This climb begins via Ingalls Lake Trail at the end of Teanaway Road north of Cle Elum. To reach the trailhead, drive Interstate 90 to exit 85, about 1 mile east of Cle Elum, then turn north on Washington Highway 970 and drive east toward U.S. Highway 97 for 6.8 miles. Turn left onto Teanaway Road (Forest Road 9737) and follow it about 23 miles to the Esmerelda trailhead at the road's end. A Northwest Forest Pass is required.

ROUTE DESCRIPTION
Hike 0.3 mile up Esmerelda Trail (FS Trail 1394) to a junction, and take a right on Ingalls Way Trail (FS Trail 1390). Continue 1.3 miles to the Longs Pass Trail junction, and take the left fork, following Lake Ingalls Trail another 3.0 miles over Ingalls Pass and down across a wide, rocky basin to Ingalls Lake. Leave the trail wherever and hike cross-country up the rocky basin toward the gap dividing the South and North peaks, to the base of the Dogtooth Spires, a cluster of rock

horns just up from the gap. In early season, a simple snow traverse from Head-light Creek Basin can be made to and up the basin to the spires, but be careful not to skirt too high to avoid downclimbing on difficult terrain to get around the South Peak. Skirt below the Dogtooth Spires to the base of the South Ridge, the popular summit route. Some climbers refer to this as the South Face route, understandable since it is more of a face climb than a ridge climb.

From the base of the spires, climb Class 3–4 gullies to a ledge. Climb cracks up the slabby orange ridge face for 2 or 3 pitches to the summit ridge, then scramble along the exposed ridge to the summit. There are several options, from 5.2 to 5.6. The crack system in the middle of the face is the popular route (5.6). An easier variation on the ridge to the right avoids the crux crack, but is a bit loose and uprotected. Bring a good selection of stoppers and cams from wired to 3 inches, and several slings.

To descend, rappel from anchors and slings directly down the ridge face. Two 60-meter rappels will reach the base of the route; a single rope will suffice but you have to make 3 to 5 rappels and do some downclimbing.

OPTIONS
The easiest route to the summit of Ingalls Peak is the Southwest Face, a Class 4 route angling left from the base of the Dogtooth Spires and ascending slabby rock to a gully and up to the summit. The South Peak, which is just barely lower than North Peak, is a much easier climb. From the Dogtooth Spires gap, scramble directly up the ridge to the summit. Expect Class 3 and some loose rock.

PRECAUTIONS
Although the South Ridge route is fairly solid, there is loose rock, especially on the approach and on the Southwest Face route. The South Ridge route may be very crowded. Expect delays and watch out for falling rock and dropped gear. There is reportedly a Class 3 scrambling descent, but it is hard to find and takes longer and it is not recommended.

46. MOUNT STUART

Elevation: 9,415 feet/2,870 meters
Route: Cascadian Couloir
Rating: Class 3
Distance: 13 miles round trip
Elevation Gain: 6,500 feet
Time: 8 to 10 hours trailhead to summit; best done as a two- or three-day trip
Maps: USGS Mount Stuart; Green Trails No. 209 (Mount Stuart) or 209S (The Enchantments)

ABOUT THE CLIMB
Mount Stuart, the highest summit of the Stuart Range and one of the dominant landmarks of the Cascade Range, is visible from nearly every high ridge and summit in the northeast and central Cascades. At 9,415 feet elevation, it is the seventh highest mountain in Washington state and the second highest non-volcanic peak next to 9,511-foot Bonanza Peak. As one of the few 9,000-foot

Mount Stuart and Sherpa Peak

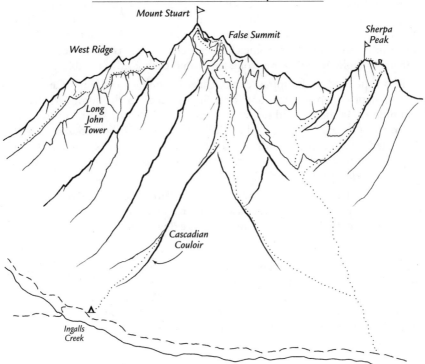

peaks in the Cascades with a non-technical scrambling route that does not require glacier travel and offering unsurpassed views of the northeastern Cascade Range, Mount Stuart is a very popular climb. The fact that Mount Stuart can be climbed in a single—albeit long—day only adds to its popularity.

The most popular and easiest route up Mount Stuart, the Cascadian Couloir, is a long snow and talus gully on the southeast flank of the mountain that has been described by some as a wonderful climb and by others as an ugly, dirty gully. It's a little of both. Down low, the couloir is sandy and gravelly; higher up, the going is open and alpine. In early season, it's largely a snow climb; by late season, it's mostly rock scrambling. Despite the fact that a one-day ascent is possible, most parties wisely make it a two-day climb with a base camp at Ingalls Creek or high bivouac in the upper basin.

There are a number of other popular routes up Mount Stuart, including the semi-classic West Ridge (III, 5.6) and the mega-classic North Ridge (III, 5.7 or IV, 5.10). Given that Mount Stuart is the highest peak in the eastern central Cascades, it has unmatched summit views of nearly the entire range, including Mount Adams, Mount Rainier, the Snoqualmie Crest peaks, Mount Daniel, Mount Hinman, the Wenatchee Mountains, the Dakobed Range, the Entiat Mountains, Mount Baker, Mount Shuksan, and Glacier Peak. You will see the peaks, lakes, and river valleys of the Stuart Range, and out across the Cle Elum Valley and Yakima River Valley.

Mount Stuart from Longs Pass. Cascadian Couloir is the gully in the lower right corner of the photo.

HOW TO GET THERE

This climb begins via Longs Pass Trail from the end of Teanaway Road north of Cle Elum. To reach the trailhead, drive Interstate 90 to exit 85, about 1 mile east of Cle Elum, then turn north on Washington Highway 970 and drive eastward toward U.S. Highway 97 for about 5 miles. Turn left onto Teanaway Road (Forest Road 9737) and follow it 23 miles to the parking area at the road's end. A Northwest Forest Pass is required.

ROUTE DESCRIPTION

Hike up Esmerelda Trail (Trail 1394) 0.3 mile to the first fork, then take a right up Ingalls Way Trail (Trail 1390). Climb 1.5 miles to a second junction, take the right fork, Longs Pass Trail, and climb another 0.5 mile to Longs Pass, elevation about 6,300 feet. Descend 1.1 miles northward from Longs Pass, down a steep, tricky rock slope or steep snow at first, then more gradually through forest into the valley bottom, and across a log over Ingalls Creek to Ingalls Creek Trail (Trail 1215). Turn right, following the trail downstream about 0.3 mile to a large meadow area on the left. There are several campsites here, popular with summit-bound climbers.

The climber's trail begins just beyond the clearing, a faint boot path angling up and left (northeast) through the meadows. Ascend meadow slopes at first, then a brushy path into the maw of the Cascadian Couloir, the obvious big gully directly above. Ascend the couloir, clambering over boulders and blocks of various sizes, and what's left of the winter snowpack. The couloir is narrow at the bottom but widens higher up. At the top of the couloir, a granite headwall and cliffs force the route left, up and over a rocky ridge, into a talus basin high on the east shoulder of Mount Stuart. There are several options here. The most direct route is to continue climbing talus or snow to the notch at the head of the basin, just east of the false summit. This is a great spot to take a break and enjoy excellent views in all directions.

From the notch, or just below, traverse left toward the false summit across granite blocks and up a steep snowfield to a ridge. The snowfield lingers through summer during years of heavy snowfall. From the ridge, there may be a confusing assortment of cairns appearing to mark several possible routes. There are two standard variations here, a low route and a high route. The low route has the least exposure; it traverses down 100 feet or so following cairns, then skirts a steep cliff band and passes through some blocks, including a tunnel between three large blocks leaning on each other. Finish with a straightforward scramble directly to the summit ridge. The high route is steeper with more exposed scrambling. The final climb to the summit is a scramble up a steeply angled face via large, weathered cracks. To descend, downclimb the route.

OPTIONS

There are numerous variations of this route. Among the more popular is the broad gully immediately right of the Cascadian Couloir, which leads directly up talus and snow slopes to the upper basin above Cascadian Couloir, essentially bypassing the couloir altogether. The next gully to the east leads up to the base of Sherpa Peak, where a traverse over an intervening ridge gains the upper basin. These approaches are recommended as early season alternatives when snow lingers in the Cascadian Couloir, or for an ascent of Sherpa Peak.

For those seeking a more technical route to the summit, the West Ridge ♦ (III, 5.4–5.6) is a long but moderate classic consisting of mostly Class 2–3 scrambling with only a few brief Class 4–5 pitches. The classic alpine route up Mount Stuart is the North Ridge (III, 5.7 or IV, 5.10), one of the entries popularized by Steve Roper and Alan Steck in *Fifty Classic Climbs in North America*. This route is more than adequately covered by several other guidebooks. For route information, refer to *Fifty Classic Climbs in North America*, *Selected Climbs in the Cascade Range*, or *Cascade Alpine Guide*.

PRECAUTIONS

Lack of water is the number one complaint on this climb. This is a long, strenuous, and often hot climb. Be sure to carry plenty of water because the mountain is dry by late season. On the ascent, some climbers leave Ingalls Creek Trail too early and end up too far west in Ulrich's Couloir or a dead-end gully in between. On the descent, be sure to descend Cascadian Couloir rather than one of the steeper, more difficult gullies farther west. The couloir and upper basin headwall are avalanche prone in winter and spring. Steep snow lingers through summer some years and may be undermined later in the season. Like other high summits east of the Cascade crest, afternoon thunderstorms are common, especially during the summer months. The route is exposed to rockfall, particularly in the couloirs and when others are climbing above. Be careful not to knock loose rocks on other climbers. Watch out for shifting talus and loose blocks. Don't underestimate the climb or overestimate the party's ability to get up and down in a day. Climbing too fast could result in symptoms of altitude sickness.

47. SHERPA PEAK

Elevation: 8,605 feet/2,623 meters
Route: West Ridge
Rating: Grade II, 5.5
Distance: 18 miles round trip
Elevation Gain: 5,600 feet
Time: 8 to 10 hours to summit
Maps: USGS Mount Stuart; Green Trails No. 209 (Mount Stuart) or 209S (The Enchantments)

ABOUT THE CLIMB

Sherpa Peak is to Mount Stuart what Little Tahoma Peak is to Mount Rainier—a significant peak in its own right but deemed by many to be a mere satellite peak. Although the peak seems a rocky nub next to Mount Stuart, at least as viewed from the south; from the north Sherpa stands out as a very distinct alpine peak. It is not nearly as popular as Mount Stuart, for obvious reasons; however, it is a pleasant, interesting climb, despite a long, tedious approach. The easiest route is the South Face, a modest Class 3–4 climb, but the better option is the West Ridge, a 400-foot Class 5 alpine rock route. An ascent of Sherpa Peak can be combined with Mount Stuart via a relatively simple traverse, although most parties are pressed for time and climb the higher peak only. If you climb light and bivouac in the upper basin, you can easily climb both Mount Stuart and Sherpa Peak in a two-day trip.

HOW TO GET THERE

Follow the directions for Mount Stuart to the trailhead for Ingalls Creek and Longs Pass at the end of Teanaway Road. A Northwest Forest Pass is required.

ROUTE DESCRIPTION

Approach via Longs Pass Trail (Trail 1229) as for Mount Stuart to the junction with Ingalls Creek Trail. Turn right and follow Ingalls Creek Trail (Trail 1215) downstream about 1 mile to a large open area below the Stuart-Sherpa col. A climber's trail leads up through the trees on the west side of this opening. If you get to the junction with Turnpike Trail, you have gone too far. An option is to hike Beverly-Turnpike Trail (Trail 1391) to the junction with Ingalls Creek Trail, then head upstream about 0.2 mile to the open area described above.

The best route up Sherpa Peak is the West Ridge (II, 5.5), an enjoyable alpine rock climb of about 400 feet from the saddle directly west of the summit. Ascend the climber's trail up the broad drainage. After gaining about 500 feet, the trail traverses to the east side of the drainage and proceeds over a ridge into the next drainage. From here, ascend directly toward the Stuart-Sherpa col. Climb straight to the first notch west of the Sherpa summit formation, scrambling over large boulders. In early season, a steep snow/ice slope just below the notch may present a problem for those without an ice ax and crampons. From the notch, ascend Class 4–5 rock on or near the ridge crest. The route is varied, offering several options. A crux gully or jam crack high on the ridge leads to within about

100 feet of the summit, from where a final easier pitch gains the top. Bring a light rack including cams to 3 inches and a few long slings.

Descend via rappel and downclimbing back to the notch, then scramble back down the way you came. Double ropes are recommended for the descent.

OPTIONS

The easiest route up Sherpa Peak is the South Face (II, 5.0), climbing the left-slanting gully to below the balanced rock, then up Class 4–5 rock to the summit. It is feasible to enchain Sherpa Peak and Mount Stuart, which is best done from a base camp at Ingalls Creek or a high bivouac en route. There are other routes up the north face of Sherpa Peak that are popular with serious alpine rock climbers and mountaineers. Refer to *Cascade Alpine Guide* for route details.

PRECAUTIONS

Nearly all precautions listed for Mount Stuart apply to Sherpa Peak. The upper basin headwalls and gullies are avalanche prone in winter and spring. The slabs below the Stuart-Sherpa col present a serious hazard when icy or snow-covered. These "death slabs" would be very hazardous to traverse in slippery conditions.

48. COLCHUCK PEAK

Elevation: 8,705 feet/2,654 meters
Route: Colchuck Glacier
Rating: Class 2–3; Grade I glacier
Distance: 14 miles round trip
Elevation Gain: 5,400 feet
Time: 5 to 6 hours trailhead to summit
Maps: Green Trails No. 209S (The Enchantments)

ABOUT THE CLIMB

Colchuck Peak is one of the major summits in the Stuart Range. Like other summits of the range, its south slopes are rocky but relatively gentle, presenting little technical difficulty, in contrast to its northern exposure, which rises in a rocky rampart nearly 3,000 feet high. Colchuck Peak is a very popular climb, owing to its craggy alpine nature and commanding summit views. There are several scrambling routes to its summit, only one of which is truly popular, and several alpine rock routes.

The Colchuck Glacier route is the most popular, and for good reason. The route combines a reasonable approach hike, a steep glacier climb, and alpine rock scrambling in an exceptional setting with rock walls rising thousands of feet on either side. Another good route, less popular but deserving more attention, is the North Buttress, a long, mostly simple alpine rock climb directly up the prominent buttress rising above Colchuck Lake. Summit views are exceptional and include an intimate perspective of the north face of Dragontail Peak and an airy view of Colchuck Lake, eastward along the Stuart Range and across the Wenatchee Mountains, with Mount Rainier and Glacier Peak looming in the distance. It is often enchained with Dragontail Peak in a one- or two-day ascent.

Norm Buckley

Mount Stuart and Colchuck Peak (foreground) from Dragontail Peak.

Enchantment Lakes Area

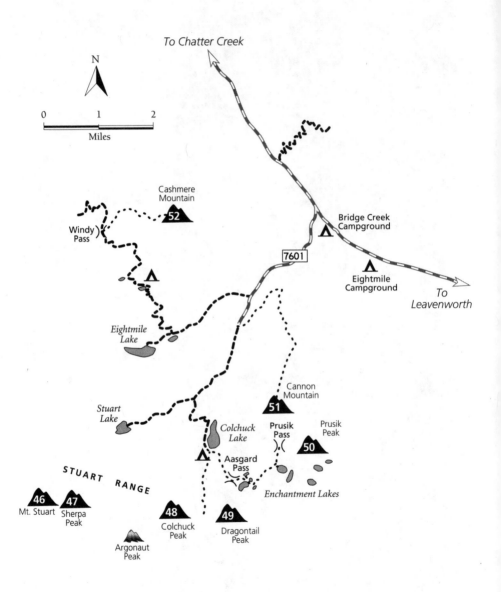

To Chatter Creek

N

0   1   2
Miles

Cashmere
Mountain

52

Windy
Pass

Bridge Creek
Campground

7601

Eightmile
Campground

To
Leavenworth

Eightmile
Lake

Cannon
Mountain

51

Stuart
Lake

Colchuck
Lake

Prusik
Pass

Prusik
Peak

50

Aasgard
Pass

Enchantment Lakes

STUART RANGE

46   47
Mt. Stuart Sherpa
Peak

Argonaut
Peak

48
Colchuck
Peak

49
Dragontail
Peak

HOW TO GET THERE

This climb begins via Mountaineer Creek Trail just south of Icicle River Road outside of Leavenworth. From U.S. Highway 2 at the west edge of the town of Leavenworth, turn onto Icicle River Road and follow it 8.3 miles to Bridge Creek Campground. Turn left and follow Forest Road 7601 for 3.9 miles to its end at Mountaineer Creek trailhead. A Northwest Forest Pass is required. If you are camping in this area, a permit is required; contact the Leavenworth Ranger Station for information.

ROUTE DESCRIPTION

The most direct and popular route up Colchuck Peak is via Colchuck Glacier and Colchuck Col, the broad saddle dividing Colchuck Peak and Dragontail Peak.

Hike up Mountaineer Creek Trail (Trail 1599) 2.4 miles to its junction with Colchuck Lake Trail (Trail 1599.1), then follow that trail another 2.1 miles to the southern shore of Colchuck Lake, elevation 5,570 feet. From Colchuck Lake, scramble up the immense, broad talus and moraine slope to the terminus of the Colchuck Glacier, an icy remnant lying in the shady canyon between the great faces of Dragontail and Colchuck.

Don at least crampons and ice ax if not a rope for the moderately steep glacier ascent, which leads seemingly forever up the narrowing canyon between the towering walls of Dragontail Peak and Colchuck Peak. The eastern lobe of the glacier rarely shows crevasses, but a late-season bergschrund or moat may present an obstacle getting off the glacier. From the head of the glacier, ascend a steep rock or snow slope to the col, elevation 8,050 feet. From the col, scramble westward up the ridge directly to the summit of Colchuck Peak. The ridge traverse is fairly straightforward Class 2-3 scrambling. The ridge is rocky and very exposed on the north side, but less so on the south side, so stay to the left of the ridge crest where necessary to skirt around the most exposed, difficult sections of the ridge. To descend, downclimb the route.

OPTIONS

The North Buttress♦ (III, Class 4-5.6) is an interesting, very alpine climb involving about 2,000 feet of blocky scrambling and easy climbing up to Class 5 in difficulty depending on the route taken.

Colchuck Peak and Dragontail Peak are often enchained in a single day or overnight with a bivouac. An excellent high traverse begins from a base camp at Colchuck Lake, ascends the North Buttress of Colchuck Peak, traverses Colchuck Col to Dragontail Peak, and descends via Aasgard Pass, or crosses over Prusik Pass and traverses out over Cannon Mountain back to the trailhead. Climbers attempting this traverse as an overnight trip should be sure they have the correct permit for their intended bivy site.

PRECAUTIONS

Because much of the Colchuck Glacier route is up a steep rock-walled canyon, there is an unavoidable risk of random rockfall from the cliffs above. Rockfall hazard is amplified when there are climbers on the cliffs above the glacier. High avalanche hazard exists in winter and early season, especially on the slopes above

Colchuck Peak and Dragontail Peak

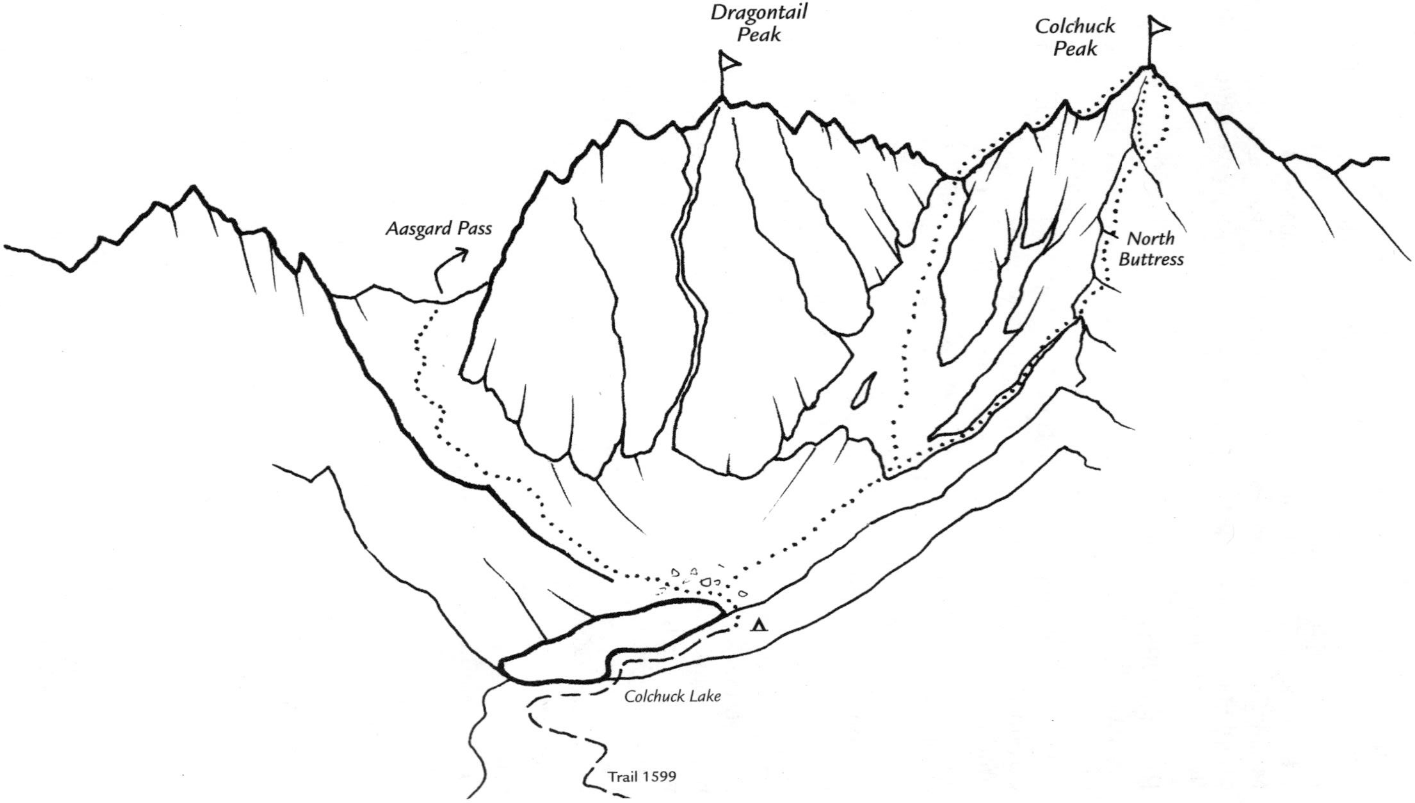

Colchuck
Peak

North
Buttress

Dragontail
Peak

Aasgard Pass

Colchuck Lake

Trail 1599

Colchuck Lake and on the glacier. Beware of shifting talus and loose rocks on the moraine slopes leading up to the glacier. Because part of the route ascends a glacier, bring a rope, crampons, and ice ax. The glacier is fairly steep and almost always icy. Crevasses rarely show on the eastern lobe of the glacier, but a late-season bergschrund or moat may be problematic. Roping up is recommended on glaciers, although this one is frequently climbed unroped.

An overnight permit is required for camping in this area between June 15th and October 15th. Refer to the section "Enchantment Basin Permits" of Appendix B, and call the Leavenworth Ranger District Office for current permit information.

49. DRAGONTAIL PEAK

Elevation: 8,840 feet/2,695 meters
Route: East Ridge via Aasgard Pass
Rating: Class 2–3; Grade I glacier
Distance: 14 miles round trip
Elevation Gain: 5,500 feet
Time: 5 to 7 hours trailhead to summit
Maps: Green Trails No. 209S (The Enchantments)

ABOUT THE CLIMB

Despite an unassuming presence from Ingalls Creek and the Enchantment Lakes, Dragontail Peak is one of the most impressive peaks of the Stuart Range, at least when viewed from the north. From here, you behold its inspiring north face, a steep, 3,300-foot high rock wall broken only by a few couloirs, ledges, and crack systems. There are some impressive Grade III, IV, and V routes here, from 5.7 to 5.11 in difficulty, featuring multiple pitches of exposed rock, mixed rock and ice, or just snow and ice, depending on season and conditions. But Dragontail is not solely the domain of hard-core climbers; it has two moderate scrambling routes to its summit. It is a feasible one-day climb but is often done as part of an extended trip to the Enchantment Lakes. Summit views include the Enchantment Peaks, Enchantment Lakes, and the Stuart Range; Mount Rainier, and Mount Adams; north to Glacier Peak, Mount Baker, and the Entiat Mountains; and an airy view down the north face to Colchuck Lake.

HOW TO GET THERE

Follow the directions for Colchuck Peak up Icicle River Road to the Mountaineer Creek trailhead. A Northwest Forest Pass is required. To camp in this area, obtain a permit in advance from the Leavenworth Ranger Station.

ROUTE DESCRIPTION

The popular route up Dragontail Peak is the East Ridge, which is usually approached via Colchuck Lake and Aasgard Pass.

Hike up Mountaineer Creek Trail (Trail 1599) 2.4 miles to its junction with Colchuck Lake Trail (Trail 1599.1), then follow that trail another 2.1 miles to the southern shore of Colchuck Lake. From Colchuck Lake, hike through the big boulders and ascend the "trail" up steep talus and rock or snow slopes to the left

Dragontail Peak East Ridge

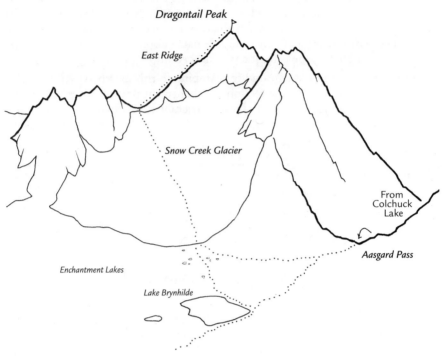

of Dragontail Peak to Aasgard Pass, the obvious broad gap immediately left of Dragontail's imposing northeast buttress. The route up Aasgard Pass is not technically difficult if you go the right way, but a routefinding error or slip at the wrong place could be disastrous. Ascend carefully, especially if snow lingers.

Once at the pass, descend briefly toward (but not all the way to) Brynhild Lake, the first big lake, called Isolation Lake on topo maps. Then, angle up and right (south) toward the westernmost lobe of Snow Creek Glacier, the large glacier remnants flanking Dragontail Peak on the northeast side. Ascend the snow slope to the broad saddle at its top, then scramble up talus or snow and easy rock along or just left (south) of the ridge leading directly to the summit. The ascent is very straightforward and enjoyable. To descend, downclimb the route.

OPTIONS

Another popular route up Dragontail Peak is via Colchuck Glacier, which is described under Colchuck Peak. From Colchuck Col, descend slightly on the south side and angle into and up a broad gully to a saddle. Cross over into Dragontail Creek Basin and ascend talus or snow slopes to the Snow Creek Glacier saddle described previously, then continue up the ridge to the summit. The traverse and descent from the upper saddle into Dragontail Creek Basin is steep and exposed snow or Class 3 rock scrambling. A traverse linking Dragontail Peak and Colchuck Peak is a popular enchainment, possible in a long day but more feasible as an overnight trip.

PRECAUTIONS

Although it follows a trail much of the way, the ascent to Aasgard Pass is steep and treacherous in places. Be very careful when ascending to the pass. The slopes leading up to Aasgard Pass are highly avalanche prone in winter and spring. There is risk of climber-caused and random rockfall as well. As always, roping up on glaciers is recommended, although most climbers don't bother because this "glacier" rarely if ever shows crevasses. You may encounter steep snow slopes below Aasgard Pass and on Snow Creek Glacier, especially in early season. Don't stray too far from the summit; it's a long way down the north face.

An overnight permit is required for camping in this area or at Colchuck Lake between June 15th and October 15th. Refer to the section "Enchantment Basin Permits" of Appendix B, and call the Leavenworth Ranger District Office for current permit information.

50. PRUSIK PEAK

Elevation: 8,000 feet/2,439 meters
Route: West Ridge
Rating: Grade III, 5.7
Distance: 18 miles round trip from Mountaineer trailhead
Elevation Gain: 4,700 feet from Mountaineer Creek trailhead to summit
Time: 8 to 10 hours from Mountaineer trailhead to summit
Maps: Green Trails No. 209S (The Enchantments)

ABOUT THE CLIMB

Although it is a mere spur ridge of Mount Temple, Prusik Peak is one of the most striking summits of the Stuart Range, at least when viewed from the proper perspective. It is also one of the most classic alpine rock climbs in the Cascade Range—and one of the most crowded. Prusik's stark white, angular granite faces and cathedral-like ridges rise abruptly from the Enchantment Plateau. It is truly one of the landmark peaks of the Alpine Lakes Wilderness. The peak graces the cover of hiking guides, photo books, and calendars. It is widely known for its airy alpine rock routes, particularly the West Ridge, the easiest summit route. Owing to this route's classic status, climbers flock here in the summer and fall, which can result in overcrowding on the West Ridge route. Prusik Peak is remote enough that a one-day ascent is not feasible for most, although very fit, obsessive climbers (and those who can't get an overnight permit) often try it anyway. Most prefer a two- or three-day ascent as part of a tour of the Enchantment Lakes. If you are lucky enough to get a permit, you might as well take your time and enjoy every aspect of the Enchantments.

HOW TO GET THERE

There are two popular approaches: Snow Lakes Trail or Colchuck Lake Trail and Aasgard Pass. The latter is the shortest approach, and consequently, the most popular, but it is more strenuous and hazardous especially in early season.

If approaching via Aasgard Pass, follow the directions for Colchuck Peak to the Mountaineer Creek trailhead, then hike up to Colchuck Lake and Aasgard

Colchuck Lake Area

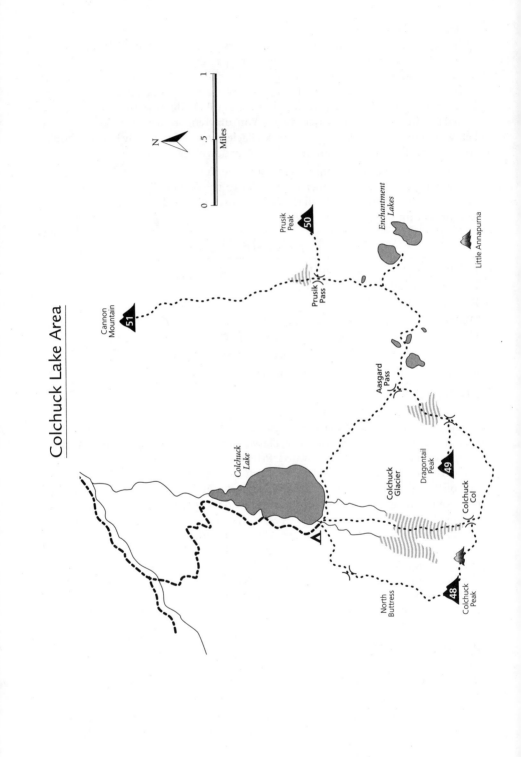

Cannon Mountain **51**

Prusik Peak **50**

Prusik Pass

Enchantment Lakes

Little Annapurna

Aasgard Pass

Colchuck Lake

Colchuck Glacier

Dragontail Peak **49**

Colchuck Col

North Buttress

Colchuck Peak **48**

N

0   .5   1
Miles

Pass as described under Dragontail Peak. From the pass, descend into the Enchantment Lakes and hike to Rune Lake (Inspiration Lake on topo maps), then follow a climber's trail northward to Prusik Pass. The "hike" to Prusik Pass via Aasgard Pass is about 9 miles and takes about five or six hours one way. Start very early if planning a one-day ascent from the trailhead.

To approach via the Snow Lakes Trail approach, park at the Snow Lakes trailhead (4.1 miles up Icicle River Road from Leavenworth) and hike Snow Lakes Trail (Trail 1553) about 6.5 miles to Snow Lakes, then continue another 4 miles through the Enchantment Lakes to Prusik Pass. This approach is a bit longer with additional elevation gain, but it is preferred by many as the safer, saner early season alternative when avalanche hazard makes the route up to Aasgard Pass too risky. Avoid Snow Lakes during "bug season."

A Northwest Forest Pass is required at each trailhead. These are high "car-prowl" trailheads, especially the Snow Creek trailhead, so leave nothing of value behind.

ROUTE DESCRIPTION

From Prusik Pass, follow the climber's trail to the right and traverse the ridge on the right (south) side until you reach the base of the West Ridge proper. Scramble up the first section of the ridge, staying fairly low and right, to reach the large balanced boulder marking the beginning of the actual climbing. Rope up and belay here, or about 20 feet above the boulder at the end of the Class 3 ledges and a small tree. The first 2 pitches (5.0–5.5) go up blocky ledges and slabby rock just below and left of the ridge crest. Follow the easiest line, which is well worn and lichen free from countless prior ascents. Belay wherever seems convenient; most parties reach the friction block in 2 pitches. From a sloping step at the base of the friction block, lead up and place protection. There is a fixed pin, but many climbers don't trust it and wisely back it up (small cams helpful). Balance your way up the slightly runout 5.7 friction moves 15 feet up and over the block, and belay as soon as convenient to avoid rope drag. Continue along the exposed ridge, then follow Class 3-4 cracks and ramps angling left, downward at first then slightly up, to a big ledge traversing below the summit block on the north side. Most parties reach the ledge in 3 pitches, although 4 pitches is a better idea to lessen rope drag.

Just across the ledge, locate an obvious short, clean jam crack in a left-facing dihedral. Climb it (5.6) to a ledge and mantel up, then lieback up a 5.6 flake to a higher ledge just below an obvious narrow chimney in the summit block. Many parties attempt the chimney on the left because it is the most obvious; however, it is much harder (5.8) than the 5.4 chimney reported in Beckey's guide. Supposedly there is a wider chimney hidden around the corner to the right. Some parties climb the crack, flake, and chimney as a single long pitch, but rope drag can be a problem. It is possible to break this section into shorter pitches. If you climb the harder chimney, it is easier sans pack and adequately protected with the right-sized gear (a #2 Camalot or equivalent).

Bring a moderate rack including cams up to 3 inches, mostly medium sizes. Double ropes are recommended for the rappel descent, although parties seem to

Prusik Peak West Ridge

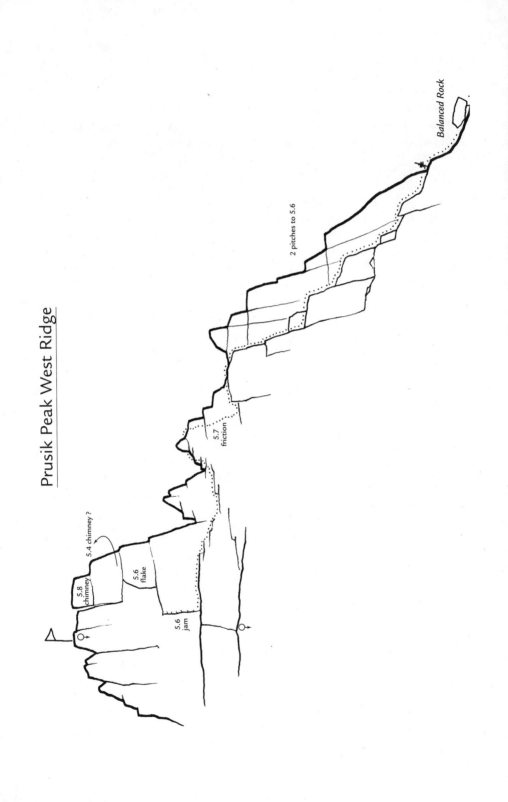

Balanced Rock

2 pitches to 5.6

5.7 friction

5.4 chimney ?

5.8 chimney

5.6 flake

5.6 jam

manage just fine with a single rope. Rock shoes recommended. To descend, find the anchor bolt about 30 feet east of the chimney and 10 feet west of the summit. Rappel to the big ledge, then continue rappelling down the north side until you can scramble back up to the beginning of the route. Double ropes reduce the number of rappels, but parties have reported that single-rope rappels and a little scrambling get you down the north side just fine. As an alternative, descending the route is feasible, although somewhat complicated and more time consuming, with a greater risk of jamming ropes and annoying other climbers.

OPTIONS
There are many other excellent routes up Prusik Peak. A few routes on the south face are among Washington's classic alpine rock climbs. Refer to *Cascade Alpine Guide* or *Selected Climbs in the Cascade Range* for details.

PRECAUTIONS
The West Ridge route is sometimes overcrowded. Rope drag is a major complaint on this route, especially on the pitch above the friction block and on the summit block. To avoid problems, climb short pitches and belay often, or bring several long slings. Check for snow at the base of the descent route, and consider carrying boots and ice ax up the climb because traversing steep snow slopes in rock shoes is no fun at best, dangerous at worst, and takes much, much longer. Climbing the summit chimney with a pack can be very awkward and difficult, so either haul packs or leave them below to be retrieved later.

Prusik Peak lies within the Enchantment Lakes Basin. An overnight permit is required for camping in this area between June 15th and October 15th. Refer to the section "Enchantment Basin Permits" in Appendix B, and call the Leavenworth Ranger District Office for current permit information.

51. CANNON MOUNTAIN

Elevation: 8,638 feet/2,633 meters
Route: Northwest Ridge
Rating: Class 2–3
Distance: 10 miles round trip
Elevation Gain: 5,300 feet
Time: 6 to 8 hours trailhead to summit
Maps: USGS Cashmere Mountain; Green Trails No. 209S (The Enchantments)

ABOUT THE CLIMB
Cannon Mountain is a big but relatively inconspicuous peak hidden at the western edge of the Lost World Plateau. Although it is one of the major peaks of the region, rising higher than its cross-canyon neighbor, Cashmere Mountain, it is concealed from nearly every lowland vantage. When you see it from the proper perspective, such as from Icicle Ridge or Lake Caroline Trail, it is quite a big mountain and somewhat appealing as a climbing objective; but by the easiest

Cannon Mountain, Northwest Ridge, and North Couloir

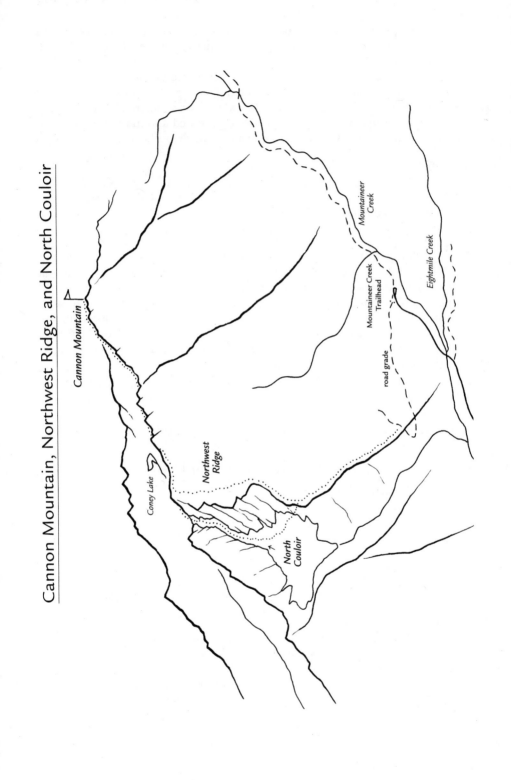

Cannon Mountain

Coney Lake

Northwest Ridge

North Couloir

road grade

Mountaineer Creek Trailhead

Mountaineer Creek

Eightmile Creek

route, it is a long, strenuous, brushy climb without an approach trail or a distinguished summit. Thus, Cannon Mountain is not especially popular and much less frequently climbed than many of its neighbors. Even on a sunny spring or summer weekend, you might have this mountain all to yourself.

The North Couloir is an enticing and enjoyable snow climb offering a good ski mountaineering descent for those so inclined. The real appeal of an ascent of Cannon Mountain is its remoteness—the solitude of traversing a high ridge and wandering the high basins and plateaus, including the Druid Plateau, which sits on Cannon's southeast shoulder. Cannon's summit provides excellent views of the Stuart Range, Enchantment Peaks, Cashmere Mountain, Glacier Peak, and other surrounding summits.

HOW TO GET THERE
Follow the directions for Colchuck Peak via Icicle River Road to the Mountaineer Creek trailhead. A Northwest Forest Pass is required.

ROUTE DESCRIPTION
There are several routes up Cannon Mountain, each having advantages and disadvantages. The route described is the Northwest Ridge, which is the least complicated route but not necessarily any easier or faster than other possible summit routes. It is not nearly as attractive or alpine in nature as the North Couloir.

From Mountaineer Creek trailhead, follow the old gated logging spur road leading northeast along the brushy, fire-scarred slopes of Cannon Mountain. The road is overgrown in places but not too difficult to follow on foot. Hike the road about 2 miles to where it is washed out. Leave the road here and ascend directly up the steep ridge, following a faint boot path and gaining about 3,300 feet in 1.5 miles. The ridge slopes, which were burned bare by the 1994 fire, are very brushy in places. Start early or this portion of the route will be insufferably hot. The upper fire line is reached about 1,000 feet below the summit ridge; from here, climb more easily through open subalpine fir and pine slopes to the rocky summit ridge at about 7,900 feet elevation. Traverse the summit ridge just over 1 mile to the summit. The ridge is mostly rocky hiking with a few talus or snow traverses that skirt the rocky points closer to the summit on the east side. Alternatively, angle down talus or snow slopes to Coney Lake, then climb the basin headwall southwest of the lake via talus and snow.

To descend, either downclimb the route or descend a different route. A traverse over Cannon Mountain, Prusik Pass, and Aasgard Pass makes for an interesting loop.

OPTIONS
A popular variation is the North Couloir, ascending the obvious broad couloir just below the north end of the summit ridge. The couloir provides a long, moderately steep early season snow route to the summit ridge. This route is not quite as direct as the ridge, but it is much more sporting and alpine in nature, and allows you to bypass much of the brush that makes the Northwest Ridge unpopular. Another feasible but long route is from the Enchantment Lakes via Prusik Pass.

PRECAUTIONS

The 1994 fire left countless burned trees and dead snags on the mountain's lower slopes that pose an obvious hazard, but also some unseen hazards. Be very careful while ascending the burned slopes. Expect some rockfall exposure while skirting rocks on the summit ridge and in the North Couloir. In early season, you may encounter steep snow, especially in the North Couloir and on the passes if approaching via Prusik Pass. Although much of the route is relatively protected, avalanche danger may exist in winter and early season, particularly in gullies, on bare slopes, and along the North Couloir. Beware of cornices that may have formed on the summit ridge.

Cannon Mountain lies within the Enchantment Lakes Basin. An overnight permit is required for camping in this area between June 15th and October 15th. Refer to the section "Enchantment Basin Permits" in Appendix B, and call the Leavenworth Ranger District Office for current permit information.

52. CASHMERE MOUNTAIN

Elevation: 8,501 feet/2,591 meters
Route: West Ridge via Windy Pass
Rating: Class 3
Distance: 17 miles round trip
Elevation Gain: 5,300 feet
Time: 6 to 8 hours trailhead to summit
Maps: USGS Cashmere Mountain; Green Trails No. 209S (The Enchantments)

ABOUT THE CLIMB

Cashmere Mountain is a great pyramid-shaped peak rising up from Icicle Creek Canyon about 10 miles west of Leavenworth. It is one of the most prominent peaks of the Cascades' eastern front range, easily seen as you drive westward on U.S. Highway 2 from Wenatchee. It is prominently visible from the town of Cashmere, hence its name. It is a fairly popular climb, mostly due to its outstanding relief, proximity to Leavenworth, and easy accessibility via a popular hiking trail that leads to within 1.5 miles and 1,300 vertical feet of its summit. At 8,501 feet elevation, it rivals the peaks of the nearby Stuart Range in elevation and views. Although the trail is a bit long for casual scramblers, and climbers tend to have their sights set on the more rugged peaks of the Stuart Range, Cashmere Mountain is an enjoyable and worthwhile climb. It is a long day climb but reasonable with a base camp at one of the lakes along the approach trail. Summit views are outstanding; a full panorama of peaks including close views of the Stuart Range, as well as the Snoqualmie Crest peaks, Mount Daniel, the Monte Cristo peaks, Glacier Peak, and the Entiat Mountains.

HOW TO GET THERE

This climb begins via Eightmile Creek Trail, just south of Icicle River Road outside of Leavenworth. From U.S. Highway 2 at Icicle Junction at the west edge of Leavenworth, turn onto Icicle River Road and follow it 8.3 miles to Bridge Creek Campground. Turn left and follow Forest Road 7601 about 3 miles to the Eightmile Creek trailhead. There is limited parking. Do not block the road or the gate. A Northwest Forest Pass is required.

Cashmere Mountain

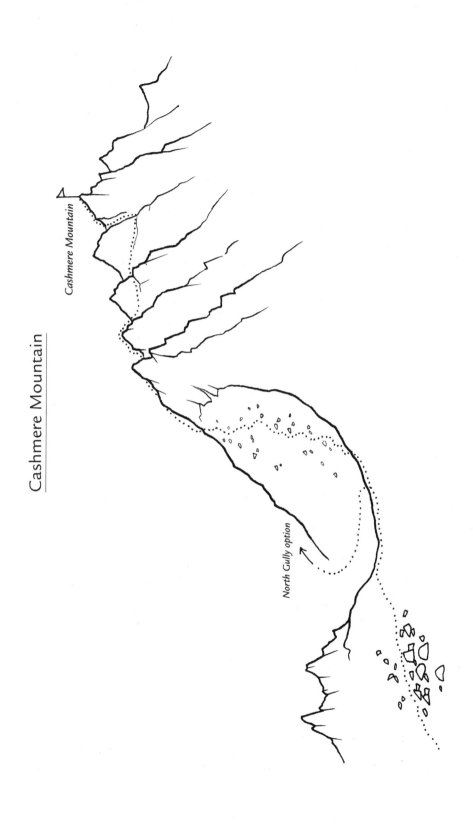

Cashmere Mountain

North Gully option

Cashmere Mountain from Windy Pass Trail.

ROUTE DESCRIPTION

Hike Eightmile Creek Trail (Trail 1552) about 2.5 miles to Little Eightmile Lake and the junction with Lake Caroline Trail (Trail 1554). Take a right and continue on Lake Caroline Trail another 2.3 steep miles up switchbacks through fire-scarred forest, go up flowery meadow slopes and down over a divide to Lake Caroline, and then travel another easy 0.6 mile to Little Caroline Lake. For those making a multi-day ascent, there are several good campsites at Lake Caroline near the outlet stream, as well as a couple of campsites at Little Caroline Lake. There is a pit toilet at Lake Caroline, the last such facilities available on the trail. From Little Caroline Lake, continue on the trail another 1.5 miles to its high point at Windy Pass, elevation 7,220 feet.

Leave the trail at Windy Pass and hike up the rocky ridge crest, northward at first then curving eastward toward the summit rocks of Cashmere Mountain. Follow a faint climber's trail for much of the way up the ridge. Bypass a few craggy ridge points on the southeast side and scramble across talus slopes and through a big talus field, then descend to the broad 7,990-foot saddle just west of the summit rocks. Snow patches may linger into summer. From the saddle, follow a faint climber's trail up the gentle rocky shoulder directly toward the first peak of the summit ridge. When things get difficult, traverse left to easier ground, staying below the steep, loose gullies, to reach the north side of the first ridge peak where broken rock leads to the first notch in the summit ridge. From the first notch, scramble directly over or around the second peak, then skirt around the third on the south side via broken ledges and slabs. Finish up a loose gully to the notch just west of the summit block where a brief rock scramble gains the exposed summit block. There are many possible route variations to the summit. Most of the route described is Class 2 scrambling with a bit of Class 3 along the summit crest, but it is easy to get off route, where you may encounter exposed, loose Class 4–5 rock. To descend, downclimb the route.

OPTIONS

An often-climbed summit variation descends northward from the 7,990-foot saddle, traverses snowfields around to the north side of the summit formation, and climbs a snow or scree gully directly to the notch west of the summit. This route is moderately steep but less exposed than the ridge route, although it still has loose rock. It is said to be a good early season route, assuming there is no avalanche danger.

PRECAUTIONS

The summit scramble is very exposed in places with abundant loose rock. It is easy to get off route onto loose, exposed Class 4–5 rock. The southern slopes and northern gullies are avalanche prone. Beware of cornices on the ridge crests. The upper mountain may be dry by late season; bring plenty of water.

53. BIG CHIWAUKUM

Elevation: 8,081 feet/2,463 meters
Route: Northwest Ridge
Rating: Class 3–4
Distance: 17 miles round trip
Elevation Gain: 5,300 feet
Time: 6 to 8 hours trailhead to summit
Maps: USGS Chiwaukum Mountains; Green Trails No. 177 (Chiwaukum Mountains)

ABOUT THE CLIMB

Big Chiwaukum is the highest of the Chiwaukum Mountains, a subrange of modestly craggy older peaks lying on the high divide separating Icicle Creek and the Nason Creek–Wenatchee River drainage, including Snowgrass Mountain. The mountain forms a long north-south crest that rises just above 8,000 feet at its midpoint with a glacier remnant below its precipitous east face. Despite its size and elevation, Big Chiwaukum is an unassuming peak. Although visible from surrounding high ridges and summits, it does not stand out like other nearby peaks. Big Chiwaukum is hardly noticed with the giants of the Stuart Range jutting up so near to the south and literally overlooked in favor of the snowy volcanoes rising to the north. Perhaps that explains why only a handful of climbers reach its summit each year.

The mountain deserves to be more popular, not only because of its height and regional importance, but because it is fairly easy to approach and is an interesting, rocky scramble despite some tedious meadow hiking. It is a feasible spring climb from Frosty Pass as soon as the Icicle River Road is passable or via U.S. Highway 2 and Wildhorse Creek Trail, the shorter approach. The ascent is strenuous but rewarding with some loose rock scrambling on the summit ridge. Summit views include the Stuart Range, Mount Rainier, the Snoqualmie Crest and Monte Cristo peaks, Mount Daniel, Glacier Peak, the Dakobed Range, the Entiat Mountains, and Bonanza Peak.

HOW TO GET THERE

The fastest approach to Big Chiwaukum is via Whitepine Trail and Wildhorse Creek Trail from U.S. Highway 2 east of Stevens Pass. Drive U.S. Highway 2 and

Big Chiwaukum and Snowgrass Mountain

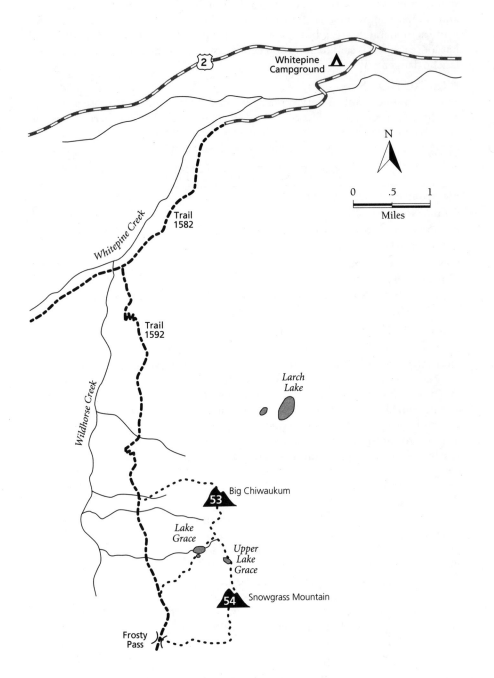

turn onto Whitepine Road about 14 miles east of Stevens Pass and 21 miles west of Leavenworth. Follow Whitepine Road (Forest Road 6950) for 3.8 miles to the trailhead at the road's end. A Northwest Forest Pass is required. Alternatively, approach via Frosty Pass Trail and Grace Lake as described under Snowgrass Mountain.

ROUTE DESCRIPTION

The route described is the Northwest Ridge, which is probably the fastest route to the summit. It is a long, strenuous meadow hike and rock scramble and feasible in a day for strong climbers who start early, although some prefer a two-day climb with a camp at Grace Lake.

Hike up Whitepine Trail (Trail 1582) about 2.3 miles to the junction with Wildhorse Trail. Follow Wildhorse Trail (Trail 1592) another 6.5 miles (mostly uphill) to the first stream crossing in the broad meadow basin directly west of the peak, elevation about 5,400 feet. By summer, this stream is the last reliable water source. About 30 feet past the stream, a way trail forks off to the left and leads up into the basin. Follow this trail briefly; when you lose the path amid game trails and brush, hike cross-country through the meadows toward the mountain. Several routes are feasible. A proven route climbs the northwest ridge, ascending left out of the basin and up the steep, flowery meadow ridge directly up toward the mountain's craggy northwest shoulder. At about 6,700 feet elevation, stay left of a subalpine fir thicket in an open, shallow gully to avoid a bushwhack through some bristly firs. At the head of the gully, where the going gets rocky, scramble right up loose scree ledges and dirt gullies, following goat trails, to gain the rocky ridge crest on the right. Continue up rocky meadow slopes just right of the craggy ridge crest for several hundred feet to a headwall below the northern peak of the summit ridge. A gully leads directly to the headwall at the north end of the summit ridge, a direct snow climb in early season but rocky and loose later on. A meadow ridge on the right side of this gully offers a feasible route as well.

Regardless of which route you take to get there, from the base of the headwall at a low band of orange-streaked rock, traverse right, scrambling across blocky ledges and gullies toward the summit pinnacle. You must cross two rock ridges. The first involves climbing a short rock step with a possible Class 5 move but not exposed. The second presents an imposing 40-foot slab, which may be passed by traversing low and climbing a short step to gain an easier gully. You can pass the second arete on the summit ridge via an interesting, exposed traverse on the east face. Once past these aretes, a rising traverse on loose rock leads to a sharp notch just north of the summit pinnacle, where a short rocky scramble gains the narrow, exposed summit. The upper ridge traverse is Class 2–3 scrambling with careful routefinding, but it could involve Class 4–5 rock if you don't follow the easiest route.

To descend, either downclimb the route or traverse off via the Southwest Slope route described under "Options." In early season, glissading down snow slopes and gullies can save considerable time, but be careful of sliding over a cliff or into rocks. When snow conditions are ripe, the northwest gully provides a 2,000-foot ski descent for experienced ski mountaineers.

Big Chiwaukum

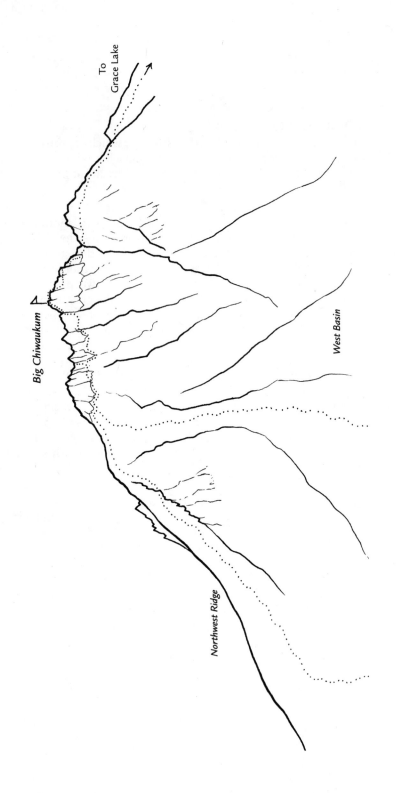

To
Grace Lake

Big Chiwaukum

West Basin

Northwest Ridge

Big Chiwaukum Summit Detail

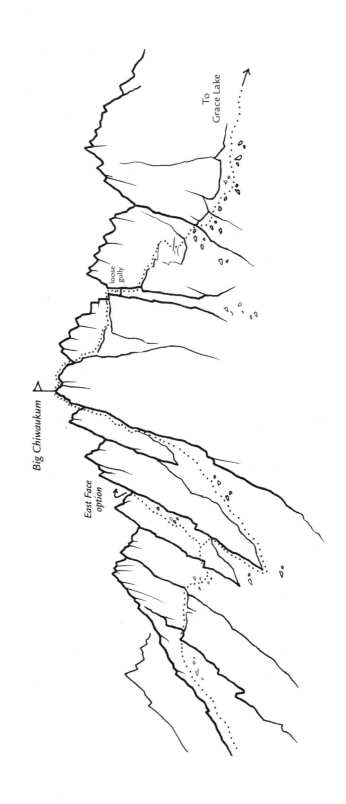

Big Chiwaukum

East Face
option

loose
gully

To
Grace Lake

OPTIONS

An easier but longer route up Big Chiwaukum is via the Southwest Slope from Lake Grace. Scramble from Grace Lake to the upper basin, then traverse talus and scree slopes northward below the summit ridge rocks, eventually crossing a wide, dirty scree gully within sight of the summit. The most direct route climbs a short Class 3 slab, then traverses ledges left to the upper right edge of a steep, loose gully. Enter the gully and climb to its top, where a short Class 3–4 step gains the summit rocks. The gully is steep, has loose rock, and is exposed at its top; only one person at a time should climb in the gully to minimize rockfall exposure. From the top of the gully, traverse ledges left and up to a short gully that leads to the notch just south of the summit, where easier, exposed scrambling completes the ascent.

An ascent of Snowgrass Mountain via the steep snowfield on the northeast face can be made from Upper Grace Lake as part of a traverse from Big Chiwaukum. Refer to the information under Snowgrass Mountain for route details.

PRECAUTIONS

The west and east side gullies and slopes are highly avalanche prone in winter and spring. Beware of cornices on the summit ridge. The summit ridge of Big Chiwaukum is craggy and has loose rock; the east face is very steep and exposed. Although the route is Class 3, a wrong turn could lead to Class 4–5 climbing on loose rock.

54. SNOWGRASS MOUNTAIN

Elevation: 7,993 feet/2,436 meters
Route: South Ridge via Frosty Pass
Rating: Class 2
Distance: 16 miles round trip
Elevation Gain: 5,200 feet
Time: 5 to 6 hours trailhead to summit
Maps: USGS Chiwaukum Mountains, Leavenworth; Green Trails No. 177 (Chiwaukum Mountains)

ABOUT THE CLIMB

Snowgrass Mountain is the second highest of the Chiwaukum Mountains, a mere 88 feet lower than its neighbor, Big Chiwaukum. The mountain is aptly named; winter and spring snows melt away each year to reveal grassy meadows on its broad south and west slopes. Although the peak is craggy on its north and east sides, Snowgrass is a simple rocky meadow hike via its southern ridge, which is frequently climbed by adventuresome hikers along Icicle Ridge Trail. Snowgrass is far more often climbed than Big Chiwaukum because of its relative accessibility from a popular hiking trail. Snowgrass Mountain is a good spring climb via the south ridge after avalanche danger has passed on the trail to Frosty Pass, which occurs at about the same time as Icicle Road is clear, by May most years. Summit views include the Stuart Range, Mount Rainier, the Snoqualmie Crest and Monte Cristo peaks, Mount Daniel, Glacier Peak, the Dakobed Range, the Entiat Mountains, and Bonanza Peak.

Snowgrass Mountain from Big Chiwaukum.

Snowgrass Mountain

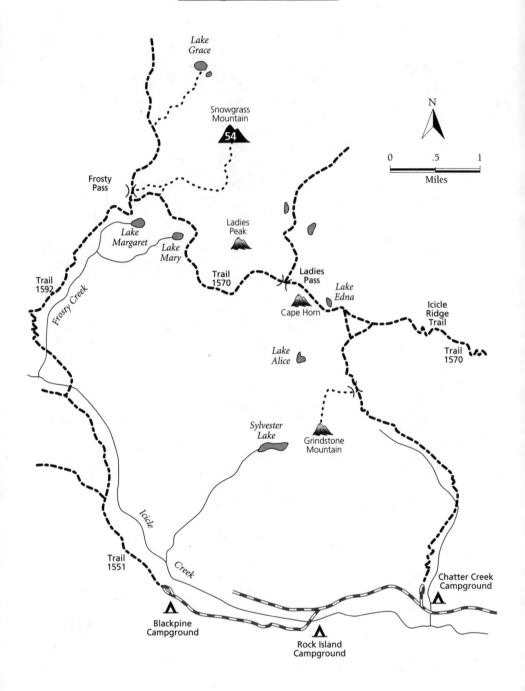

HOW TO GET THERE

Snowgrass Mountain is best approached via Frosty Pass Trail from Icicle River Road east of Leavenworth. From Leavenworth, drive Icicle River Road to the Icicle Creek trailhead at the road's end near Black Pine Campground. A Northwest Forest Pass is required.

ROUTE DESCRIPTION

Hike Icicle Creek Trail (Trail 1551) about 2.4 miles to its junction with Frosty Pass Trail (Trail 1592). Take the right fork, crossing Icicle Creek and climbing alongside Frosty Creek another 4.5 miles to Frosty Pass, elevation 5,680 feet. Leave the trail at Frosty Pass and ascend eastward up the grassy divide to the south ridge, then northward up the rocky ridge to the summit. The ridge can just as easily be approached via the meadow slopes above Lake Mary, or from the divide above Lake Mary on Icicle Ridge Trail. This is a moderately long, rocky ridge hike of about 1.5 miles, which should take little more than an hour one way from trail to summit for conditioned hikers and climbers. To descend, downclimb the route.

OPTIONS

The best route up Snowgrass Mountain, at least from a climber's perspective, is to ascend from Upper Lake Grace via the moraine and steep snowfield on the northeast face, where a short Class 3 scramble finishes up the ridge to the summit. This route, which follows an old glacier remnant, is best climbed in early season when snow fills the entire basin and allows easier climbing and a safer runout above the moraine. By late season, this is an icy slope with some nasty rocks at the bottom. To descend, traverse off via the south ridge.

PRECAUTIONS

Snowgrass Mountain is craggy and has abundant loose rock on its exposed ridges and faces, particularly on the north and east sides. Beware of winter and spring cornices on the ridge and summit. The northeast face snowfield is avalanche prone in winter and spring, and steep and icy in late season with nasty moraine rocks at the base of the slope. Self-arrest may be difficult when icy, so climb carefully.

55. BIG JIM MOUNTAIN

Elevation: 7,763 feet/2,366 meters
Route: North Slope/Ridge
Rating: Class 2
Distance: 12 miles round trip
Elevation Gain: 4,970 feet
Time: 5 to 6 hours trailhead to summit
Maps: USGS Big Jim Mountain; Green Trails No. 177 (Chiwaukum Mountains)

ABOUT THE CLIMB

Big Jim Mountain is one of the high points of Icicle Ridge. It is a commanding but gentle peak compared with its craggy neighbors across Icicle Creek Canyon

Big Jim Mountain

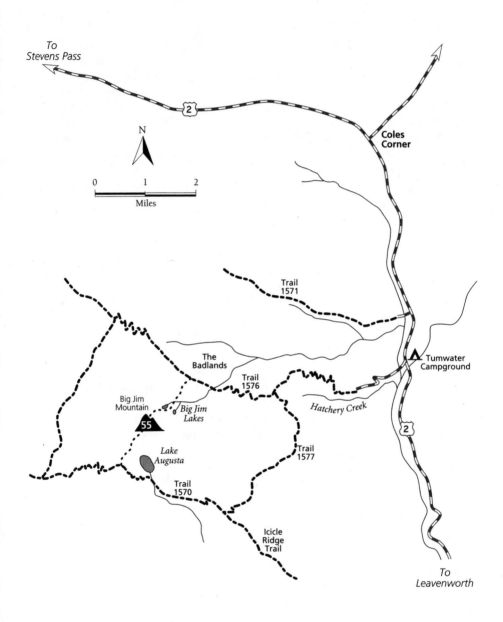

Big Jim Mountain

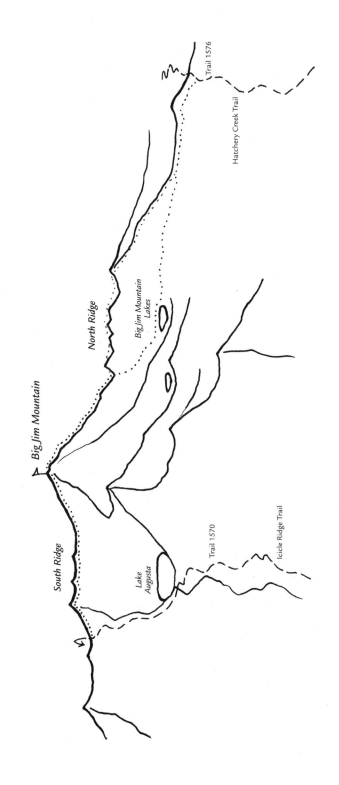

Trail 1576

Hatchery Creek Trail

North Ridge

Big Jim Mountain
Lakes

Big Jim Mountain

South Ridge

Lake
Augusta

Trail 1570

Icicle Ridge Trail

and offers a relatively easy scrambling ascent with few routefinding difficulties and great views. It is a popular winter and spring climb via its north slopes and ridges. Climbers prefer the route from Hatchery Creek Trail because of the shorter approach and easier access. Adventuresome hikers regularly make the ascent via the south ridge, a fairly short, rocky ridge hike from Icicle Ridge Trail. Summit views include the Stuart Range, Enchantment Peaks, Cashmere Mountain, Cannon Mountain, Glacier Peak, and Mount Baker.

HOW TO GET THERE
This climb begins via Hatchery Creek Trail from U.S. Highway 2 north of Leavenworth. Drive U.S. Highway 2 to Tumwater Campground, 8.7 miles from Leavenworth and 5.8 miles from Coles Corner. Find Hatchery Creek Road (Forest Road 7905) 0.1 mile south of the campground on the north side of the bridge. Follow Hatchery Creek Road for 2 miles to the trailhead. A Northwest Forest Pass is required. In winter and spring, the road may be impassable, forcing a longer approach hike from the highway.

ROUTE DESCRIPTION
The popular climbing route ascends Big Jim Mountain via the north slope from Hatchery Creek Trail. This route is most popular because it takes the least time and because it is the only route reported in *Cascade Alpine Guide*. Those willing to hike a bit farther will find a straightforward route via Lake Augusta and the south ridge.

Hike Hatchery Creek Trail (Trail 1576) about 2.2 miles to its junction with Trail 1577. Continue west 1.8 miles on Hatchery Creek Trail to an area marked on USGS maps as "The Badlands" at about 6,200 feet elevation. Leave the trail here and hike southwest through open meadows to Big Jim Mountain Lakes. From the lower lake, hike west up easy meadow and scree slopes to the north ridge, then scramble up the ridge to the summit. In winter and spring, most of the route is snow covered, allowing mostly easy snow climbing from the lakes to the summit. To descend, downclimb the route or descend the south ridge and loop out via Lake Augusta.

OPTIONS
The long north ridge can be traversed directly from the trail to the summit. It is a long traverse of about 3 miles, which consists of mostly ridge hiking, occasional easy rock scrambling, and some short Class 3 climbs to the summits of several minor peaks along the ridge. This route is said to be a very enjoyable two-day spring climb. An easier route ascends the south ridge from Icicle Creek Trail, beginning from the divide just west of Lake Augusta. This route has a longer approach but is the least complicated route up the mountain, involving about 1 mile of rocky ridge and meadow hiking with only about 400 feet elevation gain from trail to summit.

PRECAUTIONS
The steeper north and west slopes of Big Jim Mountain are avalanche prone in winter and spring. Beware of cornices on the ridges during winter and spring.

Granite Mountain from near Cathedral Pass.

56. GRANITE MOUNTAIN

Elevation: 7,144 feet/2,178 meters
Route: Robin Lakes Route
Rating: Class 2
Distance: 18 miles round trip
Elevation Gain: 3,900 feet
Time: 5 to 7 hours to summit
Maps: USGS The Cradle; Green Trails No. 176 (Stevens Pass)

ABOUT THE CLIMB

Granite Mountain is one of the highest peaks in the Wenatchee Mountains, a subrange of peaks along the divide between Deception Pass and the French Creek and Icicle Creek drainages. Given its height and central position, Granite Mountain offers nearly unsurpassed views of the Alpine Lakes Wilderness. Surrounding peaks stand out in stark relief: Mount Stuart, Ingalls Peak, Mount Rainier, Mount Adams, Lemah Peak, Chimney Rock, Mount Daniel, Mount Baker, and Glacier Peak. Alpine lakes dot the landscape on all sides. The relatively simple ascent and a strenuous approach hike make an excellent two-day climb with a bivouac at Tuck Lake or Robin Lake, although motivated scramblers can

Granite Mountain

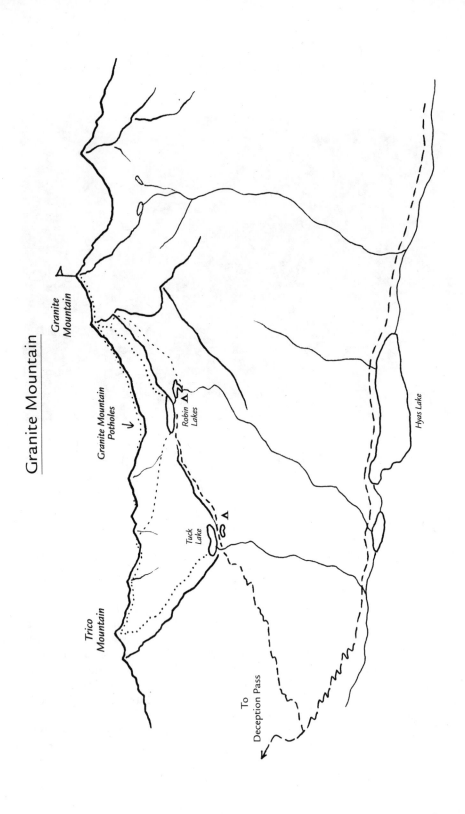

Granite Mountain

Granite Mountain Potholes

Trico Mountain

Robin Lakes

Tuck Lake

Hyas Lake

To Deception Pass

make the ascent in a reasonably long day. If you camp out at the lakes, you can climb both Granite Mountain and nearby Trico Mountain via a traverse of the ridge or the gentle slopes leading up from the lakes.

HOW TO GET THERE

This climb begins via Hyas Lake Trail at the upper end of Cle Elum River north of Roslyn. Drive Interstate 90 to exit 80 (Roslyn/Salmon La Sac) near Cle Elum, about 27 miles east of Snoqualmie Pass. Head north 2.8 miles to Washington Highway 903. Turn left and drive east on Washington Highway 903 through Roslyn and Ronald, turn up Cle Elum River Road (Forest Road 4330) along the east shore of Cle Elum Lake 16.5 miles to the pavement's end. The road forks here; take the right fork and continue another 12.4 miles to the Hyas Lake trailhead at this road's end. A Northwest Forest Pass is required. The road crosses two creeks, which are usually running high in spring and early summer, deterring some from driving all the way to the trailhead. A high-clearance vehicle is recommended. Otherwise park, ford the creeks, and walk or bike the last couple of miles to the trailhead.

ROUTE DESCRIPTION

Hike Hyas Lake Trail (Trail 1059) 4.4 miles to the junction with Tuck Lake Trail, just 0.3 mile short of Deception Pass. Tuck Lake Trail is a dusty, boot-beaten fire trail that climbs a rocky meadow slope for some 2 miles and gains 700 feet elevation. From Tuck Lake, continue up the "trail" another 1.7 miles, scrambling up roots and granite slabs to Robin Lakes, elevation 6,178 feet. There are several good campsites at and near Robin Lakes.

There are many possible routes from Robin Lakes to the summit. The most direct route contours along the upper lake's southern shore; climbs moderately steep heather and talus or snow slopes to a ridge crest; and ascends the ridge/slope to the summit. Alternatively, hike the rocky ridge from lower Robin Lakes and continue up easy connecting ridges to the summit. Expect to take about one hour from lakes to summit. To descend, downclimb the route or descend a different route back to Robin Lakes.

OPTIONS

Granite Mountain's south summit is not its highest but can be reached easily by traversing 0.6 mile from the summit along or just west of the ridge crest. Trico Mountain (6,640 feet) lies just north of Granite Mountain. It is a reasonable Class 2 scramble from Robin Lakes, often combined with an ascent of Granite Mountain with a base camp at the lakes or the more private Granite Mountain Potholes, located just over the ridge dividing Trico Mountain and Granite Mountain.

PRECAUTIONS

Beware of shifting talus. Watch out for mountain goats lingering about camp at Robin Lakes; they'll eat anything with salt, including boots and pack straps. Watch out for hunters in September and October; they tend to clog up the trailhead parking lots, among other things. Steep snow in early season; bring an ice ax.

Mount Si

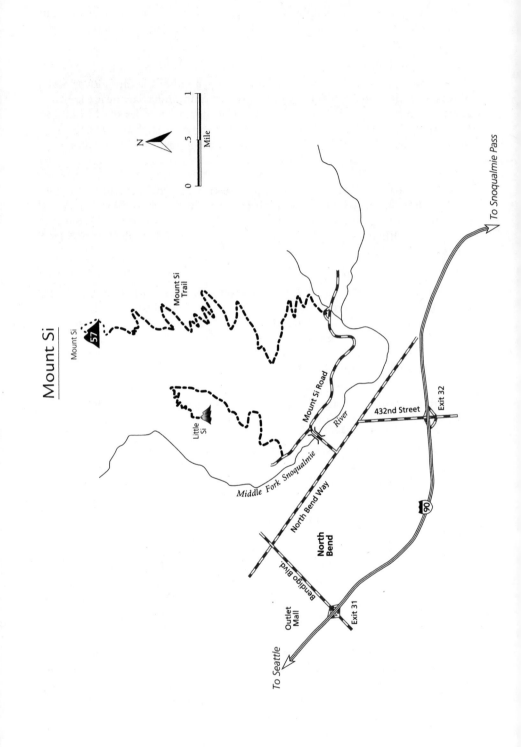

Mount Si from North Bend.

57. MOUNT SI

Elevation: 4,167 feet/1,270 meters
Route: Haystack Gully
Rating: Class 3
Distance: 9 miles round trip
Elevation Gain: 3,600 feet
Time: 3 to 4 hours to summit
Maps: USGS Mount Si; Green Trails No. 205 (Mount Si).

ABOUT THE CLIMB

Mount Si is the craggy peak rising to the northeast of the town of North Bend. It is one of Washington's most recognizable and most frequently climbed mountains due primarily to its proximity to the suburban sprawl of Puget Sound and because a popular trail leads to within a few hundred vertical feet of its summit. Hikers flock to Mount Si year round, as do mountaineers in training for bigger peaks. You'll encounter a wide assortment of hikers and climbers on the trail from families with dogs on weekend hikes to hard-core climbers shouldering 80-pound packs. The peak made a cameo appearance in the opening credits of the cult classic television show *Twin Peaks*. Mount Si's summit offers unsurpassed views of the Snoqualmie River Valley and the western front of the Cascade Range, with the skyscrapers and suburbs of Seattle and the Olympic Mountains spread out in the distance to the west, and Mount Rainier looming to the south. The final climb to the summit is rocky and exposed, but it is short and only briefly difficult, making it a very popular climb. The majority of trail hikers wisely stop at the trail's end, well short of the summit, where the views are almost as good.

Mount Si

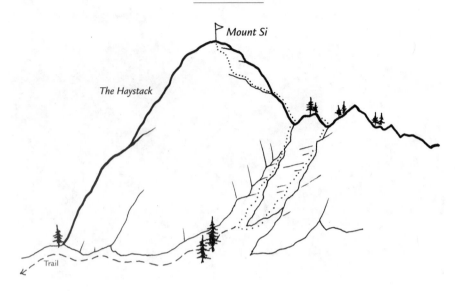

HOW TO GET THERE

This climb begins from the Mount Si trailhead just northeast of North Bend. Drive Interstate 90 to North Bend (exit 32). Once off the interstate, turn north on 432nd Street and follow it just over 0.5 mile to North Bend Way. Take a left and go 0.25 mile to Mount Si Road. Turn right and follow Mount Si Road 2.4 miles to the trailhead on the left. There is usually ample parking but the lot is often very crowded on sunny summer weekends. A Northwest Forest Pass is not required. This is a high "car-prowl" trailhead, so leave nothing of value behind.

ROUTE DESCRIPTION

The ascent begins with a 4-mile hike up Mount Si Trail, which climbs steeply up the heavily wooded south slope of Mount Si with countless switchbacks to a rocky shoulder at the foot of the summit rock formation, the Haystack. From the trail's end, traverse around the right side of the Haystack, following a well-established climber's trail into the woods and along the eastern base of the summit rocks to an obvious rocky gully on the northeast side. Scramble up the loose gully to either of two notches in the summit ridge, then traverse briefly southward on the ridge and ascend a short, exposed rock step to gain the summit. To descend, downclimb the gully and hike out via the trail.

OPTIONS

There's an old "trail" ascending from Little Si Trail directly up the southwest slope to the summit ridge. Old-timers know the way and can be seen occasionally appearing from seemingly out of nowhere. This would be a difficult route for those unfamiliar with the old trail, but it would definitely not be as crowded as the new trail.

PRECAUTIONS
Other climbers, many of whom are inexperienced day hikers, are the usual source of trouble on Mount Si. The summit scramble has loose rock, is significantly exposed, and is not recommended for inexperienced scramblers. Those planning a winter or spring ascent should bring ice ax and crampons at least; a rope and some gear (including a picket or two) are recommended because the gully is often icy and lacks a safe runout, and the summit rocks are treacherous when snow- or ice-covered. Be careful when hiking out on the trail, particularly after dark or in bad light; don't stray off the trail as other hikers have done.

58. BIG SNOW MOUNTAIN

Elevation: 6,680 feet/2,036 meters
Route: East Ridge via Hardscrabble Lakes
Rating: Class 2
Distance: 16 miles round trip
Elevation Gain: 5,300 feet
Time: 6 hours road to summit
Maps: USGS Big Snow Mountain; Green Trails No. 175 (Skykomish)

ABOUT THE CLIMB
Big Snow Mountain is one of the major peaks of the Snoqualmie River region of the western Cascade Range. Indeed, it is the highest mountain in the Alpine Lakes Wilderness west of the several 7,000-foot summits along the Snoqualmie Crest, including Chimney Rock, Summit Chief, Mount Daniel, and Mount Hinman. However, due to its relatively remote, central location, it is often overlooked by climbers and hardly known to anyone who doesn't hike or climb in the Alpine Lakes Wilderness. You can't see the mountain from any road. Although it isn't a big, rugged peak and doesn't catch the eye like Mount Thompson, Kaleetan Peak, or Mount Stuart, it has an undeniable prominence and attraction, especially when viewed from any nearby summit or high ridge.

Big Snow offers a good, basic scrambling ascent requiring some routefinding skill, with solitude and impressive views as rewards. It is a popular early season snow climb after the trail is mostly snow-free and avalanche danger has passed, and much of the climb is up moderate snow slopes. By late season, it is an enjoyable alpine scramble up steep, rocky heather slopes. Although it isn't highly visible, it has a great vantage point and provides good views of the Snoqualmie Pass peaks to the south, the Snoqualmie Crest peaks to the east, Index Peak and the Monte Cristo peaks to the north, and Glacier Peak, Mount Baker, Mount Stuart, and Mount Rainier in the distance.

HOW TO GET THERE
The most popular route, via Hardscrabble Lakes, begins about 0.5 mile west of the Dutch Miller trailhead. To get there, drive Interstate 90 to exit 34 in North Bend. Head north on 468th Avenue, past the service stations, for 0.6 mile to Middle Fork Road. Turn right and continue 0.9 mile to a fork. Stay right, taking Lake Dorothy Road (the higher road), and continue another 1.6 miles to the

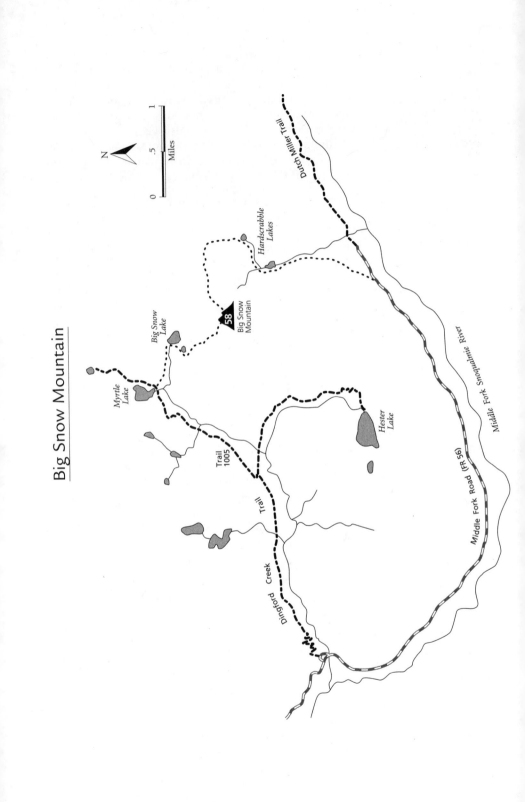

Big Snow Mountain

N

0   .5   1
Miles

Myrtle Lake

Big Snow Lake

Trail 1005

58 Big Snow Mountain

Hardscrabble Lakes

Dutch Miller Trail

Trail

Hester Lake

Dingford Creek

Middle Fork Road (FR 56)

Middle Fork Snoqualmie River

Big Snow Mountain from above Hardscrabble Lakes. The route climbs the talus gully on the right, then traverses the ridge to the summit.

pavement's end, where the road becomes Forest Road 56. Continue on Forest Road 56 another 9.5 miles, past the Middle Fork trailhead and across a bridge to the junction with Forest Road 56. Turn right staying on Forest Road 56 (may be incorrectly marked) and continue 13.2 rough miles, staying left at all forks, to the Dutch Miller trailhead at the road's end. Turn around and backtrack 0.5 mile to a turnout on the south side of the road. The turnout is large enough for several cars. A Northwest Forest Pass is not required. Although the trailhead is only about 25 miles from North Bend, the road is so bad that it takes about two hours. A high-clearance vehicle is recommended. Four-wheel drive is helpful.

ROUTE DESCRIPTION

The Northeast Shoulder via Hardscrabble Lakes is the best and most popular route. The route begins via an old logging road about 0.5 mile short of the Dutch Miller trailhead. Hike up the overgrown road for over 0.5 mile, then along a sometimes obvious, sometimes hard to follow, fishermen's trail to lower Hardscrabble Lake. Stay on the left side of Hardscrabble Creek and skirt the lower lake on the left side. Continue to upper Hardscrabble Lake, staying left of the creek and falls (take a more direct route when snow-covered). Routefinding is uncomplicated to upper Hardscrabble Lake. Most parties camp at the upper lake. From there, head northwest up forested slopes that open into talus and scree, then climb to and up the snow or talus gully to the notch just east of the northeast shoulder (Point 6,131 on USGS maps). Traverse northwest below Point 6,131 and follow the broad heather ridge to the summit. The route is simple and straightforward heather and rock scrambling with some steep snow in early season. One advantage to this route is the early views of the Snoqualmie Crest peaks, including Chimney Rock, Lemah Mountain, and others. To descend,

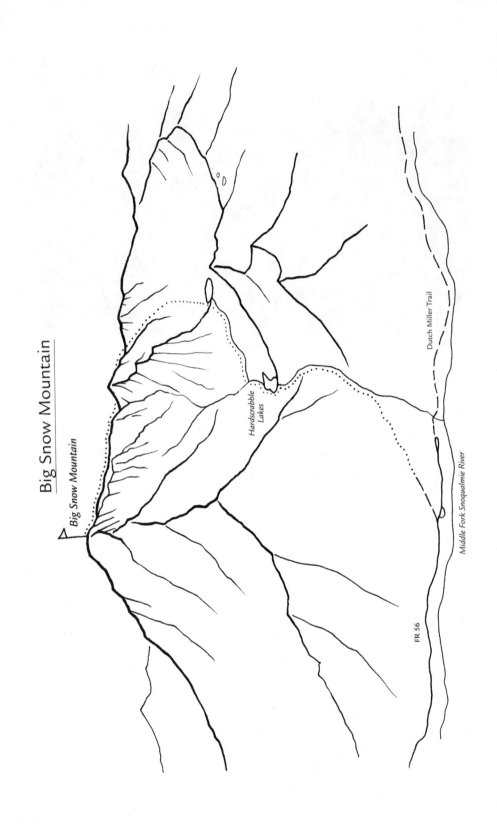

Big Snow Mountain

downclimb the route or traverse off via the Myrtle Lake route if transportation has been arranged.

OPTIONS

There are several other routes to the summit, none of which is particularly difficult. The Northwest Shoulder, commonly referred to as the Myrtle Lake route, is a popular option. It ascends from Myrtle Lake to Big Snow Lake and Snowflake Lake, then up heather and talus slopes to the summit.

PRECAUTIONS

Beware of avalanche danger in winter and early season, especially in the Hardscrabble Lakes gully and upper slopes. Beware of shifting talus and loose scree. The approach drive up Middle Fork Road is notoriously bad. Getting bumped around on the horrendously rocky road may result in whiplash or a concussion. It is only half jokingly recommended that a helmet be worn during the drive to the trailhead. Carrying a cell phone to call for assistance is recommended, although you might not get a signal in the valley.

59. McCLELLAN BUTTE

Elevation: 5,162 feet/1,573 meters
Route: South Ridge via McClellan Butte Trail
Rating: Class 2
Distance: 9 miles round trip
Elevation Gain: 3,700 feet
Time: 3 hours trailhead to summit
Maps: USGS Bandera; Green Trails No. 206 (Bandera)

ABOUT THE CLIMB

McClellan Butte is the prominent forested horn rising dramatically from the Snoqualmie River Valley about 8 miles east of North Bend. As you drive past it on Interstate 90, foreshortening makes the summit seem much closer and more precipitous than it really is. A popular hiking trail climbs 4.6 miles to the summit ridge, then a short scramble leads to the summit. Although guidebooks advise hikers to leave the summit for experienced climbers, hikers routinely ignore such advice and scramble on up to the top. The summit view is a sufficient lure, apparently, despite the fact that much of the view is of clearcut slopes to the south. Fortunately, Mount Rainier rises magnificently above and beyond the carnage, and the peaks of the Alpine Lakes Wilderness dominate the northeastern skyline. On a clear day, you may see the skyscrapers of downtown Seattle and the Olympic Mountains farther west.

HOW TO GET THERE

This climb is approached via Tinkham Road just east of North Bend off Interstate 90. Drive Interstate 90 to Tinkham (exit 42) about 8 miles east of North Bend and 10 miles west of Snoqualmie Pass. Turn south and travel 0.3 mile to the turnoff for the trailhead on the right, then continue another 0.2 mile to the trailhead. A Northwest Forest Pass is required. This is a high "car-prowl" trailhead, so leave nothing of value behind.

McClellan Butte

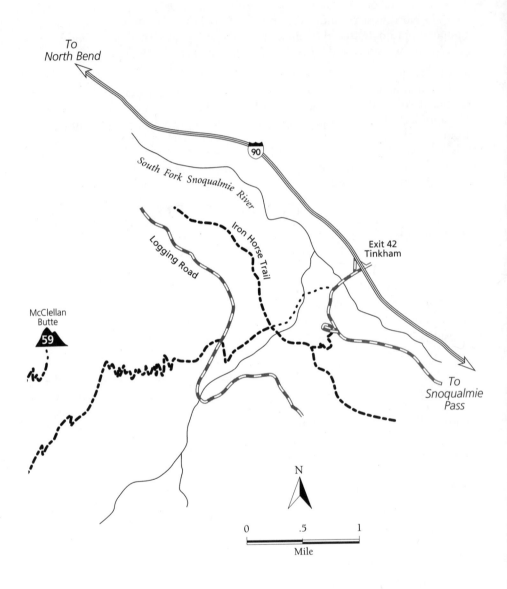

McClellan Butte from Mailbox Peak.

ROUTE DESCRIPTION

Hike McClellan Butte Trail (Trail 1015) 4.6 miles to the summit ridge. The new trail is not direct. It joins Iron Horse Trail, an old railroad grade, for a short section. From the junction with Iron Horse Trail, take a right and follow the wide path westward about 0.3 mile to rejoin McClellan Butte Trail. The strenuous trail switchbacks steeply for some distance, then traverses the eastern slope of McClellan Butte, crossing several avalanche gullies, before circling around the south slope and traversing the west slope through meadow basins and benches. The trail ends high on the summit ridge, just south of the summit rocks. From the trail's end, scramble up the slabby rocks following a well-worn route just east of the ridge crest to the summit. There are abundant small ledges and big holds that make the summit route easy to follow. To descend, scramble down the ridge and hike out on the trail.

Options

There is reportedly a direct scrambling route to the summit via the northeast ridge. The route leaves the trail at the 3,500-foot level, the top of the first series of switchbacks. Details are uncertain, but a climber's trail does leave the trail on the near side of the second gully crossing about 0.2 mile from the top of the switchbacks. This route continues up scree and mossy rock all the way to the summit ridge. This variation poses a rockfall hazard to hikers on the trail below and is not recommended.

PRECAUTIONS

In winter, spring, and early summer, crossing avalanche gullies along the trail can be very hazardous, not only due to avalanche hazard but because of slips and falls on the steep snow. More than one fatal accident has occurred here by a slip down a snow gully on the trail. Bring an ice ax and crampons before July most years. Consider belaying each party member across the gullies if there are any doubts about making a safe crossing. An ice ax is recommended.

60. GRANITE MOUNTAIN

Elevation: 5,629 feet/1,716 meters
Route: Granite Mountain Trail
Rating: Trail or Class 2
Distance: 8 miles round trip
Elevation Gain: 3,800 feet
Time: 3 to 4 hours trailhead to summit
Maps: USGS Snoqualmie Pass; Green Trails No. 207 (Snoqualmie Pass)

ABOUT THE CLIMB

Granite Mountain is the big, bald mountain rising north of Interstate 90 as it curves up the final few miles to Snoqualmie Pass. The mountain is easily distinguished by an absence of trees on its upper slopes, and of course, by the summit lookout cabin. A popular trail leads 4 strenuous miles to the summit, but there are several scrambling routes up the peak, two of which are popular with hikers and scramblers alike. The trail is long and steep, making it a popular training hike. It also provides an excellent introduction to mountain hiking and scrambling, big enough to call a real mountain, yet easy enough not to scare off would-be mountaineers. As a former lookout site, Granite Mountain offers excellent views of the other Snoqualmie Pass peaks, particularly Kaleetan Peak, Chair Peak, the Tooth, and Mount Thompson, and far away mountains including Mount Rainier, Glacier Peak, and Mount Stuart.

HOW TO GET THERE

The climb begins from Pratt Lake trailhead just west of Snoqualmie Pass on Interstate 90. Drive Interstate 90 to exit 47 (Denny Creek/Asahel Curtis), about 15 miles east of North Bend and 5 miles west of Snoqualmie Pass. Head north briefly, turn left, and continue 0.2 mile to the parking lot at Pratt Lake Trail. The parking lot serves several popular trails and can be overcrowded especially on summer weekends. A Northwest Forest Pass is required. This is a high "car-prowl" trailhead, so leave nothing of value behind.

ROUTE DESCRIPTION

Hike 1 mile on Pratt Lake Trail (Trail 1007) to the junction with Granite Mountain Trail. Continue right up Granite Mountain Trail (Trail 1016), which climbs steeply for 1 mile or so before traversing a wide avalanche gully at about the 3,600-foot level. Continue up the trail another mile or so, eventually curving around the east shoulder of the mountain and coming back toward the summit. After crossing the outlet stream of a boulder-strewn tarn (great campsite here), ascend meadow slopes to the foot of a rocky ridge. Here, the trail drops into a basin northeast of the summit and leads through the basin and up a short ridge to the summit. Hike the trail or continue west up the obvious blocky ridge, scrambling over big granite blocks and up a final talus slope to the summit

Granite Mountain

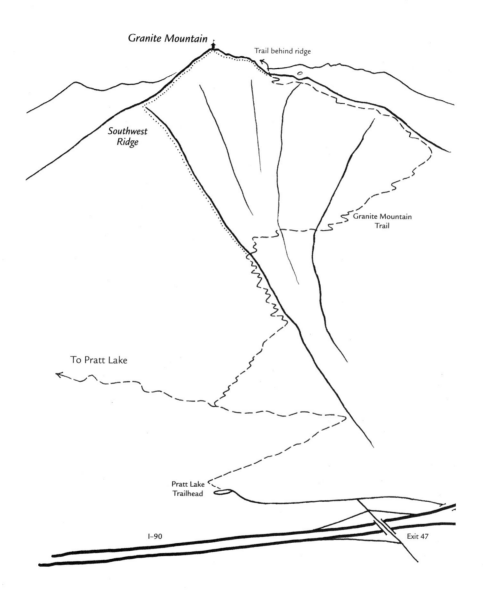

Granite Mountain

Trail behind ridge

Southwest
Ridge

Granite Mountain
Trail

To Pratt Lake

Pratt Lake
Trailhead

I-90

Exit 47

lookout. The going is mostly easy and mildly exposed with only a few easy climbing moves required to surmount or traverse around the largest blocks. To descend, hike out on the trail or scramble down the ridge and out.

OPTIONS

There is a direct scrambling route to the summit via the southwest ridge (the broad ridge west of the avalanche gully), which is the preferred winter and spring route because avalanche danger makes crossing the gully too risky. This option is preferred by some climbers even in summer and fall as a more challenging and less crowded alternative to the trail. Leave the trail at about the 3,500-foot level, just before the trail crosses the gully, and scramble upward, bearing northwest through light brush at first, then up grassy steeps and steep, rocky meadows to the rocky southwest ridge. This route is not entirely free of avalanche danger, but it is a much less risky alternative. Some loose blocks may be encountered on the climb; mind your step.

The summit lookout cabin is available for overnight rental. Contact the North Bend Ranger District Office for information.

PRECAUTIONS

The trail is not recommended in winter or spring due to severe avalanche danger in the gully. Do not cross the avalanche gully if significant snow remains on the trail or on the slopes above the gully; use the southwest ridge.

61. KALEETAN PEAK

Elevation: 6,259 feet/1,908 meters
Route: South Ridge
Rating: Class 2
Distance: 12 miles round trip
Elevation Gain: 4,000 feet
Time: 4 to 5 hours trailhead to summit
Maps: USGS Snoqualmie Pass; Green Trails No. 207 (Snoqualmie Pass)

ABOUT THE CLIMB

Kaleetan Peak is the prominent, sharply pointed peak rising above Melakwa Lakes, directly opposite Chair Peak. Kaleetan (or "kahlîtan") means arrow in the Chinook jargon, and the peak is aptly named. It is easily recognized from any west side vantage and can be picked out from surrounding peaks from many miles away due to its distinct profile. Kaleetan is an appealing peak from a climbing perspective because an easy scrambling route leads to impressive summit views. Kaleetan is a popular scramble but a long one compared to others around Snoqualmie Pass. There are over 10 miles of hiking just getting to the peak and back from the trailhead, not counting the climb itself, yet it is well worth the effort. Kaleetan Peak also has a very good, moderately popular rock route climbing its North Ridge, which provides something a bit more challenging for those who deem the scrambling route too easy. Summit views are good, especially of the surrounding peaks and valleys, although Chair Peak somewhat obstructs the views of peaks to the northeast.

Kaleetan Peak

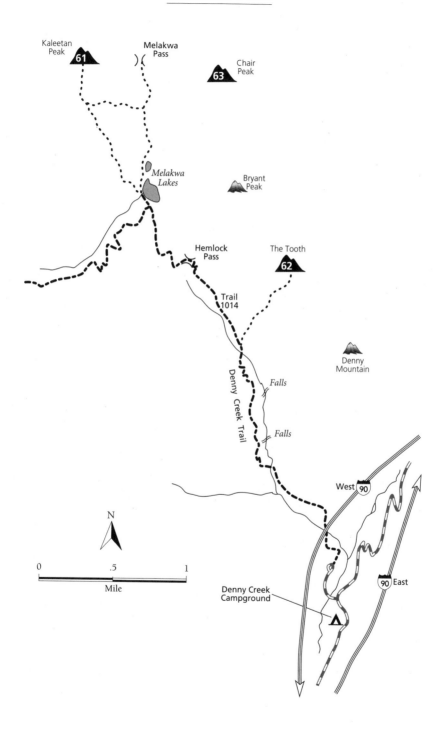

Kaleetan Peak

61

Melakwa Pass

Chair Peak

63

Melakwa Lakes

Bryant Peak

Hemlock Pass

The Tooth

62

Trail 1014

Denny Mountain

Falls

Denny Creek Trail

Falls

West **90**

N

0   .5   1
Mile

90 East

Denny Creek Campground

Kaleetan (left) and Chair Peaks from Granite Mountain.

Kaleetan Peak

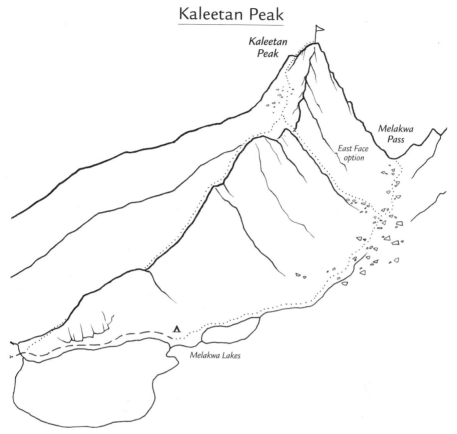

HOW TO GET THERE

The climb begins from Denny Creek trailhead near Denny Creek Campground just east of Snoqualmie Pass. Drive Interstate 90 to exit 47 (Denny Creek/Asahel Curtis), about 15 miles west of North Bend and 5 miles west of Snoqualmie Pass. Head briefly north, turn right, and follow Denny Creek Road eastward under the freeway overpass, curving northward for about 2 miles to Denny Creek Campground. A spur road on the left just past the campground entrance leads 0.25 mile to the Denny Creek (Melakwa Lakes) trailhead. A Northwest Forest Pass is required. This is a high "car-prowl" trailhead, so leave nothing of value behind.

ROUTE DESCRIPTION

Hike Denny Creek Trail (Trail 1014) all the way up and over Hemlock Pass to Melakwa Lakes, supposedly 4.5 miles but it feels longer. A steep cliff rises above the western shore of lower Melakwa Lake. Leave the shore trail just past the outlet logjam and follow the side trail leading to the toilet. Before you get to the toilet, a climber's trail forks off and leads up the forested ridge slopes to a high point at about 5,700 feet elevation. Then travel along the ridge crest before dropping down to the left into a high basin. An ascent along the ridge crest proper involves some steep, loose rock climbing. Ascend left of and below the upper ridge rocks into the upper basin below Kaleetan's summit, bearing left across snow or talus to the head of the basin and the base of a rocky gully that gives access to a final short summit scramble. A climber's trail leads much of the way up the slope. To descend, downclimb the route.

OPTIONS
The 700-foot East Face is a good winter and spring route assuming stable snow conditions. Hike to Melakwa Lakes and continue past the upper lake into the basin toward Melakwa Pass. Just before the final ascent to the pass, climb directly up a moderately steep snow gully to a break in the ridge at about 5,600 feet elevation, then traverse the upper basin and continue to the summit as for the Southeast Ridge route. Naturally, this route is not recommended during periods of avalanche hazard because it climbs an obvious avalanche slope. The route is a steep, loose dirt and rock scramble later in the year.

The North Ridge route♦ (II, 5.2) is a moderately popular route that traverses from Mount Roosevelt via continuous, exposed scrambling, some very loose rock, and a little bit of Class 5 climbing.

PRECAUTIONS
The upper slopes are highly avalanche prone in winter and spring. There is rockfall potential on the east face and upper slopes. A creek crossing at about 1 mile in on the approach hike may be difficult in spring and early summer; there is no bridge, so cross carefully. Also be careful if hiking out after dark; there are dangerous cliffs along the trail.

62. THE TOOTH

Elevation: 5,600 feet/1,707 meters
Route: South Face
Rating: Grade II, 5.2–5.3
Distance: 5 miles round trip
Elevation Gain: 2,500 feet
Time: 3 to 4 hours
Maps: USGS Snoqualmie Pass; Green Trails No. 207 (Snoqualmie Pass)

ABOUT THE CLIMB
The Tooth is the second summit of the group of peaks ascending from Denny Mountain to Chair Peak. It is a small, rocky peak that neatly resembles a canine tooth from nearly every surrounding vantage, hence the name. The Tooth is visible briefly from Interstate 90 as you drive eastbound toward Snoqualmie Pass and is unmistakable from the Snow Lake Trail. This is a very popular climb due to its proximity to the Seattle area, the fast and easy approach, the solid rock, and—to borrow a Fred Beckey term—its "distinctly alpine nature." The peak is so accessible that some climbers make an ascent early in the day before going to work or in the evening after work. The small, flat summit area is a popular bivouac site. The Tooth's South Buttress, one of the classic alpine rock climbs of the Cascade Range, is more often climbed than the easier route up the north ridge. The popularity of The Tooth makes it a crowded climb, so much so that the popular route resembles a sport crag on sunny summer weekends. If you don't like waiting in line to climb a wilderness mountain route, come early or on

The Tooth and Chair Peak

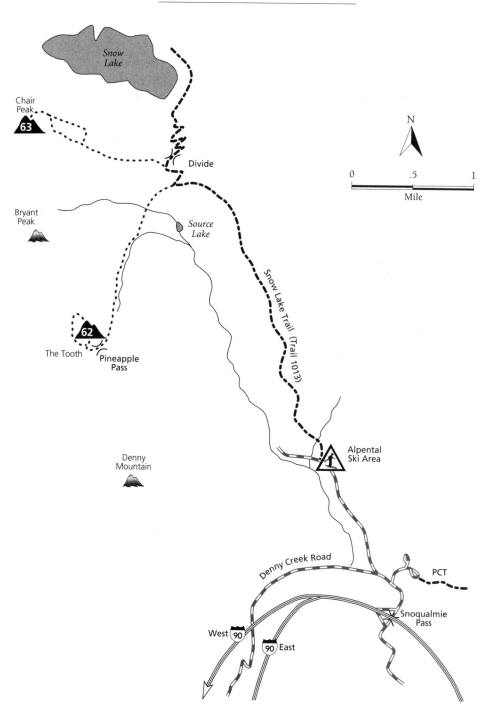

The Tooth from Snoqualmie Mountain.

The Tooth

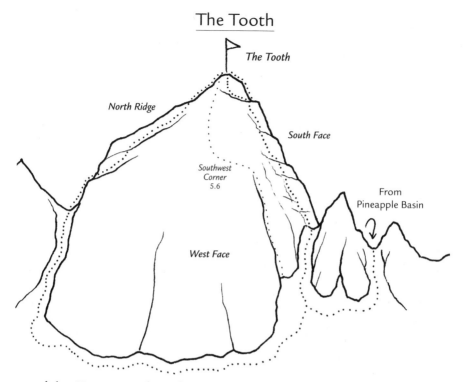

a weekday. You may not have the mountain all to yourself, but at least you won't have to fight the crowds.

HOW TO GET THERE

The climb begins from the Snow Lake trailhead at the Alpental parking lot just northwest of Snoqualmie Pass. Drive Interstate 90 to exit 52 (Snoqualmie Pass West Summit), then turn north and follow Alpental Road northwest 1.4 miles to the ski area parking lot, where the Snow Lake Trail begins. A Northwest Forest Pass is required. This is a high "car-prowl" trailhead, so leave nothing of value behind.

ROUTE DESCRIPTION

Hike up Snow Lake Trail (Trail 1013) approximately 2 miles to where the trail switches back above Source Lake. Leave the trail and follow a climber's trail across the basin headwall above Source Lake (snow traverse until late summer) and up the obvious gullies leading into the talus basin beneath The Tooth's imposing east face. Traverse the talus, aiming for the gap beneath the prominent south buttress. To attain the gap, either scramble directly up a gully (loose Class 3 and not recommended) or surmount the easier saddle just south ("Pineapple Pass") like everyone else and skirt around to the gap from the west side. An approach via Denny Creek Trail is longer, involves bushwhacking, and is understandably less popular.

The route climbs the south face directly from the gap, ascending exposed but mostly solid rock from ledge to ledge. The first pitch or two is low Class 5 rock and very enjoyable. Much of the rest of the route is Class 3–4 rock. High on the face is "the Catwalk," the popular variation traversing left across an exposed ledge (although a direct route up flakes and ledges is just as feasible). There is a popular 5.6 variation on the final pitch to the summit. The climb involves 3 or 4 roped pitches, depending on frequency of belays, and a bit of scrambling between roped pitches. The route has been rated as easy as Class 4 and as difficult as 5.6, depending on the route taken, but the general consensus is that it is 5.2 or 5.3 via the line of least resistance. A 50-meter rope, light rack, and a few long slings should suffice for protection and belay anchors. The summit is flat but small and very exposed; the east face drops away some 600 feet to the talus below.

To descend, rappel or climb back down the south face (double ropes recommended) or traverse the north ridge, staying just west of the crest on sloping Class 2–3 ledges until you are forced to downclimb a short step to a notch (about 30 feet of Class 4 downclimbing). From here, easier scrambling down a dirty gully leads to a climber's trail skirting beneath the west face and back to the base of the south face.

OPTIONS
An easier but less popular climb is the North Ridge. Approach to Pineapple Pass, then follow a climber's trail around below the west face to the north side. Climb a gully to a notch in the ridge and follow a 30-foot Class 4 traverse up and right to easier climbing on slabs and ledges along the west side of the ridge to the summit. Bring a rope, a few pieces of gear, and slings to belay the Class 4 section, which is a bit steep and exposed for unroped climbing.

PRECAUTIONS
Due to its popularity, this climb is often overcrowded. There are only so many belay ledges and anchors, so if there are climbers on the route, be patient or climb a different route. The summit is very exposed. Stay roped up and tied in, especially when the summit area is crowded. The slopes above Source Lake are highly avalanche prone. Beware of cornices on the ridgeline during winter and spring.

63. CHAIR PEAK

Elevation: 6,238 feet/1,901 meters
Route: Northeast Buttress
Rating: Grade II, Class 4
Distance: 8 miles round trip
Elevation Gain: 3,100 feet
Time: 4 to 5 hours to summit
Maps: USGS Snoqualmie Pass; Green Trails No. 207 (Snoqualmie Pass)

ABOUT THE CLIMB
Chair Peak, the highest summit of the Denny Mountain group, is only slightly less popular than The Tooth as a climbing objective despite a slightly shorter approach. Although it is not the highest peak in the immediate vicinity of Snoqualmie Pass, it is much more craggy and striking than other nearby mountains,

Chair Peak (left) and Kaleetan Peak from Snoqualmie Mountain.

and a much more appealing climb. The peak is often swarming with climbers on sunny summer and fall weekends, especially on the popular routes. The favorite route is the Northeast Buttress, a 400-foot Class 4 rock climb, but there are several other routes up the peak. Chair Peak has a well-founded reputation for loose rock, although most of the actual climbing is on reasonably sound rock. Chair Peak's summit offers commanding views of the surrounding area, including views north to Glacier Peak and Mount Baker, west to Mount Stuart, and south to Mount Rainier.

HOW TO GET THERE
Approach as for The Tooth to the Alpental parking lot and Snow Lake trailhead. A Northwest Forest Pass is required. This is a high "car-prowl" trailhead, so leave nothing of value behind.

ROUTE DESCRIPTION
Hike up Snow Lake Trail (Trail 1013) approximately 2.5 miles. Leave the trail just before the Snow Lake divide and hike cross-country, following a climber's trail or snow up the broad basin leading southwest, directly toward Chair Peak's imposing east face. Pass the "Footstool" (or "Thumb Tack"), a small, rocky bump in the basin, and continue up the basin to the foot of the east face. For the Northeast Buttress route, ascend the gully (loose rock or snow) to the right and up to the ridge crest at the foot of the buttress. Alternatively, from the base of the Footstool, angle sharply right and scramble up rocky heather slopes and ledges to the top of the divide, then hike along the north side of the divide to the base of the buttress. This is a less obvious approach route that is easier and less exposed than the gully.

From the base of the buttress, climb a blocky gully that begins just down and right of the divide. The gully angles right at first, then straightens up. From the top of the gully, continue up the blocky, low-angle face above, angling left up exposed, slabby ledges toward a cluster of trees near the prow of the northeast buttress proper. Alternatively, if the gully is clogged with climbers, you can take a shortcut directly up the slabby arete about 40 feet left of the gully. This variation is not as well protected as the gully (a sling may be tied around a rock horn), but it is no more difficult. From the top of the slabby face, climb through the trees, scramble up steep, eroded, rocky heather slopes and around to the south side of the summit stack, and then go up easy, loose rock to the summit. The route involves about 400 feet of rock climbing up the gully and slabby face, mostly exposed Class 3 with some Class 4 sections. The angle is moderate, the climbing is relatively easy, and the rock is mostly sound, but the exposure is significant enough that most parties belay much if not all of the ascent.

To descend, most parties scramble back down the rocky meadows to the cluster of trees at the top of the northeast buttress face, then alternately rappel and scramble down the route. A double-rope rappel from the trees, a bit of downclimbing to the head of the gully, and another double-rope rappel will bring you to the base of the buttress. Bring slings to back up or replace old, worn rappel slings.

Chair Peak

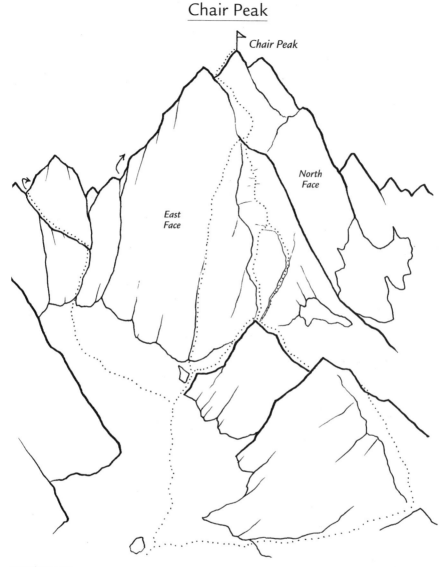

OPTIONS

A more difficult alpine rock route ascends the East Face (II, 5.5) directly, a fairly straightforward climb following the line of least resistance. The route is adequately protected but subject to rockfall, particularly from climbers above. Bring a light rack up to 2.5 inches and several slings. A helmet is recommended.

The North Face is a popular winter route when snow and ice conditions are favorable. Refer to *Selected Climbs in the Cascade Range* for route details. This route is often very crowded due to its popularity. An increasingly popular winter alternative is to climb the Northeast Buttress route.

PRECAUTIONS

The Northeast Buttress route is very popular and can become overcrowded, especially on sunny summer weekends. Rockfall is a major hazard on Chair Peak, particularly climber-caused rockfall, so helmets are highly recommended. Because of rockfall hazard, belaying and staying tied in at belay ledges is recommended. A snowfield along the base of the Northeast Buttress may linger late into the summer, requiring a short bit of snow climbing to get on the rock. Those climbing Chair Peak in winter or spring should be wary of the slopes above Source Lake and below Chair Peak, which are very avalanche prone. Do not attempt Chair Peak during periods of avalanche hazard. Climbers have been killed by avalanches here, and there have been many lucky escapes. In recent years, Alpental Ski Area has been running a cat track from the ski area to Source Lake in the winter, allowing a shorter and probably safer approach for winter ascents of The Tooth and Chair Peak, at least to the end of the cat track.

64. SNOQUALMIE MOUNTAIN

Elevation: 6,278 feet/1,913 meters
Route: Alpental Slope Trail
Rating: Class 1
Distance: 4 miles round trip
Elevation Gain: 3,100 feet
Time: 2 to 3 hours
Maps: USGS Snoqualmie Pass; Green Trails No. 207 (Snoqualmie Pass)

ABOUT THE CLIMB

Snoqualmie Mountain is the highest peak in the immediate vicinity of Snoqualmie Pass, but you might not even notice this featureless mountain from the pass. Beckey describes it as a "bulky, amorphous mass"—i.e., a big blob, which is apt enough. Despite its unassuming, seemingly formless presence, its prominent spur ridge that terminates with Guye Peak, and its craggy-but-hidden northwest face, Snoqualmie is a worthwhile, enjoyable alpine scramble. Due to Snoqualmie Mountain's relative lack of features, it has many feasible summit routes.

The easiest route is a mere hike, making Snoqualmie Mountain one of the easiest high summits in the Snoqualmie Pass region. Its upper slopes are joyous hiking through rocky heather meadows with increasingly superlative views culminating with the panorama of high peaks visible from the summit, including sublime views of the Snoqualmie Pass peaks, as well as more distant giants like Mount Rainier, Mount Stuart, and Glacier Peak. Snoqualmie Mountain is a popular winter and spring climb, but it has high avalanche hazard, especially on its southern slopes above the Alpental Ski Area. The south slope routes are shelled with avalanche-control artillery, making them a poor choice in early season. Fortunately, there are other winter and spring routes that are not subjected to aerial bombardment.

HOW TO GET THERE

Approach as for The Tooth to the Alpental parking lot and Snow Lake trailhead. A Northwest Forest Pass is required. This is a high "car-prowl" trailhead, so leave nothing of value behind.

Snoqualmie Pass Area

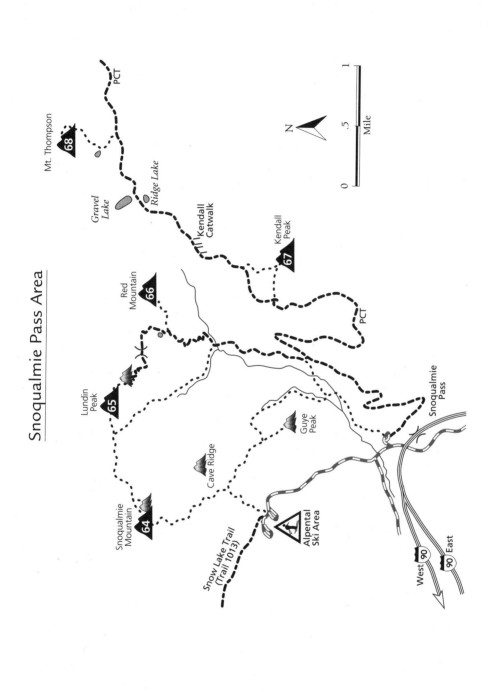

ROUTE DESCRIPTION

The route described climbs a rugged trail up the south slope from Alpental Ski Area. This is the quickest route to the summit, but it is recommended only in summer and fall after all avalanche danger has passed. From the Alpental parking lot, start hiking up the service road toward the Snow Lake trailhead; but about 100 feet before you reach the trailhead and just before crossing the stream, look for an unmarked trail leading right and up across a brushy slope. Follow this trail, which climbs steep brush and forest slopes, for about 0.7 mile to an overgrown talus basin. The trail forks here. As a sign indicates, the right fork leads to Guye Peak; the left fork, to Snoqualmie Mountain. (The "trail" leading directly left is a high route to Snow Lake and the trail to Snoqualmie Mountain climbs more up than left from here.) Take the left fork and continue up the trail, ascending the rocky slope into hemlock forest. Traverse left to a stream gully on a ledge above a steep drop-off (seasonal waterfall) and cross it, then climb rocks and roots up the left side of the gully back into forest. About 1.2 miles up the trail (at about 4,900 feet elevation), the trail turns west up the ridge toward Snoqualmie Mountain. Hike up rocky heather meadow slopes along the ridge. The trail is dusty and eroded in places low on the ridge but improves as you climb higher. Continue up the ridge, following the trail another 0.7 mile to the summit ridge. Stay left and hike briefly to the westernmost of the rounded summit points.

OPTIONS

There are several options for approaching this climb, especially in winter and spring when the Alpental slope of Snoqualmie Mountain is highly avalanche prone. For the most common route, hike in from Commonwealth Basin and up the broad gully north of Guye Peak.

According to the USGS map, the western hump is the summit. However, a sharp rock peak about 150 yards northeast of the summit hump seems to be just as high, if not higher. Even if it's not the summit, the rock peak is much more appealing from a climber's perspective. There is a fairly simple but not quite obvious scrambling route to the top.

An ascent of the north summit of Guye Peak is straightforward from Cave Ridge. An enchainment linking Guye Peak, Snoqualmie Mountain, Lundin Peak, and Red Mountain can be done in a single day or with a bivouac. The route is mostly rugged off-trail hiking and Class 2 scrambling, except Lundin Peak (Class 4). Bring a rope, slings, and a light rack for Lundin Peak; a helmet is recommended.

PRECAUTIONS

Nearly every route up Snoqualmie Mountain is subject to avalanche hazard in winter and spring. The Alpental slope of Cave Ridge is especially avalanche prone, even in spring if significant snow lingers on the ridge above. The slope is shelled by avalanche-control artillery during the winter so big avalanches don't cut loose and wipe out the Alpental Ski Area development. A long cornice lingers on the ridge in spring, posing a threat to climbers on the slopes below. Use the Commonwealth Basin approach or the Lundin Peak gully in winter and spring, and then only during periods of little or no avalanche danger. When descending in snow or bad weather, beware of cliffs and cornices on the ridges.

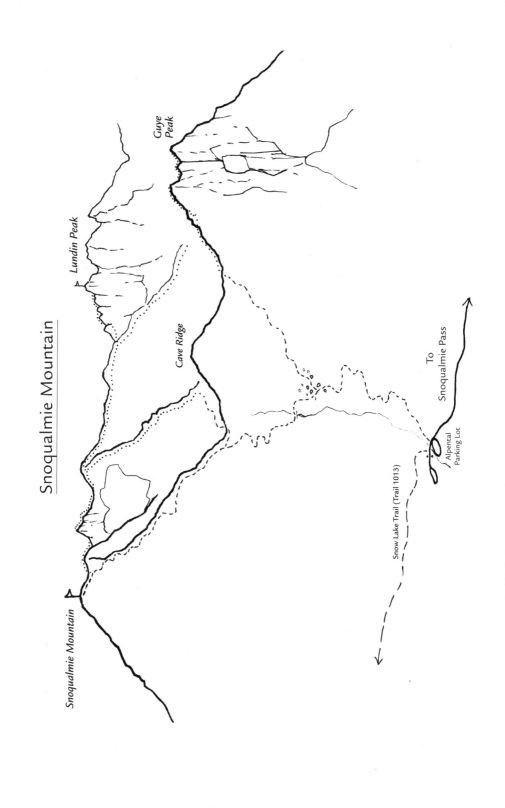

Snoqualmie Mountain

Guye Peak

Lundin Peak

Cave Ridge

Snoqualmie Mountain

Snow Lake Trail (Trail 1013)

Alpental Parking Lot

To Snoqualmie Pass

Lundin Peak from Kendall Peak.

65. LUNDIN PEAK

Elevation: 6,057 feet/1,846 meters
Route: East Peak
Rating: Grade I, Class 4
Distance: 10 miles round trip
Elevation Gain: 3,000 feet
Time: 4 to 5 hours to summit
Maps: USGS Snoqualmie Pass; Green Trails No. 207 (Snoqualmie Pass)

ABOUT THE CLIMB

Lundin Peak is really only a craggy high point on the east ridge of Snoqualmie Mountain, but it is an attractive, distinctive peak when viewed from Common-wealth Basin and Kendall Peak. This climb is popular mostly due to its accessibility, relatively easy climbing, and tremendous exposure. It is commonly climbed in conjunction with its neighbors, Red Mountain and Snoqualmie Mountain. Climbing groups sometimes use Lundin Peak as a basic instruction climb, which can leave the popular route literally tied up for hours. Hikers can follow a climber's trail to the 5,700-foot east summit, which provides excellent views.

Scramblers may balk at an unroped ascent due to a section of loose rock descending from the false summit and very exposed climbing on the summit ridge, while experienced climbers may eschew use of a rope because the climbing, though exposed, is never very difficult. The latter should take heed of the several fatalities that have occurred on Lundin Peak. An unroped fall here would assuredly be fatal. Summit views include Mount Rainier to the south, Glacier Peak to the north, Mount Thompson and Chimney Rock to the east, a close look at Snoqualmie Mountain, Red Mountain, and Kendall Peak, and down Commonwealth Basin to Snoqualmie Pass.

HOW TO GET THERE

The approach is via Commonwealth Basin just north of Snoqualmie Pass. Drive Interstate 90 to exit 52 (Snoqualmie Pass West Summit), then north briefly toward Alpental Road. In just over 0.1 mile from the freeway exit, turn right into the parking lot for the PCT. Stay right at the fork to reach the PCT trailhead. A Northwest Forest Pass is required. This is a high "car-prowl" trailhead, so park and leave nothing of value behind.

ROUTE DESCRIPTION

Hike the PCT about 2.4 miles to the junction with Commonwealth Trail (or take the old trail and save about 1.4 miles of hiking), then take a left and follow Commonwealth Trail to its end at the sign TRAIL ABANDONED, just before the saddle dividing Lundin Peak and Red Mountain at mile 4.8, elevation 5,300 feet. Continue westward from the saddle up a climber's trail that ascends a rocky heather slope to a false summit (about 5,700 feet) of Lundin Peak. The climbing route begins here.

From the false summit, you can either rappel or scramble to the notch 70 feet below. The scrambling route is not obvious and involves fairly exposed Class 3 downclimbing with loose rock. Leave the climber's trail about 25 feet below the false summit at a flat spot with whitish gravel and descend a steep, loose gully about 40 feet, then traverse a heather ledge northward to the notch. View the route from the false summit before you head down the gully so you know where you're going. If you start traversing too early, you'll end up on an exposed, blocky dead-end ledge. From the notch, ascend a slabby rock ridge briefly, then cross over and follow a climber's trail up a sloping heather shelf around the east and north side of the middle summit. Scramble down a dirty gully to the second notch, then up an easy, boulder-strewn heather slope on the southeast side of the summit formation, angling right to the base of the final summit rocks. Scramble up easy ledges to the ridge crest, then ascend the slabby rock ridge directly to the summit. The final ridge is not technically difficult, but it has a couple of tenuous moves and is severely exposed. Bolts with huge hangers ("safety holds" according to the memorial plaque glued to the rock) provide convenient protection. The route is easy enough that nobody should need to grab the bolts, which offer little more than a false sense of security when used as handholds.

To descend, either downclimb or make a short rappel and scramble back the way you came to the false summit.

OPTIONS

In early season, a direct approach can be made to the main summit notch via a steep snow gully on the south side. To get there, you have to leave the Commonwealth Trail at the last stream crossing, just before the switchbacks, and contour around the ridge and up the creek drainage into the steep basin directly below

Lundin Peak

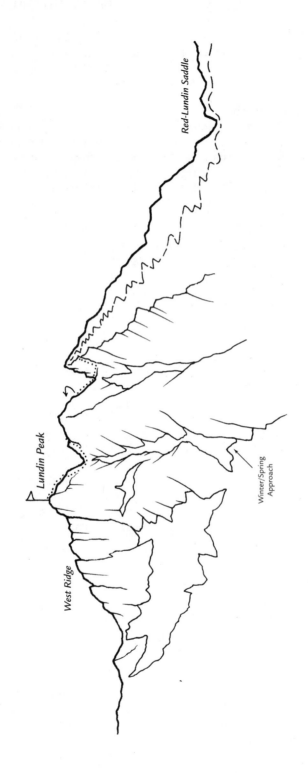

Red-Lundin Saddle

Lundin Peak

Winter/Spring
Approach

West Ridge

Lundin's south face. This is a major avalanche chute and should not be ascended during periods of avalanche danger. If you come this way, beware of rockfall, especially if climbers are on the route above you. In late season, there is too much brush, scree, and loose rock to recommend this approach.

PRECAUTIONS

The scramble down from the first false summit to the notch is exposed Class 3 with loose rock. Only one person at a time should descend the gully in order to reduce the risk of being hit by climber-caused rockfall. The final climb to the summit is rated Class 3 by some, Class 4 by others. It is not really technically difficult but involves some delicate climbing with severe exposure. If you elect to rappel the summit ridge, be careful. The ridge is narrow and slabby, and exposed on either side; a pendulum off either side could be trouble.

66. RED MOUNTAIN

Elevation: 5,890 feet/1,795 meters
Route: Southwest Slope
Rating: Class 2–3
Distance: 9 miles round trip
Elevation Gain: 3,000 feet
Time: 3 to 4 hours trailhead to summit
Maps: USGS Snoqualmie Pass; Green Trails No. 207 (Snoqualmie Pass)

ABOUT THE CLIMB

Red Mountain is a prominent peak lying at the head of Commonwealth Basin just north of Snoqualmie Pass. Due to an overabundance of iron oxide in its rock, Red Mountain has a rusty tint that easily distinguishes it from other nearby peaks. The mountain has a classic pyramid shape when viewed from Commonwealth Basin, which combined with its colorful appearance and high relief makes it seem bigger than it really is. Red Mountain is seriously undercut on its north side, where steep, loose cliffs drop off hundreds of feet—a sharp contrast to its gradually angled south and west slopes. As a climbing objective, Red Mountain is attractive and popular, especially in early season, when much of the loose rock on the ascent is snow-covered. The climbing route is relatively short but strenuous, steadily gaining 1,000 feet of elevation on the final climb—after already gaining 1,900 feet on the trail. But Red Mountain's prominence, easy accessibility and good views, particularly of Mount Rainier and east to Mount Thompson and the Snoqualmie Crest peaks, make it a very worthwhile climb.

HOW TO GET THERE

Approach as for Lundin Peak via Commonwealth Trail from the PCT trailhead at Snoqualmie Pass. A Northwest Forest Pass is required. This is a high "car-prowl" trailhead, so park and leave nothing of value behind.

ROUTE DESCRIPTION

The route described is the Southwest Slope, the most popular summit route, probably because it is the easiest and most accessible.

Red Mountain from Kendall Peak.

Red Mountain

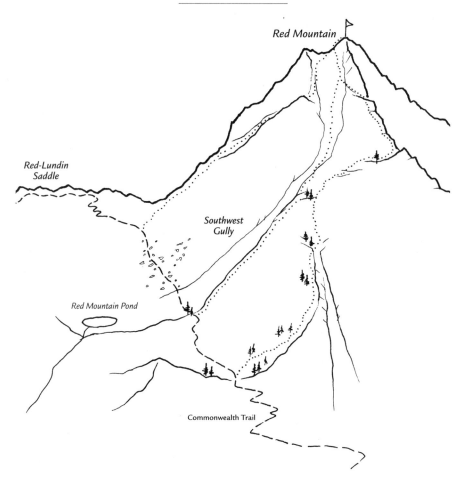

Hike the PCT about 2.4 miles to the junction with Commonwealth Trail (or take the old trail and save 1.4 miles of hiking), then take a hard left and follow Commonwealth Trail another 1.7 miles, climbing a series of switchbacks up a wooded ridge, where the trail finally levels off at a small basin. The basin is about 0.5 mile below the saddle and about 300 feet before the trail traverses talus slopes above Red Mountain Pond. The climbing route begins here.

A faint climber's trail leads off to the right just where the trail dips downhill into the basin. The trail contours up and right through huckleberry, mountain ash and thinning mountain hemlock and silver fir for 100 yards or so to the left edge of a shallow, rocky gully. It's easy to lose the trail here, so just bushwhack to the right toward the gully if you get lost. Ascend the left (west) side of the gully several hundred feet, then up a series of brushy and grassy rock ledges, passing close to nearly every cluster of trees on the face. About halfway to the summit, the route makes a long traverse to the right on a ledge, passing behind a large tree and up to the rocky ridge forming the right skyline. Scramble up the ridge a short distance, then bear left across ledges and rocky heather slopes to the head of the broad southwest gully. Ascend the rocky gully to the summit.

The usual route is fairly defined by the lack of loose rock. If you lose the route, don't worry. You can scramble up pretty much wherever the going looks easiest, staying left, near the broad gully on the southwest face. If you're off route, you will encounter more loose rock, and possibly some more difficult scrambling (up to Class 3) in places, but nothing of serious difficulty unless you purposely or foolishly choose the most difficult line. If you come in early season, ascend snow up the southwest gully as far as it goes; avoid the gully during periods of avalanche danger.

OPTIONS

There are several other routes up Red Mountain, but the standard route has less loose rock. In early season, the route climbs the southwest gully or on the ribs on either side of the gully. The gully and upper slopes are highly avalanche prone and should not be attempted during periods of avalanche danger.

PRECAUTIONS

There is quite a bit of loose rock on Red Mountain. Be especially careful not to knock loose rock down on your companions or other climbers. Spring and early summer ascents are popular because snow covers much of the loose rock and provides an obvious, direct route. However, winter and spring avalanche danger can be very high, especially on the upper slopes and in the southwest gully. Avalanches really get ripping down the gully on warm, wet spring days.

67. KENDALL PEAK

Elevation: 5,784 feet/1,763 meters
Route: North Ridge
Rating: Class 2–3
Distance: 11 miles round trip
Elevation Gain: 2,750 feet
Time: 3 to 4 hours
Maps: USGS Snoqualmie Pass, Chikamin Peak; Green Trails No. 207 (Snoqualmie Pass)

ABOUT THE CLIMB

Kendall Peak is a broad, craggy mountain rising to the northeast above Snoqualmie Pass. From the west, Kendall Peak rises gradually from deep forest to talus slopes and culminates in a rocky summit pyramid. From the east, Kendall presents a different aspect—a long, rocky ridge with steep, imposing buttresses and menacing cliffs falling away hundreds of feet. From most vantages, Kendall does not appear to be a particularly attractive or inspiring peak, but since the PCT was re-routed to within a short distance of its summit, Kendall has become a more popular and accessible peak, with an interesting scrambling route. Most parties climb a brushy route up the west slope, but there is a much more interesting rock scramble along the north ridge. The scrambling route is exposed and varied, climbing a rocky ridge crest about 0.5 mile from the PCT to the summit. Views include a close look at Mount Thompson, plus Chikamin Peak and Lemah Mountain, Alta Mountain, Hibox, and the Three Queens across the valley, Mount Stuart poking up to the east, Mount Rainier to the south, and the Snoqualmie Pass peaks across Commonwealth Basin.

HOW TO GET THERE

The approach is via the PCT from Snoqualmie Pass. Drive Interstate 90 to exit 52 (Snoqualmie Pass West Summit) and drive north toward Alpental Road. In just over 0.1 mile from the interstate, turn right onto the road leading to the PCT parking lot. Stay right at the fork to reach the PCT trailhead. A Northwest Forest Pass is required. This is a high "car-prowl" trailhead, so park and leave nothing of value behind.

ROUTE DESCRIPTION

The route described is the North Ridge. It is not the easiest or fastest route, but it is a personal favorite because it is a true scrambling route. The going is mostly easy, but sometimes you'll encounter exposed rock scrambling. This is not just a brushy dirt hike like the popular summit route.

Hike up the PCT north about 5 miles to the gap in the ridge dividing the Commonwealth Creek and Gold Creek drainages (at about 5,400 feet). Here you get your first view of the east face of Kendall Peak. Come early; the PCT is fully exposed to afternoon sun and is a hot, miserable climb late on a summer day. If you hike the first part of the old Commonwealth Trail instead, you save about 1.4 miles of hiking each way. If you don't know where the old trail begins, take the PCT on the way in and the old Commonwealth Trail on the way out. The old trail is not maintained but it is regularly used by hikers and climbers and should be fairly passable.

From the gap, scramble up the rocky ridge, first in a southwest direction, staying mostly left of the ridge crest, for several hundred feet to where the ridge levels out some and angles southward. Continue southward along the rocky summit ridge, or closely right of the crest, all the way to the summit. There are a few places where you must either climb over rock points on the upper ridge or skirt around them on the west side. The standard route up the ridge is well worn, fairly clear of loose rock, and mostly easy to follow. The ridge is very exposed on the east side and heavily fractured, so when in doubt, stay on the west side rather than on the crest. After passing over or around a few craggy rock peaks on the ridge, with a few Class 3 sections unless you skirt very low around the rocks, hike up easy rock slopes to reach the summit.

OPTIONS

The easier, more direct route ascends a brushy gully and dirt and rocky slopes directly from final switchbacks high on the west face of Kendall Peak. Leave the trail at the higher switchback opposite a silvered stump and scramble pretty much straight up the slope to the summit ridge, just north of the summit. In winter and spring, the PCT is impassable, so the route begins from Commonwealth Basin and climbs gullies all the way to the summit. Naturally, the gullies are major avalanche paths, so avoid them during periods of avalanche danger.

Kendall Peak

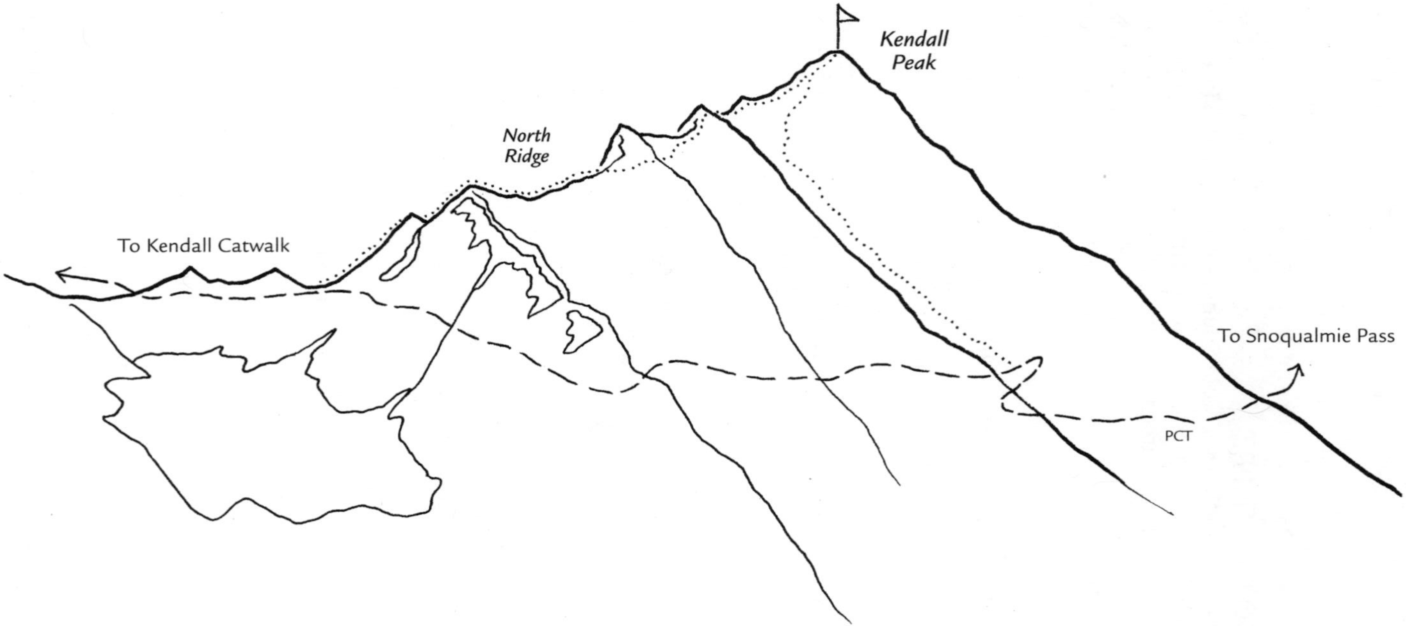

To Snoqualmie Pass

PCT

Kendall
Peak

North
Ridge

To Kendall Catwalk

The routes are long snow climbs, fairly popular but not highly recommended due to avalanche hazard.

PRECAUTIONS
The east face of Kendall Peak is very precipitous, and the ridge crest is very exposed and loose in places; so when the going along the ridge gets tough or loose, keep to the gentler west side. The more directly you tackle the ridge, the more difficult the climbing. Although it's relatively easy going, there are a couple of places on the ridge where you're rock climbing. There is abundant loose rock on the ridge, so be very careful not to knock rocks down on your companions or on hikers on the PCT below. The gullies are highly avalanche prone in winter and spring. Beware of cornices on the ridge.

68. MOUNT THOMPSON

Elevation: 6,554 feet/1,998 meters
Route: East Ridge
Rating: Class 3–4
Distance: 20 miles round trip
Elevation Gain: 3,600 feet
Time: 6 to 8 hours trailhead to summit
Maps: USGS Snoqualmie Pass and Chikamin Peak; Green Trails No. 207 (Snoqualmie Pass)

ABOUT THE CLIMB
Mount Thompson is one of the sentinels of the Alpine Lakes Wilderness, the veritable king of the Snoqualmie Pass peaks. The mountain's bell shape stands out prominently even among higher peaks nearby, making it a magnet for photographers and climbers alike. It is also one of the most remote peaks in the Snoqualmie Pass region considering the length of the approach hike. The standard approach is about 9 miles, easy hiking on the PCT but still a long approach, making for a strenuous one-day climb. Most climbers make the ascent in one day, though, because the prospect of hiking so far with overnight gear seems less desirable than the other option. Despite its long approach, Mount Thompson is one of the most popular of the Snoqualmie Pass peaks, with an enjoyable scrambling route up the East Ridge, a classic Class 5 route up the West Ridge, and unsurpassed views of nearby peaks along the Snoqualmie Crest and beyond.

HOW TO GET THERE
Although it is not the shortest way to reach Mount Thompson, the PCT offers the least complicated and least strenuous approach route. Approach as for Kendall Peak via the PCT trailhead at Snoqualmie Pass. A Northwest Forest Pass is required. This is a high "car-prowl" trailhead, so leave nothing of value behind.

ROUTE DESCRIPTION
Hike the PCT 7 miles to Gravel Lake, which makes a good base camp for those making a two-day climb. (Hiking the first section of the old Commonwealth Trail saves about 1.4 miles of hiking each way.) From Gravel Lake, continue along

Norm Buckley

Mount Thompson and Edds Lake from Chikamin Peak. The route climbs the ridge slope facing the camera.

Mount Thompson East Ridge

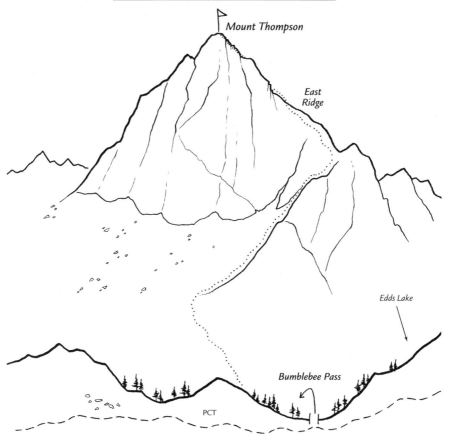

the PCT another 2 miles to Bumblebee Pass, a small saddle on the ridge crest above Alaska Lake. Leave the trail and cross the saddle, then descend into the basin on the other side. Steep snow may complicate this descent; an ice ax is recommended and crampons may be helpful. Contour across the basin above Edds Lake to the base of the south face of Mount Thompson (the long, sloping ridge on the right). Angle up a gully leading right toward the east ridge. The gully forks near the top; stay right. Once on the ridge, a climber's trail leads up the rocky heather meadow slope to an exposed viewpoint on the north side of Mount Thompson. Continue up heather meadows with some easy rock scrambling to near the top. Just below the summit, the going becomes rocky and steep. Ascend steep, solid rock to a rappel station about 20 feet below the summit. This section is probably Class 4; some parties will want to belay on the way up and rappel on the descent. The route seems a bit easier if you stay in the heather that borders the slabby ridge on the right. The final 20 feet to the summit is easy scrambling.

To descend, downclimb the route. Some parties make a single rappel from just below the summit to avoid downclimbing the last bit of rock.

OPTIONS
Technical climbers will probably prefer the good, moderately popular rock route up the West Ridge (III, 5.6)♦.

PRECAUTIONS
Steep snow may linger all summer on the north side of Bumblebee Pass. The slopes above Edds Lake and below the south face are avalanche prone in winter and spring, and exposed to rockfall. The final bit of scrambling is short but fairly exposed climbing that is considered by many climbers to be Class 4. Bring a rope and some slings in case a belay or rappel is desired.

69. ALTA MOUNTAIN

Elevation: 6,240 feet/1,902 meters
Route: South Ridge Climber's Trail
Rating: Class 1
Distance: 12 miles round trip
Elevation Gain: 3,500 feet
Time: 4 to 5 hours trailhead to summit
Maps: USGS Chikamin Peak; Green Trails No. 207 (Snoqualmie Pass)

ABOUT THE CLIMB
Alta Mountain is the high point of the divide between Gold Creek and Kachess Lake. Although not a particularly high peak, it rises dramatically from Gold Creek Valley in a 3,000-foot rampart. Alta Mountain is one of the easiest and most popular off-trail summits in the Snoqualmie Pass region, and it is the starting point of a superb high traverse. A way trail leads all the way to the summit, and hikers regularly make the ascent without difficulty. Although not technically difficult, the summit of Alta Mountain offers one of the best viewpoints in the Snoqualmie Pass region, making it a very worthwhile climb. Summit views include Kendall Peak, Mount Thompson, Chikamin Peak, Lemah Mountain, the Three Queens, and Hibox Mountain, Mount Stuart, Mount Hinman, Mount Daniel, Mount Baker, and Mount Rainier, to name only a few.

HOW TO GET THERE
This route begins from Rachel Lake trailhead just off of Interstate 90 east of Snoqualmie Pass. Drive Interstate 90 to Kachess Lake (exit 62). Turn north on Forest Road 49 and follow it about 6 miles to Kachess Lake and Kachess Campground. Turn left on Forest Road 4930 and follow it 4.5 miles to the Rachel Lake trailhead. A Northwest Forest Pass is required.

ROUTE DESCRIPTION
Hike Rachel Lake Trail (Trail 1313) some 3.9 miles to Rachel Lake, elevation 4,640 feet. Continue up the trail from the lake a short 0.5 mile to a trail junction at the crest of Rampart Ridge. Take the right fork and hike northward along Rampart Ridge toward Lila Lake, a secluded lake set below the rocky subalpine slopes of Alta Mountain. Where the trail forks, stay on the high trail, which leads northward along the ridge crest about 1 mile to the summit of Alta Mountain.

Alta Mountain

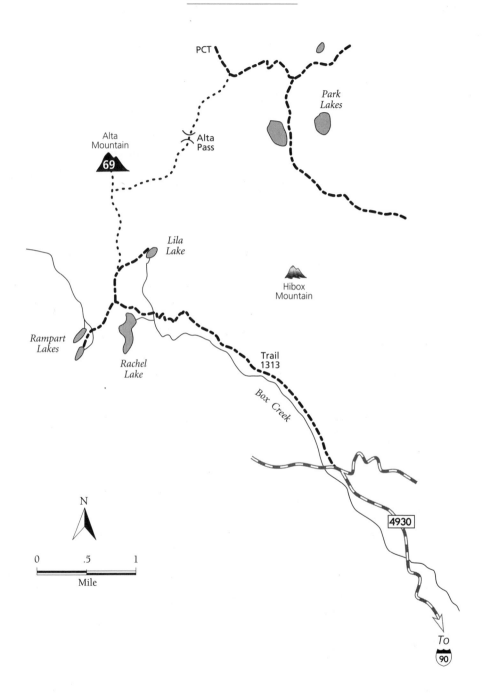

PCT

Park
Lakes

Alta
Mountain

69

Alta
Pass

Lila
Lake

Hibox
Mountain

Rampart
Lakes

Rachel
Lake

Trail
1313

Box Creek

4930

N

0   .5   1

Mile

To

90

Alta Mountain.

Matt Robertson

The trail climbs over one false summit after another until you finally arrive at the real summit.

OPTIONS

An excellent high traverse leads northward along Rampart Ridge across Alta Pass to Park Lakes or Chikamin Pass. This traverse is just over 2 miles, and is very popular. A climber's trail can be followed much of the way. The only drawback is that you must arrange transportation. Get someone to drop you off at Rachel Lake trailhead and pick you up in a day or two at the PCT trailhead at Snoqualmie Pass or Mineral Creek trailhead. Otherwise, you'll have to hike back along the ridge, not a bad thing really.

PRECAUTIONS

The ridge slopes are avalanche prone in winter and spring. Beware of cornices on the ridge.

70. CHIKAMIN PEAK

Elevation: 7,000 feet/2,134 meters
Route: South Slope
Rating: Class 3
Distance: 14 miles
Elevation Gain: 4,100 feet
Time: 6 hours
Maps: USGS Chikamin Peak; Green Trails No. 207 (Snoqualmie Pass)

ABOUT THE CLIMB

Chikamin Peak is the prominent, angular peak rising at the head of Gold Creek Valley, easily seen from Interstate 90 near the Hyak exit. It is probably the easiest of the several 7,000-foot summits along this portion of the Snoqualime Crest in terms of climbing and routefinding difficulty, as well as route length and complexity of approach. Although the approach hike is fairly long, the PCT passes to within about 1,000 vertical feet of Chikamin Peak's summit, greatly simplifying the ascent. It is often climbed by hikers passing on the PCT and by climbers as part of a multi-day, multi-peak trip. The elevation of Chikamin Peak is listed as 6,926 feet, but the USGS topo map clearly shows the highest point, the sharp peak in the middle of the summit ridge, to be just over 7,000 feet high. Whatever the actual elevation, Chikamin is an enjoyable climb, best done as an overnight trip but feasible in a long day. Like most other summits included in this guide, Chikamin Peak offers spectacular views, especially of the Snoqualmie Crest peaks, Mount Daniel, Mount Stuart, and Mount Rainier. Chikamin means both "metal" and "money" in the Chinook jargon, depending on how it is pronounced.

HOW TO GET THERE

The best approach is via Mineral Creek and Park Lakes. Drive Interstate 90 to exit 80 (Roslyn/Salmon la Sac) near Cle Elum, then head north 3 miles to Washington Highway 903. Turn left and follow Washington Highway 903 east through Roslyn and Ronald, then north along the shore of Cle Elum Lake to Cle Elum

Snoqualmie Crest Peaks

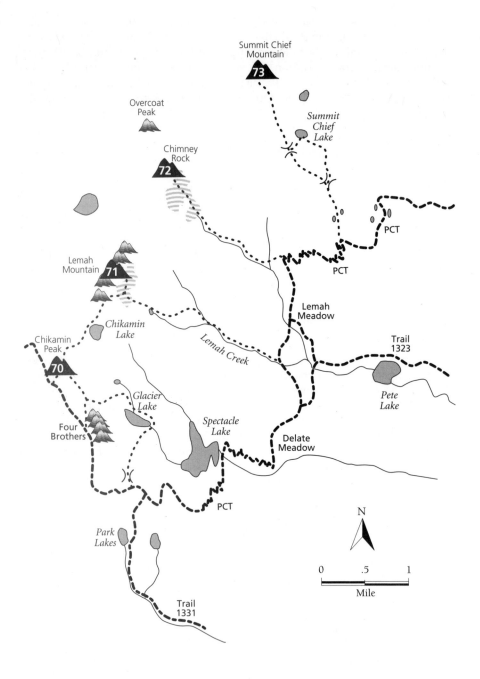

Summit Chief
Mountain
73

Overcoat
Peak

*Summit
Chief
Lake*

Chimney
Rock
72

PCT

Lemah
Mountain
71

PCT

Lemah
Meadow

Chikamin
Peak

*Chikamin
Lake*

Lemah Creek

Trail
1323

70

*Glacier
Lake*

*Spectacle
Lake*

*Pete
Lake*

Four
Brothers

Delate
Meadow

N

PCT

*Park
Lakes*

0   .5   1
Mile

Trail
1331

South Slope, Chikamin Peak. The Four Brothers are on the right.

River Campground. Turn left on Forest Road 46 and follow it for 10 unpaved miles over Cooper Pass and down to Mineral Creek trailhead. A Northwest Forest Pass is required. Hike Mineral Creek Trail (Trail 1331) about 4.7 miles to Park Lakes and join the PCT shortly above the lakes, then continue southwest on the PCT about 1 mile to Chikamin Pass, the high divide on Alta-Chikamin Ridge, and descend a short distance into Ptarmigan Park.

ROUTE DESCRIPTION

The route described is up the south slope, the shortest in terms of off-trail climbing because the PCT passes so close to the mountain, but every approach hike is long. Hike your choice of approaches to Ptarmigan Park, the large subalpine meadow in the basin below the southwest face of Chikamin Peak, about 5,400 feet elevation. There are several feasible routes on the south slope, none of which is necessarily better than another. The most obvious route is up the prominent gully directly south of the summit, which in early season provides a moderate 1,200-foot snow climb to the summit ridge, where a short rock scramble gains the summit.

In late season, a better route begins directly below the leftmost of the Four Brothers rock formations. Angle up the left edge of the talus slopes to heather slopes and a broad gully leading to the ridge, then scramble up the southeast ridge to the summit. The route is mostly easy talus and rocky heather meadow with some rock scrambling up ledges and gullies to the summit. There are several other feasible routes from Ptarmigan Park, but they are not as easy to find or follow from below. If you can't find the "correct" route, just hike and scramble up the meadows by whichever route looks best; with careful routefinding, no extraordinary difficulties should be encountered. Expect to take one or two hours from the PCT to the summit by any route. Descend the way you came, or via another route if you didn't like your route of ascent.

Chikamin Peak

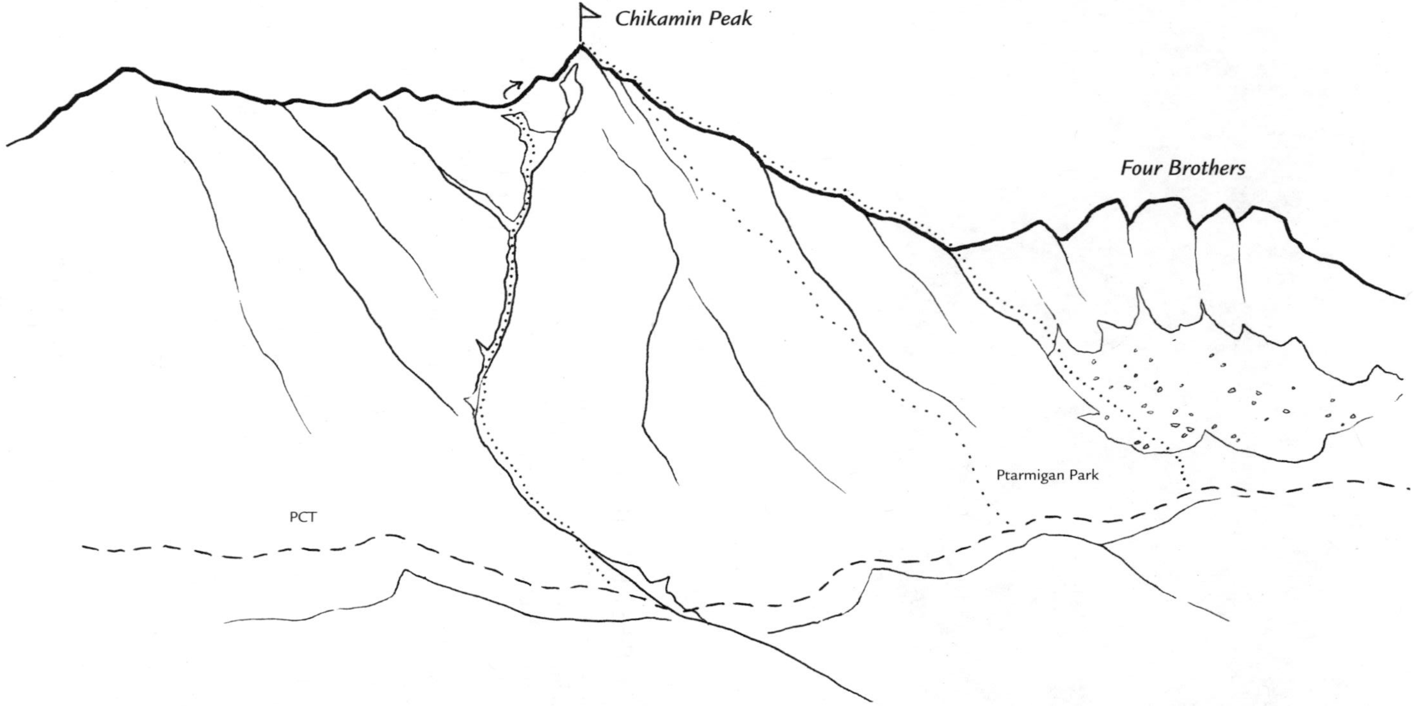

Chikamin Peak

Four Brothers

Ptarmigan Park

PCT

Chikamin Peak Glacier Lake Option

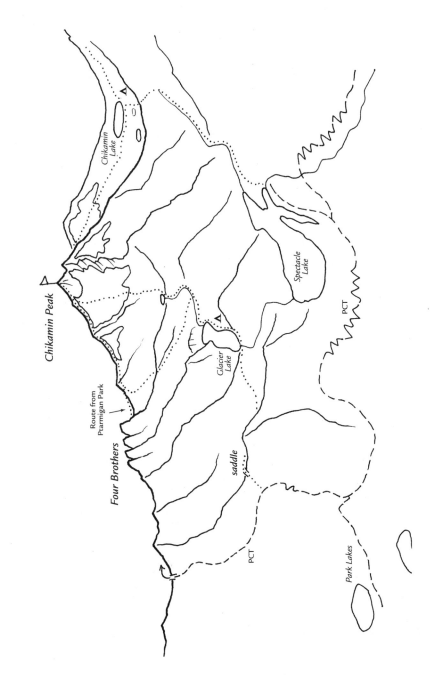

Chikamin Peak

Chikamin Lake

Four Brothers

Route from Ptarmigan Park

Glacier Lake

saddle

Spectacle Lake

PCT

PCT

Park Lakes

OPTIONS
Glacier Lake route ◆ is longer but recommended as easier to find and follow. It ascends the northeast slopes of Chikamin Peak above Spectacle Lakes. See map on page 273.

PRECAUTIONS
The southwest face of Chikamin Peak is avalanche prone in winter and spring and should not be climbed during periods of avalanche hazard. Beware of undermined snow in gullies and rockfall down the gullies.

71. LEMAH MOUNTAIN

Elevation: 7,512 feet/2,290 meters
Route: Lemah Glacier and East Gully
Rating: Class 4; Grade I glacier
Distance: 16 miles round trip
Elevation Gain: 4,700 feet
Time: 8 to 10 hours trailhead to summit
Maps: USGS Chikamin Peak

ABOUT THE CLIMB
Lemah Mountain is one of the more distinguishable peaks of the Snoqualmie Crest peaks. Lemah means "hand" in the Chinook jargon. With its five "fingers" jutting up to an altitude of over 7,000 feet, Lemah can be seen from every high ridge and summit for miles around. Although seemingly dwarfed by its neighbor, Chimney Rock, both in altitude and in stature, Lemah Mountain offers a very alpine climbing experience over snow and glacier ice and easy rock to a high ridge and exposed summit. Because it is an easier climb than Chimney Rock, Lemah is a much more popular ascent. Each of the five fingers has an independent summit route, and a traverse has been done across all five summits. Summit views are spectacular, including Chimney Rock, Mount Daniel, Mount Stuart, Mount Rainier, and sweeping views of the alpine lakes, valleys, and ridges on both sides of the crest.

HOW TO GET THERE
The usual approach is via Cooper River Trail and Pete Lake just west of Cle Elum Lake. Drive Interstate 90 to exit 80 (Roslyn/Salmon la Sac) near Cle Elum, then head north 3 miles to Washington Highway 903. Turn left and follow Washington Highway 903 east through Roslyn and Ronald, then north along the shore of Cle Elum Lake to Cle Elum River Campground. Turn left on Forest Road 46 and follow it for 4.8 unpaved miles to Cooper Lake. Take the right fork, toward Owhi Campground and continue 1.2 miles to the road's end and the Cooper River (Pete Lake) trailhead. A Northwest Forest Pass is required.

ROUTE DESCRIPTION
Hike the Cooper River Trail (Trail 1323) for 4 relatively flat miles to Pete Lake. Continue another 1.2 miles, staying left at all forks, to meet the PCT. Take a right, heading north on the PCT for about 1 mile to Lemah Creek. Leave the trail before crossing the footbridge and hike cross-country up the creek about 1.1

Lemah Mountain

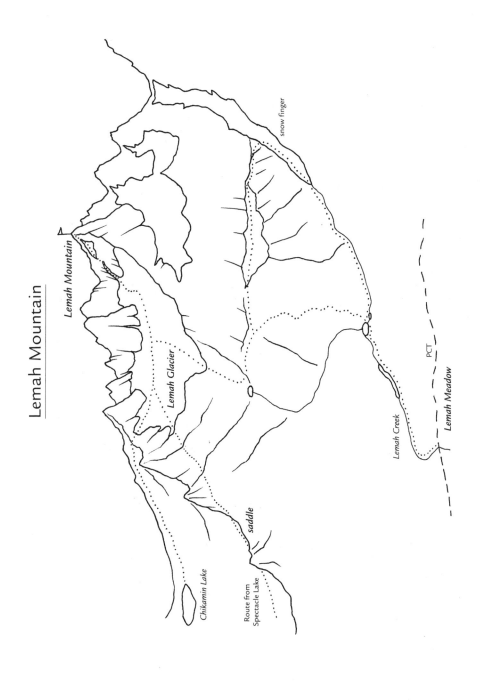

Lemah Mountain

snow finger

Lemah Mountain

Lemah Glacier

saddle

Chikamin Lake

Route from
Spectacle Lake

Lemah Creek

PCT

Lemah Meadow

miles to the head of Lemah Creek valley. From here, two routes lead to the glacier. Continue up Lemah Creek via the prominent snow gully leading northwest, then angle southward across a shelf and up moraine slopes to the glacier. Or, climb the slopes directly west from the valley to the glacier.

However you get there, rope up and ascend the glacier, entering a broad basin between the southern two of Lemah's false summits (Lemah One and Two). Contour northward, traversing around the east buttress of Lemah Two, and ascend a snow slope and chute to the upper snowpatch on Lemah's east face. The chute is the crux of the climb, involving steep snow/ice or difficult rock scrambling (at least Class 3, some say Class 4). Continue up snow or easy rock to the slight notch in the summit ridge, then scramble up the ridge to the summit of the middle peak (Lemah Three).

To descend, downclimb the route. Some parties rappel down the chute rather than downclimb Class 3-4 rock.

OPTIONS

An alternative approach begins from Spectacle Lake. This route is less direct and requires more cross-country hiking. From the PCT, skirt Spectacle Lake's northern shore, then hike cross-country up the stream basin leading west toward the Chikamin-Lemah divide. About 0.5 mile from the lake, ascend subalpine slopes northward to a broad saddle, then continue up the ridge, staying left of the rocky ridge point, to a higher saddle just below Lemah's southeast rocks. Scramble around the rocky ridge and contour to the glacier.

Each of Lemah's five fingers can be climbed via Class 2-4 routes, but it might take a couple of days to climb them all because of separate approach routes. Refer to *Cascade Alpine Guide* for route details. A complete traverse of the five summits has been reported (V, 5.4).

PRECAUTIONS

The slopes leading up to the glacier and upper chute are avalanche prone in winter and spring. There is rockfall hazard in the approach gullies, the chute, and below the upper buttresses. The glacier is relatively uncrevassed but should be crossed with caution; roping up is recommended. The chute is a Class 4 rock climb in late season, prompting many climbers to belay, particularly on the descent.

72. CHIMNEY ROCK

Elevation: 7,634 feet/2,327 meters
Route: East Face Direct
Rating: Grade IV, Class 5.6; Grade II–III glacier
Distance: 16 miles round trip
Elevation Gain: 4,800 feet
Time: Best done as a two- or three-day climb
Maps: USGS Chikamin Peak, Big Snow Mountain

ABOUT THE CLIMB

Chimney Rock is the highest of the Snoqualmie Crest peaks and probably the most difficult summit of the group, accessible only by ascending a steep glacier

Climber on East Face Direct, Chimney Rock.

and several pitches of steep technical rock. It is also the most striking, a dark rock citadel jutting up above the other peaks. Because of its prominence, Chimney Rock is a much sought-after summit, but there is no easy route to the summit of Chimney Rock, which makes it much too serious for mere scramblers and most climbers.

The first ascent was made by Art Winder, Forest Farr, and Laurence Byington in 1930, somewhat by accident. The party had climbed the east face chimney to the notch and summited the lower south summit, but had all but dismissed the final climb as impossible. Then they discovered a "blind chimney" giving access to a key ledge, from which an improbable ascent up a difficult chimney and "sheer rock face" gave access to the summit chimney. Fortunately, two of the party had the foresight to bring rubber-soled shoes, making possible the technical climbing that gained the summit.

Although its easiest route is frequently reported as a Class 4 climb, Chimney Rock is a serious mountaineering objective by any route with continuous, exposed Class 4–5 climbing. There have been a number of accidents on Chimney Rock. Although the standard route is easy enough climbing-wise, the routefinding is not easy and the commitment factor is high. The route reported here is East Face Direct (Grade IV, 5.6), the classic route up the mountain. The East Face route is slightly easier but is still a Class 5 climb with all of the seriousness and commitment of the direct route. Because the direct route is regarded by those who have climbed it as one of the best alpine rock routes in the region, it is given priority here. If you go to all the trouble of approaching this peak, you might as well climb the best route to the summit because you probably won't be back anytime soon.

Chimney Rock East Face Routes

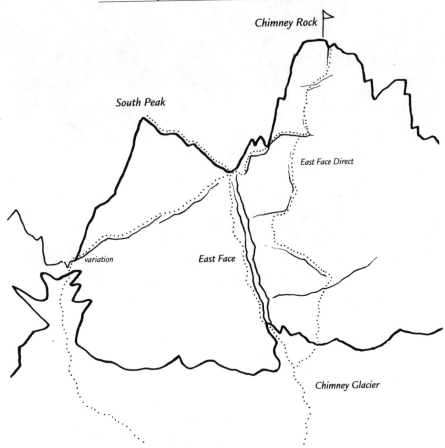

HOW TO GET THERE

Drive Interstate 90 to exit 80 (Roslyn/Salmon la Sac) near Cle Elum, then head north 3 miles to Washington Highway 903. Turn left and follow Washington Highway 903 east through Roslyn and Ronald, then north along the shore of Cle Elum Lake to Cle Elum River Campground. Turn left on well-marked Forest Road 46 and follow it for 4.8 unpaved miles to Cooper Lake. Take the right fork toward Owhi Campground and continue 1.2 miles to the road's end and the Cooper River (Pete Lake) trailhead. A Northwest Forest Pass is required.

ROUTE DESCRIPTION

East Face Direct, which is regarded as the classic route up Chimney Rock, is not the easiest. The route is commonly approached from the east side via Cooper River Trail. From the trailhead, hike Cooper River Trail (Trail 1323) for 4 relatively flat miles to Pete Lake. Continue to the far end of the lake, hiking another 2.1 miles, staying right at all forks, to meet the PCT at Lemah Meadow. Continue north on the PCT about 0.7 mile to the start of the switchbacks leading up to

Chimney Rock East Face Direct

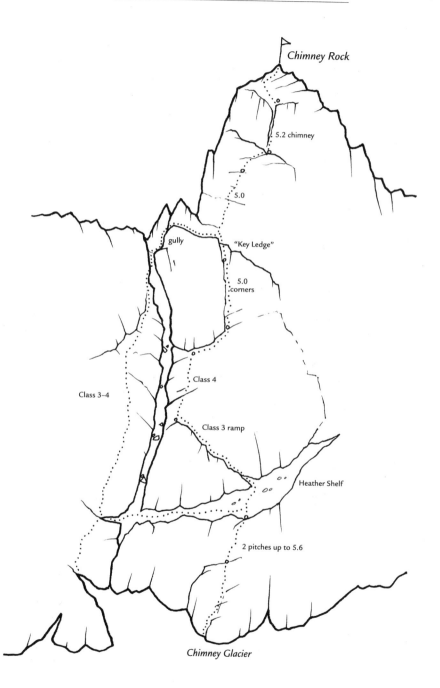

Chimney Rock

5.2 chimney

5.0

gully

"Key Ledge"

5.0 corners

Class 4

Class 3–4

Class 3 ramp

Heather Shelf

2 pitches up to 5.6

Chimney Glacier

Vista Lakes. Leave the trail at the first switchback and follow a climber's trail west; cross the creek and continue up the obvious gully just right of the creek descending from Chimney Glacier; pass waterfalls at about 4,400 feet and head into the basin above to the terminus of Chimney Glacier. Most parties camp here. Rope up and ascend the glacier, bearing right and up the icefall to the base of the east face, or via a central gully up the rock slope just left of the gully, which is easier but not as entertaining, especially if the icefall is "in shape."

The route begins almost directly below the summit, about 100 feet right of a broad gully (usually has a bergschrund). Climb a slabby rock buttress via 2 or 3 pitches of clean rock (up to 5.6 in difficulty) to a broad ledge. Scramble up the ledge, avoiding loose rock, to a higher ledge leading to the left. Follow the ledge to near the southern edge of the face, then climb up the obvious dihedral system (Class 4 and low 5) to a small bench below a headwall. Trend right and climb around an awkward corner, then go straight up a pretty dihedral and continue directly up to a bench about 400 feet below the summit (this is the "key ledge" described in Beckey's guide). From the bench, climb up and left on a small ramp, then go directly up steep Class 4–5 rock to the summit headwall. Traverse right on easy but exposed ledges to the base of an obvious chimney right of a clean headwall. Ascend the chimney (5.2). After 1 pitch, the chimney deepens. Here, you can exit on the face on the left or stay in the chimney and climb behind a big chockstone, then scramble to the summit.

To descend, rappel and downclimb the route or the East Face route. Bring double ropes, crampons, ice ax, one or two ice screws, and a medium rack of mostly medium size gear, plus several slings and a couple of pins in case you get off route and have to rappel or lower off.

OPTIONS
The East Face is the easiest route up Chimney Rock. It is reported as Class 4 but has low Class 5 climbing on the final pitches to the summit. Approach as for East Face Direct to the base of that route. Traverse left on the glacier to the base of the obvious gully splitting the east face. Climb the blocky gully and Class 3–4 slabs and ledges just left all the way to the notch south of the summit block. Traverse down and right from the notch and climb a hidden Class 4 chimney to a narrow, traversing ledge (the "key ledge"). Traverse the ledge briefly right onto the east face and join the East Face Direct for the final 3 pitches to the summit. An alternative approach to the east face notch involves climbing the glacier gully to the notch just south of the south peak, then traversing the shelf/ledge system right and up across the east face of the south peak to the upper notch. This option is Class 3–4, with loose rock and not recommended when snowy or icy.

PRECAUTIONS
Although technically easy as alpine rock routes go, this climb is long and complicated, both on the way up and on the way down. The approach is long and involved with significant off-trail travel and elevation gain. Routefinding can be difficult enough in good weather; if the weather turns bad, it can become all but impossible. Don't attempt Chimney Rock during questionable weather. Climbing is steep, sustained, and not always well protected. Snow or ice can linger on the route well into summer. Loose rock is abundant; spontaneous rockfall is

common. Be careful not to knock rocks down on your companions or other climbers. The climbing is continuously steep and exposed in places, with long runouts between protection, requiring a high level of confidence. Start early to avoid being caught on the route after dark. If you are climbing the icefall, a second ice tool will be helpful. Many climbers simul-climb a majority of the route, which saves significant time over belaying every pitch but requires great care and confidence.

73. SUMMIT CHIEF MOUNTAIN

Elevation: 7,464 feet/2,275 meters
Route: Southeast Ridge via Vista Lakes
Rating: Class 2–3
Distance: 22 miles round trip
Elevation Gain: 4,500 feet
Time: 8 to 10 hours to summit
Maps: USGS Big Snow Mountain, Mount Daniel; Green Trails No. 175 (Skykomish) and 176 (Stevens Pass)

ABOUT THE CLIMB

Summit Chief Mountain is another of the high peaks of the Snoqualmie Crest subrange. Despite its forbidding appearance from the west side, its summit can be reached via a relatively simple scramble on the east side. Although Summit Chief is an excellent alpine scramble, it is not especially popular due mostly to its relative inaccessibility. The shortest approach hike is about 9 miles, not counting cross-country hiking to the peak. Factor in driving time, and Summit Chief is out of reach as a one-day climb for most. Summit Chief is a reasonable overnight climb, though, great for an extended weekend including ascents of Lemah Mountain and Chikamin Peak. Summit views are spectacular, and include a close look at Chimney Rock and Mount Daniel, as well as a panorama of other high peaks such as Mount Stuart and Mount Rainier.

HOW TO GET THERE

The best approach is via Copper River Trail as described under Chimney Rock. A Northwest Forest Pass is required.

ROUTE DESCRIPTION

From the trailhead, hike Cooper River Trail (Trail 1323) for 4 relatively flat miles to Pete Lake. Continue 1.1 miles beyond Pete Lake to a trail junction, then take the right trail fork and hike 0.6 mile to the PCT at Lemah Meadow. Hike north on the PCT about 4.5 miles, including 3.5 miles of switchbacks that gain about 2,000 feet elevation, to the ridge crest at about 5,400 feet elevation. The trail reaches Vista Lakes, a cluster of tarns set in a high subalpine meadow just below the ridge crest. There are good bivy sites here. Leave the trail and hike northward up the ridge to a saddle at about 5,700 feet elevation, then follow the ridge crest northwest to Summit Chief Pass (or drop down and contour to Summit Chief Lake, then climb to the pass). Continue up the snow slopes just right (north) of the ridge crest into a snow basin just below the summit. Cross over the ridge and ascend a shallow rocky gully just left of the crest to the summit.

Summit Chief Mountain

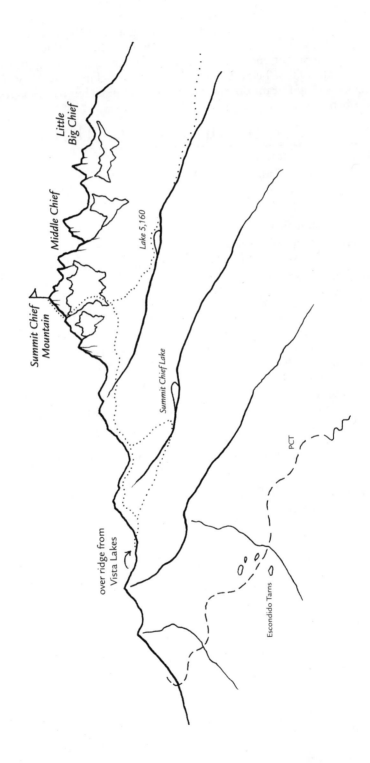

Summit Chief Mountain

Middle Chief

Little
Big Chief

Lake 5,160

Summit Chief Lake

over ridge from
Vista Lakes

PCT

Escondido Tarns

OPTIONS
Middle Chief (7,120 feet elevation) is the rock peak between Summit Chief and Little Big Chief. A Class 3 scramble up the north ridge is reported. An ascent of 7,225-foot Little Big Chief is a fairly straightforward Class 4 climb directly from Dutch Miller Gap. A traverse directly linking these three summits appears possible but has not been reported. Refer to *Cascade Alpine Guide* for route details.

PRECAUTIONS
The slopes below Summit Chief Mountain are avalanche prone in winter and spring. There is some rockfall exposure on the final climb to the summit.

74. MOUNT HINMAN

Elevation: 7,492 feet/2,284 meters
Route: West Ridge via La Bohn Gap
Rating: Class 2
Distance: 19 miles round trip
Elevation Gain: 5,200 feet
Time: 7 to 8 hours; best done as a two-day climb
Maps: USGS Mount Daniel; Green Trails No. 175 (Skykomish) and 176 (Stevens Pass)

ABOUT THE CLIMB
Mount Hinman is a significant but relatively unassuming peak in the heart of the Alpine Lakes Wilderness. Although Hinman is a distinct peak—at 7,492 feet it is one of the highest in the central Alpine Lakes Wilderness—it is generally regarded as barely more than a high point on the Mount Daniel summit ridge. It is visible only from surrounding summits and high ridges; and although glaciated and very alpine in nature, Hinman lacks the abruptness and cragginess of Mount Daniel. Like Daniel, Mount Hinman is a fairly remote glaciated peak of volcanic origin, but it is less rugged, easier to climb, and popular with adventuresome hikers and alpine scramblers approaching from Necklace Valley or Dutch Miller Trail. Mount Hinman can be climbed in a long day but is more popular as an overnight climb with a base camp at Williams Lake, Necklace Valley, or near La Bohn Gap. It offers good summit views, including the Snoqualmie Crest peaks to the south, Mount Stuart, Glacier Peak, and of course, Mount Daniel.

HOW TO GET THERE
The usual approach is via the Middle Fork Snoqualmie River and Dutch Miller Trail. Drive Interstate 90 to exit 34 in North Bend. Head north on 468th Avenue Southeast, past the service stations, for 0.6 mile to Southeast Middle Fork Road. Turn right and continue 0.9 mile to a fork. Stay right, taking Lake Dorothy Road (the higher road), and continue another 1.6 miles to the pavement's end where the road becomes Forest Road 56. Continue on Forest Road 56 another 9.5 miles, past the Middle Fork trailhead and across a bridge to the junction with Forest Road 56. Turn right on Forest 56 and continue 13.2 rough miles, staying left at all forks, to the trailhead at the road's end. A Northwest Forest Pass is required. Although only about 25 miles from North Bend, the road is so bad that it takes about two hours to drive to the trailhead. A high-clearance vehicle is recommended. Four-wheel drive is helpful.

Mount Hinman

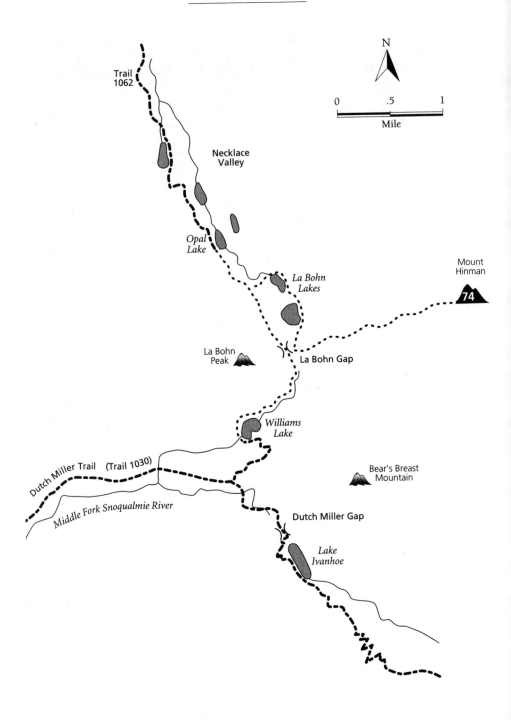

N

0   .5   1
Mile

Trail
1062

Necklace
Valley

Opal
Lake

La Bohn
Lakes

Mount
Hinman

74

La Bohn
Peak

La Bohn Gap

Williams
Lake

Dutch Miller Trail   (Trail 1030)

Bear's Breast
Mountain

Middle Fork Snoqualmie River

Dutch Miller Gap

Lake
Ivanhoe

ROUTE DESCRIPTION

Hike 6.8 miles up Dutch Miller Trail (Trail 1030) to the junction with Williams Lake Trail junction, then take the left fork and continue 0.6 mile to Williams Lake. Follow the old miner's trail around the lake's western shore and up along the inlet stream to Chain Lakes Basin. It's easy to lose the trail here; it begins just left of the entrance to the mine at the head of Williams Lake. Hike past the many small alpine lakes, then scramble up snow or heather and talus slopes to La Bohn Gap, elevation about 5,600 feet. There are several campsites at Williams Lake, in Chain Lakes Basin, and near La Bohn Gap. From La Bohn Gap, ascend heather and talus or snow slopes up to the crest of Mount Hinman's west ridge, then traverse eastward along the rocky ridge to the summit. The ridge is easy by climbing standards, with only a few sections of easy scrambling and a bit of loose blocky talus climbing near the top. Most of the ridge is just hiking on rock and snow with minimal exposure, similar to Mount Daniel's Southeast Ridge route but not nearly as long.

OPTIONS

La Bohn Gap may be approached via Necklace Valley Trail (Trail 1062). Some prefer this approach because it offers a shorter, gentler drive with just a bit more hiking. Considering the time it takes just to drive up Middle Fork Road, this may be the best option. Get an early start if you plan to climb Hinman in a day using this approach; and because this hike is so scenic, plan on taking two or three days. Drive U.S. Highway 2 to Foss River Road (Forest Road 68), about 2 miles east of Skykomish (just east of the ranger station). Follow Foss River Road for 1.1 paved miles to a fork where a sign points the way to various trailheads, including the one for East Fork Foss River Trail (Trail 1062). Take the right fork, continuing 3 gravel miles on Forest Road 68 to the trailhead parking lot on the left. Hike 8 miles to Necklace Valley, then continue on the way trail leading southward from Opal Lake to the basin below La Bohn Gap. Ascend to the gap directly via the obvious steep snow slope, or via a less obvious rock scramble to La Bohn Lakes, then continue up the west ridge to the summit. This is best done as an overnight climb with a camp at La Bohn Gap or Opal Lake. Definitely bring an ice ax and crampons for the snow slope below La Bohn Gap.

A high traverse of Mount Hinman and Mount Daniel is feasible assuming you can arrange transportation. The best direction is west to east.

PRECAUTIONS

The slopes leading up to La Bohn Gap are avalanche prone in winter and spring. Beware of cornices on the ridge and loose blocks and shifting talus. The approach drive via Middle Fork Road is notoriously bad. Getting bumped around on the rough, rocky road may give you whiplash or a concussion. Tie your gear down and hang on tight! The drive will abuse your car even more, so have a good towing plan. Bring a cell phone to call for assistance in case you bottom out, but don't count on getting a signal. The approach from Necklace Valley is recommended if you have any doubts about driving up Middle Fork Road; the hike is a little bit longer, but the drive is much shorter and less likely to result in injury to you or your car. The scramble up from Necklace Valley to La Bohn Gap is steep; a fatality has been reported here, so climb with care.

Mount Hinman

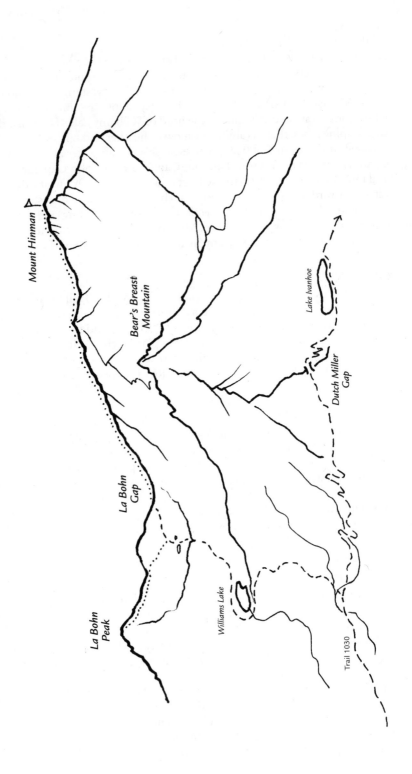

Mount Hinman

Bear's Breast
Mountain

La Bohn
Gap

La Bohn
Peak

Williams Lake

Lake Ivanhoe

Dutch Miller
Gap

Trail 1030

75. MOUNT DANIEL

Elevation: 7,986 feet/2,434 meters
Route: Hyas Creek Glacier/Southwest Ridge East
Rating: Class 3; Grade I or II glacier
Distance: 15 miles round trip
Elevation Gain: 5,000 feet
Time: 7 to 8 hours trailhead to summit
Maps: USGS Mount Daniel; Green Trails No. 176 (Stevens Pass)

ABOUT THE CLIMB

Mount Daniel is the highest summit of the Cascade crest between Stevens Pass and Snoqualmie Pass. It is a broad glaciated peak of volcanic origin punctuated with several craggy rock points and ridges. It is reminiscent of Mount Olympus, both in elevation and remoteness, although it is an easier climb, much less strenuous, and not as heavily glaciated. Unlike Olympus, Daniel is feasible in a single day although it is more popular as an overnight climb; and like Olympus, Daniel is hidden from view except from the high ridges and summits of the surrounding range.

Mount Daniel has three popular routes: Hyas Creek Glacier, Southeast Ridge, and Lynch Glacier. The former is the easier and faster route, but Lynch Glacier seems to be more popular, largely because the Mountaineers require climbers to summit via that route to earn credit for the peak as a glacier climb. The summit elevation is uncertain. It is reported as high as 7,986 feet and as low as 7,960 feet. USGS maps show East Peak at 7,960 feet elevation, but West Peak is clearly higher. Whatever the true elevation, Mount Daniel's summit views are an outstanding panorama of the interior peaks of the Cascades, all of the giants of the range, including Mount Rainier, Mount Adams, Mount Stuart, Bonanza Peak, Glacier Peak, Mount Baker, Mount Shuksan, the Monte Cristo peaks, and the surrounding peaks of the Alpine Lakes Wilderness.

HOW TO GET THERE

Drive Interstate 90 to exit 80 (Roslyn/Salmon la Sac) near Cle Elum, about 27 miles east of Snoqualmie Pass. Head north 2.8 miles to Washington Highway 903. Turn left and drive east on Washington Highway 903 through Roslyn and Ronald, then up Cle Elum River Road (Forest Road 4330) along the east shore of Cle Elum Lake for 16.5 miles to the pavement's end. The road forks here; take the right fork and continue another 12.3 miles to the Cathedral Pass trailhead on the left just 0.1 mile from the road's end. A Northwest Forest Pass is required. The road crosses two creeks, which are usually running high in spring and early summer, deterring some from driving all the way to the trailhead. A high-clearance vehicle is recommended. Otherwise you may have to park, ford the creeks, and walk the last couple of miles to the trailhead.

ROUTE DESCRIPTION

Hike Cathedral Pass Trail (Trail 1345) about 4 miles to its junction with the PCT. Take the left fork and switchback up over Cathedral Pass and down the other side. At the second switchback, not far below the pass, a spur trail departs, traversing the steep, rocky slopes below Cathedral Rock for about 0.7 mile to

Mount Daniel

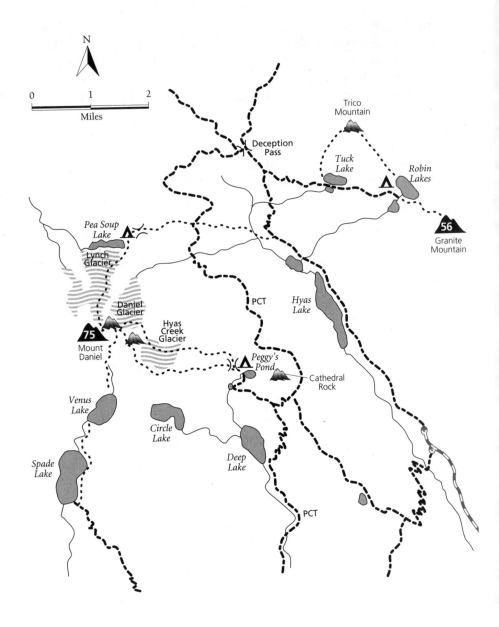

Mount Daniel and Lynch Glacier from Daniel Ridge camp.

Peggy's Pond. This is about 5 miles from the trailhead. Peggy's Pond is a small, deep lake at the base of Cathedral Rock's west face, not the small pond just past the foundation of the old miner's cabin. There are numerous abused bare ground sites near Peggy's Pond and in the moraine meadows just north. This is a heavily abused area, so please camp in designated sites only and make use of the pit toilet when the need arises.

From Peggy's Pond, two routes are popular, the Southeast Ridge and the Hyas Creek Glacier, both of which are discussed below.

To climb the Southeast Ridge route, follow the trail leading northwesterly past Peggy's Pond toward a small wooded saddle about 150 yards northwest of the lake. Just before the saddle, a climber's trail leads up through the meadows toward a small rock buttress. Follow the trail, which skirts the rock buttress on the left and ascends heather and talus slopes upward. (You can also follow a goat trail directly west up the ridge from the saddle.) There are a few bivy sites low on the ridge with lean-looking marmots to keep you company. Hike and scramble up rock or snow to the ridge crest; there are many possible route variations here, ranging from steep snow to Class 3 rock scrambling. Once to the ridge crest, hike and scramble along a well-worn path on or near the rocky crest to a broad 7,000-foot saddle above Hyas Creek Glacier. Continue up the steepening ridge, occasionally traversing on the south side of the crest (scree or snow and a few moves of loose Class 3 scrambling). You can follow a faint climber's trail much of the way, but it is easy to lose in a couple of places, especially if snow lingers, and most easily on the descent. At 7,500 feet elevation, scramble down steep, loose scree on the south side of the ridge to a gap at the head of a gully above some craggy tufa pinnacles (the core of the old volcano), then climb steep scree slopes on the other side of the gap to a rocky point just southeast of East Peak (Point 7,662). There

Gordon Schryer

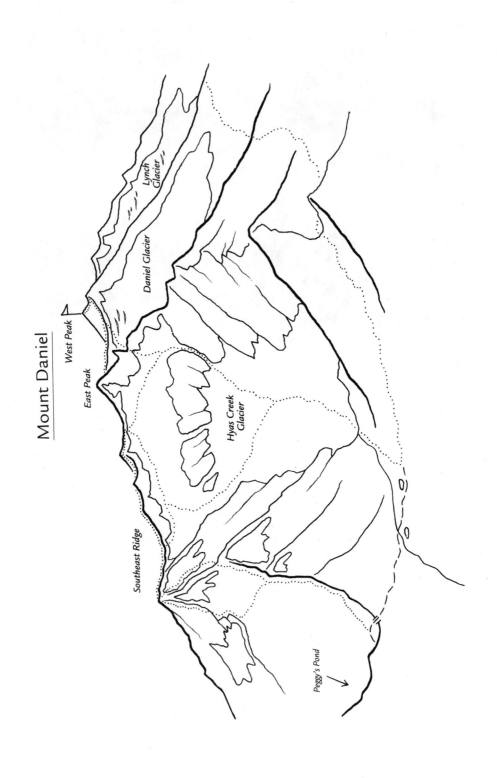

Mount Daniel

West Peak

East Peak

Lynch Glacier

Daniel Glacier

Southeast Ridge

Hyas Creek Glacier

Peggy's Pond

is some loose rock here—a bit tenuous when patchy snow or icy. This upper ridge can be bypassed by crossing over at the 7,000-foot saddle and traversing snow slopes on the north side of the ridge to the East Peak saddle (steep snow, ice ax recommended). Continue to the broad saddle south of East Peak and up briefly to the shoulder of East Peak, then traverse easy snow or tedious scree slopes south of East Peak, around an intervening ridge to the low point of the long ridge dividing East Peak and West Peak. Continue westward along the ridge to the first summit point (Middle Peak, 7,970 feet elevation), then along the ridge crest to the 7,986-foot West Peak, the true summit.

Hyas Creek Glacier route (sometimes referred to as Daniel Glacier route) also begins from Peggy's Pond. It is probably the easiest and fastest route up the mountain, but it is pretty much a snow slog and not as scenic or interesting as the other routes. Follow the trail past Peggy's Pond and across the small divide into a broad glacial meadow with several tarns. Take the first left fork in the meadow and follow a climber's trail westward along a creek and up through moraines to the terminus of Hyas Creek Glacier, a permanent snowfield that rarely shows crevasses. Ascend the gentle glacier, then climb the obvious steep snow chute on the right (or one of many variations more directly up the headwall, especially in early season when snow covers the loose rock) to the upper snow slopes below East Peak. Two variations are popular here. The first and most popular contours right below the obvious big spire on the northeast ridge, then traverses the upper slopes of Daniel Glacier, skirting crevasses, to the upper saddle and west along the ridge to Middle Peak and West Peak. The second option angles left, traversing snow slopes below East Peak to the broad saddle between East Peak and Point 7,662, then continues as for the Southeast Ridge route to the summit.

OPTIONS

The 7,960-foot East Peak is a popular objective, probably climbed as often as the true summit, especially by climbers who see how far away the summit is and decide to quit, but still want to say they climbed something. It is most easily ascended via obvious snow slopes and rock ridges on the east side via Hyas Creek Glacier or the Southeast Ridge. The Lynch Glacier route is somewhat remote but very popular. Refer to *Cascade Alpine Guide*.

PRECAUTIONS

The Southeast Ridge may involve some moderately steep, exposed snow climbing above rocks and cliffs. Cornices form on the Southeast Ridge, so don't get too close to the edge if climbing snow along the crest. There is some exposed ridge walking, a few loose Class 3 traverses, and several loose scree sections on the ridge. Hyas Creek Glacier route has steep snow and may show late-season crevasses. The Daniel Glacier variation has crevasses; roping up is recommended. All routes have avalanche-prone slopes. The snow chute above Hyas Creek Glacier narrows to nothing by late season and can be undermined. One party reported seeing a bear high on the Hyas Creek Glacier during late summer; they are likely to lurk around Peggy's Pond, although mosquitos and biting flies are the chief complaint here. Also troublesome are late-season hunters, who clog up the trailhead parking lot and shoot up the woods starting in late September most years.

South Cascades Locator Map

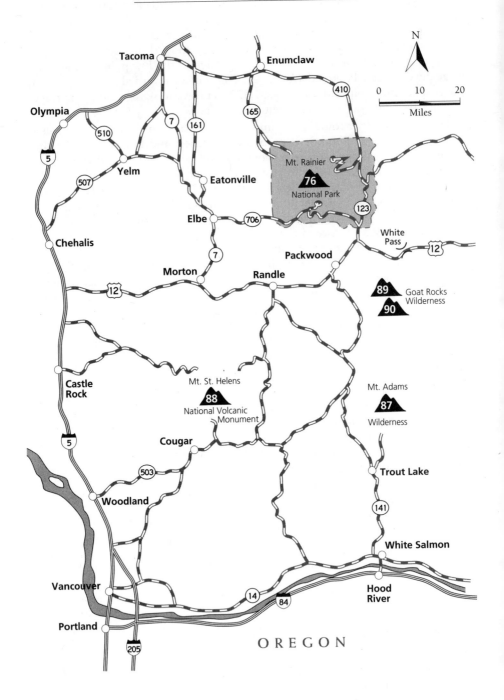

The South Cascades

Aside from the high volcanoes, Mounts Rainier, Adams, and St. Helens, the South Cascades pale in comparison with the rugged, icy North Cascades. The region is characterized by a few big, glaciated volcanoes rising above a sea of nondescript, forested mountains. A few pockets of craggy peaks rise above the clearcuts and timber, including the Goat Rocks and high ridges east of Mount Rainier. However, with the exception of the volcanoes and a few wilderness summits, there is very little here to interest climbers. But what is here is of very great interest to climbers. Mount Rainier and Mount Adams, the state's highest and second highest summit, respectively, and Mount St. Helens, a world famous volcano due to its catastrophic eruption in 1980, are climbed by thousands annually.

As climbing objectives, the peaks of the South Cascades offer limited variety, either big volcano climbs or loose scrambles. Due to the nature of the rock, which is mostly crumbly volcanic rock, there is little if any worthwhile technical climbing in this region. A majority of climbers set their sights on the volcanoes for obvious reasons. However, there are several worthy peaks scattered throughout the range, mostly within Mount Rainier National Park and Goat Rocks Wilderness. Most of these can be climbed via scrambling routes, most of them via relatively simple ridge hikes and scree gullies.

Due to the nature of the rock, climber-inflicted rockfall is common in the South Cascades, especially in gullies and on open faces; and scramblers and climbers are advised to wear helmets at all times on any route climbing on or below rock. Because of the generally poor rock quality, many of these summits are popular in spring and early summer when snow offers relatively easy and safe passage over otherwise loose rock. However, snow climbing has its own risks. Generally, more climbing accidents are attributable to slips and falls on snow and to avalanches than to rockfall. Many snow slopes and gullies do not have a safe runout, leaving climbers little time to self-arrest before sliding into rocks or over cliffs. Nearly every peak has avalanche danger in winter and spring, sometimes well into summer during years of heavy snowfall. Crampons and an ice ax should be carried by all members of your party well into summer, particularly if your intended route ascends a gully or north-facing slope.

A Cascades Volcano Pass is required for ascents of Mount Adams and Mount St. Helens. A separate permit is required for Mount Rainier. Details are included where appropriate and in Appendix B. For additional information about permits and climbing routes, contact the NPS or Forest Service, or log on to the appropriate Web site listed in Appendix C.

Austin Post/USGS

Mount Rainier and Little Tahoma Peak.

Mount Rainier National Park

Mount Rainier National Park is the primary destination of South Cascades climbers and scramblers for good reason. The state's highest mountain, the centerpiece of the park, is ringed by many ridges and summits that offer a variety of scrambling and climbing opportunities. Some of the best non-volcano climbing in the South Cascades is found in Mount Rainier National Park, as well as hundreds of miles of scenic hiking trails. A sampling of those climbs and scrambles is included in this guide. For more information about the many hikes, scrambles, climbs, and ski and snowshoe tours in Mount Rainier National Park, refer to *Adventure Guide to Mount Rainier* or one of the other guides listed in Appendix D.

Driving Directions
In western Washington, all roads lead to Mount Rainier National Park. At least it may seem that way when you look at a road map. Despite a confusing assortment of state, federal, and interstate highways, only five main highways lead to the park: U.S. Highway 12 and Washington Highway 410, 7, 123, and 165. The following directions should assist you in getting where you want to go in the park. These are not the only routes to reach the park but the easiest to describe and follow for those who have not discovered the many back roads and shortcuts.

Longmire and Paradise
Lying high on the south slopes of Mount Rainier, Paradise is the primary tourist area of Mount Rainier National Park and the starting point of many hiking trails and climbing routes. The road leading to Paradise is open year round but gated at night during the winter months. If you are coming from Seattle or Tacoma, follow Washington Highway 7 south from Tacoma to the town of Elbe, then continue east on Washington Highway 706 past Ashford and the park headquarters to the Nisqually Entrance. If you are coming from Portland or southwest Washington, follow U.S. Highway 12 east to Morton, then head north on Washington Highway 7 to Elbe and continue east on Washington Highway 706 to the Nisqually Entrance. If you are coming from Enumclaw, follow U.S. Highway 410 south to Cayuse Pass, then continue south on Washington Highway 123 to the Stevens Canyon Entrance. Head west up Stevens Canyon and past Reflection Lakes to the turnoff for Paradise. If Longmire is your destination, keep going west past the turnoff for Paradise. Finally, if you are coming from eastern Washington, follow U.S. Highway 12 west from Yakima over White Pass, then turn north on Washington Highway 123 to the Stevens Canyon Entrance and continue to Paradise or Longmire.

Sunrise and White River
Like Paradise, Sunrise occupies a high meadow with inspiring views of Mount Rainier. It is a very popular tourist destination and the starting point for many hiking trails and climbing routes. The road to Sunrise is open during the summer and fall months only, closing after the first major snowfall each year and not reopening until Memorial Day most years. If you are coming from Seattle, follow Washington Highway 169 (the "Maple Valley Highway") south from Renton to

Mount Rainier National Park

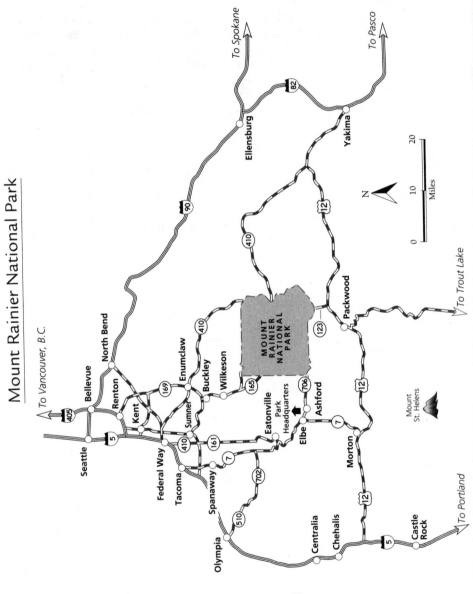

A 1920s climbing party on upper Nisqually Glacier, Mount Rainier.

Enumclaw. From Tacoma, follow Washington Highway 410 east to Enumclaw. From there, continue east then south via Washington Highway 410 about an hour to the park boundary. White River Road forks off to the right about 5 miles inside the park. If coming from eastern Washington, follow Washington Highway 410 from Yakima over Chinook Pass to Cayuse Pass and the junction with Washington Highway 123. Continue north on Washington Highway 410 about 3 miles to the turnoff for White River. If coming from southwestern Washington, follow U.S. Highway 12 to Packwood, then turn north on Washington Highway 123 and continue over Cayuse Pass and down Washington Highway 410 about 3 miles to the turnoff for White River. The White River Entrance is about 2 miles from the turnoff.

Carbon River and Mowich Lake

Carbon River and Mowich Lake are the only two areas accessible by road in the northwest corner of Mount Rainier National Park. Both roads are unpaved, and Carbon River Road is occasionally closed for repairs due to flood damage. The only road leading to Carbon River and Mowich Lake is Washington Highway 165. To get there, make your way to Buckley, a small town just southwest of Enumclaw. You can reach Buckley directly via Washington Highway 410 east from Tacoma or south from Enumclaw. From Buckley, head south on Washington Highway 165, which leads through the mining towns of Wilkeson and Carbonado. If you need a permit, visit the NPS office in Wilkeson. Nearer the park boundary, the highway crosses the historic Fairfax Bridge, which is sometimes closed for repairs or restoration. Just across the bridge, the road forks. Carbon River Road is on the left and leads to the Carbon River Entrance. The right fork leads 16 bumpy miles to Mowich Lake.

Peaks of Mount Rainier National Park

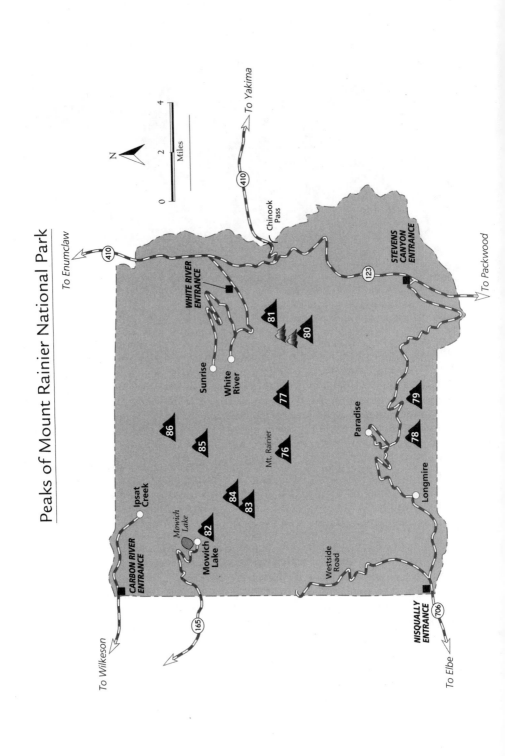

Park Entrance Fees

Park entry fees are required at all entry stations (Nisqually, Stevens Canyon, White River, and Carbon River) unless you arrive very early or very late when the entry stations are closed. There is no entry fee for Mowich Lake or for travel on Washington Highway 410 or 123. Entry fees are presently:

- $5.00 for a single person entry by foot, bicycle, motorcycle, or bus. Valid seven days. Persons sixteen and under get in free.

- $10.00 for a single vehicle entry. Includes vehicle and all occupants. Valid for seven days.

- $20.00 for a one-year pass. Valid one year from the month of purchase.

- $10.00 for a Golden Age Passport. Valid one year from the month of purchase. Access to all federal fee areas for persons sixty-two and older.

- $50.00 for a Golden Eagle Passport, a lifetime pass for U.S. residents sixty-two and older. Valid at all federal fee areas.

- Free Golden Access Passport, a lifetime pass for U.S. citizens or permanent residents who are blind or permanently disabled.

Other fees apply within Mount Rainier National Park. Auto camping fees ($10 to $14 per night) are charged at all campgrounds. Reservations are required at Ohanapecosh Campground and Cougar Rock Campground between July 1 and Labor Day; for details call (800) 365-2267, fax (301) 722-1174, or write to National Park Reservation Service, P.O. Box 1600, Cumberland, MD 21502. All other campgrounds are on a first-come, first-served basis.

Park entry fees are subject to change. Contact Mount Rainier National Park at (360) 569-2211 or log on to the park Web site at www.nps.gov/mora for current fee information.

Wilderness Permits and Climbing Permits

A wilderness permit program is in effect at Mount Rainier National Park. From May through September, overnight hikers must obtain a wilderness permit. This permit is free at last check, but call ahead to be sure. If you want to register in advance, a $20 fee applies. No permit is required for day use other than the park entry fee.

A climbing permit is required for persons climbing Mount Rainier and venturing onto the glaciers or above 10,000 feet elevation within the park. The climbing permit fee is presently $15. An annual pass is available for $25, a good investment for those who plan on climbing Mount Rainier or Little Tahoma Peak more than once a year.

As always, permit requirements and fees are subject to change. Just remember to call ahead and bring some cash with you so you don't get turned away at the gate. For current information about hiking and climbing permits, contact the NPS by telephone at (360) 569-2211, by e-mail at MORAinfo@nps.gov, through the internet at www.nps.gov/mora, or by mail at Mount Rainier National Park, Tahoma Woods, Star Route, Ashford, WA 98304-9751.

Wilderness Preservation

Because Mount Rainier National Park receives more than 2 million visitors annually, the landscape is subject to overuse and careless abuse. For this reason, I have omitted some popular scrambles and high traverses, particularly in the areas of Sunrise, Spray Park, and Indian Henry's Hunting Ground. Paradise, Sunrise, and other popular subalpine meadows and alpine zones throughout the park, and indeed throughout the Cascades and Olympics, are barely recovering from adverse impacts suffered decades ago. When visiting fragile areas of the park, please stay on the trail as much as possible and practice low impact techniques to avoid further adverse impacts.

76. MOUNT RAINIER

Elevation: 14,411 feet/4393 meters
Route: Disappointment Cleaver/Emmons Glacier
Rating: Class 2–3; Grade II glacier
Distance: 12 miles round trip.
Elevation Gain: 9,000 feet
Time: Best done as a three-day climb
Maps: USGS Mount Rainier East and West, and Sunrise; Green Trails No. 269 (Mount Rainier West) and 207 (Mount Rainier East)

ABOUT THE CLIMB

Mount Rainier is the crown jewel of the Cascade Range. Certainly other Cascade peaks have their charms, but Rainier stands supreme as a climbing objective. At 14,411 feet elevation, it is the highest summit in the Cascade Range, and is visible from nearly every high ridge, summit, and city for over 100 miles. It is one of the most heavily glaciated peaks in the range, so the mountain remains stark white throughout the year, giving it an unmistakable presence and an undeniable appeal. The mountain is the dominant landmark of the Puget Sound region, visible to millions of Washington residents, thousands of whom attempt to reach its summit each year. The uniqueness and grandeur of Mount Rainier and its surrounding peaks and forests were recognized early enough that the mountain was preserved as a national park on March 2, 1899.

More than 4,000 people climb Mount Rainier each year, and over 10,000 attempt the climb. About 30 percent of climbers are guided via Disappointment Cleaver or Emmons Glacier, although there are a number of popular routes on all sides of the mountain. The rating, distance, elevation gain, and time listed on the table are for Disappointment Cleaver. Emmons Glacier is longer with more elevation gain.

Because of its prominence and attractiveness to climbers, Mount Rainier has been the site of many climbing accidents and fatalities. Although it is only slightly more hazardous than some of the other peaks in this guide, the sheer volume of climbers coupled with the mountain's size, high elevation, steep glaciers, loose rock, and rapid weather fluctuations greatly increase the statistical chances of an accident occurring. Every year it seems at least a few people are killed while

Mark S. Dale

Sunrise on Ingraham Glacier, Mount Rainier.

climbing Mount Rainier. Approach the climb with safety first, and be prepared to turn back if conditions become unsafe.

Because of its height and proximity to the Pacific Ocean, Mount Rainier truly creates its own weather. The mountain stands directly in the path of prevailing marine winds. These winds funnel moist air across the glaciers, resulting in weather that seems unique to the mountain, including the onset of sudden storms. This accounts for the high annual snowfall on the mountain and the number of climbers who are lost or stranded on the mountain during storms every year.

Mount Rainier, consisting of twenty-six glaciers covering more than 35 square miles, has the largest single-mountain glacier system in the United States outside of Alaska. However, Mount Rainier's mantle of ice belies its fiery origins. Mount Rainier is a stratovolcano that, like many other high volcanoes of the Cascade Range, lies dormant but not extinct. Geologists speculate that the mountain once rose to a height of more than 16,000 feet, but that a subsequent violent eruption, possibly like Mount St. Helens in 1980, blasted over 2,000 feet off the top and left a wide crater, which later erupted to form the present cone and two well-preserved craters that now make up the summit area. It is predicted that Mount Rainier will erupt again in the future with possible catastrophic results.

Climbing Mount Rainier is subject to many rules and regulations. Climbers going higher than 10,000 feet are required to register and obtain permits in advance and to check out upon their return. Permits are $15 per climb or $25 for a season pass. The NPS limits the number of climbers occupying high camps, such as Camp Muir and Camp Schurman, and permits are issued on a first-come, first-served basis, so arrive early or register in advance. Party size is limited to twelve persons. Climbers under the age of eighteen years must have written parental consent. Parties of two or more are required above high camps. Solo climbers must obtain advance permission from the park superintendent. Guiding for a fee is prohibited except by authorized guide services. Use of blue bags to pack out human waste is mandatory. Any violation of these regulations is punishable by a fine. For more information about climbing Mount Rainier, log on to the NPS Web site or refer to one of the other resources listed in Appendix C.

HOW TO GET THERE

Driving directions to Mount Rainier are included at the beginning of this section. If you are climbing Disappointment Cleaver, follow the directions to Paradise. Register and obtain your climbing permit at Longmire or Paradise ranger stations. If you are climbing Emmons Glacier, follow the directions to White River. Register and obtain your climbing permit at the White River entry station.

ROUTE DESCRIPTIONS

There are dozens of routes to the summit of Mount Rainier, but two routes, Disappointment Cleaver and Emmons Glacier, have gained popularity over the years, primarily due to easy access, convenient high camps, and lack of technical difficulty. Both routes are included here.

Disappointment Cleaver (also called the "D.C." or "Muir Route") is the most popular route up Mount Rainier, primarily because it is the standard guided route to the summit, and also because it is the most accessible of the two "easy" routes. This climb begins at Paradise and ascends the Skyline Trail for about 2 miles, nearly to Panorama Point, to the junction with Pebble Creek Trail, then leads up that trail to the Muir Snowfield. In early season, much of the trail is snow-covered; but unless you come after a snowfall, there will usually be a well-defined path to follow. From the trail's end, ascend the Muir Snowfield to Camp Muir, elevation 10,100 feet, the usual bivouac site for summit-bound climbers. The shelter is available on a first-come, first-served basis; it holds twenty-five people and has an emergency radio inside. If there's no room at the shelter, find a tent site. There is a limit of 110 people per night at Camp Muir. Please use the toilets here to avoid contaminating this heavily used area. Other regulations apply to Camp Muir; find out about them when registering at the ranger station.

A note on the approach to Camp Muir. It is very easy to become disoriented here during poor visibility. Many hikers, climbers, and skiers have vanished on the Muir Snowfield. The tendency is to follow the natural fall line, which unfortunately leads onto the Nisqually Glacier or down steep, avalanche-prone slopes, above Paradise Glacier. A simple compass reading can help prevent you from getting lost between Camp Muir and Paradise. The NPS provides an information sheet that has compass bearings for the ascent to and descent from Camp Muir. Be sure to get one and keep it handy in case the weather turns bad.

From Camp Muir, traverse northward across the Cowlitz Glacier toward 10,640-foot Cathedral Gap, an obvious gap in the ridge at the far side of the glacier. Continue through the gap via snow or scree and across the Ingraham Glacier to Ingraham Flats, a flat area on the glacier about halfway to Disappointment Cleaver. Ingraham Flats is a popular alternative campsite, allowing a shorter ascent on summit day. There is a limit of thirty-five people per night

USGS

allowed at Ingraham Flats. From here, there are two popular options. In early season, some climbers prefer to ascend the Ingraham Glacier directly from the flats. This involves climbing through an icefall, which becomes more hazardous later in the season. By June or July, most climbers opt for the Disappointment Cleaver itself. The route passes below a notorious icefall just before the cleaver. Move quickly to avoid prolonged exposure to this hazard. Ascend the cleaver, following snowfields and scree to the head of the cleaver at about 12,300 feet elevation, the traditional make-or-break point of the climb. The route continues up the glaciers, weaving through crevasses, over snow bridges, and across or around the bergschrund to the rim of the east crater. The route varies from season to season and year to year, depending on snow and crevasse conditions. Sometimes you can go straight up from the cleaver to the summit; often the route angles left up to the head of Gibraltar Rock, then up to the crater rim. Some climbers call the crater rim the "summit" and head back down, although the true summit, Columbia Crest, is a simple and literally breathtaking walk across the crater or along the crater rim. Columbia Crest is merely a pumice ridge dividing the east and west craters, but it's as high as you can get in Washington, and indeed, in the entire Cascade Range.

The Emmons Glacier is the largest of Mount Rainier's glaciers, descending in a broad, heavily crevassed sheet down the northeast flank of the mountain, nearly 2 miles from the summit to its terminus at the headwaters of the White River. Although the route is referred to as Emmons Glacier (also called the "Schurman Route" after the popular campsite), the route involves climbing on both the Emmons and Winthrop Glaciers. This climb begins at White River Campground, following the Glacier Basin Trail 3.5 miles to its end, then continuing via a climber's trail up an old moraine to the terminus of Inter Glacier. Rope

USGS

up and ascend the glacier, crossing or skirting several crevasses midway up, to the saddle dividing Mount Ruth and Steamboat Prow. From here, either descend scree slopes to the Emmons Glacier and continue up the glacier to Camp Schurman, or continue nearly to the top of Steamboat Prow and descend Class 2–3 gullies just below and left of the prow to Camp Schurman, elevation 9,500 feet. Camp Schurman is the customary bivy site for summit-bound climbers on the Emmons Glacier route.

From Camp Schurman, ascend directly up the glacier, staying approximately in the middle of Emmons Glacier and Winthrop Glacier. Several hundred feet above Camp Schurman is Emmons Flats, a broad, relatively flat area at about 9,800 feet, which is a popular alternate bivouac site. Continue up the glacier, ascending the corridor of unbroken snow and ice between the glaciers as high as possible (usually to about 11,200 feet) to where the route steepens and crevasses force a detour. Most parties angle right up the Winthrop Glacier toward the col dividing Liberty Cap and Columbia Crest in order to skirt the bergschrund.

Some are able to cross it directly, although by late season this is usually not an option. Some contour left toward Disappointment Cleaver to outflank the bergschrund. The route varies from year to year depending on glacier and crevasse conditions. However the bergschrund is negotiated, continue up firn slopes to the crater rim and on to Columbia Crest.

For both routes, descend the route of ascent. Most parties have a hard enough time descending their route of ascent during poor weather, so don't make things harder by descending by a different route.

OPTIONS
There are a number of other popular routes up Mount Rainier. The best are probably the Furher Finger and Kautz Glacier on the south side, the Tahoma Glacier on the west, and Liberty Ridge♦—the mountain's most classic route—on the north. For information about climbing these routes, refer to *Adventure Guide to Mount Rainier, Climbing the Cascade Volcanoes*, or one of the other guidebooks listed in Appendix D.

PRECAUTIONS
Approach Mount Rainier with this in mind. More people have died on Mount Rainier than on any other mountain in the Cascade Range with the possible exception of Mount Hood. In fact, on average, at least one or two people are killed in climbing accidents on Mount Rainier each year, primarily due to avalanches and slips on steep glacier ice, but occasionally due to falls into crevasses, rockfall and icefall, hypothermia, and altitude sickness. Mount Rainier is subject to sudden changes in weather and getting caught unprepared in a storm high on the mountain has led to innumerable rescues and evacuations. Simply put, there is no guaranteed safe route to the summit of Mount Rainier. Climb at your own risk.

Although Disappointment Cleaver and Emmons Glacier are relatively easy compared with other routes on Mount Rainier, they are by no means "easy" routes without risk. Both are serious mountaineering routes with unavoidable hazards. On Disappointment Cleaver, the principal hazards are avalanches, icefall where the route traverses the Ingraham Glacier to the cleaver, crevasses, rockfall below and on the cleaver and other rock formations, weather, and altitude. Avalanches and icefalls have claimed many lives on this route. On June 11, 1981, eleven people were killed in a single accident when blocks of ice avalanched onto several guided parties as they crossed the Ingraham Glacier. There have been other accidents and close calls below the icefall. Rockfall on Disappointment Cleaver is an unavoidable hazard, especially climber-caused rockfall. Countless climbers have slipped and fallen on the glacier, sometimes dragging their ropemates with them into crevasses.

The Emmons Glacier has also had its share of climbing accidents, many involving slips and falls on ice, particularly in late summer when the snow has melted leaving a hard, slippery ice surface on the steep upper glacier slopes. Avalanches, icefall, and falls into crevasses are common too. Snow bridges are generally unreliable; cross them prepared for a plunge into the crevasse. Descend as soon as possible because the afternoon heat weakens snow bridges, loosens rock, and destabilizes snow slopes, increasing the risk of an accident. Many fatigued climbers have slipped or tripped on the descent and fallen, dragging their ropemates with them, often with fatal results. On any route, be very careful on the descent, when you are more likely to make a fatigue-induced mistake.

Because of its lofty elevation, climbers on Mount Rainier frequently suffer symptoms of acute mountain sickness (AMS), high altitude pulmonary edema (HAPE), and high altitude cerebral edema (HACE). Climbers rushing from the city to high camp in the afternoon and to the summit the next morning are at the highest risk. Don't try for an ascent from sea level to the summit in under twenty-four hours; take your time. It is recommended that climbers acclimatize before their summit bid. Climbers suffering symptoms of AMS, HAPE, or HACE should descend immediately.

An ice ax, crampons, and a helmet are required, as is roping up on the glaciers. Everyone in the climbing party should be proficient in and prepared for self-arrest and crevasse rescue. Wanding the route during the ascent is recommended, especially if weather may deteriorate, as it all too often does. Check route conditions before your climb, either at the ranger station or on-line at www.nps.gov/mora/climb/climb.htm.

Mount Rainier is a serious endurance test, so get yourself in very good physical condition before you attempt the climb. Get an early start from high camp. Carry plenty of water with you on summit day. Be prepared for anything, especially the onset of bad weather and for the possibility of crevasse rescue or an unplanned bivouac.

Before climbing Mount Rainier, you should read Dee Molenaar's book, *The Challenge of Rainier*, which contains a history of nearly every fatal accident on Mount Rainier. If you know what mistakes other climbers have made, hopefully you won't repeat them. Check current route and weather conditions before your climb. They are posted at various ranger stations and on the NPS Web site.

77. LITTLE TAHOMA PEAK

Elevation: 11,138 feet/3,395 meters
Route: Whitman Glacier
Rating: Class 3; Grade I glacier
Distance: 12 miles round trip
Elevation Gain: 8,600 feet
Time: 10 to 12 hours trailhead to summit; best done as a two-day climb
Maps: USGS Mount Rainier East; Green Trails No. 270 (Mount Rainier East)

ABOUT THE CLIMB
Little Tahoma Peak is a satellite peak of Mount Rainier. Although Little Tahoma seems insignificant compared with its lofty neighbor, at least from a distance, it is in fact the third highest peak in Washington State. It is moderately popular and involves relatively easy glacier climbing with just a bit of loose rock scrambling to the summit, although that little bit is very loose and very scary, so much so that the Mountaineers give credit for the climb even if you stop well short of the summit. Little Tahoma's reputation for loose rock is well deserved.

Little Tahoma Peak from above Camp Schurman.

Like many other Cascades volcanoes, Little Tahoma's rock varies between shattered and rotten, or worse.

A major rockfall from the north face deposited millions of cubic yards of debris on the Emmons Glacier. A 1959 route up the north face went unrepeated, and even then was considered a death route. The craggy, rotten West Ridge was one of the "last great problems" on Mount Rainier until it was finally climbed in 1981 in full winter conditions. However, even though the rotten rock was covered by ice, the first ascent party experienced rockfall. The summit scramble is no exception. Expect loose rock and wear a helmet.

Except for the summit scramble, Little Tahoma is an enjoyable, relatively mild glacier climb. Even from below the summit, the views are exquisite, but from the top they are unsurpassed. You will get a frightening look down to the Emmons Glacier and Ingraham Glacier and views across the entire eastern part of Mount Rainier National Park, with several big volcanoes including Mount Adams, Mount Hood, Mount St. Helens, and Mount Baker rising in the distance. Because it involves glacier travel above 10,000 feet elevation, climbing Little Tahoma Peak requires a permit, which is available at the White River Ranger Station.

HOW TO GET THERE

This climb begins via Summerland Trail from White River Road. Follow the directions to White River Entrance. Pay the entry fee, register, and obtain a climbing permit at the entry station, then continue another 2.9 miles up White River Road to the Summerland trailhead on the left. Parking is limited and often overcrowded on sunny summer weekends. Be sure to park in designated areas only and off the road.

Little Tahoma Peak and Cowlitz Chimneys

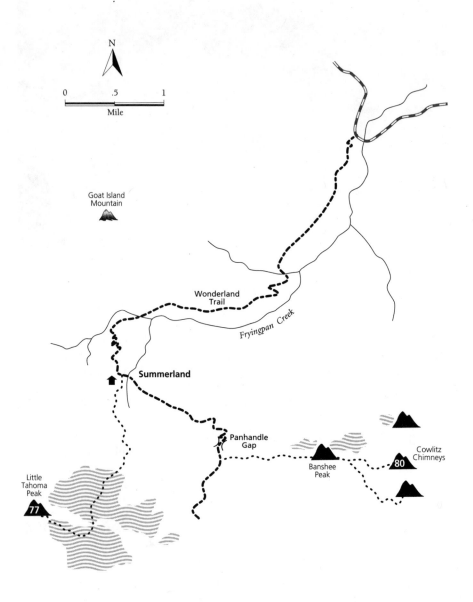

N

0 .5 1
Mile

Goat Island
Mountain

Wonderland
Trail

Fryingpan Creek

Summerland

Panhandle
Gap

Cowlitz
Chimneys

80

Banshee
Peak

Little
Tahoma
Peak

77

Little Tahoma Peak

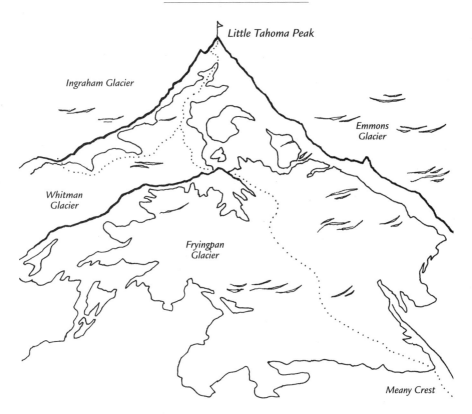

Little Tahoma Peak

Ingraham Glacier

Emmons
Glacier

Whitman
Glacier

Fryingpan
Glacier

Meany Crest

ROUTE DESCRIPTION

Hike 3.5 miles up the trail to Summerland, one of the more popular subalpine meadows of Mount Rainier National Park. The trail is steep and strenuous in places. Continue up through the meadow to the stone shelter hut. Some parties hike in during the afternoon and camp here, others bivouac higher up on the glacier, and still others grind it out to the summit and back in a single day.

A climber's trail leads up the meadow slope behind the shelter and continues across the moraines and up over Meany Crest to the Fryingpan Glacier, so named because it is shaped like a frying pan, or at least some old-time miner thought so. Stick to the trail here; do not shortcut across the fragile meadows. From Meany Crest, rope up and ascend the glacier, angling right toward the obvious 9,060-foot saddle in the ridge dividing Fryingpan Glacier and Whitman Glacier. Cross the saddle and descend onto the Whitman Glacier, then ascend to the head of the glacier, staying right of the bergschrund. Continue up a snow finger and a rocky gully to a gap below the summit horn, then traverse across and up frightfully loose, exposed rock to the summit.

To descend, downclimb the route. Glissading on the glaciers is not recommended because of crevasses.

OPTIONS

Little Tahoma Peak can be approached from Paradise via a long traverse below Anvil Rock and Camp Muir, which involves crossing the Ingraham Glacier and ascending a gully to reach the Whitman Glacier. This route is longer, is not as popular, and has more significant glacier travel than the route from Summerland. Telemark skiers "flock" (well not quite flock, but . . .) to the glaciers of Little Tahoma Peak in spring. Winter and spring ski ascents are popular, although there is avalanche hazard and hidden crevasses lurking under the snow.

PRECAUTIONS

Fryingpan Glacier and Whitman Glacier are not the most fearsome of the park's glaciers, but they do have many crevasses and sinkholes, so rope up and be prepared to effect a crevasse rescue before venturing onto the glaciers. The glacier slopes are avalanche prone in winter and spring. Loose rock is abundant on Little Tahoma Peak, so take care to avoid knocking loose rock down on other climbers or pulling off a hold and falling to your demise. Spontaneous rockfall is a distinct possibility. The final summit climb is on very loose rock with very significant exposure down the north face. Some parties belay the most exposed sections, although careful rope management will be necessary to avoid starting rockfall. Most parties elect to forego the summit proper and call it a climb at the top of the glacier.

78. PINNACLE PEAK

Elevation: 6,562 feet/2,000 meters
Route: South Gully
Rating: Class 2
Distance: 4 miles round trip.
Elevation Gain: 1,500 feet
Time: 2 hours trailhead to summit
Maps: USGS Mount Rainier East; Green Trails No. 270 (Mt. Rainier East)

ABOUT THE CLIMB

Pinnacle Peak is the centerpiece of the Tatoosh Range, a jagged old mountain range rising in sharp relief directly south of Paradise. An attractive rock horn reminiscent of the Matterhorn, Pinnacle Peak is one of the most popular summits in the park. Although not technically difficult, the summit scramble is steep and exposed with loose rock and rockfall potential, which makes it unsuitable for inexperienced hikers. Still, despite its dangers, many adventuresome hikers head for the summit, primarily because it offers one of the most commanding views of the Nisqually River Valley, Paradise Meadows, and south slopes of Mount Rainier, as well as views of the South Cascades, including Mount Adams, Mount St. Helens, the Goat Rocks, and Mount Hood.

HOW TO GET THERE

This climb begins via Pinnacle Saddle Trail from Stevens Canyon Road. Drive to the Nisqually Entrance, then follow Paradise Road to the turnoff for Paradise. Stay to the right and continue about 1.3 miles on Stevens Canyon Road to

Pinnacle Peak from Pinnacle Saddle Trail.

Paradise Area Mount Rainier

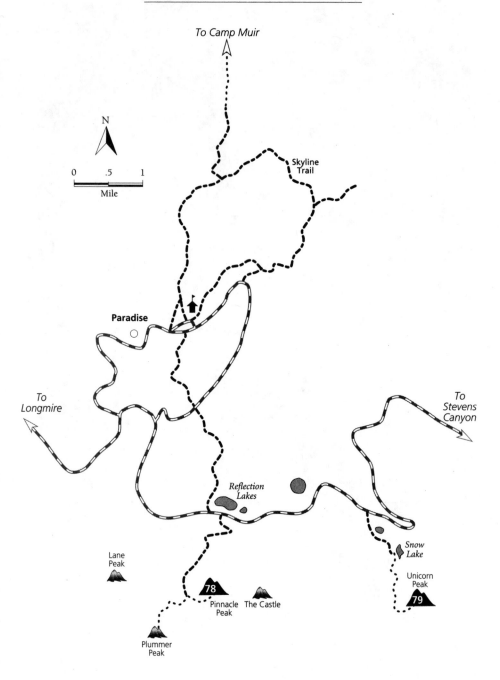

Pinnacle Peak

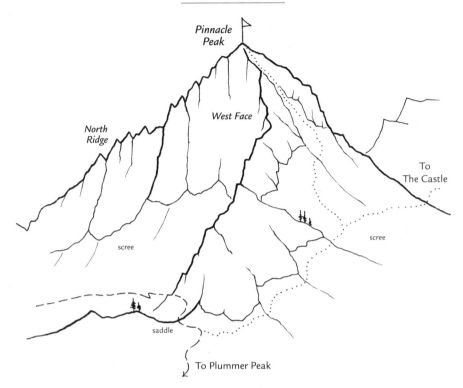

Reflection Lakes. If approaching from the east, drive to Stevens Canyon Entrance and follow Stevens Canyon Road to Reflection Lakes. Park in the wide paved parking area on the left next to the lakes. The trailhead is directly across the road from Reflection Lakes.

ROUTE DESCRIPTION

Hike up the 1.5 mile trail to Pinnacle Saddle. From the saddle, traverse east along the south side of the divide, following the well-established climber's trail. The trail soon forks; take the left fork, which veers upward onto the rocky south face. Ascend slabby rock to the right side of a rock tower, then climb a steep gully on the right to the upper slopes and continue via easy, broken rock to the airy summit.

OPTIONS

An easier climb continues up a way trail leading south from the saddle to the summit of 6,370-foot Plummer Peak, a popular ascent with good views of the Goat Rocks, Mount Adams, and Mount St. Helens. This is mostly a simple hike with only a little bit of easy scrambling required. Because Pinnacle Peak is such a short climb, you might as well climb Plummer Peak too.

A single-day traverse may be made eastward along the Tatoosh Range crest. This would include Pinnacle Peak, The Castle, Foss Peak, and Unicorn Peak.

PRECAUTIONS

Casual hikers are advised not to climb Pinnacle Peak. Although the route is not technically difficult, it is steep and exposed with much loose rock. A slip in the wrong place could easily be fatal. Rockfall is also a major concern on Pinnacle Peak. Random and climber-caused rockfall has caused injuries here. Large parties are discouraged, and helmets are recommended. The slopes below Pinnacle Peak are very avalanche prone in winter and spring. Summer lightning storms seem to target Pinnacle Peak; so if a storm is coming, descend from the summit and high ridges immediately. Stay well back from the ridge crest; the west face drops off steeply, and loose rock can make footing unreliable. Fatalities have occurred on Pinnacle Peak, so be careful.

79. UNICORN PEAK

Elevation: 6,917 feet/2,108 meters
Route: Snow Lake Route
Rating: Class 4–5.0
Distance: 5 miles round trip
Elevation Gain: 1,900 feet
Time: 3 to 4 hours trailhead to summit
Maps: USGS Mount Rainier East; Green Trails No. 270 (Mount Rainier East)

ABOUT THE CLIMB

Unicorn Peak is the distinct horn rising above Snow Lake near the eastern end of the Tatoosh Range. It is, in fact, the highest summit of the Tatoosh Range yet not among the most popular, probably because it has a longer, more difficult approach. Given the choice between a 1.5-mile trail and short rock scramble up Pinnacle Peak and a long ridge traverse or gully scramble to Unicorn Peak, most opt for Pinnacle Peak. Of course, that means Unicorn Peak is less crowded, a plus if you seek a greater sense of solitude and adventure.

The route is mostly easy, involving snow and scree climbing with a short, enjoyable rock scramble up the pronounced summit horn. Perhaps the term "scramble" is inappropriate here because there are fairly exposed Class 5 moves on the summit climb. Competent rock climbers will make quick work of it, but most will want the security of a top-rope to complete the ascent and to rappel instead of climbing down, especially if weather and route conditions are less than perfect. Unicorn is a popular late spring and early summer climb after avalanche hazard has passed. Enjoy impressive views from the summit, south to the Goat Rocks, Mount Adams, and Mount St. Helens, and north to Mount Rainier, of course.

HOW TO GET THERE

This climb begins via Snow Lake Trail from Stevens Canyon Road. From the Nisqually Entrance, follow Paradise Road to the turnoff for Paradise, then continue about 3 miles on Stevens Canyon Road (about 1.4 miles past Reflection Lakes) to the Snow Lake trailhead. If you are coming from the east, drive to

Summit horn, Unicorn Peak (right), with Mount Rainier in the background.

Stevens Canyon Entrance and follow Stevens Canyon Road to Snow Lake trail-head. Park in a turnout on the south side of the road.

ROUTE DESCRIPTION

Hike the 1.5-mile trail to Snow Lake. There are several possible routes from Snow Lake. The most direct and popular is to ascend the steep headwall directly south of the lake to the saddle just west of Unicorn Peak's summit horn. The first part of the ascent is via a steep left-angling snow gully, which leads to a talus basin and a second broad gully. Ascend talus and scree and a perennial snowfield high in the upper basin to the upper saddle, elevation about 6,600 feet. Routefinding is not ordinarily difficult because you can follow a climber's trail much of the way. In early season, the gully and upper slopes are an easy snow climb but avalanche prone. In late season, expect loose rock in the gullies. From the saddle, traverse the easy ridge to the southwest side of the summit pinnacle where a short, steep, exposed rock climb gains the summit. Bring a rope and a light rack for the summit climb. To descend, downclimb or rappel from the summit, then descend to Snow Lake and hike out.

OPTIONS

A popular high traverse is to begin from Pinnacle Saddle and ascend Pinnacle Peak, The Castle, Foss Peak, and Unicorn Peak in a single day. You may also traverse southward to Stevens Peak and Tatoosh Peak.

PRECAUTIONS

Loose rock and steep snow are the major hazards on the approach, particularly on the headwall slopes above Snow Lake. The route can be dangerous due to

Unicorn Peak

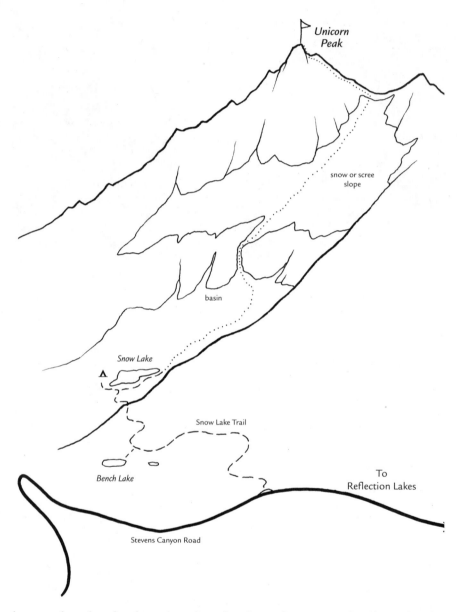

loose rock and avalanches, also when there's patchy snow and rock. Avalanche hazard is high in winter and spring, especially in the gullies and the upper basin. A fatality has occurred here, so be careful. The summit pinnacle is fairly solid but has some loose rock and is exposed. Many climbers feel that the summit horn is too steep and exposed in places to scramble up unroped.

80. COWLITZ CHIMNEYS

Elevation: 7,421 feet/2,262 meters
Route: West Side via Panhandle Gap
Rating: Class 2–3
Distance: 15 miles round trip
Elevation Gain: 4,400 feet
Time: 6 to 8 hours trailhead to summit
Maps: USGS Mount Rainier East; Green Trails No. 270 (Mount Rainier East)

ABOUT THE CLIMB

Cowlitz Chimneys is the collective name of a group of rock peaks and spires forming an extension of the Cowlitz Divide on the east side of Mount Rainier, just east of Panhandle Gap. There are three chimneys. The South Chimney (or Main Chimney) is the largest and highest of the group, rising to an elevation of 7,605 feet and dominating the view looking east from Panhandle Gap. The 7,015-foot North Chimney is a steep rock spire with no easy route to its summit. The 7,421-foot Middle Chimney is an easy ridge traverse from the Wonderland Trail near Panhandle Gap. Being the easiest, the Middle Chimney is the most popular. If views are what you are after, the Middle Chimney provides those in abundance, including extraordinary views of Little Tahoma Peak and the eastern parkland of Mount Rainier. The views from the South Chimney are similar; so considering the extra distance, greater difficulty, and higher risk involved, an ascent of the Middle Chimney is probably the best option. The North Chimney is the most difficult of the three; all routes involve complex approaches and Class 5 rock climbing. Due to the local topography, it would be a difficult undertaking to climb all three of the Cowlitz Chimneys in a single day.

HOW TO GET THERE

This climb begins via the Summerland Trail from White River Road. Drive Washington Highway 410 to the turnoff for White River, then head to the White River entry. Continue 2.9 miles up White River Road to the Summerland trailhead. Parking is limited, especially on summer weekends. Come early to avoid parking problems. Be sure to park off the road and only in designated parking areas. If there is no parking, choose another hike or climb.

ROUTE DESCRIPTION

Hike up the Wonderland Trail 4.5 miles to Summerland, one of the most beautiful and popular subalpine meadows on Mount Rainier's north side. Continue up the trail another 1.5 miles to Panhandle Gap, the highest point of the Wonderland Trail at just over 6,900 feet. Leave the Wonderland Trail just south of Panhandle Gap and traverse the big, easy meadow ridge over the top of Banshee Peak (about 7,400 feet). You are likely to encounter mountain goats here.

To climb the Middle Chimney, descend briefly into the basin just southwest of the Middle Chimney. Then straightforward snow and rock scrambling leads several hundred feet to the summit.

OPTIONS

The South Chimney has a complex scrambling route. A blow-by-blow description can be found in *Cascade Alpine Guide*. There are a few other routes

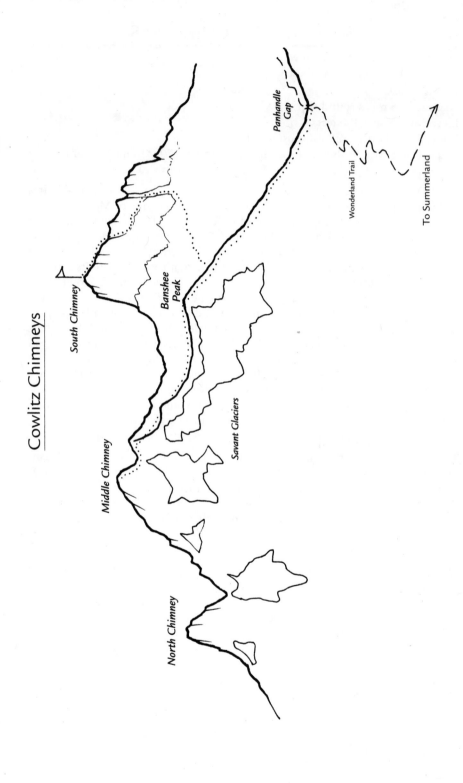

Cowlitz Chimneys

South Chimney

Middle Chimney

North Chimney

Banshee Peak

Savant Glaciers

Panhandle Gap

Wonderland Trail

To Summerland

approaching and climbing the Cowlitz Chimneys from the east via Chinook Pass. These are more complicated to approach and not as popular except in winter and spring when they provide the easiest access to the chimneys. The North Chimney has a few Class 5 routes that are rarely climbed.

PRECAUTIONS
The slopes leading to Panhandle Gap and across the upper basins are avalanche prone in winter and spring. Snow patches linger until late summer. The Middle Chimney has some loose Class 2 scrambling.

81. TAMANOS MOUNTAIN

Elevation: 6,790 feet/2,070 meters
Route: Southeast Ridge
Rating: Class 2
Distance: 10 miles round trip
Elevation Gain: 3,100 feet
Time: 3 to 4 hours to summit
Maps: USGS Sunrise; Green Trails No. 270 (Mount Rainier East)

ABOUT THE CLIMB
Tamanos Mountain is a rocky pyramid rising to the west above Owyhigh Lakes. It is a very popular scramble and a good early season snowshoe climb via its southeast ridge. This climb begins with a popular hiking trail to a high saddle, then climbs through flowery subalpine meadows, and is punctuated with a short rock scramble to the summit. It offers a fairly easy ascent with just a bit of rock scrambling, and wide views of the northeast corner of Mount Rainier National Park, including Little Tahoma Peak, Cowlitz Chimneys, and Governor's Ridge. Small parties are encouraged because large parties tend to trample the meadows. Early season ascents are recommended so you climb on snow as much as possible.

HOW TO GET THERE
This climb begins via Owyhigh Lakes Trail from White River Road. Follow the directions to the White River Entrance. Continue about 2.2 miles beyond the entry station to the Owyhigh Lakes trailhead. Parking is limited and can be crowded on sunny summer weekends. Be sure to park only in designated areas. If there is no parking, try a different hike or climb.

ROUTE DESCRIPTION
Hike the trail 3.5 miles to Owyhigh Lakes. Continue briefly beyond the lakes to the broad 5,350-foot saddle dividing Barrier Peak and Tamanos Mountain. Leave the trail and hike first northwest then north up the grassy slopes and ridge crest to the summit rocks, which are easily surmounted via a short rock scramble. To descend, downclimb the route or traverse out via the northest ridge.

OPTIONS
A route ascends the northeast ridge of Tamanos Mountain, leaving the trail at the final switchback at 5,240 feet elevation. It is longer and less straightforward

Tamanos Mountain

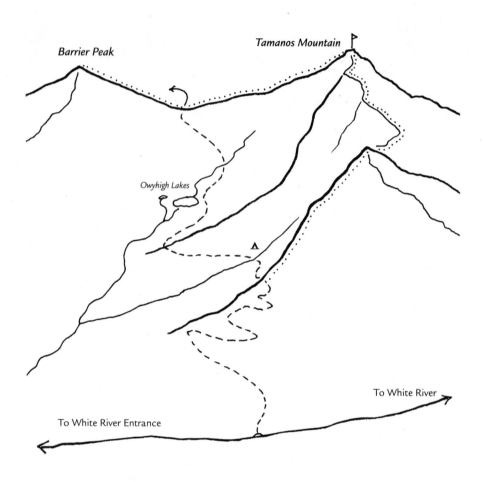

than the route up the southeast ridge, and thus not as popular, but some climbers prefer the northeast ridge in the winter because it avoids crossing the worst avalanche slopes. From the Barrier-Tamanos divide, an ascent of Barrier Peak is fairly simple and straightforward via Class 2 scrambling up the ridge.

PRECAUTIONS
Small parties are recommended to avoid trampling the meadow slopes leading up from the Barrier-Tamanos divide. This is a popular snowshoe ascent but has avalanche danger, especially when traversing below the east slope. Beware of cornices on the ridge crest.

82. FAY PEAK

Elevation: 6,492 feet/1,979 meters
Route: East Slope
Rating: Class 2-3
Distance: 4 miles round trip
Elevation Gain: 1,600 feet
Time: 2 hours to summit
Maps: USGS Mowich Lake; Green Trails No. 269 (Mount Rainier West)

ABOUT THE CLIMB

Fay Peak is the attractive rocky summit visible to the southeast from Mowich Lake. It is officially the highest summit of a cluster of peaks located between Mowich Lake and Spray Park, although its east ridge rises about 30 feet higher than the summit. The peak is named after Fay Fuller, the first woman to climb Mount Rainier. She made her historic ascent in 1892. Fay Peak offers a straightforward scrambling ascent from any direction, although the fastest route is via Knapsack Pass Trail and the eastern basin slopes. It is one of a handful of minor peaks that can be climbed during a one-day loop hike and traverse that includes Mother Mountain, Mount Pleasant, and Hessong Rock. Fay Peak and its neighbors all offer inspiring views of Mowich Lake, Mist Park, Spray Park, and Ptarmigan Ridge. A traverse over Knapsack Pass, climbing summits along the way, is a popular spring snowshoe or ski tour.

HOW TO GET THERE

This climb begins from Mowich Lake. From Buckley, follow Washington Highway 165 past Wilkeson and across the Fairfax Bridge. Take a right turn at the fork and follow the unpaved road to Mowich Lake. There is plenty of parking, although it can be crowded on sunny summer weekends.

ROUTE DESCRIPTION

From the Mowich Lake parking area, hike through the campground and follow the trail on the left down along the outlet stream and right along the lakeshore to the ranger cabin. Continue past the ranger cabin, along the lakeshore at first, and find a way trail leading up the slopes above the lake. If you seem to be wandering forever along the lakeshore, you probably missed the trail. Follow the way trail into a rocky basin below Knapsack Pass. About halfway up the basin, leave the trail and head west across the basin and up a broad rocky gully to the upper slopes of Fay Peak. Alternatively, follow the way trail almost to Knapsack Pass, then traverse the grassy slopes up and right (staying below the cliffs) to the southeast ridge of Fay Peak (which at 6,520 feet elevation is actually higher than the summit of Fay Peak) and continue along the ridge to the summit. Either way, easy rock scrambling leads to the summit. To descend, downclimb the route of ascent or traverse off a different way.

OPTIONS

Another route that is not as popular ascends from Fay Creek on the north side of Fay Peak. An ascent of the 6,478-foot Mother Mountain is easily made. Follow

Fay Peak from Mowich Lake.

Mount Rainier, Mowich Lake, and Spray Park Area

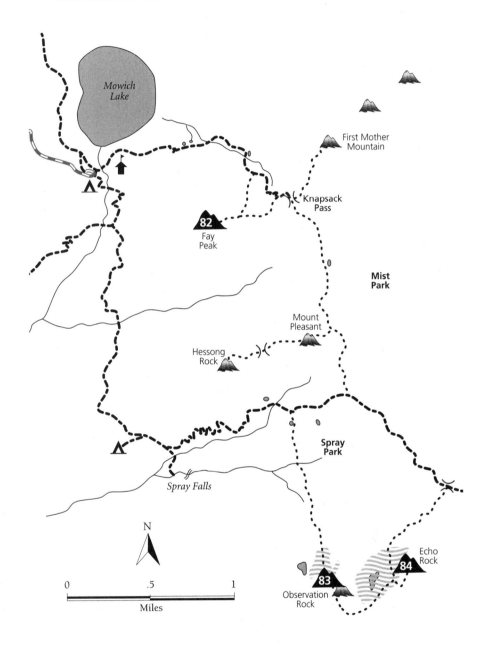

Mowich
Lake

First Mother
Mountain

Knapsack
Pass

82
Fay
Peak

Mist
Park

Mount
Pleasant

Hessong
Rock

Spray
Park

Spray Falls

N

Observation
Rock

83

84

Echo
Rock

0   .5   1

Miles

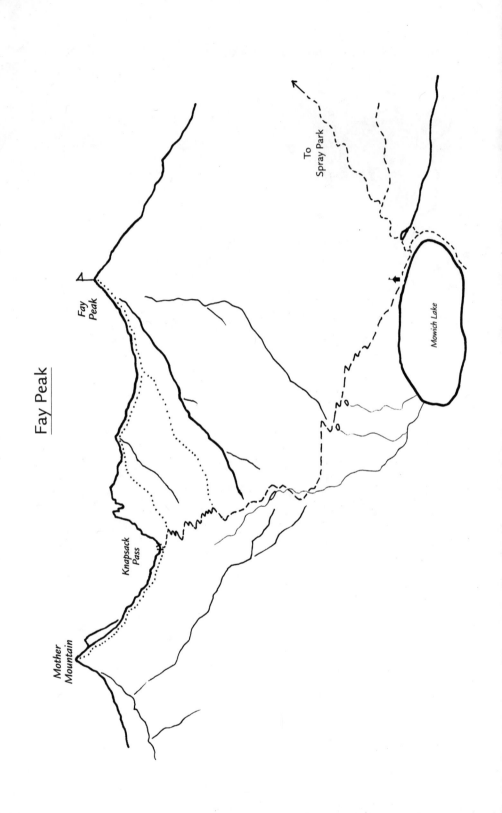

Fay Peak

the climber's trail east from Knapsack Pass, then scramble up the ridge to the summit. If you descend from Knapsack Pass and hike across Mist Park, you can climb the 6,454-foot Mount Pleasant by hiking up its east ridge, then traversing west along the ridge crest to the 6,385-foot Hessong Rock. This one-day traverse of Mother Mountain, Fay Peak, Mount Pleasant, and Hessong Rock is a popular venture and loops out through Spray Park via the Wonderland Trail. Due to restoration efforts, the NPS prefers that hikers do not use the steep trail descending to Spray Park from the saddle between Hessong Rock and Mount Pleasant, so please try to find an alternative descent route. Early season ascents, when snow covers the meadows, are preferred.

PRECAUTIONS

This climb is not especially difficult or dangerous, although there is some loose rock to avoid. In winter and spring, the basin slopes below Knapsack Pass and upper slopes of Fay Peak are avalanche prone. The summit rocks are slippery when wet.

83. OBSERVATION ROCK

Elevation: 8,364 feet/2,550 meters
Route: Flett Glacier via Echo Rock Col
Rating: Class 2 with minimal glacier travel
Distance: 13 miles round trip
Elevation Gain: 3,800 feet
Time: 4 to 6 hours trailhead to summit
Maps: USGS Mowich Lake; Green Trails No. 269 (Mount Rainier West)

ABOUT THE CLIMB

Observation Rock is an old dacite plug on the northwest flank of Mount Rainier. Because of its commanding position at the head of Spray Park and the attractive mantle of snow and ice, it seems a much more distinct summit than it really is. Once you get there, you find it is merely a bump on a long pumice ridge. Even so, Observation Rock is a very worthwhile and enjoyable climb. It is a good introductory ascent for novice mountaineers, requiring basic routefinding and snow travel skills without unreasonable exposure or difficulty. It also offers a commanding view of Spray Park and surrounding peaks, of the foreboding north face of Mount Rainier, across the Puget Sound lowlands to Tacoma and Seattle, and across the water to the peaks of the Olympic Range.

HOW TO GET THERE

This climb begins via the Wonderland Trail from Mowich Lake. Follow Washington Highway 165 past Wilkeson and across the Fairfax Bridge. Take a right turn at the fork and follow the unpaved road to Mowich Lake. There is plenty of parking, although it can be crowded on sunny summer weekends.

ROUTE DESCRIPTION

Hike the Wonderland Trail through Spray Park about 4.5 miles to its highest point at the 6,300-foot divide between Spray Park and Seattle Park. A climber's trail leads up the ridge. Follow the trail (or hike up snowfields during early season to avoid adverse impacts) about 1 mile up the divide to the moraines of the Flett

Observation Rock and Echo Rock

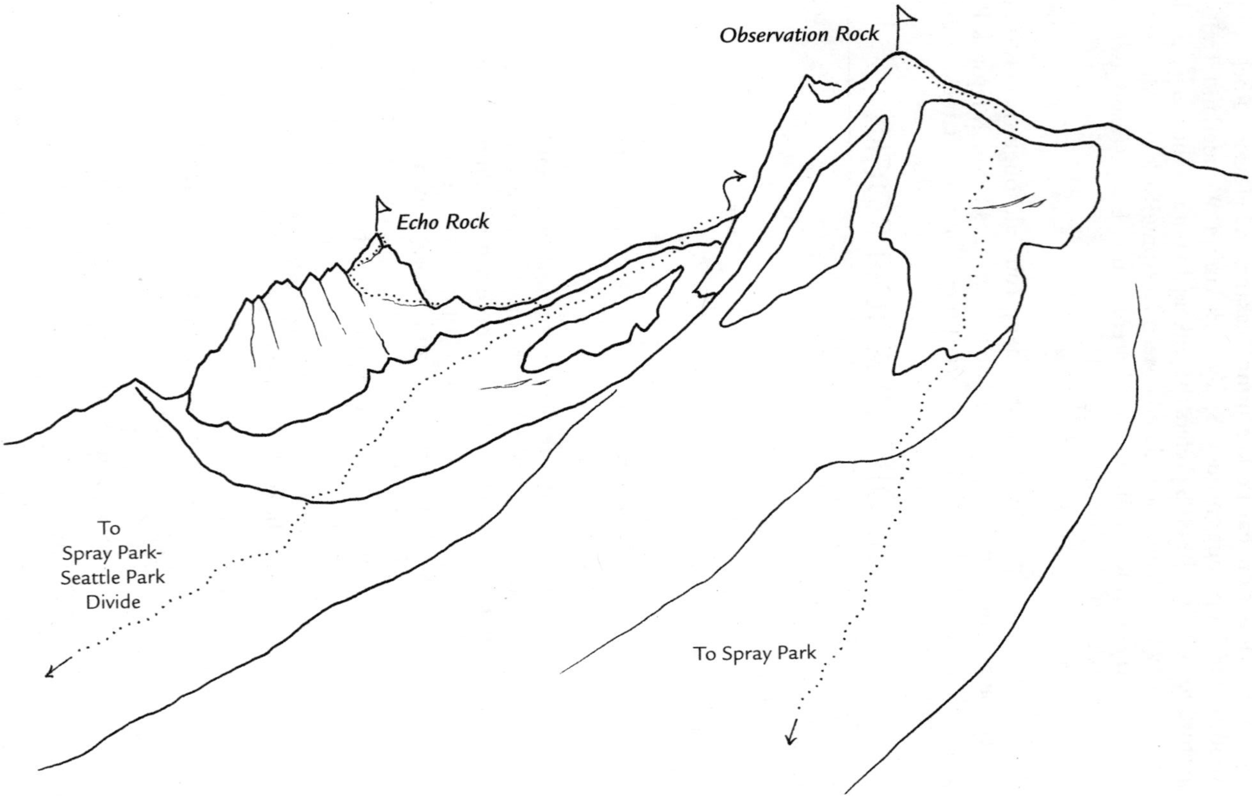

Observation Rock

Echo Rock

To Spray Park

To
Spray Park-
Seattle Park
Divide

Echo Rock (left) and Observation Rock dwarfed by Mount Rainier.

Glacier. Cross over a loose terminal moraine, then drop down to the foot of the glacier. Ascend the glacier to its head (easier on the left side closer to Echo Rock), then traverse westward up snow and scree to a pumice ridge directly south of the summit. Follow the pumice ridge northward, via a boot track to the summit. A false summit just south of the true summit can be reached via a short rock scramble.

OPTIONS

Several alternate routes exist, all involving extended cross-country travel from Spray Park. These routes are best done in early season when snow allows easy and low-impact travel. The western lobe of the Flett Glacier is an obvious and popular route, ascending about 1,000 feet of moderately steep snow or firn up the north face. This is an increasingly popular early winter ice climb with 2 or 3 pitches of steep (50- to 60-degree) ice. This lobe of the glacier is avalanche prone in early season and shows crevasses later in the year. A spring ski descent down this slope to Spray Park would be a great way to complete the climb.

PRECAUTIONS

Although the Flett Glacier is fairly stagnant, it does show crevasses in late season and has caves and sinkholes hidden beneath its harmless-looking surface. The slope above the glacier is steep and can be treacherous when icy. If you ascend Observation Rock via the cirque directly below the craggy east face, beware of rockfall. This route also has some steep snow slopes, which can be trouble when icy.

In order to avoid adverse impacts, the NPS prefers that climbers not follow the social trails leading up from Spray Park. If possible, stay on snowfields or rocks. Be careful not to trample sensitive plants in this area. One careless step can cause damage that will last hundreds of years. Come in early season when snow covers the meadows and allows easy passage without adverse impacts. Please camp on snow and do not move rocks to construct windbreaks or clear ground. A permit is required for overnight camping.

84. ECHO ROCK

Elevation: 7,862 feet/2,396 meters
Route: Southwest Gully
Rating: Class 3
Distance: 12 miles round trip.
Elevation Gain: 3,300 feet
Time: 4 to 6 hours to summit
Maps: USGS Mowich Lake; Green Trails No. 269 (Mount Rainier West)

ABOUT THE CLIMB

Echo Rock is a craggy old dacite plug located low on Ptarmigan Ridge just east of Observation Rock. It is one of the most visible of Mount Rainier's satellite peaks, especially when viewed from Seattle. For this reason, it used to be known as "Seattle Rock." There's a reason it is called Echo Rock, which you will no doubt discover if you have chatty people in your group. Whatever you call it, Echo Rock is still a popular ascent despite its sinister appearance and deserved reputation for loose rock. The rock isn't all loose, but there are some loose blocks poised and ready to be knocked off by careless climbers. Otherwise, the route is enjoyable and straighforward. Like its neighbor Observation Rock, Echo Rock provides exhilarating views of Spray Park and Mount Rainier, and across to Old Desolate and Moraine Park. Those seeking only views may prefer to climb Observation Rock, which is a much easier and safer ascent, although most who come this far end up climbing both Observation Rock and Echo Rock.

HOW TO GET THERE

This climb begins via the Wonderland Trail from Mowich Lake. Follow Washington Highway 165 past Wilkeson and across the Fairfax Bridge. Take a right turn at the fork and follow the unpaved road to Mowich Lake. There is plenty of parking, although it can get crowded on sunny summer weekends.

ROUTE DESCRIPTION

Hike the Wonderland Trail through Spray Park about 4.5 miles to its highest point at the divide between Spray Park and Seattle Park (about 6,300 feet). A social trail leads up the ridge. Follow the trail (or hike up snowfields during early season to avoid adverse impacts) about 1 mile up the divide to the moraines of the Flett Glacier. Cross over a loose terminal moraine, then drop down to the foot of the glacier. Ascend the glacier past its steepest point, then stay left on the gentler slopes, traversing beneath the cliffs of Echo Rock. Continue just past Echo Rock, then angle left to the pumice ridge saddle directly south of the rock and follow a climber's trail northward, toward the rock, passing several large dacite boulders. Ascend a blocky slope up and left to the southwest corner of Echo Rock, then traverse a ledge system around and left to a steep, blocky gully.

Echo Rock from Spray Park.

Scramble up the gully, which leads to an exposed ridge high on the north side of the summit formation. Angle back southward, across a ledge on the west side of the summit pinnacle, then scramble up a final steep wall to the summit block. For all of its traversing, the route is fairly straightforward. The summit is a narrow, exposed block. Standing on the summit proper would be a dangerous undertaking for those without circus training. To descend, downclimb the route.

OPTIONS
An ascent of Observation Rock is a popular option. Experienced scramblers and climbers with a permit may continue up the ridge to the 10,331-foot high point below Ptarmigan Ridge.

PRECAUTIONS
All precautions for Observation Rock apply to Echo Rock. In addition, there is a lot of loose rock on Echo Rock. Wear a helmet, and be careful of knocking rocks loose onto other climbers and avoid pulling up on a loose hold.

85. OLD DESOLATE

Elevation: 7,137 feet/2,175 meters
Route: Moraine Park Gully
Rating: Class 2–3
Distance: 15 miles round trip
Elevation Gain: 4,900 feet
Time: 4 to 6 hours to summit
Maps: USGS Mowich Lake; Green Trails No. 269 (Mount Rainer West)

ABOUT THE CLIMB
Old Desolate is a massive, rocky old mountain rising above Mystic Lake on the north side of Mount Rainier. Its slopes are uniformly barren and talus strewn, giving the mountain a sinister aspect when viewed from the Wonderland Trail as it passes Mystic Lake and Moraine Park. Although the craggy ridges and steep gullies of the mountain's south face are less than inviting, the northern slopes offer a fairly easy scrambling route to the summit. This is not one of the best alpine scrambles in Mount Rainier National Park. This is pretty much a talus climb up a fairly obscure peak. However, Old Desolate offers a spectacular close-up view of the north face of Mount Rainier, as well as an airy view of Mystic Lake and the surrounding parkland, including what must be the most desolate of all of Mount Rainier National Park's subalpine meadows, upper Moraine Park. In that respect, at least, it is a very interesting and worthwhile scramble.

HOW TO GET THERE
This climb begins via the Wonderland Trail from Carbon River trailhead. Drive Washington Highway 165 past Wilkeson and across the Fairfax Bridge. At the fork, stay left and follow the paved road to the Carbon River Entrance. Continue to Ipsut Creek Campground and park at the Carbon River trailhead at the road's end. Carbon River Road has suffered flood damage in recent years and is sometimes closed for repairs. If so, park and walk or mountain bike up the road from the entry station to the trailhead.

Old Desolate and Sluiskin Mountain

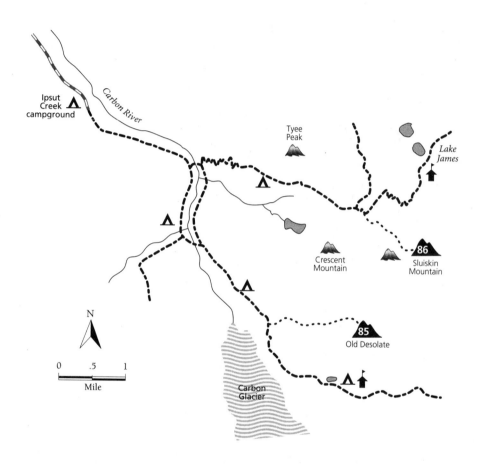

Ipsut Creek campground

Carbon River

Tyee Peak

Lake James

Crescent Mountain

86 Sluiskin Mountain

N

0   .5   1
Mile

85 Old Desolate

Carbon Glacier

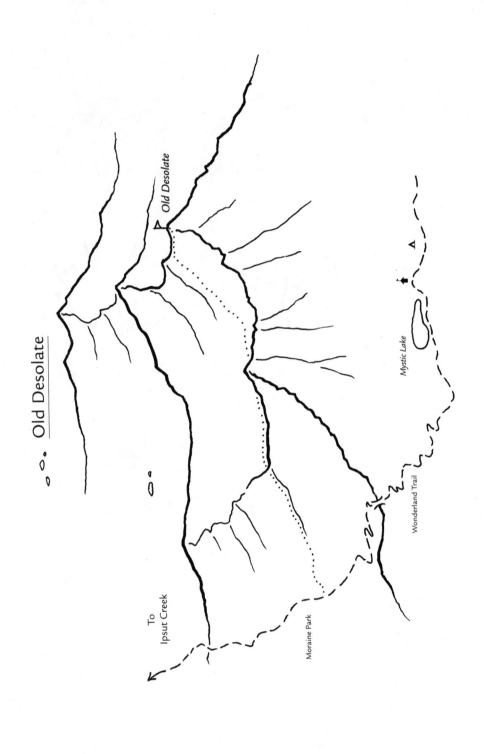

Old Desolate

To Ipsut Creek

Moraine Park

Mystic Lake

Wonderland Trail

Old Desolate

ROUTE DESCRIPTION

Hike up Carbon River Trail 3 miles to a suspension bridge spanning the Carbon River. Cross the bridge and continue up Wonderland Trail another 3 uphill miles until the trail levels off in a broad meadow of lower Moraine Park. As soon as you enter the meadow, leave the trail and hike carefully eastward, taking care to avoid trampling sensitive plants or skittish marmots. Find a rocky gully leading up the steep, wooded slope, and ascend carefully to avoid knocking loose rocks down on your companions. At the top of the gully, you'll reach the barren plateau of upper Moraine Park. Stay on rocks at the southern fringe of the plateau to avoid damaging this very fragile meadow. The highest summit of Old Desolate lies to the southeast. Traverse eastward, along the base of the broad talus slope, and ascend a broad gully to the saddle just north of the highest point. A short talus scramble and rocky ridge traverse lead to the summit. To descend, downclimb the route, or wander northward across Moraine Park and the reclusive Elysian Fields, then over Crescent Mountain to Windy Gap and hike out from there.

OPTIONS

There are several possible routes up Old Desolate. An obvious option is to ascend the ridge directly from the Moraine Park-Mineral Park divide. This route involves endless talus scrambling to the ridge crest, then about 0.5 mile of exposed Class 2–3 scrambling along the ridge crest to the true summit. Staying on the ridge crest proper involves Class 4 and occasionally Class 5 climbing; it is easier if you skirt the rock buttresses on the less exposed north side, staying low on talus rather than on the ridge. Many climbers forego the true summit and scramble to the 6,995-foot high point at the west end of the summit ridge, which directly overlooks Mystic Lake and Willis Wall, a most scenic spot.

PRECAUTIONS

The approach gully from Moraine Park has loose rock. The talus slopes are very unstable in places. Early season ascents would be favored, except for avalanche hazard on the approach hike and upper slopes. Be careful not to trample the meadows, especially the upper plateau of Moraine Park, one of the most fragile alpine meadows in the park.

86. SLUISKIN MOUNTAIN

Elevation: 7,026 feet/2,142 meters
Route: North Slope via Windy Gap
Rating: Class 3
Distance: 16 miles round trip
Elevation Gain: 5,000 feet
Time: 6 to 8 hours trailhead to summit
Maps: USGS Mowich Lake; Green Trails No. 269 (Mount Rainier West)

ABOUT THE CLIMB

Sluiskin Mountain is a prominent rock peak rising above the parkland meadows of northern Mount Rainier National Park, just east of Windy Gap on the Northern Loop Trail. The peak is named after Sluiskin, the native guide who led

Sluiskin Mountain

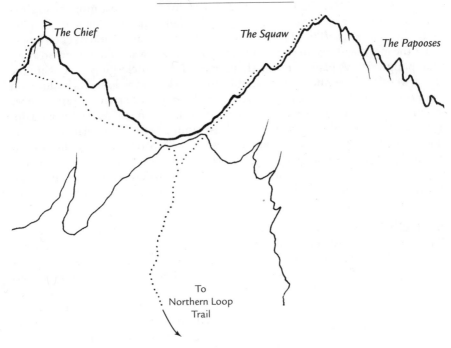

The Chief

The Squaw

The Papooses

To
Northern Loop
Trail

Philemon Van Trump and Hazard Stevens to Mount Rainier during their first ascent of the mountain in 1870. It has two summits, The Chief (7,026 feet) and The Squaw (6,911 feet), with several smaller pinnacles and towers, dubbed The Papooses, descending along the ragged western ridgeline. Despite its craggy and imposing appearance, especially from the south, Sluiskin offers a reasonable scrambling route on its north side. Summit views are wide with a panorama of subalpine meadows spread out beneath you and Mount Rainier looming in nearby.

HOW TO GET THERE
This climb begins via the Wonderland Trail from Carbon River trailhead. Drive Washington Highway 165 past Wilkeson and across the Fairfax Bridge. At the fork, stay left and follow the paved road to the Carbon River Entrance. Continue to Ipsut Creek Campground and park at the Carbon River trailhead at the road's end. The Carbon River Road is sometimes closed due to flood damage. If so, park and walk or mountain bike up the road from the entry station to the trailhead.

ROUTE DESCRIPTION
Hike Carbon River Trail 1.5 miles to a trail junction. Cross the Carbon River here via footlogs. If the trail is impassable due to washouts, cross the river via the swinging bridge another 1.5 miles up the trail and follow the trail on the other side of the river back downriver to the junction. Either way, follow the Northern Loop Trail another 4.5 miles as it climbs steeply and seemingly endlessly up dark,

forested slopes and through the steep grassy meadows below Yellowstone Cliffs to Windy Gap, elevation about 5,800 feet. Here, Sluiskin Mountain is unmistakable. Descend the trail from the gap about 0.3 mile to a basin, then leave the trail and hike cross-country toward the broad snow gully below the saddle dividing The Chief and The Squaw. Ascend the gully to the saddle. From the saddle, scramble westward across easy rock slopes on the north side of The Chief and around to and up the northeast corner to the summit. The final scramble to the summit is steep and exposed Class 3, but only briefly difficult. To descend, downclimb the route.

OPTIONS
An ascent of The Squaw is easier (Class 2). From the saddle, follow the east ridge more or less directly to the summit. The several rock pinnacles on the west ridge of The Squaw ("The Papooses") may also be climbed according to *Cascade Alpine Guide*, but they are rarely if ever climbed.

PRECAUTIONS
The north gully is avalanche prone in winter and spring and may be icy on cold early season mornings. The summit scramble is exposed and has loose rock.

87. MOUNT ADAMS

Elevation: 12,276 feet/3,742 meters
Route: South Spur
Rating: Class 1–2
Distance: 12 miles round trip
Elevation Gain: 6,700 feet
Time: 8 to 10 hours
Maps: USGS Mount Adams West and East; Green Trails No. 367S (Mount Adams)

ABOUT THE CLIMB
The third highest of the Cascade volcanoes, Mount Adams ("Washington's forgotten volcano") rises above the rounded foothills and plateaus of the eastern Cascades, much farther east than its neighboring volcanoes. It is not a precipitous peak, but a broad dacite dome, and is nearly invisible except from the interior of the south Cascades and south-central Washington. Mount Adams was observed by Lewis and Clark's expedition in 1805, but it was mistaken for St. Helens. Later explorers and cartographers frequently confused the two mountains.

In 1839, the mountain was officially named for President John Adams as part of Hall Kelley's "President's Range," a scheme to rename all of the volcanoes down the coast after U.S. presidents (which had limited success as Adams apparently was the only peak named under this scheme, and this due to a cartographer's error). Although botanist David Douglas was said to have climbed the mountain shortly after his arrival in the region in 1825, the first ascent of Mount Adams is credited to an 1854 party, including A.G. Aiken, E.J. Allen, Andrew

Mount Adams (1958). The South Spur route follows snowfields on the right skyline.

Birge, and B.F. Shaw. For a time, there was a manned lookout cabin atop Mount Adams, which was built with the help of horse and mule pack trains. The remains of the lookout still stand, supported by a mass of old snow inside its frame. For a brief time, a sulphur mine was in operation at the summit, but it proved to be unprofitable.

The volcano is believed to have begun forming about half a million years ago, and the most recent cone building was within the last 25,000 years. Geologists suspect that the mountain is almost entirely composed of dark andesite, which is a bit more resistant to erosion than other volcanic materials. The mountain has displayed little evidence of its volcanic birth during the past two hundred years, other than summit fumaroles, but there have been other geological events, most notably large rockfalls in 1997. Continued volcanic activity is thought unlikely, but Mount Adams is very prone to future rockfalls and mudslides.

As a climbing objective, Mount Adams is one of the most popular summits in Washington's Cascades, mostly because it is the second highest peak in the state and is the easiest to climb of the high volcanoes. This, of course, has resulted in overcrowding on the most popular route, as well as environmental damage. The Forest Service is in the process of formulating a plan to reduce overcrowding and preserve the wilderness aspect of Mount Adams, which may involve implementation of a permit system. Mount Adams is a very popular spring climb, especially with ski mountaineers.

HOW TO GET THERE

Drive to the town of Trout Lake and register at the ranger station. From Trout Lake, drive up Forest Road 8040 to Cold Springs Campground and continue to

Mount Adams South Climb

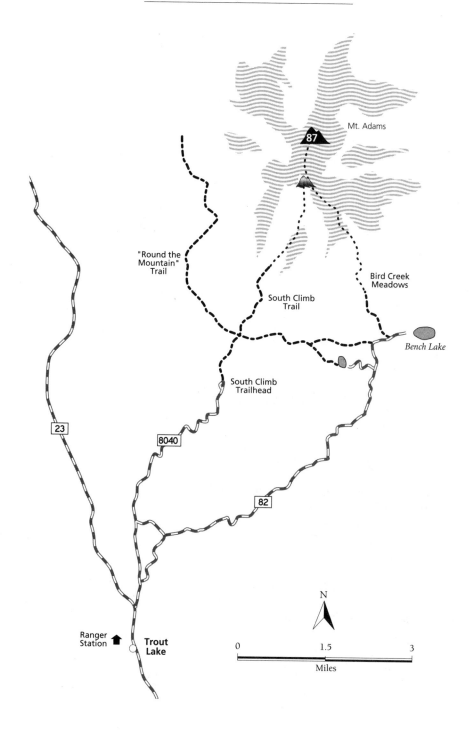

Mt. Adams

87

"Round the Mountain" Trail

Bird Creek Meadows

South Climb Trail

Bench Lake

South Climb Trailhead

23

8040

82

N

Ranger Station

Trout Lake

0   1.5   3

Miles

Mount Adams

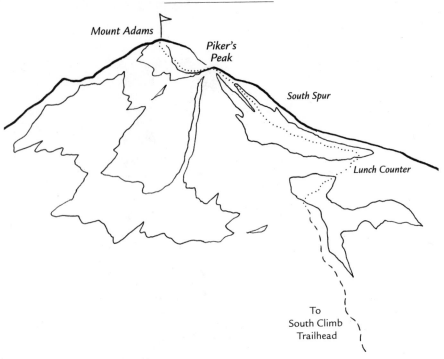

Mount Adams
Piker's Peak
South Spur
Lunch Counter
To South Climb Trailhead

the South Climb trailhead. The road is well marked and easy to follow but gets a little bumpy near the end. There is limited parking. Check current access and permit status before your climb. A Cascades Volcano Pass is required.

ROUTE DESCRIPTION

The South Spur or "South Climb" is the most popular and least technical route on Mount Adams. Mules made the ascent on a regular basis during the mining era. Dozens of climbers daily make the climb on spring and summer weekends. The route is a long, long snow slog most of the season with absolutely no technical difficulty.

Hike South Climb Trail to the left edge of the tiny Crescent Glacier to reach the "Lunch Counter," a flat area at about 9,000 feet elevation. Continue up Suksdorf Ridge via easy snowfields or pumice ridges to the 11,657-foot false summit dubbed "Piker's Peak," after an inscription on a rock. Continue across a gentle saddle to the true summit, which seems eternally far away but should take you only another hour to attain. The cupola of the old summit lookout is still there, frozen in place in the summit ice cap.

OPTIONS

There are several other popular routes to the summit of Mount Adams, and if you've done the South Climb already, you should want to help alleviate overcrowding of that route by climbing a different route next time. The North Ridge,

Mazama Glacier, and Adams Glacier are all worthy of your attention. Refer to *Climbing the Cascade Volcanoes* or *Cascade Alpine Guide* for details.

PRECAUTIONS

Although the route does cross the summit ice cap, if you stay on the route, crevasses are usually not a problem. Glissading, skiing, and snowboarding are popular methods of descent, but glissading accidents regularly occur. Play it safe, and don't glissade unless snowcover is sufficient to provide a safe runout. Also, don't glissade while wearing crampons.

A Cascades Volcano Pass is required for this climb; details are provided in Appendix B. Permit and registration requirements are likely to change in the future, so be sure to call ahead for current access status and permit requirements. Contact Mount Adams Ranger District Office, Trout Lake, WA 98650; (509) 395-3400.

88. MOUNT ST. HELENS

Elevation: 8,365 feet/2,550 meters
Route: Ptarmigan Trail
Rating: Class 1–2
Distance: 6 miles round trip
Elevation Gain: 4,000 feet
Time: 6 to 8 hours to summit
Maps: USGS Mount St. Helens; Green Trails No. 364S (Mount St. Helens)

ABOUT THE CLIMB

Mount St. Helens hardly needs an introduction. St. Helens is a poor reminder of the once-symmetrical cone rising above the placid waters of Spirit Lake. The formerly interesting summit climb, too, has been reduced to a strenuous snow and pumice hike. The pre-eruption volcano rose to a height of 9,677 feet and was first ascended by Thomas J. Dryer, founder of *The Oregonian*, and his party in 1853. Post-1980 ascents were made prior to the opening of the "Red Zone," and a few parties were arrested and fined for their derring-do. The first post-eruption ascent was probably made during the winter of 1981 and 1982; illegal ascents were certainly made during the spring of 1982 and after. The first legal post-eruption ascent of Mount St. Helens was not made until 1987.

Most visitors to Mount St. Helens prior to 1980 thought impossible the eventual eruption that blew off over 1,000 feet of the mountain's summit and devastated the surrounding landscape. The mountain had not been active during the previous century, aside from a few long-forgotten outbursts of steam and ash, and there was no evidence to the casual observer that the mountain was not dormant. Geologists, however, had as early as 1975 predicted a possible violent eruption in the near future.

In March 1980, the mountain gave its first sign of awaking in 123 years with an earthquake measuring over 4.0 on the Richter Scale. The earthquakes continued daily, growing stronger and more frequent, until they occurred almost

Robert Kimmell/USGS

Mount St. Helens, May 18, 1980.

continuously without pause between one another. On March 27, Mount St. Helens erupted. This, however, was a minor eruption that merely opened up the summit crater and sent a steam and ash cloud 7,000 feet high. A second crater opened within a week of the first eruption, and the mountain began to swell measurably. Harmonic tremors began occurring more frequently, indicating that magma was moving beneath the volcano. The mountain was poised and ready for a major eruption.

"Where were you when the mountain blew?" In the quiet of early morning on May 18, 1980, an earthquake registering 5.1 on the Richter Scale caused an enormous landslide as the north side of Mount St. Helens collapsed and slid toward Spirit Lake. This collapse literally uncorked the pressure that had built up within the mountain and caused upward and outward explosions of gas, ash, and pyroclastic projectiles that killed everything within 0.5 mile radius of the north side of the mountain (the "Eruption Impact Area") and shot an ash cloud 14 miles into the stratosphere. Pyroclastic material as hot as 1,600 degrees F poured down the mountain at speeds estimated at 100 miles per hour, cushioned by compressed air, burning everything that was left intact from the eruption. Water from displaced lakes, mixed with ash, snow, ice, and assorted volcanic debris, generated catastrophic mudflows that wiped out bridges, logging equipment, and buildings.

This brief account of the events of May 18 and the days to follow hardly captures the eruption of Mount St. Helens in all its glory. If you wish to learn more about historical or geological Mount St. Helens, please consult Appendix D for further references, visit the Johnston Ridge Observatory, view any of dozens of films chronicling the eruption, or better yet, visit the northern portion of the monument to get a firsthand look at the destructive legacy of the May 1980 eruption. If you visit the mountain, you will see that the barren wilderness created by the eruption is quickly coming back to life.

As noted previously, the way to the summit of Mount St. Helens is no longer challenging, but it is certainly much more popular. Forest Service estimates put the number of post-eruption ascents at about 12,000 as of September 1987. Permits are reserved months in advance for the climb. Don't expect solitude here. Early-season ascents are recommended, as snow climbing is usually preferable to slogging up endless pumice slopes. Ski mountaineers flock to St. Helens in the spring and early summer. Tourists and casual hikers will probably want to wait until after the snow is gone before climbing the mountain. The summit provides excellent views of the surrounding volcanoes—Rainier, Adams, Hood—and the geologic spectacle of the crater, lava dome, and blast zone.

HOW TO GET THERE

To reach the routes, drive about 4 miles west from the town of Cougar on Washington Highway 90, then head north on the well-marked Forest Road 83, the main drag into Mount St. Helens National Volcanic Monument. The road forks in about 3 miles. Take the left fork, Forest Road 81. In another 1.5 miles, reach the junction with Forest Road 830, where a sign points the way to the Climbers Bivouac. Follow this steep, bumpy, unpaved road another 2 miles or so to the bivouac area and trailhead.

Mount St. Helens

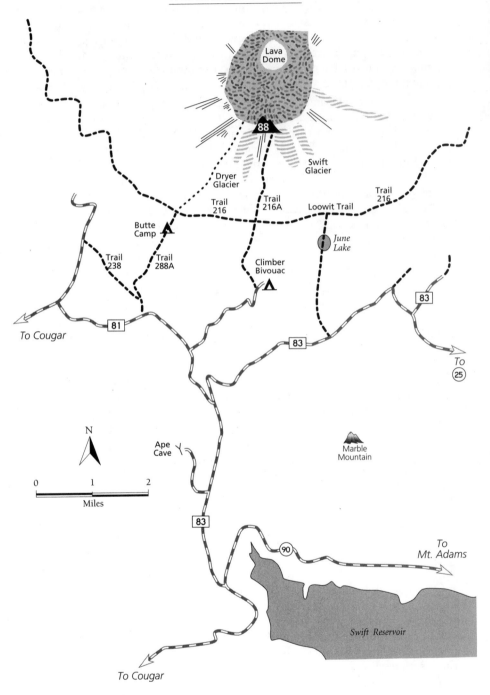

Lava Dome

88

Swift Glacier

Dryer Glacier

Trail 216

Trail 216A

Loowit Trail

Trail 216

Butte Camp

June Lake

Trail 238

Trail 288A

Climber Bivouac

81

To Cougar

83

83

83

To 25

N

Ape Cave

Marble Mountain

0   1   2
Miles

83

90

To Mt. Adams

Swift Reservoir

To Cougar

ROUTE DESCRIPTION

Begin from the bivouac area via Ptarmigan Trail (Trail 216A), which leads 2 gradual uphill miles to Loowit Trail (Trail 216) at timberline. From there, the climber's trail continues more or less directly up the mountain, crossing lava flows and levees and ascending the pumice ridge to the crater rim. The route is marked with poles for easy routefinding. Attain a saddle between the true summit and a false summit. The true summit is about 0.2 mile to the west, an easy traverse along the ash-covered rim.

OPTIONS

Although Mount St. Helens is most popular as a spring and summer climb, it is also a good winter climb during stable snow conditions. It is very popular with ski mountaineers during spring months. During spring, before the road to the Ptarmigan trailhead is open, park at the Sno-Park lot on Forest Road 83 and ski or snow hike in to the route. The route is marked in winter and spring. Follow the markers faithfully during poor weather, and stay close on the descent so you don't end up too far from the car.

PRECAUTIONS

Climbers should be wary of the crater rim, which is quite unstable and prone to avalanching. Stay on the south slope of the rim, well back from the rim itself. Be sure to bring sun and wind protection, as well as gaiters and goggles to keep ash out of your boots and eyes. An ice ax and crampons are recommended depending on snow cover. Don't forget Mount St. Helens is an "active" volcano. Even though geologists can better predict eruptions, an eruption could still occur without much warning. The lava dome is still growing, and it has been blown off several times already. In the event of an eruption, descend immediately, avoiding gullies and depressions, and breathe through a moist cloth if ash overwhelms you. Cornices form on the summit ridge; be wary in winter and spring. During winter and spring, and especially during poor visibility, stay close to the trail markers. If you descend the wrong way, you could end up far from the trailhead. The slopes of Mount St. Helens are avalanche prone in winter and spring.

A Mount St. Helens Climbing Pass is required for all travel above timberline. From November 1 to May 14, simply register at Jack's Restaurant before and after your climb. Jack's is located about 5 miles west of Cougar on Washington Highway 503. Between May 15 and October 31, climbing passes are issued on a first-come, first-served basis, so come early. Beginning in February, mail-in applications to monument headquarters are accepted, and seventy permits per day are issued by this process. An additional forty permits are issued from Jack's Restaurant. Direct your inquiries and permit requests to Mount St. Helens National Volcanic Monument Headquarters, Route 1, Box 369, Amboy, WA 98601; (360) 247–5800. They'll send you a packet of information about climbing Mount St. Helens along with your application. Permits go fast, so get yours early! Permits are valid for thirty-six hours, allowing overnight camping prior to the ascent. Climbers must sign in and check out too, even if they already have a permit. You may purchase an annual pass, which is good for climbs of Mount Adams, too. For details, contact Mount St. Helens National Volcanic Monument.

Emergencies should be reported to Mount St. Helens National Volcanic Monument Headquarters, (360) 247–5473; or dial 911.

Goat Rocks

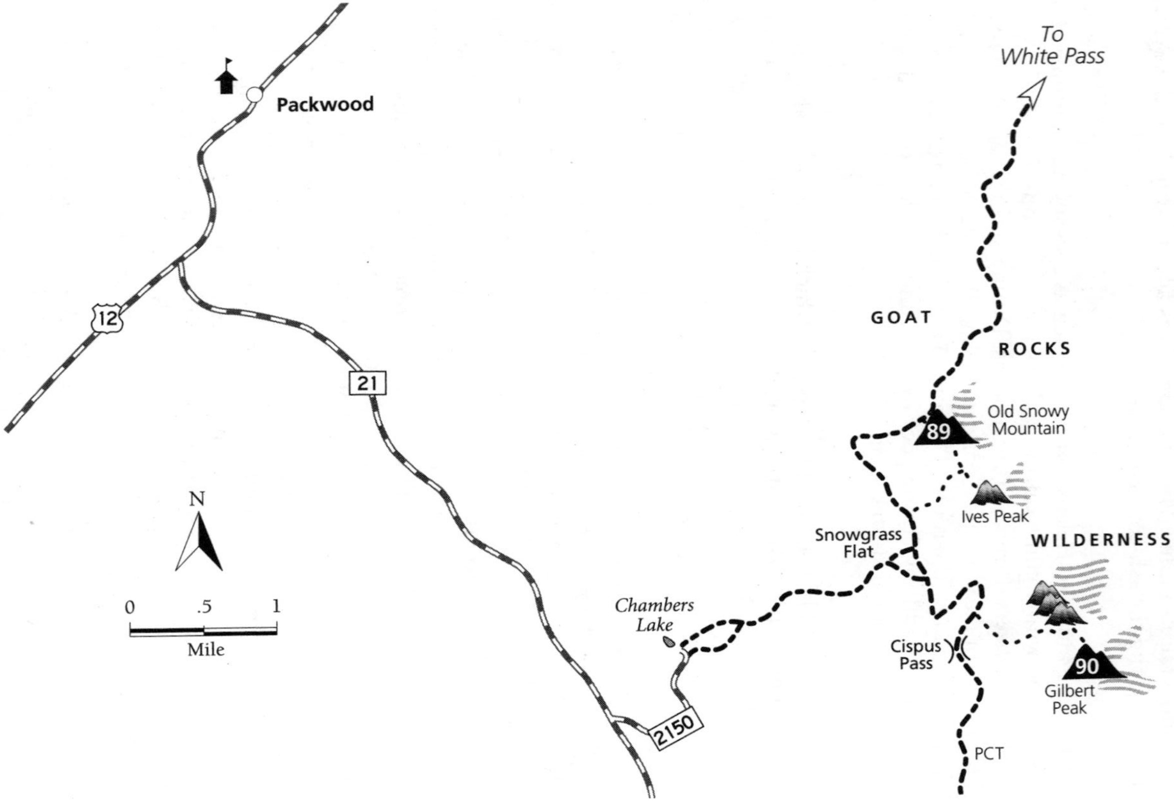

Packwood

12

21

2150

Chambers
Lake

Snowgrass
Flat

Cispus
Pass

PCT

**GOAT
ROCKS**

89

Old Snowy
Mountain

Ives Peak

WILDERNESS

90

Gilbert
Peak

To
White Pass

N

0   .5   1
Mile

89. OLD SNOWY MOUNTAIN

Elevation: 7,930 feet/2,417 meters
Route: Climber's Trail
Rating: Class 1–2
Distance: 14 miles round trip
Elevation Gain: 3,600 feet
Time: 5 to 6 hours to summit
Maps: USGS Old Snowy Mountain; Green Trails No. 303 (White Pass) and 335 (Walupt Lake)

ABOUT THE CLIMB

Old Snowy is one of the sentinels of the Goat Rocks Wilderness. Although not the highest summit of the group, it is the most accessible, easiest to climb, and therefore, the most popular. The peak has a reputation of being remote with a long approach. Although it takes most climbers a few hours to drive to the trailhead, Old Snowy can readily be climbed in a day. It has a variety of routes, including talus scrambling, glacier climbing, and a trail. The two popular routes begin from Snowgrass Flat, a meadow basin just southwest of the peak, and hike the highest segment of the PCT in Washington to within a short distance of the summit. It is a good spring ski ascent, assuming favorable snow conditions. Summit views are far and wide, including close views south to the Goat Rocks, Mount Gilbert, and Mount Adams, east to Mount St. Helens, and north to Mount Rainier.

HOW TO GET THERE

Goat Rocks Wilderness is located south of White Pass and just east of the town of Packwood on U.S. Highway 12. The shortest approach is via Snowgrass Flats Trail (Trail 96), which begins just southeast of Packwood. Drive U.S. Highway 12 to the turnoff for Johnson Creek Road (Forest Road 21), about 3 miles southwest of "downtown" Packwood. Follow Forest Road 21 about 13.5 miles to Hugo Lake, then take a left at the fork and follow Forest Road 2150 nearly 1 mile to Chambers Creek. Take the next left fork, just across the creek, staying on Forest Road 2150 and following it about 2 miles to the Forest Road 405 loop, which leads to the Snowgrass Flat trailhead. You can also continue to the end of Forest Road 40 spur and Goat Ridge trailhead. A Northwest Forest Pass is required.

ROUTE DESCRIPTION

Hike Snowgrass Flat Trail (Trail 96 or 96A) about 4 miles to Snowgrass Flat, elevation about 5,800 feet. From Snowgrass Flat, hike Snowgrass Flat Trail (Trail 96 or 97, your choice) east about 0.8 mile to join the PCT, then hike northward up the PCT. About 1.4 miles north from Trail 96 junction, the PCT reaches its high point at about 7,200 feet elevation, where it contours the upper slopes of Old Snowy Mountain above the Packwood Glacier. Leave the trail here and hike up easy rocky slopes to the summit ridge, then scramble to the summit. A boot track leads most of the way to the summit. Only a short section of blocky scrambling is required to reach the top. To descend, downclimb the route or traverse off toward the Snowy-Ives col and out.

Old Snowy Mountain

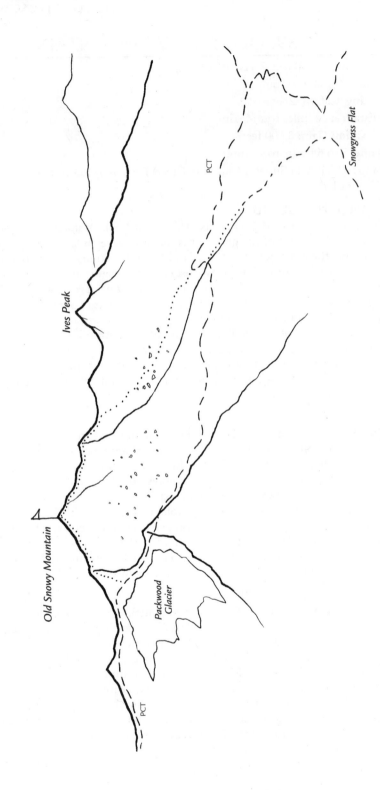

Old Snowy Mountain

Ives Peak

PCT

PCT

Packwood
Glacier

Snowgrass Flat

OPTIONS

It is possible to scramble directly up talus and scree slopes to the summit from just about anywhere on the west slope, but loose talus and scree make these options less enjoyable than the standard route. Another route ascends Old Snowy via the McCall Glacier on the northeast side of the mountain from the North Fork Tieton River and Glacier Basin. This is a more alpine route, involving glacier travel and rock scrambling. Ives Peak (7,940 feet) may be climbed from the saddle via Class 3 rock scrambling. Refer to *Cascade Alpine Guide* for route details.

PRECAUTIONS

Old Snowy has some loose talus and rotten rock. The PCT is impassable to hikers until late July most years. Expect snow in early season most years and through summer in years of heavy snowfall. There is avalanche hazard in winter and early season, especially above Snowgrass Flat and on the mountain's upper slopes.

90. GILBERT PEAK

Elevation: 8,184 feet/2,484 meters
Route: Northwest Gully via Cispus Basin
Rating: Class 3
Distance: 16 miles round trip
Elevation Gain: 3,600 feet
Time: 6 to 8 hours trailhead to summit
Maps: USGS Old Snowy Mountain; Green Trails No. 303 (White Pass) and 335 (Walupt Lake)

ABOUT THE CLIMB

Gilbert Peak is the highest summit of the Goat Rocks, a high ridge of craggy volcanic peaks located about 25 miles southeast of Mount Rainier. Like Old Snowy, Gilbert Peak (also referred to as Mount Gilbert or Mount Curtis Gilbert) has a reputation for being a remote peak, but in reality it is easily approached via Snowgrass Flat Trail and the PCT. The approach drive is long, but the approach hike is quite reasonable, making Gilbert feasible in a weekend trip. Also like Old Snowy, Gilbert Peak has several scrambling routes to its summit, mostly scree scrambling with glacier traverses on the mountain's eastern flanks. However, the routes are relatively long and have more objective difficulty and hazard, especially loose rock. Because of this, Gilbert is not the most popular summit of the Goat Rocks. Early season ascents are favored because snow still allows easy passage over scree and loose rock. Most who visit the Goat Rocks climb several summits over a long weekend or extended trip. If you have time to spare, plan on spending at least four or five days to climb and explore this beautiful wilderness area.

HOW TO GET THERE

Approach as for Old Snowy Mountain to Snowgrass Flats trailhead. A Northwest Forest Pass is required.

Gilbert Peak

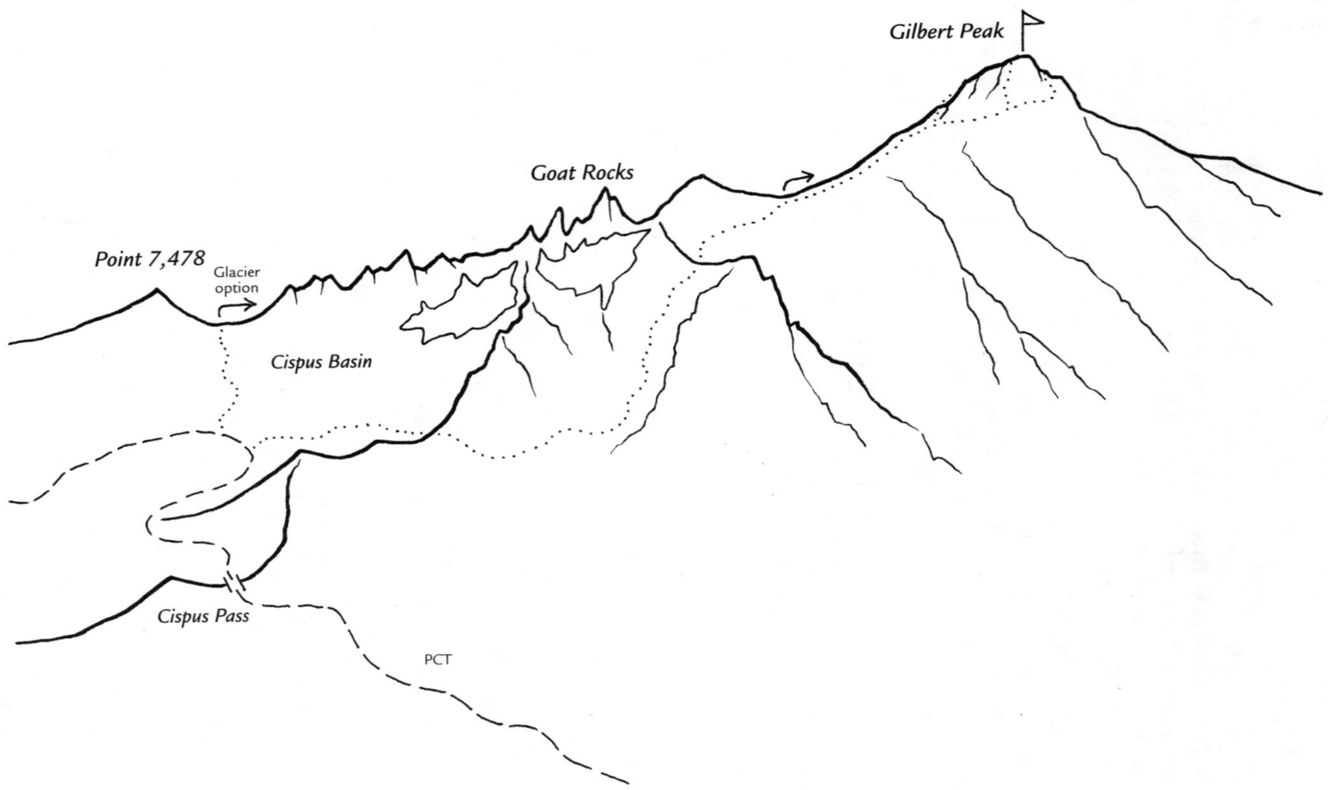

Gilbert Peak

Goat Rocks

Point 7,478

Glacier
option

Cispus Basin

Cispus Pass

PCT

ROUTE DESCRIPTION
Hike Snowgrass Flat Trail (Trail 96 or 96A) about 3.7 miles to the junction at Snowgrass Flat, then take the right fork (Trail 97) and follow it for about 0.4 mile to the junction with the PCT. Hike westward then southward on the PCT about 2.2 miles into flowery Cispus Basin, elevation about 6,160 feet. Leave the trail in the basin and hike up scree or snow slopes to the saddle (about 6,800 feet) just east of Cispus Pass. Drop down and contour scree slopes eastward, then up an obvious broad scree and rock gully that leads to the northwest shoulder of Gilbert Peak at about 7,600 feet elevation, just southwest of the rocky pinnacles of Big Horn and Little Horn. Do not climb into the snow basin below these horns; skirt around them on the southwest side to the upper ridge. From this shoulder, the rest of the route is a straightforward hike up the broad, sandy ridge to the summit formation. A brief, loose scramble up the summit rocks completes the ascent. There are several viable routes to the summit on the west, south, and southeast sides, which involve about 80 feet of rock scrambling. To descend, downclimb the route.

OPTIONS
A variation of this climb begins from Cispus Pass and ascends north-northeast to the pass (about 7,200 feet) just east of Point 7,478 (north of the Big Horn–Little Horn group). Then the route traverses around to the east side of the Goat Rocks, across a broad glacier, and up and over a saddle (about 7,700 feet) to gain the upper ridge. This is a more strenuous option but has less loose rock and is more alpine in character. Roping up on the glacier is recommended. A bergschrund or moat may be difficult to pass in late season.

Gilbert Peak can be approached and climbed from the east via Tieton River Road (Forest Road 1000 and 795) and Conrad Meadows Trail (Trail 1120). The route goes up the Mad Glacier to the summit. This may be the fastest option for those approaching from the east via U.S. Highway 12. Refer to *Cascade Alpine Guide* for route details.

PRECAUTIONS
Like all the summits of the Goat Rocks, Gilbert Peak has abundant loose and rotten rock, perhaps more than its share. Beware of rockfall, especially when traversing below the Goat Rocks and climbing the broad gully leading to the crest. There is avalanche hazard in winter and spring, particularly on the slopes of Cispus Basin and in the access gully. If you climb one of the glacier routes, bring crampons and rope up on the glaciers, which have crevasses.

Summit formation, Mount Olympus.

Olympic Mountaineering

The
Olympic Mountains

The Olympic Mountains are one of the most unique mountain "ranges" in the world. Not a mountain range in the traditional sense, the Olympics are the result of local uplifting of suboceanic rock resulting from the collision of several large and small tectonic plates. The Olympic Mountains were quite literally squeezed up from beneath the sea, resulting in the formation of an isolated cluster of enfolded peaks and valleys dramatically rising nearly 8,000 feet only a few miles from the Pacific Ocean. Glaciers and rivers have carved out deep, long valleys, adding to the high relief of the Olympics. The uniqueness of this region was preserved by the creation of Olympic National Park in 1938. All of the summits included in this guide are located within the park or within one of the several designated wilderness areas bordering the park.

As climbing objectives, the Olympic Mountains offer variety, from easy scrambles to moderate alpine rock climbing, snow, ice and glacier climbing, and high traverses. While a majority of climbers set their sights on Mount Olympus, literally the crown jewel of the Olympic Mountains, there are dozens of other worthy peaks scattered throughout the range. Most Olympic peaks can be climbed via scrambling routes, most of them via relatively simple ridge hikes and scree gullies. Only a few Olympic peaks require technical rock climbing, although Class 4–5 routes exist on many peaks. For the most part, the routes featured in the Olympics are snow and rock scrambles, and only the most classic glacier and alpine rock routes are included in this guide. Climbers seeking more challenging routes should refer to the *Climber's Guide to the Olympic Mountains*, the comprehensive climbing guide to the region.

The rock formations of the Olympic Mountains are primarily shales, sandstone, soft basalts, and pillow lava, all of which are generally loose and broken, some very much so. While good rock does exist, the majority of Olympic Mountain rock is unreliable for climbing. Climber-inflicted rockfall is common in the Olympics, especially in gullies and on open faces; and scramblers and climbers are advised to wear helmets at all times on any route climbing on or below rock— that is, pretty much everywhere on any climb in the Olympics. Many routes feature fairly easy but exposed scrambling on shattered rock where pulling off a loose hold or being hit by a falling rock could be disastrous. Because of this, climbers must exercise great care while climbing and scrambling in the Olympics.

Because of the generally poor rock quality, many Olympic summits are most popular in spring and early summer when snow offers relatively easy and safe passage over otherwise loose rock. However, snow climbing has its own risks.

351

Olympic Mountaineering

Climbers traversing summit rocks, Mount Olympus.

More climbing accidents in the Olympics are attributable to slips and falls on snow and to avalanches rather than to rockfall. Many snow slopes and gullies do not have a safe runout, leaving climbers little time to self-arrest before sliding into rocks or over cliffs. Nearly every peak has avalanche danger in winter and spring, sometimes well into summer during years of heavy snowfall. Crampons and an ice ax should be carried by all members of your party well into summer, particularly if your intended route ascends a gully or north-facing slope.

Climbing Safely in the Olympic Mountains

During the past several years, there have been an increasing number of climbing accidents in the Olympic Mountains, including several fatalities. As a result, the NPS has focused attention on climbing safety and has suggested several safety tips for climbers.

This information can be found on the Olympic National Park climbing home page at www.nps.gov/olym/wic/climb.htm. Current trail information and climbing route conditions are available from the Wilderness Information Center in Port Angeles. Ranger stations may also be able to provide current route conditions.

Driving Directions

U.S. Highway 101 nearly encircles Olympic National Park and is the primary access route to the climbs listed in this section. Getting to U.S. Highway 101 is fairly straightforward but can be costly or time consuming—or both—for those who live across Puget Sound and must either drive the long way around or take a ferry.

If you are approaching from the south, drive Interstate 5 to Olympia, then west on U.S. Highway 101. If you are climbing Mount Olympus, you will want to continue west on U.S. Highway 12 to Hoquiam, then rejoin U.S. Highway 101 and drive up the west side of the Olympic Peninsula to the turnoff for Hoh River. For all other climbs, stay on U.S. Highway 101 from Olympia and drive up the east side of the peninsula.

If you are approaching from Tacoma and are climbing Mount Olympus, follow U.S. Highway 12 west from Olympia, then north up U.S. Highway 101 to Hoh River. If you are climbing Mount Washington, The Brothers, Mount Constance, or other peaks among them, follow U.S. Highway 101 north from Olympia. If you are climbing the Royal Basin Peaks, Mount Angeles, or Mount Carrie, follow Washington Highway 16 north to Bremerton, continue north to Port Gamble, cross the Hood Canal Bridge, and follow Washington Highway 104 and U.S. Highway 101 north.

If you are approaching from Seattle, either drive through Tacoma or Olympia, or take a ferry across Puget Sound. The Bainbridge Island ferry and Edmonds-Kingston ferry connect with Washington Highway 104, which leads across the Hood Canal Bridge to U.S. Highway 101. From here, a short drive in either direction gives access to all of the peaks in this section except Mount Olympus. If you are climbing Mount Olympus, continue on U.S. Highway 101 through Port Angeles and Forks to the Hoh River.

Olympic Mountains Locator Map

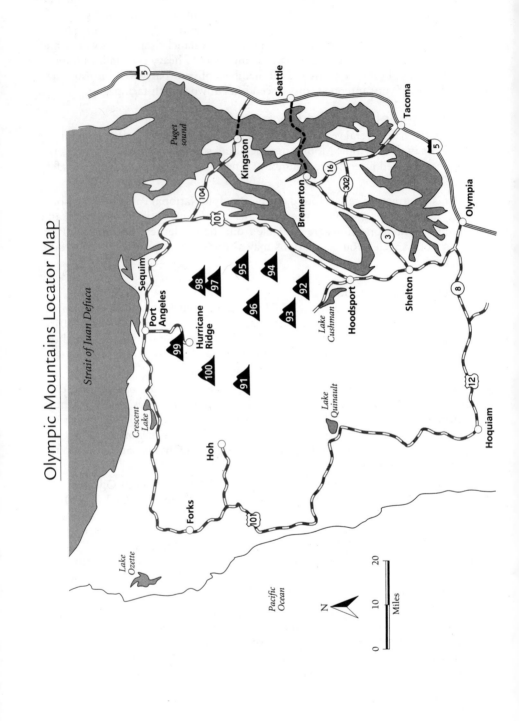

Summit photo, Mount Olympus.

If you are coming from north Puget Sound or Vancouver, B.C., you can take the Keystone Ferry from Whidbey Island and connect with U.S. Highway 101 just east of Sequim. If you are coming from Vancouver Island, a ferry connects Victoria with Port Angeles.

For schedule and rate information for Washington State Ferries and the Victoria-Port Angeles ferry, call 1-888-808-7977 or 206-464-6400, or log onto the Washington State Ferries Web site at block www.wsdot.wa.gov/ferries/.

Olympics Permit Requirements

A wilderness camping permit is required for all overnight stays in undeveloped areas of Olympic National Park. Permits may be obtained from the Wilderness Information Center, or from several ranger stations. Self-registration permits are also available at several trailheads throughout the park. There is a $5.00 wilderness use fee for a permit to camp overnight in the wilderness, plus an additional $2.00 per person per night. There is no additional charge for visitors sixteen years of age or under. Annual passes are available for frequent visitors for $30, plus $15 for each additional household member. You can also get a free annual pass by volunteering sixteen hours of your time through the Olympic Volunteers in Park program. In addition, a $10 park entrance fee is charged at Staircase, Hurricane Ridge, Sol Duc, Elwah, and Hoh River, or you can purchase an additional $20 pass. Remember, fees are subject to change, so whatever you do, bring lots of cash when you visit Olympic National Park so you can afford your wilderness experience.

In addition, a pass is required when parking at Olympic National Forest trailheads. Northwest Forest Passes cost $5.00 per vehicle per day or $30.00 for an annual pass. Refer to Appendix B for details.

Several areas of Olympic National Park are subject to quotas and may require advance reservations for overnight camping. Presently, the only quota areas included in this guide are Lake Constance, Flapjack Lakes, and Hoh River. Call the Wilderness Information Center at (360) 452-0300 for quota information or to make reservations for your visit. Day use is not subject to fees, quotas, or permits—at least, not yet!

For more information about permits, fees, and wilderness trip planning, contact the Superintendent, 600 East Park Avenue, Port Angeles, WA 98362; call. Olympic National Park Visitor Center at (360) 452-0330 or the Wilderness Information Center at (360) 452-0300; or log onto the park service Web site at www.nps.gov/olym/home.htm.

In Case of Emergency
In case of emergency, dial 911 or call the park service at (360) 452-0300.

91. MOUNT OLYMPUS

Elevation: 7,965 feet/2,429 meters
Route: Blue Glacier
Rating: Class 3; Grade II glacier
Distance: 44 miles round trip
Elevation Gain: 7,400 feet
Time: 6 to 8 hours from Glacier Meadows to summit; best done as a three-day climb
Maps: USGS Mount Olympus; Green Trails No. 134 (Mount Olympus)

ABOUT THE CLIMB
Mount Olympus is literally the crown jewel of the Olympic Mountains. It not only is the highest and most heavily glaciated peak of the Olympics, but it lies near the geographic center of the range. Olympus, named for the fabled home of the gods of Greek mythology, is one of the most remote of the Olympic Mountains. Although Olympus rises to within a stone's throw of 8,000 feet elevation, it is so thoroughly enfolded within the range that it is practically invisible except from the highest surrounding ridges and summits.

The approach hike is 18 miles long, one of the longest approaches of any peak in Washington. Despite the tedium of hiking so far carrying a heavy load of climbing and backpacking gear and supplies for the usual three-day ascent, the approach rarely deters climbers from the task. Hundreds of climbers annually brave blisters, cramps, and shoulder-strap bruises to trudge up the trail to base camp at Glacier Meadows, then summon the will to arise early the next morning, stiff joints, sore muscles and all, and continue another 3,700 vertical feet to the summit. As testament to its popularity, Mount Olympus accounts for an estimated 90 percent of guided climbs in the entire range of the Olympic Mountains.

The first ascent of Mount Olympus was made by a party of eleven climbers on August 13, 1907. After searching for evidence of an earlier claimed ascent and finding none, they concluded they had made the first ascent. "With a mighty

Olympic Mountaineering

Climbers resting on Snow Dome, Mount Olympus.

cheer and then a song," they set about building a cairn, placing a summit register, and taking photos. Modern climbers usually dispense with the mighty cheer
and song, and the summit cairn is well established, but taking photos is still a
highly popular summit activity. In clear weather, the view from the summit will
likely surpass your expectations. Like the first ascent in 1907, it is not uncommon to find a dozen or more climbers on the summit together on sunny summer weekends.

Perhaps Olympus epitomizes the alpine climbing ideal more than many of the
peaks in this guide that can easily be climbed and descended in a single day. It is
not an ascent to be rushed, but savored, and not a peak to be "bagged," but
experienced. It is a mountain with more intrinsic challenges and more lasting
rewards. Unlike many other sought-after peaks, Mount Olympus cannot simply
be pointed to from the lowlands while you brag "I climbed it." If climbers brag
after an ascent of Mount Olympus, it is usually something like "I never have to
hike the Hoh River Trail again!"

The recommended climbing season is from late June through early September
most years, although good conditions often exist from the middle of spring into
fall. Winter ascents are rare due to the long approach and avalanche hazard.

HOW TO GET THERE
Drive U.S. Highway 101 to mile 178.5 and Upper Hoh Valley Road, about 12
miles south of the town of Forks and 21 miles north of Kalaloch. Follow Upper
Hoh Valley Road about 18 miles to the road's end at Hoh Rainforest Visitor Cen-
ter, a very popular tourist destination with two loop trails through the famed
Olympic rain forest.

Mount Olympus

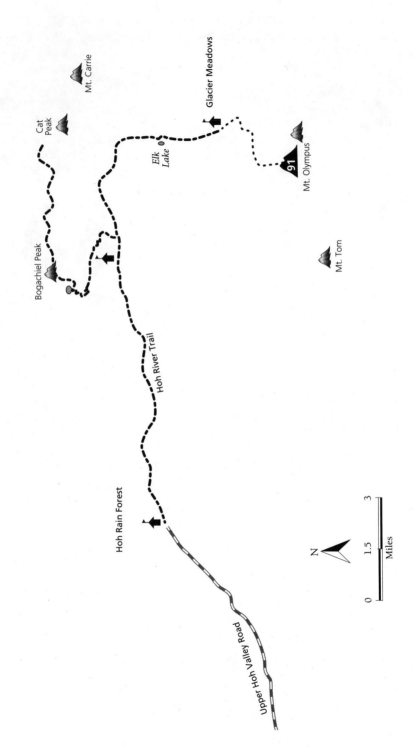

Mt. Carrie

Cat
Peak

Glacier Meadows

Bogachiel Peak

Elk
Lake

Mt. Olympus

91

Mt. Tom

Hoh River Trail

Hoh Rain Forest

Upper Hoh Valley Road

N

0   1.5   3
Miles

From here, follow Hoh River Trail as far as it goes, 17.5 miles to Glacier Meadows, elevation 4,200 feet. There are numerous camps and shelters along the way, but climbers traditionally camp at Glacier Meadows, about 1 mile below the Blue Glacier. Permits are required; they are issued at the Hoh Rainforest Visitor Center.

ROUTE DESCRIPTION

From Glacier Meadows, continue up a broken trail 0.9 mile to the easternmost lateral moraine of the Blue Glacier. Cross the moraine and drop down to the glacier, then rope up and traverse to the west side of the glacier to the base of Caltech Ridge. Ascend to Snow Dome, a broad, largely uncrevassed lobe of the glacier north of the West Peak. The usual route from the glacier to Snow Dome is up a snow gully and Class 2 slabs. Once you see the research station atop Snow Dome, ascend directly there. A westerly traverse along the northern edge of the glacier is recommended until you see the research station because there are hidden crevasses south of the main route on Snow Dome that have eaten many climbers over the years. During poor visibility, you may have trouble finding the route to the research station.

From Snow Dome, continue up the gentle glacier, skirting crevasses, to the head of upper Blue Glacier. Aim for the narrow col dividing West Peak (the pointy rock peak on the right) and the false summit (the little rock hump on the left). In early season, it may be possible to climb directly to the col via a steep firn slope. A late-season bergschrund usually blocks direct access to the col, forcing an end-around. If so, from the schrund, head southeast along the north side of the Five Fingers rock formation for about 700 feet, then traverse over the Five Fingers. This involves moderately steep firn slopes, a late-season moat crossing, and some loose rock scrambling. Getting off the snow and onto the rock, and vice-versa, can be tricky. There are several possible routes around or across the Five Fingers. Staying on the east side is the shortest route. After crossing the Five Fingers, you end up about 200 yards east of the false summit. Head west to the north side of the false summit and climb it via a Class 4 rock chute, then descend the other side, dropping about 200 feet into a snow bowl separating the false summit and West Peak. Traverse south then east on the summit tower to access the southeast ridge, then climb about 100 feet of Class 4 rock up the ridge to the summit.

OPTIONS

In early season, when snow obscures the trail above Glacier Meadows, some parties descend to the glacier sooner. The Snow Dome area may also be reached via one of the icefalls farther up the glacier.

There are several routes up West Peak. One option climbs the northwest corner from the top of the firn slope. Angle up steep, blocky ledges, then traverse easier rock to the spiny northwest arete and up to the summit. This variation is Class 4, fairly easy climbing but very exposed, especially on the arete. A more direct variation climbing the north face of the summit tower involves 50 feet of 5.4 climbing on dubious rock.

The Middle Peak and East Peak of Mount Olympus can be climbed along with the Main Peak, provided you have time to linger and don't have to rush back to camp and hike out right away. Refer to the *Climber's Guide to the Olympic*

Mount Olympus

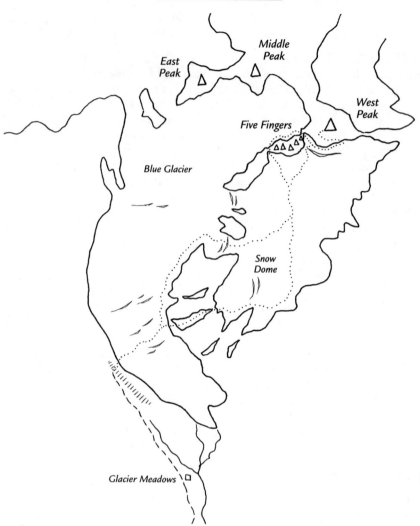

Mountains for route information on these and other peaks in the vicinity of Mount Olympus.

PRECAUTIONS

The Hoh River Trail is one of the most popular hikes in Olympic National Park, and Mount Olympus is one of the most popular climbs in the park, so don't be upset when you find a lot of people on the trail and climbing route. The approach hike is long and can be tedious, and the climbing route is fairly long as well. Don't try this one if you aren't in shape or you'll suffer. (You'll suffer anyway, just maybe not as much if you're in shape.) Choice of footwear can make a big difference. Blisters have turned back as many climbers as bad weather.

Mount Olympus West Peak and False Summit

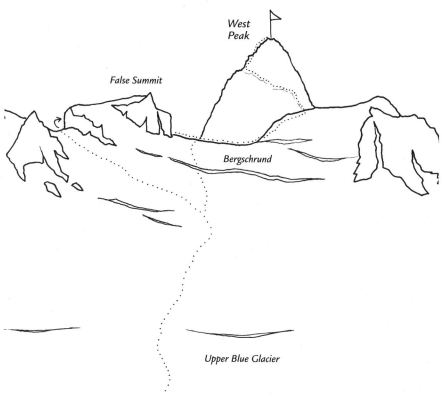

The Blue Glacier is fairly mild as glaciers go, but it has crevasses lurking beneath its sometimes harmless-looking surface. Rope up and know how to effect a crevasse rescue. There is avalanche hazard during winter and early season. Climbing the Main Peak and its satellites involves fairly exposed and notoriously loose rock. As the first ascent party reported, "There was some real climbing here, every climber having to be extremely careful not only to keep from falling, but also not to loosen and start rock on the people below." Take care yourself, not only of your handholds and footholds, but also to avoid raining rocks down on your companions and other climbers. There are some big loose blocks that could do quite a bit of damage. Crossing moats can be difficult and dangerous. Ice ax and crampons required; helmet highly recommended.

Climbers are requested to register prior to their climb at the Glacier Meadows Ranger Station. Climbers should sign out after their climb. Registration sign-out may become mandatory. A "blue bag" policy is in effect on Mount Olympus climbing routes, including the Blue Glacier. The free bags are available at the climber's registration box at Glacier Meadows. Used bags may be dropped in a container on the lateral moraine about 1 mile above Glacier Meadows.

Mount Washington

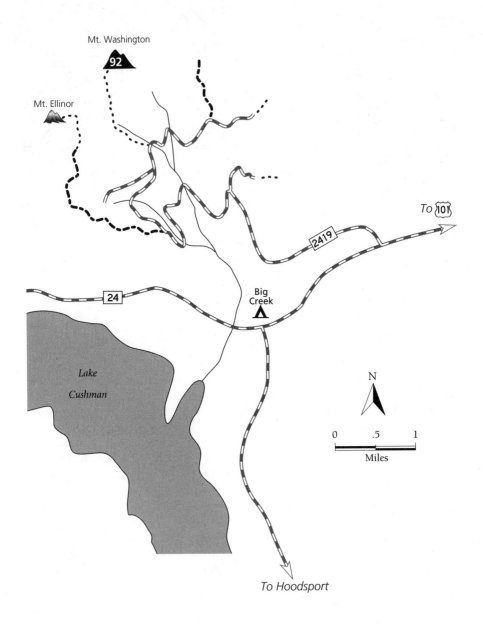

Mt. Washington

92

Mt. Ellinor

To 101

2419

24

Big
Creek

Lake
Cushman

N

0   .5   1
Miles

To Hoodsport

Matt Robertson

Mount Washington. The route climbs the big gully left of the summit.

92. MOUNT WASHINGTON

Elevation: 6,255 feet/1,907 meters
Route: Big Creek Gully
Rating: Class 2–3
Distance: 5 miles round trip
Elevation Gain: 3,300 feet from road to summit
Time: 4 to 6 hours from road to summit
Maps: USGS Mount Washington; Green Trails No. 167 (Mount Steel) and 168 (The Brothers)

ABOUT THE CLIMB

Mount Washington is the prominent peak rising immediately north of Mount Ellinor. It is one of the most popular summits in the Olympic Mountains, most likely due to its commanding presence and easy accessibility from Puget Sound. Given the absence of a summit hiking trail, Mount Washington offers some measure of routefinding challenge, although the usual route is fairly straight-forward under most conditions. The mountain supposedly resembles George Washington's profile when viewed from across Puget Sound, hence the name. The summit provides superlative views of the interior peaks and the Puget Sound lowlands, and across to Mount Rainier and other peaks of the Cascade Range.

HOW TO GET THERE

Drive U.S. Highway 101 to Hoodsport, then head northwest on Lake Cushman Road (Forest Road 44) about 9 miles, past the entrance to Lake Cushman State

Mount Washington

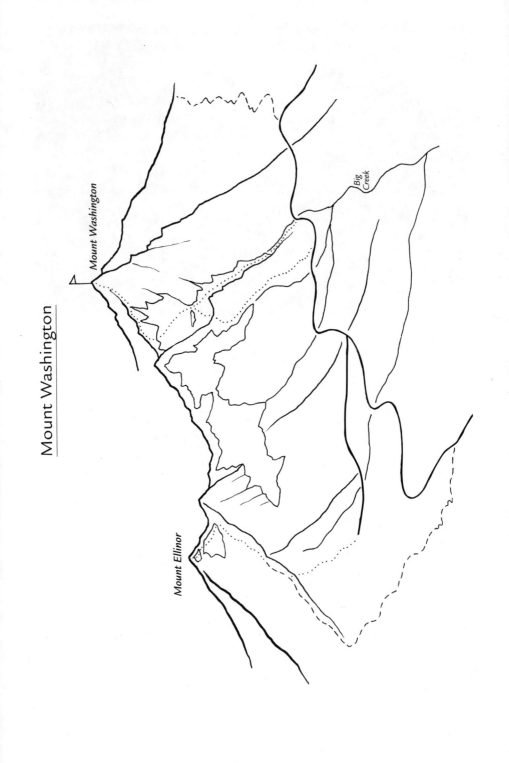

Mount Washington

Mount Ellinor

Big Creek

Park, to the junction with Forest Road 24. Turn right and continue east on Forest Road 24 about 1.7 miles to Forest Road 2419. Alternatively, from U.S. Highway 101 north of Hoodsport, follow Forest Road 24 west about 6.6 miles to Forest Road 2419. However you get there, follow Forest Road 2419 nearly 5 miles up and across the Big Creek watershed to Mount Ellinor trailhead, then continue about 1.5 miles to a spur road just before the road crosses one of the branches of Big Creek. If you pass a waterfall, you've gone too far. Park at the established turnout.

ROUTE DESCRIPTION

There are several popular routes on Mount Washington's east slopes. The most popular is the Big Creek route, which begins from Forest Road 2419 about 0.25 mile north of the spur road. Ascend the middle fork of Big Creek up a broad stream gully, then right to the summit ridge. Follow a way trail up into a basin below the south ridge, then ascend the obvious gully through the headwall directly to the ridge. Continue northward up the ridge to the summit rocks, which may be surmounted directly from the south or via a traverse across a ledge on the east side of the summit block and a short scramble from the north. Early season snow simplifies the ascent greatly, but even in late season, the route is fairly direct and enjoyable

OPTIONS

There are a number of other routes to the summit of Mount Washington, most involving Class 3–4 climbing on fairly solid rock. Refer to *Climber's Guide to the Olympic Mountains* for details. An ascent of Mount Ellinor is an easy hike and scramble via a rugged trail.

PRECAUTIONS

There is severe avalanche hazard in winter and early season. Loose rock is abundant, and party-inflicted rockfall in the gully and below the summit block is common. An avalanche may have obliterated part of the approach trail, which would make routefinding a bit challenging for a short distance.

93. MOUNT CRUISER

Elevation: 6,104 feet/1,861 meters
Route: South Corner
Rating: Grade II, 5.0
Distance: 16 miles round trip
Elevation Gain: 5,300 feet
Time: 7 to 10 hours to summit; best as a two- or three-day climb
Maps: USGS Mount Skokomish; Green Trails No. 157 (Mount Steel)

ABOUT THE CLIMB

Mount Cruiser is the highest summit of Sawtooth Ridge, a craggy escarpment rising due east of Flapjack Lakes. Mount Olympus notwithstanding, Mount Cruiser is probably the classic climb of the Olympic Mountains, definitely one of the best rock climbs in the range. The fact that it is pictured on the cover of the Olympics

Mount Cruiser Approach

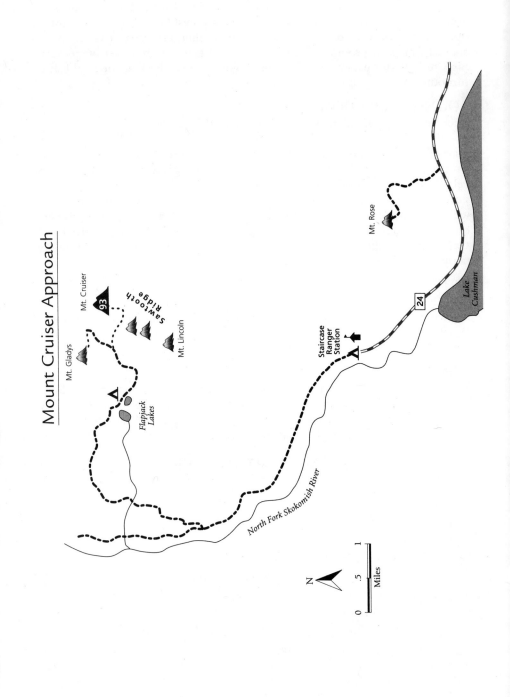

Mt. Gladys

Mt. Cruiser

93

Sawtooth Ridge

Mt. Lincoln

Flapjack Lakes

North Fork Skokomish River

Staircase Ranger Station

Mt. Rose

24

Lake Cushman

N

0   .5   1
Miles

climbing guide has certainly not diminished the climb's popularity. There is no scrambling route to its summit. The easiest route is a technical rock climb, easy as rock climbs go but no place for mere scramblers. The rock is fairly solid by Olympics standards. The approach includes a steep snow gully, making crampons and ice ax necessary. Considering the length of the approach hike and the amount of equipment required for this climb, it may seem like too much for just a pitch or two of easy rock climbing. Sure, a lot more climbing can be had with less work at your local cragging area, but Cruiser is a worthwhile climb for summit-minded climbers, and the approach isn't all that bad. The climb can be done in a single long day by ambitious climbers, although most make it a two-day climb with a base camp at Flapjack Lakes, assuming they can get a permit to camp in this popular area. Making the climb during the week will increase your chances of obtaining a permit.

HOW TO GET THERE

From U.S. Highway 101 at Hoodsport, drive west on Lake Cushman Road (Forest Road 44) about 9 miles, past the entrance to Lake Cushman State Park, to the intersection with Forest Road 24. Alternatively, from U.S. Highway 101 at Jorsted Creek, drive west on Forest Road 24 about 8.3 miles to the intersection with Lake Cushman Road. From here, follow Forest Road 24 west along the north shore of Lake Cushman to its end at Staircase Ranger Station. Follow a short paved road uphill from the ranger station to the North Fork trailhead. A Northwest Forest Pass is required.

Hike Staircase Loop Trail on the northeast bank of the North Fork Skokomish River about 1 mile to a junction with the Rapids Loop Bridge Trail. Stay to the right and continue another 2.5 miles to the junction with Flapjack Lakes Trail. Stay right again and climb for about 3.5 miles to the junction with Black and White Lakes Trail at the head of Donahue Creek. Take yet another right and follow the trail 0.5 mile to Flapjack Lakes, the traditional base camp for climbing on Sawtooth Ridge. Limited permits are available for camping at Flapjack Lakes; they are issued at the Staircase Ranger Station.

ROUTE DESCRIPTION

From Flapjack Lakes, continue up the trail leading southeast toward Sawtooth Ridge. Leave the trail just below Gladys Pass and ascend the obvious steep snow gully leading up to the notch at the base of The Needle, the sharp spire located just south of Mount Cruiser. From the notch ("Needle Pass"), traverse northward about 0.25 mile, following a faint climber's trail across ledges and easy rock to the base of Mount Cruiser's summit block. Ascend the gully on the left, leading up to the base of a big chockstone, then chimney up behind the chockstone and out the cannon hole to the top of the chockstone, the standard belay ledge for the South Corner. Traverse right across the top of the chockstone to the base of the summit spire and belay. Alternatively, you can climb unprotected easy Class 5 up the wall right of the chockstone to reach the belay platform directly. From the belay platform, turn the corner and ascend slabby rock just right of the rib. Clip a manky old bolt and climb 35 feet to where you can place a #3 Camalot under a flake, then run it out 30 feet more to anchors just below the summit. Class 4 climbing reaches the summit.

Mount Cruiser South Corner

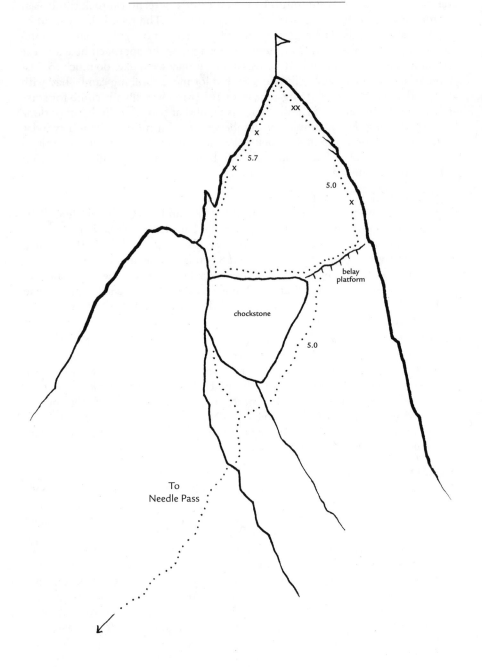

xx

x

5.7

x

5.0

x

belay
platform

chockstone

5.0

To
Needle Pass

Bring a small rack of chocks and slings for protection, including a #3 Camalot or equivalent. To descend, downclimb back to the anchors and rappel down to the belay platform. You have to swing in to the belay platform. Double ropes required for the rappel.

OPTIONS
The Needle is an obvious option that offers a fun Class 5.3 climb to its summit from the notch. The Southwest Corner route is another good option. From the left end of the chockstone, just above the cannon hole, climb up and left to the base of an obvious flake, then up the corner. The route is 5.7 and protected by two bolts. Although it is run out, this route is much more enjoyable than the South Corner route. To descend, rappel the South Corner route.

PRECAUTIONS
The gully leading up to The Needle usually has steep snow or ice. The rock on Mount Cruiser is generally sound, but rockfall may still be experienced in the gully and on the summit formation, especially party-inflicted rockfall in the gully.

94. THE BROTHERS

Elevation: 6,866 feet/2,093 meters
Route: South Chute
Rating: Class 3
Distance: 14 miles round trip
Elevation Gain: 6,200 feet
Time: 7 to 10 hours to summit
Maps: USGS The Brothers; Green Trails No. 158 (The Brothers)

ABOUT THE CLIMB
As viewed from Seattle, The Brothers is perhaps the most distinguishable peak of the Olympic Mountains. Its angular slopes, twin summits separated by a sharp gap, and bold relief make it easily recognizable from almost anywhere around Puget Sound. Probably for this reason as much as any, The Brothers is a popular climb. Actually, the South Brother is the popular climb. It is best done as an early season snow climb; by late season, loose rock mars the route. A traverse from the North Brother to the South Brother is somewhat popular, although it is more demanding than many climbers suspect. The climb is feasible in a long day with an early start from the trailhead, but it is best done as an overnight climb with a high camp above Lena Lake. Summit views are spectacular, including the interior peaks of the Olympic Mountains, as well as eastward across Puget Sound to Seattle and the Cascade Range.

HOW TO GET THERE
Drive U.S. Highway 101 to mile 318 to Hamma Hamma Road (Forest Road 25), which is between Quilcene and Hoodsport. Follow Forest Road 25 west about 8 miles to the Lena Lake trailhead. Hike about 3 miles up Lena Lake Trail (Trail 810) to Lena Lake, then follow along the lakeshore, staying right at the first trail

The Brothers

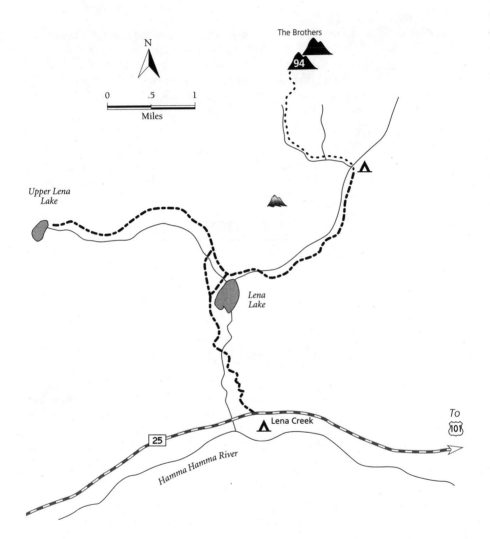

N

0   .5   1
Miles

The Brothers

94

Upper Lena
Lake

Lena
Lake

Lena Creek

To
101

25

Hamma Hamma River

The Brothers

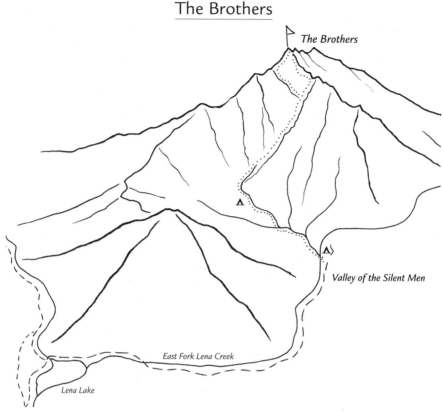

junction, to a junction with Trail 821. Follow Trail 821 up the East Fork Lena Creek (up the "Valley of the Silent Men") another 3 miles or so to the climber base camp at the "trail's end" at Lena Forks. Early season windfalls and snow may slow your progress on the approach.

ROUTE DESCRIPTION

From the base camp at Lena Forks, cross the east fork and continue up the western branch of the creek, following a climber's trail. Cross the creek on the uphill (north) side of the feeder stream so you end up on the north side and avoid a second stream crossing. About 1 mile up this canyon, there is a bench just below the first cliffs that provides a convenient, usually uncrowded camp. (This bench is the first avalanche meadow mentioned in the Olympics climbing guide.)

Traverse the meadow and cross a ridge to the foot of the obvious gully, the South Chute, which leads northwest toward the summit ridge. The Olympics climbing guide describes the ridge as being a "minor tree-covered ridge," but recent avalanches have wiped out most of the trees. Ascend the South Chute (usually snow until late summer) into a basin and stay right, passing below the notorious Hourglass debris chute. Scramble eastward up easy rocks across a "ledge" to a spot dubbed Lunch Rock, which is below a cluster of "small trees" that are no longer so very small. From here, continue north (more than 200 yards) to where an easy traverse leads left back into the upper South Couloir. Some parties bivy just above Lunch Rock. Ascend the South Couloir, a moderately steep snow chute, to a headwall at about 6,000 feet elevation. Turn right and traverse beneath the headwall to a ridge where you can see several spires. There are several gullies here to confuse you. The southernmost chute is the standard route. Climb up the gully, ascend a short chimney, and finish with a short scramble up a talus slope to complete the ascent.

OPTIONS
From the south summit, a Class 4 traverse reaches the 6,800-foot north summit. This traverse can be done in a single day from base camp at Lena Lake. It is a fairly serious undertaking. There are other routes up The Brothers, although few are popular. Refer to the *Climber's Guide to the Olympic Mountains* for route details.

PRECAUTIONS
Expect snow on the approach hike to Lena Forks until late June most years. This can complicate the approach hike, especially the stream crossings. Use care when crossing snow bridges and downed trees. There is severe avalanche hazard in winter and early season and rockfall exposure in the gully and on the upper slopes. Although the summit scramble is not technically difficult, routefinding can be complicated. Many parties try the wrong gullies to the ridge. As a general rule, if the going gets at all difficult, you are off route.

95. MOUNT CONSTANCE

Elevation: 7,743 feet/2,360 meters
Route: South Chute
Rating: Class 3
Distance: 8 miles round trip
Elevation Gain: 5,300 feet
Time: 5 to 8 hours to summit
Maps: USGS Mount Deception, The Brothers, and Mount Townsend; Green Trails No. 136 (Tyler Peak)

ABOUT THE CLIMB
Mount Constance is the third highest of the Olympic Mountains and the highest of the Olympic peaks visible from Seattle. The craggy peak, which is composed of old, loose basalt and pillow lava, has a variety of minor summits, pinnacles, spires, and faces, and features several of the range's most difficult alpine rock routes. Fortunately, there are a few scrambling routes to the summit as well, although none is particularly easy, safe, or recommended. Mount Constance's routes are generally exposed and hazardous. Climbers have been killed in accidents here. As far as routefinding goes, Mount Constance is one of the most complex peaks of the Olympic Mountains. Although there are relatively easy routes to the summit, they are not immediately obvious and will put your routefinding skills to the test. All things considered, Mount Constance is not a casual ascent. It should only be attempted by experienced climbers and alpine

Mount Constance and Mount Anderson

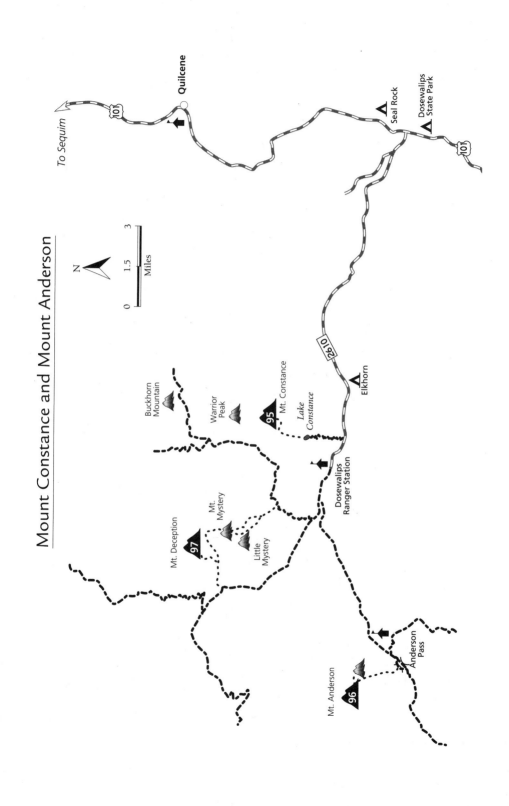

scramblers, preferably in the company of someone who has climbed it before. Despite the hazards, Mount Constance is a popular climbing objective, mostly because of its prominence and accessibility from Puget Sound. The summit offers unsurpassed views of Puget Sound and the interior peaks.

HOW TO GET THERE

Drive U.S. Highway 101 to mile 306.1 just north of the town of Brinnon (between Quilcene and Hoodsport). Follow Forest Road 2610 (Dosewalips Road) westward up the Dosewalips River for 14.2 miles to the Lake Constance trailhead. The trail is not well marked; it begins at a small trail sign beside Constance Creek. Hike up the steep, rugged boot-beaten trail 2.2 miles to the lake, elevation 4,700 feet. One hiking guide describes the hike as "little more than a climbing route . . . typified by brutal uphill pitches choked with roots and exposed boulders." There are a few campsites on the north shore of the lake; permits are issued at Dosewalips Ranger Station.

ROUTE DESCRIPTION

From Lake Constance, ascend northward up Avalanche Canyon, the broad, steep-walled gully directly north of the lake. About 0.75 mile up the canyon, scramble up the South Chute, the main gully on the right, which leads to the lowest notch in the ridge just south of a distinctive twin-peaked spire known as the Cat's Ears. Traverse around the south side of the Cat's Ears and continue along the east side of the ridge below Point Schellin to an obvious gully. Ascend the gully (steep scree or snow) to a notch in the east-west ridge, then go down the gully on the other side to a talus field. Continue northward toward the steep cirque that holds the "Terrible Traverse." To get there, cross two distinct snow or talus slopes, each with off-route gullies heading up toward the ridge crest. If visibility is poor, follow a compass bearing north, staying out of the gullies until you reach the steep cirque. Follow a big ledge system up to a distinct rock outcrop. This is the Terrible Traverse. It is exposed but not terribly difficult. Rock climbers should have no trouble, but skiers should expect to be scared. After that, traverse to the summit rocks. Climb the north side of the summit pinnacle, which involves a couple of Class 4 moves. To descend, downclimb the route.

OPTIONS

There are several variations to the South Chute route. The most obvious is the North Chute, which ascends a prominent gully about 0.5 mile farther up Avalanche Canyon. This is a steep, narrow chute (full of "nasty, rotten rock, ice, snow, and generally rotten climbing" according to a local guide) that leads to the main ridge just south of the South Summit where you join the South Chute route. Mount Constance also has several Class 4 and Class 5 routes, although the rock is generally not reliable.

PRECAUTIONS

The trail to Lake Constance is steep and not maintained. This is definitely not a family hike. Even conditioned hikers and climbers will feel the strain of 2 miles of unrelenting climbing. Pace yourself so you have some strength left for the real climbing. The trail has some rock scrambling and is not recommended when wet

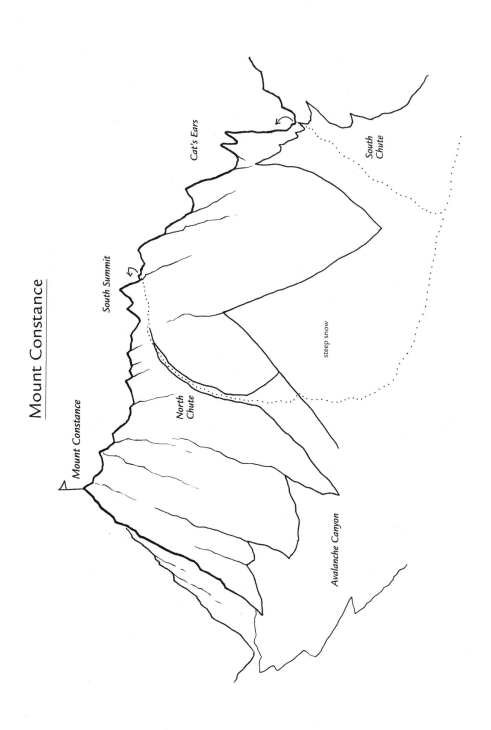

Mount Constance

Mount Constance

South Summit

Cat's Ears

North Chute

steep snow

South Chute

Avalanche Canyon

Mount Constance (East Face)

Mount Constance

South Summit

Cat's Ears

or snow covered. There is abundant loose rock on Mount Constance, so wear a helmet and climb carefully to avoid knocking rocks down on your companions and other climbers. The scrambling is very exposed in places. Early season snow patches can be treacherous. Steep, rotten snow and ice can make for hazardous going, especially in the North Chute. There is avalanche hazard in Avalanche Canyon, all gullies, and in the upper cirque in early season.

96. MOUNT ANDERSON

Elevation: 7,321 feet/2,232 meters
Route: Anderson Glacier
Rating: Class 2; Grade I glacier
Distance: 27 miles round trip
Elevation Gain: 5,900 feet
Time: Best done as a two- or three-day climb
Maps: USGS Mount Steel, Chimney; Green Trails No. 167 (Mount Steel)

ABOUT THE CLIMB

Mount Anderson is one of the major interior peaks of the Olympic Mountains. It is also one of the most remote climbs in the Olympics, not quite as remote as Mount Olympus, but certainly out there. Mount Anderson is a significantly glaciated, craggy peak. There are several summit routes; but due to typically unreliable Olympic rock, the best routes climb the glaciers and snow as much as possible. Early season ascents are preferred by most to take advantage of snow cover. The true summit is referred to as "West Peak," while the lower summit is "Mount Anderson." Of the two, Mount Anderson is the most popular, although each may be fairly easily ascended via Flypaper Pass and the Eel Glacier. The main obstacle to a successful ascent of Mount Anderson is the approach trail. In recent years, the trail has not been maintained, and several windfalls have made passage difficult enough to deter climbers from approaching the peak. When the trail is clear, Mount Anderson is feasible as a two-day climb, although it is a strenuous undertaking best done in three days, allowing a full day for the approach hike, another day for the summit climb, and a third day to hike out. Mount Anderson's central position within the Olympic Mountains means it has one of the best viewpoints in the range. Assuming good weather, nearly every high summit of the Olympics is visible from its summit.

HOW TO GET THERE

Drive U.S. Highway 101 to mile 306.1 in the town of Brinnon on the Dosewalips River between Hoodsport and Sequim. Turn west on Dosewallips Road (Forest Road 2610) and follow it 15.5 miles to the trailhead at the road's end.

Hike up Dosewalips River Trail 1.4 miles to the junction with Anderson Pass Trail at Dose Forks. Take the left fork and hike west up the West Fork Dosewalips River another 9.2 miles to Anderson Pass, elevation 4,464 feet. Follow a climber's trail northward up a steep forested ridge to the foot of the Anderson Glacier. Many parties camp at Siberia Camp, a shelter just 0.5 mile below Anderson Pass. If you are climbing Mount Anderson in two days, camp at the foot of the glacier.

Mount Anderson

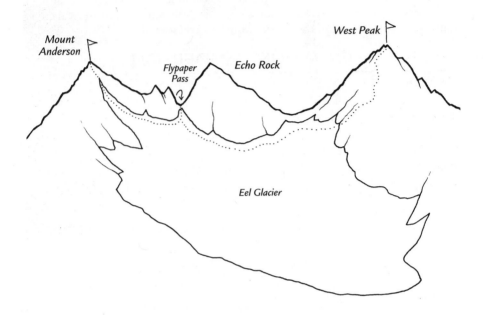

ROUTE DESCRIPTION

Ascend the Anderson Glacier to Flypaper Pass, the obvious gap, reached via a steep, strenuous couloir. Descend 200 feet from Flypaper Pass to the Eel Glacier and turn right, then traverse below rock towers and ascend the southeast arm of the glacier and snow slopes above to the west slope of Mount Anderson. Continue directly up the rotten rock ridge to the summit.

OPTIONS

If you are climbing the higher West Peak (elevation 7,365 feet), cross over Flypaper Pass and descend to the Eel Glacier, then traverse northwest under a big cliff of rotten rock, staying as high as possible on the glacier. When you reach a steep, rotten shoulder of the West Peak, turn north and continue until you reach a ledge that gains the northeast shoulder. Follow the rotten summit ridge southward to the top.

PRECAUTIONS

There is avalanche hazard in winter and early season, especially on the slopes below Flypaper Pass and on the upper slopes. There is abundant loose, rotten rock on Mount Anderson and the West Peak. The trail is not well maintained and may be impassable. Contact the park service prior to your climb to make sure the trail is passable.

Climber on the Snow Finger, Mount Deception.

Olympic Mountaineering

97. MOUNT DECEPTION

Elevation: 7,788 feet/2,375 meters
Route: Royal Basin Route
Rating: Class 2–3
Distance: 18 miles round trip
Elevation Gain: 5,300 feet
Time: Best done as a two- or three-day climb
Maps: USGS Mount Deception; Green Trails No. 136 (Tyler Peak)

ABOUT THE CLIMB

Mount Deception is the second highest peak of the Olympic Mountains if you exclude the east summit of Mount Olympus, which is slightly higher but does not qualify as a distinct mountain by most accounts. Although Mount Deception may be ascended by several moderate scrambling routes, the climbing is steep, exposed, and quite serious. Mount Deception has been the scene of several fatal accidents and has gained a reputation as one of the more dangerous Olympic peaks. These accidents involved slips on snow where the climber was unable to self-arrest quickly and fell, as well as falls on loose rock. You may encounter loose rock and steep snow, so exercise good judgment and great care to climb safely on Mount Deception. This is not an appropriate climb for inexperienced climbers. Given a preference, most climbers choose an early season ascent of Mount Deception to avoid the worst of the loose rock.

HOW TO GET THERE

Drive U.S. Highway 101 to mile 267.4 near Sequim Bay State Park. Turn south on Palo Alto Road. Follow Palo Alto Road about 6 miles to the pavement's end.

Mount Deception and Mount Clark

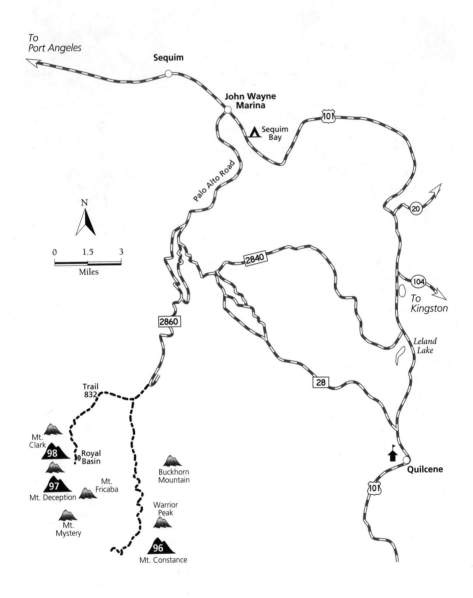

Mount Deception

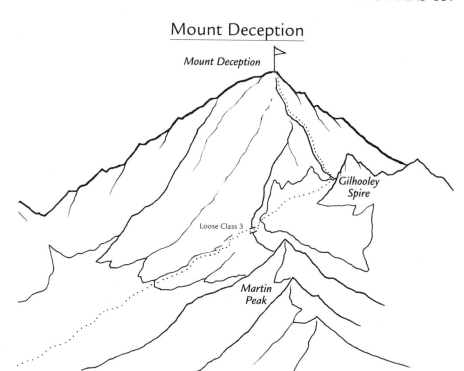

Continue on Forest Road 28 another 3 miles to Forest Road 2860. Take a left and follow Forest Road 2860 about 7.1 miles to a fork. Avoid Forest Road 2870 and stay on Forest Road 2860, which descends another 1.5 miles to the Upper Dungeness trailhead.

ROUTE DESCRIPTION

Hike the Upper Dungeness Trail 1 mile to a fork with Royal Basin Trail and take the right fork (Trail 832). Continue on Royal Basin Trail another 6 miles to Royal Lake. There are several campsites at or near Royal Lake. The area is popular, though, so come early to get a site. Permits are required to camp in Royal Basin; contact Olympic National Park for current permit information.

From Shelter Rock at Royal Lake, follow the climber's trail leading southward into upper Royal Basin. The trail levels off and meanders through alpine meadows and beautiful alpine tarns. Scramble across a boulder field to the main snow slopes south and west from the upper meadows. From the snow slopes, ascend directly to the col between Mount Deception and Martin Peak. The ascent to the col is via moderate snow slopes in early season and nightmarishly loose Class 3 rock later in the season. Several people have died descending this section, so be very careful here.

From the col, follow the ridge south and around to the upper snow slopes of the Deception Glacier, just left of Gilhooley Spire, a rotten rock tower. Proceed up a very steep snow finger just left of Gilhooley Spire, then ascend the easy ridge southeast to the summit.

OPTIONS
The Deception Creek route on the mountain's south side may be used, especially if you want to combine an ascent of Mount Deception with an ascent of Mount Mystery. The route is much easier and less exposed to loose rock but has a longer approach and is not often climbed. Refer to *Climber's Guide to the Olympic Mountains* for route details.

PRECAUTIONS
The route is steep and will likely involve snow and loose rock climbing. Rockfall is likely, so wear a helmet. An ice ax is recommended; crampons if hard snow. Be extremely careful while climbing Mount Deception, particularly while descending the loose Class 3 section below the col. The NPS doesn't want another dead climber here, or anywhere else for that matter. If you are camping in Royal Basin, camp only at established campsites and be prepared to defend your food against hungry bears. A bear-resistant food container is highly recommended. Bugs are notoriously voracious during summer months. This is a heavily used area, so do your best to avoid adverse impacts. Permits are required for overnight camping in Royal Basin.

98. MOUNT CLARK

Elevation: 7,528 feet/2,295 meters
Route: Surprise Basin Route
Rating: Class 3
Distance: 17 miles round trip
Elevation Gain: 5,000 feet
Time: Best done as a two- or three-day climb
Maps: USGS Mount Deception; Green Trails No. 136 (Tyler Peak)

ABOUT THE CLIMB
Mount Clark is one of the high summits of The Needles, a cluster of craggy peaks located above Royal Basin and just north of Mount Deception. Although not the highest peak of The Needles, Mount Clark is considered one of the best scrambles in the Olympics. Its western route from Surprise Basin is a classic by Olympics standards, mostly because the rock is fairly solid and the route is exposed and interesting rather than the usual shattered-rock walk up or death scramble found on many other Olympic peaks. The north ridge from Belvedere Basin is also a good route, slightly more difficult but on fairly sound rock. There are several other good climbs and scrambles among The Needles, more than enough to keep a climber busy for a week or more. Because of the popularity of this area, a permit is required to camp in Royal Basin. Although day trips are feasible despite the 7-mile approach hike, climbers visiting Royal Basin are advised to spend several days here exploring and climbing at their leisure.

HOW TO GET THERE
Drive U.S. Highway 101 to mile 267.4 near Sequim Bay State Park. Turn south on Palo Alto Road. Follow Palo Alto Road about 6 miles to the pavement's end.

Mount Clark

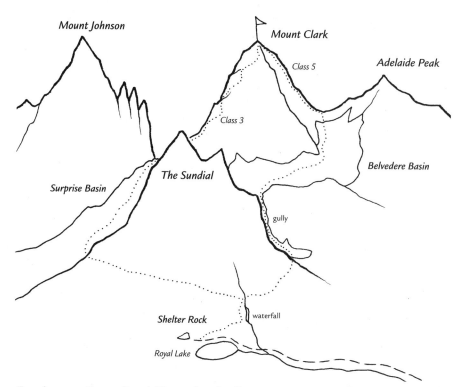

Continue on Forest Road 28 another 3 miles to Forest Road 2860. Take a left and follow Forest Road 2860 about 7.1 miles to a fork. Avoid Forest Road 2870 and stay on Forest Road 2860, which descends another 1.5 miles to the Upper Dungeness trailhead.

Hike Upper Dungeness Trail 1 mile to a fork with Royal Basin Trail, then take the right fork (Trail 832). Continue on Royal Basin Trail another 6 miles to Royal Lake. There are several campsites at or near Royal Lake. The area is popular, though, so come early to get a site. Permits are required to camp in Royal Basin; contact Olympic National Park in advance for current permit information.

ROUTE DESCRIPTION

Surprise Basin route is the popular scramble. Begin from Shelter Rock at Royal Lake. Hike west across a meadow and find a climber's trail on the left side of the waterfall. This leads to a boulder field. Go left to the base of Surprise Basin, then ascend scree and snow to the pass at the head of the basin. From the pass, follow a shelf and gullies on the right to the notch between Mount Clark and the Sundial. Then continue westward up the ridge and face, ascending ledges, gullies, and broken rock to the summit. This route is Class 3, with some loose rock. An alternate approach is to ascend the Belvedere Basin route to the basin, then traverse southward to the Clark–Sundial notch. To descend, downclimb the route.

OPTIONS

A better route, but more technical, is the Belvedere Basin route (II, 5.0). It also begins from Shelter Rock. Hike west across a meadow and find a climber's trail on the left side of the waterfall. This leads to a boulder field. Climb right through the boulders and follow a shelf below a cliff band until you reach a meadow west of the Sundial. Turn left and descend into a snow basin, then ascend a long snow finger (scree gully in late season) to Belvedere Basin, the snow basin lying between Mount Clark and Adelaide Peak. Cross the basin and ascend to the col dividing Mount Clark and Adelaide Peak. From here, about 300 feet of slabby Class 4–5 rock climbing leads up to the summit ridge where easy scrambling gains the summit. To descend, either downclimb the route or scramble down the Surprise Basin route.

PRECAUTIONS

Expect steep snow climbing and loose rock scrambling on all routes. If you are camping in Royal Basin, camp only at established campsites and be prepared to defend your food against hungry bears. A bear-resistant food container is highly recommended. Bugs are notoriously voracious during summer months. This is a heavily used area, so do your best to avoid adverse impacts. Permits are required for overnight camping in Royal Basin.

99. MOUNT ANGELES

Elevation: 6,454 feet/1,967 meters
Route: Mount Angeles Climbers' Trail
Rating: Class 2–3
Distance: 8 miles round trip
Elevation Gain: 1,200 feet
Time: 2 to 3 hours to summit
Maps: USGS Mount Angeles; Green Trails No. 135 (Mount Angeles)

ABOUT THE CLIMB

Mount Angeles, the highest summit between Hurricane Ridge and the Strait of Juan de Fuca, offers a nearly unparalleled panoramic view of the interior range, including the nearby glaciated peaks, Mount Carrie and Mount Olympus and nearly every high peak of the range, as well as the entire northern coast of the Olympic Peninsula, and on a clear day, the Pacific Ocean. Mount Angeles is an easy climb as scrambles go, and exceedingly popular. It is a popular local "mountain run," often climbed by local climbers before or after work. Given its proximity to the Hurricane Ridge Visitor Center, the "trail" route is frequently climbed by determined hikers, and even a few tourists manage to reach the summit, although the mountain is far too craggy and exposed to recommend to any but experienced scramblers. Because the Hurricane Ridge Road is open year round (as conditions permit), Mount Angeles is a popular winter and spring climb, but it is subject to extremes in weather and avalanche hazard. It is a very good spring and summer scramble.

One of the main attractions of Mount Angeles is the mountain goats, which have found this high ridge to be more to their liking than any other within the

Mount Angeles

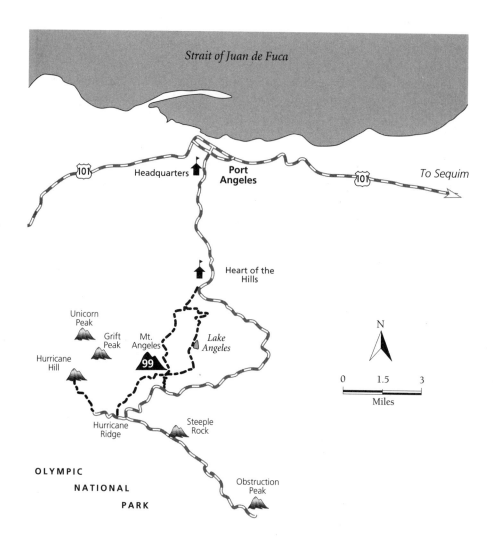

Strait of Juan de Fuca

101

Headquarters

Port Angeles

101

To Sequim

Heart of the Hills

Unicorn Peak

Grift Peak

Mt. Angeles

99

Lake Angeles

Hurricane Hill

Hurricane Ridge

Steeple Rock

Obstruction Peak

OLYMPIC

NATIONAL

PARK

N

0   1.5   3

Miles

Mount Angeles

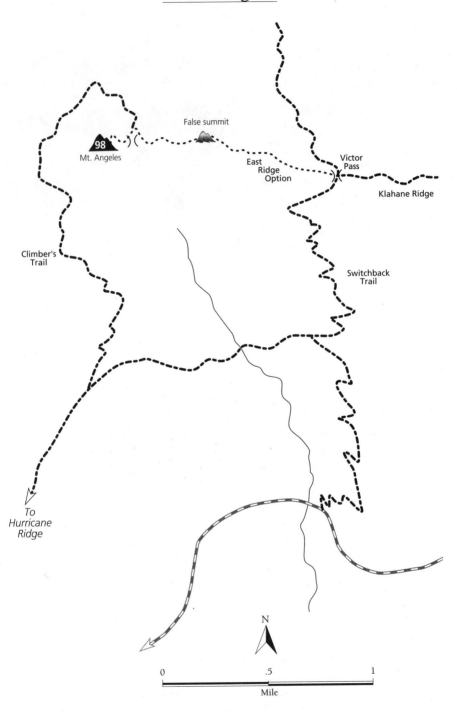

False summit

98
Mt. Angeles

East
Ridge
Option

Victor
Pass

Klahane Ridge

Climber's
Trail

Switchback
Trail

To
Hurricane
Ridge

N

0   .5   1
Mile

Mount Angeles

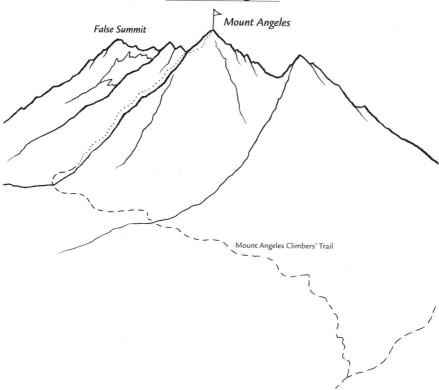

park. The goats were introduced to the Olympic Mountains in the 1930s to provide "sport" for local hunters. Hunting was banned with the establishment of Olympic National Park, and the goat population exploded due to a lack of predators, which resulted in a great deal of environmental damage due to erosion and overgrazing. So, during the 1980s, a program began that deported goats back to the Cascade Range and was followed by the eradication of the remaining goats. Predictably, the mountain goat population has decreased substantially since then. On Mount Angeles, you stand a fair chance of seeing one or more of these curious creatures up close and personal, although the goats, having understandably grown wary of humans, tend to avoid the mountain these days.

HOW TO GET THERE

Drive U.S. Highway 101 to Port Angeles. Follow Hurricane Ridge Road 15 miles from Port Angeles (about 10 miles from the park entry station) to the turnout on the right at the Switchback trailhead. Both routes described begin from here. The climber's trail can be approached via the Mount Angeles Trail from Hurricane Ridge, although there are far too many tourists on this trail to recommend it to fellow climbers.

ROUTE DESCRIPTION

If you are making the ascent via the climber's trail, hike up Switchback Trail about 0.8 mile to the junction with Mount Angeles Trail. Take the left fork and traverse meadows and scree slopes southwest about 0.5 mile to a signed fork marking the start of the trail to Mount Angeles. Take a hard right and follow the trail southward up steep subalpine slopes into a rocky meadow just southwest of the summit. The trail is faint here and easy to lose in poor weather; a cairn may help steer you back on track. Resist the urge to climb the trail leading up the scree slopes to the notch just southeast of the summit; there is a route, but it's Class 4–5 rock climbing. Instead, pick up the trail leading through trees on the opposite side of the meadow. The trail winds around the meadowy west slopes and up a long scree gully, skirting cliffs to gain the gap immediately northeast of the summit, where a brief rock scramble leads to the summit. A loose scree trail leads all the way up the gully to the gap. The summit scramble isn't steep but is a bit exposed and loose.

OPTIONS
The East Ridge route (Class 3–4) ✦ is more challenging. This route is popular with scramblers and climbers.

PRECAUTIONS
Although Mount Angeles is mostly a pedestrian route via the climber's trail, accidents are not uncommon. A slip in the wrong place or getting knocked off balance by a loose rock could prove fatal even on the easy route. The trail is easy to lose in a couple of places, especially in poor weather. The summit rocks may be slippery when wet. There is loose scree in the gully and loose rock near the summit, plus rockfall hazard, especially climber-caused, in the gullies and from the summit rocks. Weather is unpredictable on Mount Angeles. Storm clouds can roll in quickly, and windy conditions should be expected (they don't call it Hurricane Ridge for nothing). Bring a wind/rain shell even on perfect summer days, and definitely during cool, windy weather.

100. MOUNT CARRIE

Elevation: 6,995 feet/2,132 meters
Route: High Divide Trail Route
Rating: Class 3
Distance: 26 miles round trip
Elevation Gain: 5,100 feet
Time: Best done as a two- or three-day climb
Maps: USGS Mount Carrie; Green Trails No. 134 (Mount Olympus)

ABOUT THE CLIMB
Mount Carrie is one of the central high peaks of the Olympic Mountains. Although it does not quite rise to 7,000 feet elevation, local relief and abundant glaciation make it one of the dominant peaks visible from Hurricane Ridge. Carrie is not a technical peak. It is pretty much a long ridge climb with a difficult approach hike and only a bit of scrambling. Mount Carrie's summit views rival those of Mount Olympus, better because you get a close view of Olympus and a panorama of the high peaks of the Olympic Mountains. Because of a long approach, Mount Carrie is not feasible as a day climb unless you're a very fast,

Mount Carrie

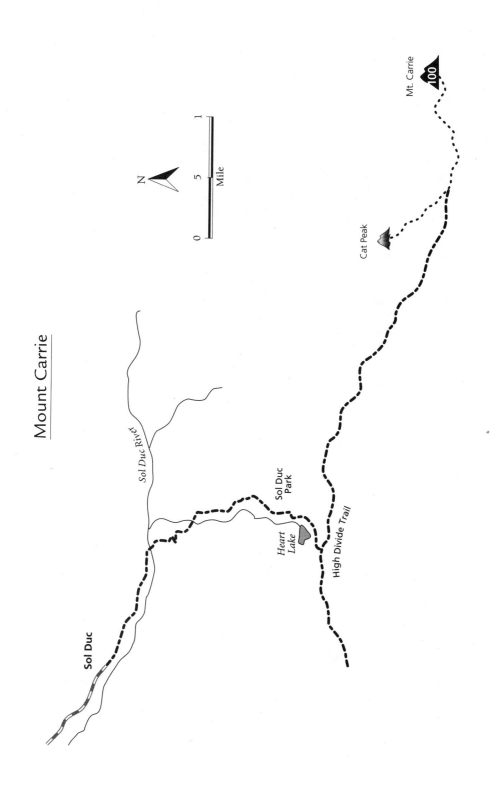

Sol Duc

Sol Duc River

Sol Duc Park

Heart Lake

High Divide Trail

Cat Peak

Mt. Carrie

100

N

0   5   1
Mile

Olympic Mountaineering

Mount Carrie and Carrie Glacier.

strong hiker. It is probably best done as a three-day climb with a high camp along the ridge. It is also a remote, challenging winter and spring ascent, but it is not often climbed in winter due to inaccessibility and avalanche hazard.

HOW TO GET THERE

Drive U.S. Highway 101 to Sol Duc River Road, about 1.6 miles west of Crescent Lake and 4.2 miles east of Klahowya Campground (via Forest Road 2918). Follow the road about 13 miles, past Sol Duc Campground and ranger station, to the road's end and the Sol Duc River trailhead.

ROUTE DESCRIPTION

Hike up Sol Duc River Trail past the shelter and Sol Duc Falls, then continue up the river about 5 miles to the junction with Appleton Pass Trail. Take the right fork and continue about 0.5 mile to Upper Sol Duc Camp, then cross the river and climb another 3 miles through Sol Duc Park and past Heart Lake to a junction with the High Divide Trail.

From the High Divide Trail, head southeast on the primitive trail to Cat Peak for about 3 miles to the trail's end at a signpost. Although this is a primitive trail, it is not difficult to follow because it leads along the ridge crest toward Cat Peak. From the trail's end, continue traversing the west slopes of Cat Peak via "the Catwalk," an exposed and narrow "trail" consisting of Class 2 scrambling along a knife-edge ridge. Once across to the far side, about 1.5 miles along, reach Boston Charlie's Camp, an underused campsite at the saddle dividing Cat Peak and Mount Carrie. This is a good campsite, often used by climbers traversing the Bailey Range. From here, follow a fading climber's trail up the ridge toward Mount Carrie's summit, trending east then angling back north as you approach the

Mount Carrie

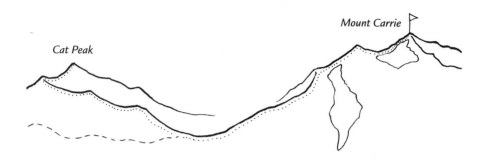

summit rock bands. In early season, these are gentle snow slopes, but they avalanche quite readily. In late season, it's a straightforward scramble through heather and broken rock bands.

OPTIONS
An ascent of Cat Peak (5,940 feet) is a fairly simple undertaking, easily combined with an ascent of Mount Carrie. The glaciers lying north of Mount Carrie offer highly recommended spring backcountry skiing, but the slopes are avalanche prone, and there are crevasses; experts only. Cat Peak is the northernmost summit of the Bailey Range. The Bailey Range Traverse is one of the best high traverses in the Olympic Mountains. Refer to *Climber's Guide to the Olympic Mountains* for details about the Bailey Range Traverse.

PRECAUTIONS
The route is fairly easy and direct, but the Catwalk is exposed with loose rock. There is avalanche and cornice hazard in winter and spring.

Appendix A: Transportation Information

Stehekin and Holden Village Transportation

A few of the peaks included in this guide, and a great many other hikes and climbs in the North Cascades, are most easily approached from Lake Chelan via the town of Stehekin and the Holden Village. These approaches require taking a ferry up 55-mile-long Lake Chelan, then getting a ride on a shuttle bus or van from town to the trailhead. If you are hiking or climbing in this region, you are advised to make transportation arrangements in advance.

The *Lady of the Lake* ferry provides morning service from Chelan and Field's Point Landing (about 16 miles up the west shore of Lake Chelan). The ferry departs at about 8:30 A.M. from Chelan taking about two hours to arrive at Lucerne (port of Holden Village) and three hours to Stehekin, with a ninety-minute layover in Stehekin before returning to Chelan. Express service to Stehekin takes about two hours but costs about twice as much. During summer months, a high-speed catamaran makes the voyage in just over an hour but costs about twice as much again as the express ferry. The slow boat usually gets you to Stehekin in plenty of time to catch the shuttle bus. Schedule and ticket information for the ferry is available on-line at www.ladyofthelake.com or by calling (509) 682–2224. Parking is cheaper at Field's Point Landing, about $4.00 per day or $20.00 per week at last check. Parking is also available in Chelan for a slightly higher fee.

Holden Village is a Lutheran retreat located at the southeast edge of North Cascades National Park and the northeast edge of Glacier Peak Wilderness. To get there, take Lady of the Lake ferry to the town of Lucerne. A Holden Village driver meets the regular morning ferry and express ferry to drive you the 12 miles from Lucerne to the village. The driver will also take you from Holden Village to Lucerne in time for the afternoon return ferry if you hike out to the village in time. Plan on arriving at Holden Village by 12:30 P.M. if you want to catch the afternoon run. Holden Village recommends that you write ahead of time to let them know of your planned date of arrival and departure, so they can be sure to have a driver pick you up, especially if you are hiking in from the west.

There are no camping facilities in the village, and while unregistered guests are welcome, there may be no accommodations available. If you do get stranded overnight at Holden Village, the current rate is just over $50 per night. Finally, there are no phones in Holden Village, meaning emergency evacuation is slow and difficult. The village is an affirmed place of sabbath, meaning cell phones are not welcome in Holden Village, and persons coming into the village are encouraged not to bring them and asked not to use them. If you have packed a cell phone along in case of emergency, keep it packed away until you absolutely need it. For more information, write to Registrar, Holden Village, HC00 Stop 2, Chelan, WA 98816-9769.

Stehekin is a remote town located at the north end of Lake Chelan and at the east edge of the North Cascades. To get there, take the Lady of the Lake ferry. A shuttle bus to trailheads and campground leaves Stehekin about one hour after the ferry's arrival. From there, a NPS van continues up to various North Cascades trailheads. You have to make reservations for the NPS van if you want to be sure to get a ride; call (360) 856-5700, extension 340, line 14, for reservations and current fares. The NPS van begins service by late July most years. No reservations are required for the Stehekin bus, but you have to pay to ride. Have some extra cash along in case the bus stops at the bakery. For more information about bus and shuttle service, road conditions, and accommodations, contact Stehekin Lodge at (509) 682-4494, or North Cascades National Park, Golden West Visitor Center, at (360) 856-5700 extension 340, line 14.

Washington State Ferries

Driving to climbs in the Olympic Mountains (or driving to the Cascades from the Olympic Peninsula) may require taking a ferry across Puget Sound. For schedule and rate information for Washington State Ferries and the Victoria–Port Angeles ferry, call (888) 808-7977 or (206) 464-6400, or log onto the Washington State Ferries Web site at www.wsdot.wa.gov/ferries/.

Appendix B: Permits and Passes

Enchantment Basin Permits

Because of the overwhelming popularity of the Enchantment Lakes, permits are required for overnight stays from June 15 through October 15 each year. There are separate permits for the Enchantment Lakes, Stuart Lake, Colchuck Lake, Snow Lake, and Eightmile Lake. These requirements affect Mount Stuart, Sherpa Peak, Argonaut Peak, Colchuck Peak, Dragontail Peak, Prusik Peak, Cannon Mountain, Cashmere Mountain, and other summits in the region bordered by Icicle Creek and Ingalls Creek. The Forest Service issues a limited number of permits each day. The majority of permits are issued to those who mail in applications and permit fees. Processing of permit applications begins on March 1. Applications cannot be postmarked prior to February 21. The permit fee is currently $3.00 per person per day. The remaining permits are issued on a lottery basis at the Leavenworth Ranger District Office beginning at 7:45 A.M. You can obtain a permit application by calling (509) 548-6977 or by downloading a permit application from the Forest Service Web site listed in Appendix C: For More Information.

Fortunately, the permit requirement affects only a few of the peaks included in this guide and does not affect day use of these areas. You still have to fill out and carry a self-issue day use permit, but as long as you're not camping, you can roam to your heart's content through the Enchantments and surrounding wilderness. You can also obtain an overnight permit for one of the adjoining areas, allowing you to camp closer to the Enchantments. Contact the Forest Service for current permit applications, fees, and requirements.

Northwest Forest Pass

Ostensibly to provide a "simpler, easier way to support recreation" in the national forests, the Forest Service implemented its program Northwest Forest Pass in May 2000. This program, like its predecessor, the Trail Park Pass, requires hikers and climbers using trails and other designated "fee sites" in forests and parks in the Pacific Northwest to purchase and display a pass in their vehicle parked at or near a trailhead. An annual pass is $30.00; a daily pass is $5.00. The Northwest Forest Pass is available from the Forest Service and many outdoor retail stores throughout the Pacific Northwest. For more information about ordering or purchasing a Northwest Forest Pass, contact your nearest ranger district office or log on to the forest service's Web site at www.fs.fed.us/r6/mbs/nwpass/order.htm or www.fs.fed/us/mbs/nwpass/vendors.htm.

Cascades Volcano Pass

Effective July 1999, visitors climbing above 7,000 feet elevation in the Mount Adams Wilderness are required to purchase and display a Cascades Volcano Pass. The pass costs $10 for a midweek climb, $15 for a weekend climb, and $30 for an annual pass good for multiple ascents of Mount Adams and Mount St. Helens. The pass is available at the Mount Adams Ranger Station, and trailheads for the South Climb, Killen Creek, and Divide Camp as well as on-line at at www.fs.fed.us/gpnf/. For more information, contact Cascade Volcano Pass, Mount Adams Ranger District, 2455 Highway 141, Trout Lake, WA 98650; (509) 395-2501.

Appendix C: For More Information

National Park and National Forest Office Phone Numbers

North Cascades National Park
Main Office: (360) 856-5700
Marblemount: (360) 873-4500
Stehekin: (509) 682-2549

Mount Rainier National Park
Main Office: (360) 569-2211
Nisqually: extension 2390
Carbon River: extension 2358
Sunrise: extension 2357
White River: extension 2356
Ohanapecosh: extension 2352
Paradise: extension 2314

Olympic National Park
Main Office: (360) 452-4501
Road and Weather Information: (360) 452-0329
Elwah: (360) 425-9191
Hoh: (360) 374-6925
Sol Duc: (360) 928-3380
Staircase: (360) 877-5569

Mount Baker–Snoqualmie National Forest
Main Office: (425) 744-3200
Darrington: (360) 436-1155
Glacier: (360) 599-2714
Sedro Woolley: (360) 856-5700
North Bend: (425) 888-1421
Skykomish: (360) 677-2414
Verlot: (360) 691-7791
White River: (360) 825-6585

Wenatchee National Forest
Main Office: (509) 622-4335
Chelan: (509) 682-2576
Cle Elum: (509) 674-4411
Lake Wenatchee: (509) 763-3103
Entiat: (509) 784-1511
Naches: (509) 653-2205

Gifford Pinchot National Forest
Main Office: (360) 750-5000
Mount Adams: (509) 395-2501
Packwood: (360) 494-5515
Amboy-Yale-Cougar: (360) 347-5473
Mount St. Helens: (360) 750-3961
Randle: (360) 497-1100
Goat Rocks: (360) 750-5000

Okanogan National Forest
Main Office: (509) 422-2704
Twisp: (509) 997-2131
Winthrop: (509) 996-2266
Tonasket: (509) 486-2186

National Park and National Forest Office Addresses
Leavenworth Ranger District Office
600 Sherbourne Street
Leavenworth, WA 98826
(509) 548-6977

Cle Elum Ranger District Office
803 West 2nd Street
Cle Elum, WA 98922
(509) 674-4411

White River Ranger District Office
853 Roosevelt Avenue East
Enumclaw, WA 98022
(360) 825-6585

Cowlitz Valley Ranger District Office
10024 U.S. Highway 12
P.O. Box 670
Randle, WA 98377
(360) 497-1100

Mount Adams Ranger District Office
2455 Highway 141
Trout Lake, WA 98650
(509) 395-3400

Mount St. Helens National Volcanic Monument
42218 Northeast Yale Bridge Road
Amboy, WA 98601
(360) 247-3900

Naches Ranger District Office
10061 Highway 12
Naches, WA 98937
(509) 653-2205

Packwood Information Center
13068 U.S. Highway 12
Packwood, WA 98361
(360) 494–0600

Olympic National Forest Headquarters
1835 Black Lake Boulevard SW
Olympia, WA 98512–5623
(360) 956–2400

Hoodsport Ranger District Office
150 North Lake Cushman Road
P.O. Box 68
Hoodsport, WA 98548
(360) 877–5254

Quilcene Ranger District Office
295142 Highway 101 South
Quilcene, WA 98376
(360) 765–2200

Forks Ranger District Office
437 Tillicum Lane
Forks, WA 98331
(360) 874–6522

North Cascades National Park
Wilderness Information Center
7280 Ranger Station Road
Marblemount, WA 98267
(360) 873–4500, extension 39

North Cascades Visitor Center
Newhalem, WA
(206) 386–4495

Golden West Visitor Center
Stehekin, WA
(360) 856–5700, extension 340, line 14

Mount Baker Ranger District Office
2105 State Route 20
Sedro Woolley, WA 98284
(360) 856–5700

Glacier Public Service Center
Glacier, WA 98244
(360) 599–2714

Darrington Ranger District Office
1405 Emmons Street
Darrington, WA 98241
(360) 436–1155

Methow Valley Ranger District Office
502 Glover Street
P.O. Box 188
Twisp, WA 98856
(509) 997-2131

Winthrop Visitor Information Center
Building 49, Highway 20
24 West Chewuch Road
Winthrop, WA 98862
(509) 996-4000

Entiat Ranger District Office
2108 Entiat Way
P.O. Box 476
Entiat, WA 98822
(509) 784-1511

Skykomish Ranger District Office
74920 Northeast Stevens Pass Highway
P.O. Box 305
Skykomish WA 98288
(360) 677-2414

Lake Wenatchee Ranger District Office
22976 State Highway 207
Leavenworth, WA 98826
(509) 763-03103

Internet Resources and Links

Climbing Washington www.climbingwashington.com/ (the Web site inspired by this guide, includes route information and updates, links, and more to come).

Mount Rainier National Park: www.nps.gov/mora/climb/climb.htm (Mount Rainier National Park climbing home page).

North Cascades National Park: www.nps.gov/noca/climbing.htm (North Cascades climbing home page).

Olympic National Park: www.nps.gov/olym/wic/climb.htm (Olympic National Park climbing home page).

USDA Forest Service: www.fs.fed.us/r6/mbs/recreport/recrep_home.htm (Mount Baker-Snoqualmie National Forest recreation home page, includes trail conditions, links, and contact information for forest service offices); www.fs.fed.us/gpnf/ (Gifford Pinchot National Forest, includes Mount St. Helens and Mount Adams climbing and permit information); www.fs.fed.us/r6/olympic/ (Olympic National Forest); www.fs.fed.us/r6/oka/ (Okanogan National Forest and Pasayten Wilderness); www.fs.fed.us/r6/wenatchee/recreat/recmain.html (Wenatchee National Forest recreation home page).

Mount St. Helens National Volcanic Monument: www.fs.fed.us/gpnf/msh-nvm/climbing/ (Mount St. Helens climbing information).

Washington Trails Association: www.wta.org/wta/ (trail news and conditions, photo gallery, trip reports, and on-line hiking guide).

USGS Geographic Names Information System (GNIS): www.mapping/usgs.gov/www.gnis/gnisform.html (database of geological information, includes summit elevation, location, and links to maps, aerial photos, and other resources).

Microsoft TerraServer: www.terraserver.microsoft.com (USGS and satellite aerial photos and topo maps).

Rainier Mountaineering, Inc.: www.rmiguides.com/htmldocs/route.asp (interactive route information for Disappointment Cleaver route and current weather conditions for Mount Rainier).

Washington State Department of Transportation Real Time Road and Weather Traveler Information ("Weather Beta"): www.wsdot.wa.gov/Rweather.

Boeing Alpine Society: ww.boealps.org/newnewmainwin.asp (club newsletter, includes trip reports, photos, and links).

The Mountaineers: www.mountaineers.org/ (all about the state's oldest and largest outdoor club, includes scrambling and climbing course information, a bulletin board, and climbing schedules).

Mountainwerks Cascadian Climbing Adventures: http://www.mountainwerks.com/cma/ (trip reports for many climbs and scrambles, photos, and links).

North Cascades Climbing Resource: http://www.ac.wwu.edu/~berdind/index.html (route descriptions and photos).

Tom's Climbing Records: http://www.tumtum.com/climbing/ (trip reports and Route Descriptions of many peaks in the Cascades).

Phil's Trip Reports: http://praxis.etla.net/~philfort/ (humorous trip reports and photos).

Seattle Post–Intelligencer "Getaways": http://seattlepi-i.nwsource.com/getaways/hike/ (articles by Karen Sykes about hiking trails and scrambles, and other hiking and climbing related articles).

Mountaineering and Outdoor Images by Bob Bolton: http://members2.clubphoto.com/robert198786/ (excellent photo gallery of several Cascades peaks including Ptarmigan Traverse).

Washington Climbing Links: http://www.geocities/com/Yosemite/2899/climbing.html (links to nearly every national park and forest service climbing site, plus trail and weather links).

Weather and Avalanche Information

Cascade Ski Report: (206) 624–0200

Crystal Mountain Ski Report: (360) 634–3771

Mount Baker: (360) 599–2714

Mount Rainier: (360) 569–2211

Monte Cristo and Glacier Peak: (360) 436–1155

Olympics: (360) 452–0329

Stevens Pass: (360) 677–2414

Stevens Pass Ski Report: (360) 634–1645

Washington State Avalanche Line: (206) 526–6677

Oregon/South Cascades Avalanche Line: (503) 326–2400

Washington State Department of Transportation Real Time Road and Weather Traveler Information ("Weather Beta"): http://test.wsdot.wa.gov/rwis/.

Guide Services

The following is a list of selected climbing schools and guide services in Washington. It is not a complete list. If you do not see a guide service listed for your region, or an area you are interested in visiting, consult your phone directory or visit the American Mountain Guide Association Web site at www.amga.com/.

Alpine Ascents International
121 Mercer Street
Seattle, WA 98109
phone: (206) 378–1927, fax: (206) 378–1937
e-mail: Climb@AlpineAscents.com

American Alpine Institute, Ltd.
1515 12th Street N-3
Bellingham, WA 98225
phone: (360) 671–1505
e-mail: info@aai.cc

Cascade Alpine Guides & Adventures, LLC
2208 NW Market Street, Suite 504
Seattle, WA 98107
phone: (206) 706–1587, fax: (206) 706–1621
e-mail: info@cascadealpine.com

Mount Rainier Alpine Guides, LLC
c/o Ashford Mountain Center
P.O. Box T
Ashford, WA 98304
phone: (360) 569–2604
e-mail: www.rainierguide.com

Olympic Mountaineering
140 West Front Street
Port Angeles, WA 98362
phone: (360) 452–0240
e-mail: olymtn@olymtn.com
Web site: www.olymtn.com

Pro Guiding Service
909 Northeast 6th
North Bend, WA 98045
phone: (425) 831-5558
e-mail: martinv@accessone.com
Web site: www.proguiding.com/

Rainier Mountaineering, Inc.
535 Dock Street, Suite 209
Tacoma, WA 98402
phone: (360) 569-2227 (summer) or (253) 627-6242 (winter)
Web site: www.rmiguides.com/

Appendix D: Further Reading

Selected References
Beckey, Fred: *Cascade Alpine Guide, Climbing and High Routes, 1: Columbia River to Stevens Pass* (3rd edition, Mountaineers 2000); *2: Stevens Pass to Rainy Pass* (2nd edition, 1989); *3: Rainy Pass to Fraser River* (2nd edition, 1995).

Beckey, Fred and Van Steen, Alex: *Climbing Mount Rainier, The Essential Guide* (AlpenBooks Press 1999).

Beckey, Fred: *Challenges of the North Cascades* (2nd edition, Mountaineers 1996).

Copeland, Kathy and Craig: *Don't Waste Your Time in the North Cascades* (Wilderness Press 1996).

DeGraw, Robert: *Secrets of Si—The Mount Si Guidebook* (Ro-De Publishing 1995).

Gauthier, Mike: *Mount Rainier: A Climbing Guide* (Mountaineers 1999).

Goldman, Peggy: *75 Scrambles in Washington* (Mountaineers, 2001).

Molenaar, Dee: *Challenges of Mount Rainier: A Record of Explorations and Ascents, Triumphs and Tragedies* (Mountaineers 1979).

Manning, Harvey and Spring, Ira: *50 Hikes in Mount Rainier National Park* (4th edition, Mountaineers 1999); *100 Hikes in Washington's Glacier Peak Region* (3rd edition, Mountaineers 1996); *100 Hikes in Washington's North Cascades National Park Region* (3rd edition, Mountaineers 2000); *100 Hikes in Washington's South Cascades and Olympics* (3rd edition, Mountaineers 1998).

Manning, Harvey and Spring, Ira and Vicky: *100 Hikes in Washington's Alpine Lakes* (3rd edition, Mountaineers 2000).

Molvar, Erik: *Hiking in Olympic National Park* (Falcon Publishing 1995); *Hiking the North Cascades* (Falcon Publishing 1998).

Mountaineers: *Mountaineering: The Freedom of the Hills* (6th edition, Mountaineers 1997).

Nelson, Jim and Potterfield, Peter: *Selected Climbs in the Cascade Range, Volumes 1 and 2* (Mountaineers 1992, 2000).

Olympic Mountain Rescue: *Climber's Guide to the Olympic Mountains* (3rd edition, Mountaineers 1987).

Schneider, Heidi and Skjelset, Mary: *Hiking Mt. Rainier National Park* (Falcon Publishing 1999).

Smoot, Jeff: *Adventure Guide to Mount Rainier* (Falcon Publishing 1999); *Climbing the Cascade Volcanoes* (Falcon Publishing 1999); *Hiking Washington's Alpine Lakes Wilderness* (Falcon Publishing 2002).

Selected Maps
Official Washington State Highway Map (Washington Department of Transportation 1998).

Rand McNally 1998 Road Atlas (Rand McNally & Company 1998).

Washington Atlas & Gazetteer (DeLorme Mapping Company 1988).

Alpine Lakes Protection Society: The Alpine Lakes Wilderness and surrounding management unit, Central Cascade Mountains of Washington State, 1:100,000 scale topographic map (USGS–based with trail data).

Northwest Interpretive Association: Northside, Eastside and Southwest Hiking Guide to Mount Rainier National Park (USGS–based topo maps with detailed trail descriptions and data).

Pargeter's Maps (Richard Pargeter): The North Cascades West, The North Cascades East, The North Central Cascades, The Olympic Mountains (pictorial landform maps with road and trail information).

Molenaar's Maps (Dee Molenaar): Mount Rainier (pictorial landform map with road, trail, and climbing route information).

USDA Forest Service: Mt. Baker–Snoqualmie National Forest Visitor Map (1988); Mount Adams Wilderness topo map (1988); Olympic National Forest and National Park map and recreation guide (1998); Pasayten Wilderness topo map (1991); Henry M. Jackson Wilderness topo map (1991); Chelan-Sawtooth Wilderness topo map (1991).

USGS and Green Trails Maps listed in each chapter. USGS maps may be viewed online via the Microsoft Terraserver at www.terraserver.microsoft.com; Green Trails Maps may be previewed and ordered on-line at www.greentrails.com/.

TOPO! Interactive Maps on CD-ROM: North Cascades, Mount Baker, and Surrounding Wilderness Areas; Seattle, Mount Rainier, and Central Cascades; and Olympic Peninsula, San Juan Islands, and Puget Sound. Preview on-line at www.topo.com/.

About the Author

Jeff Smoot has been hiking and climbing in Washington for twenty-five years. He contributes articles to magazines such as *Climbing* and *Rock & Ice*. He is the author of four guidebooks, including *Climbing the Cascade Volcanoes*, *Rock Climbing Washington*, and *Adventure Guide to Mount Rainier*.